Pasting Up Protest

McGill-Queen's Iberian and Latin American Cultures Series
Series editor: Nicolás Fernández-Medina

The McGill-Queen's Iberian and Latin American Cultures Series is committed to publishing original scholarship that explores and re-evaluates Iberian and Latin American cultures, connections, and identities. Offering diverse perspectives on a range of regional and global histories from the early modern period to twenty-first-century contexts, the series cuts across disciplinary boundaries to consider how questions of authority, nation, revolution, gender, sexuality, science, epistemology, avant-gardism, aesthetics, travel, colonization, race relations, religious belief, and media technologies, among others, have shaped the rich and complex trajectories of modernity in the Iberian Peninsula and Latin America.

The McGill-Queen's Iberian and Latin American Cultures Series promotes rigorous scholarship and welcomes proposals for innovative and theoretically compelling monographs and edited collections.

1 Populism and Ethnicity
Peronism and the Jews of Argentina
Raanan Rein
Translated by Isis Sadek

2 What Would Cervantes Do?
Navigating Post-Truth with Spanish Baroque Literature
David Castillo and William Egginton

3 The Pen, the Sword, and the Law
Dueling and Democracy in Uruguay
David S. Parker

4 From the Theater to the Plaza
Spectacle, Protest, and Urban Space in Twenty-First-Century Madrid
Matthew I. Feinberg

5 Death in the Snow
Pedro de Alvarado and the Illusive Conquest of Peru
W. George Lovell

6 Configurations of a Cultural Scene
Young Writers and Artists in Madrid, 1918–1930
Andrew A. Anderson

7 Beyond Intimacy
Radical Proximity and Justice in Three Mexican Poets
Christina Karageorgou-Bastea

8 Patriarchy's Remains
An Autopsy of Iberian Cinematic Dark Humour
Erin K. Hogan

9 Pasting Up Protest
The Art of Memorializing Violence in Mexican Printmaking
Annik Bilodeau

The Art of Memorializing Violence in Mexican Printmaking

Pasting Up Protest

ANNIK BILODEAU

McGill-Queen's University Press
Montreal & Kingston • London • Chicago

ISBN 978-0-2280-2558-0 (paper)
ISBN 978-0-2280-2559-7 (ePDF)
ISBN 978-0-2280-2560-3 (ePUB)

Legal deposit fourth quarter 2025
Bibliothèque et Archives nationales du Québec

Printed in Canada on acid-free paper.

This book has been published with the help of a grant from the Federation for the Humanities and Social Sciences, through the Awards to Scholarly Publications Program, using funds provided by the Social Sciences and Humanities Research Council of Canada.

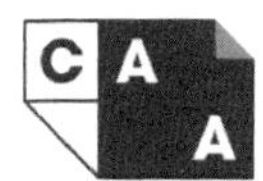

Publication of this book has been aided by a grant from the Wyeth Foundation for American Art Publication Fund of CAA

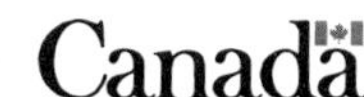

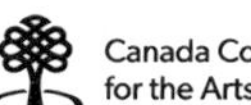

We acknowledge the support of the Canada Council for the Arts.
Nous remercions le Conseil des arts du Canada de son soutien.

McGill-Queen's University Press in Montreal is on land which long served as a site of meeting and exchange amongst Indigenous Peoples, including the Haudenosaunee and Anishinabeg nations. In Kingston it is situated on the territory of the Haudenosaunee and Anishinaabek. We acknowledge and thank the diverse Indigenous Peoples whose footsteps have marked these territories on which peoples of the world now gather.

Library and Archives Canada Cataloguing in Publication

Title: Pasting up protest : the art of memorializing violence in Mexican printmaking / Annik Bilodeau.
Names: Bilodeau, Annik, author
Series: McGill-Queen's Iberian and Latin American cultures series ; 9.
Description: Series statement: McGill-Queen's Iberian and Latin American cultures series ; 9 | Includes bibliographical references and index.
Identifiers: Canadiana (print) 20250184796 | Canadiana (ebook) 20250184842 | ISBN 9780228025580 (paper) | ISBN 9780228025597 (ePDF) | ISBN 9780228025603 (ePUB)
Subjects: LCSH: Art—Political aspects—Mexico. | LCSH: Street art—Political aspects—Mexico. | LCSH: Street art—Social aspects—Mexico. | LCSH: Artists—Political activity—Mexico. | LCSH: Artists— Mexico—Interviews. | LCSH: Art and social action—Mexico. | LCSH: Violence in art. | LCSH: Disappeared persons in art. | LCSH: Missing persons in art. | LCSH: Collective memory in art. | LCSH: Memorialization—Mexico.
Classification: LCC N72.P6 B55 2025 | DDC 701/.030972—dc23

This book was designed and typeset by studio oneonone in Minion 11/14.
Copyediting by Ryan Perks.

McGill-Queen's University Press
Suite 1720, 1010 Sherbrooke St West, Montreal, QC, H3A 2R7

Authorized safety representative in the EU: Mare Nostrum Group BV, Mauritskade 21D, 1091 GC Amsterdam, the Netherlands, gpsr@mare-nostrum.co.uk

Contents

Table, Figures, and Plates

Table

Figures

Plates

Preface

Nos quisieron enterrar, pero no sabían que éramos semillas.
(They tried to bury us, not knowing we were seeds.)
– Mexican protest slogan

In Latin America, one slogan has been repeatedly deployed in political demonstrations since the 1960s. Its appeal lies both in its power and in the lack of resolution to the crisis to which it calls attention. "Nos quisieron enterrar, pero no sabían que éramos semillas" (They wanted to bury us, not knowing we were seeds)[1] has been seen on hand-held signs, banners, and sometimes even bodies in Mexico from the Dirty War of the 1970s to the Ayotzinapa disappearances in 2014. More recently it has even been taken up by the movement against gender-based violence and femi(ni)cides. The slogan is reactivated demonstration after demonstration, death after death. The metaphor of seeds is an apt one to describe activism around missing persons in Mexico; one missing person spurs hundreds into action, and decade after decade, new generations of activists rise, ready to take on this ongoing battle. Activism takes many shapes.

The first time I encountered this slogan and the metaphor of seeds to describe Mexican activism was shortly after the 2014 events in Ayotzinapa (Guerrero), where forty-three students were disappeared, likely by the state and the army. I was in the middle of my PhD studies in Spanish American literature when those whom we now commonly call "the forty-three" disappeared. As a young teacher myself, I felt a kinship with them, despite our very different circumstances. The hashtag #Vivos LosLlevaronVivosLosQueremos (They took them alive, we want them back alive) was trending on social media, and calls for action were often accompanied by pictures of the various wheat paste posters that many artists were plastering on the streets across Mexico. I started saving them on my computer, hoping to use them in class. The book you are holding was probably already taking shape.

Like many scholars, after defending my dissertation I was able to pursue new academic interests. As I was waiting to defend, a friend lent me *Getting Up for the People: The Visual Revolution of* ASAR*-Oaxaca* (2014), Mike Graham de la Rosa and Suzanne Michele Schadl's book about the role that ASARO played in the 2006 uprising in Oaxaca. I rolled my eyes – not at the topic, but at the mere idea of reading yet another book – but my friend assured me that I would love it. I accepted, assuming it would join the pile of books I was hoarding, but which I had been unable to find time to read. Since starting my PhD program, reading purely for pleasure had rarely been possible. Despite my initial reaction, I read *Getting Up for the People* in a single sitting.

I was immediately mesmerized by ASARO's prints, both their simplicity and their denunciatory aspects. I did not consider myself much of an activist. And yet, looking at these prints, absorbing them, taking them in, I felt compelled to do *something* to change the situations ASARO were denouncing. While I shared their anger, I knew myself well enough to know that I was not about to travel to Oaxaca and start demonstrating against human rights violations, low wages, or landlessness. So instead I continued researching the collective and gathering and reflecting on their prints; and eventually, I did travel to Oaxaca to conduct interviews with members of the group. Looking back, I now realize that this is the moment my scholarly activism was born. Research became my way to participate.

Pasting Up Protest is as much a scholarly endeavour as it is a militant one. I firmly believe that denouncing the violence enacted on women and student activists, as well as the impunity enjoyed by perpetrators and the inaction of Mexican authorities, is necessary; a duty for everyone who studies the country. Especially from my privileged position as a Canadian scholar. I am not risking my life in doing so; I am only reporting on the work others do. It is, in a way, the least I can do as a Latin Americanist. But more important than calling out the Mexican government, I showcase artists and activists who live the fight. I admire the dedication and boldness of these artists and activists who risk everything to denounce injustices – often their freedom, sometimes their lives.

During my first summer of fieldwork in Oaxaca, in 2019, the more time I spent poring over the reports written by the Grupo Interdisciplinario de Expertos Independientes (Interdisciplinary Group of Independent Experts) for the Ayotzinapa case, photographing street art, and meeting with artists, the angrier I became. Reading about the events that had unfolded in Ayotzinapa and the impunity afforded to the authorities meant I was also reading about feminicides, whose perpetrators often go unpunished too. And I became even angrier. I was angry that I could spend days, weeks reading about the history of student activists and women killings to get a better understanding of social, historical, political causes, and that while the phenomena were thoroughly documented, there did not seem to be a way to put an end to that violence. There is a wealth of literature on juvenicides and feminicides in Mexico, myriad measures have been implemented by successive governments, and yet …

Up until the summer of 2019, my anger was very theoretical, book-based. This safe emotional distance, while necessary at the beginning, might actually have been keeping me from really tapping into the anger of the streets and using it to fuel my writing. I was hitting the stacks, compiling a database of images used in protests against violence targeting youths and women, writing about artworks and posters, juggling with theories. Up until August 2019, I had never felt the energy of the street, nor the power of a freshly painted stencil denouncing state violence. I was working on Ayotzinapa, four to five years after the mass disappearances, and while demonstrations were still gathering Mexicans by the thousands, in the state of Oaxaca they had somewhat subdued. Bluntly put, I did not have lived experience with the clamour of the streets. I kept telling myself that it was a good thing not to study current events. While I could not be fully detached from my topic – the same way I had been during my PhD years; I mean, I loved the novels I analyzed, but they did not keep me awake at night – the lack of opportunity to watch protests unfold afforded me what I thought was a safe distance from the violence. I was working from a very privileged place.

I acknowledged the power of anger – in protests and for my writing – toward the end of my first fieldwork research trip. I was in Mexico City when the Brillanteada, the Glitter Protest, occurred on 16 August 2019. My research assistant and I were intrigued by the calls to gather at the Glorieta de los Insurgentes, a major roundabout in Mexico City, but since federal laws stipulate that it is illegal for foreigners to participate in protests, even peaceful ones, we refrained from attending.[2] Instead, we went to see the protest artworks the next day.

Quite a lot of pink glitter – the newest weapon in Mexican activists' tool kit – had gathered in the water channels and sewer grids, and the once grey walls of the metro station were but a memory. And only then, faced with hundreds of poorly erased slogans, inscriptions, and stencils, did I fully take in the outrage, the anger that the rape of two teenaged girls by police officers had unleashed. It was at that moment that something really clicked for me.

The Brillanteada was called after two Mexico City teenaged girls came forward accusing uniformed police officers of rape at the beginning of August 2019. Unsurprisingly, the women's accusations were not treated seriously, neither by the authorities nor by the media. The cases followed a typical slut-shaming pattern: The victims' names were released, and the media, the police, and members of the public questioned their behaviour and attire, as well as the mere fact they were even outside the night they were assaulted. Should they not have been at home, where they would have been safe?

Seeing that the officers were not going to be indicted, feminist activist groups organized online, and staged a first, smaller in-person protest on 12 August in front of the attorney general's office in Mexico City. During a press conference called in the hopes of shooing away the protesters, Security Minister Jesús Orta Martínez explained that investigations were still ongoing. This answer did not convince anyone in attendance. He called the protesters "radicals"; they then proceeded to douse him in pink glitter.[3] I had never considered the radicality of glitter until then.

Despite assurances offered by Orta Martínez that the two rape cases would be investigated properly, a larger demonstration was called for Friday, 16 August. It was nicknamed La Brillanteada, a cheeky reference to the pink glitter – *brillantina*, in Spanish – the protesters had used on the security minister, and which they were planning on using again during the march. The activists gathered at the Glorieta de los Insurgentes, a metro station and major roundabout in Mexico City, close to the Paseo de la Reforma, Mexico City's best-known avenue. The peaceful march quickly turned violent: A male photographer was assaulted, businesses were vandalized, their windows smashed, and the headquarters of the city police were set on fire.

As I stood at the entry of the Glorieta de los Insurgences the next day, mesmerized, the only coherent thought I could form in my mind was that those white patches hiding the protesters' slogans and signs screamed as loudly as, if not louder than, the words spray-painted and stenciled the night before. Both the discourse and the erasure of the discourse were a stunning sight. It was one thing to intellectually understand anger, but quite another to witness its aftermath. Even more disconcerting was how quickly the authorities were moving in to erase the traces of the demonstration. I should not have been surprised; I knew this happened after every single protest – I had read about it! – but it was still enraging to see.

And yet, the pièce de résistance was still to come. The night before, the demonstrators had made their way to the Ángel de la Independencia, the monument celebrating the country's independence from Spain in 1822.[4] Upon reaching it, protesters proceeded to cover its base with colourful stencils and inscriptions. Intending to follow in their footsteps, we soon learned through social media that the monument had been boarded up – in less than twelve hours. Once again, it told as loud a story of silencing as the half-erased stencils we had seen earlier.

Strictly speaking, it is true that property was damaged. The Ángel, a beloved symbol of Mexican national identity, having also been tagged, would remain unavailable to the public for the foreseeable future.[5] Some Mexicans felt this as an attack on the nation itself. And while I do not condone the tagging of historical monuments, I learned in the weeks after the supposed desecration of the Ángel that spray paint is fairly easy to remove from marble and bronze statues, as it does not corrode the surface.[6] Unlike the twenty women who are killed in Mexico every day, the Ángel would be fine.

The discussions and media coverage around the Glorieta and Ángel protests followed another classic pattern: People were more upset about the destruction of properties and monuments than about the omnipresent rape culture in Mexico, the high rate of female homicides, and the impunity that aggressors, rapists, and killers enjoy. And the more the debates raged, the more I was rolling my eyes and getting upset. The discourse of politicians, and even some left-wing intellectuals, revolved around physical damage to buildings and public spaces, never around the women to whom the protest gave a voice, those who, as one of the slogans eloquently put it, "no volvieron" ("por las que no volvieron," for those who did not come back.).

Even President Andrés Manuel López Obrador demanded that demonstrations be peaceful, and historical monuments respected, ironically giving more respect to the statue of Nike, the goddess of victory – a metaphorical woman – than to women of flesh and blood.[7]

And while I was dismayed at the content presented in the media, at least there was some media coverage. People were talking about gender-based violence. I could not say the same about Ayotzinapa. Things had been silent for a while on that front, and would be until August 2022, when Mexican Undersecretary for Human Rights Alejandro Encinas finally confirmed what we all suspected: the forty-three Ayotzinapa students had been killed in September 2014, and military personnel had been involved. Parents and activists who have been calling this a state crime were right all along. It did not come as a surprise, but it still angered me.

It is this anger that has kept me going, especially as this investigation grew more taxing. I have always believed that keeping a safe distance from my topic was the best way for me to do research, but this investigation proved otherwise.

I hear you, fellow cynics. Can a book make a difference? Yes and no. Research will never replace the political will of states to ensure the well-being of their citizens. Nor can it be a substitute for militancy and citizen demands that the state respect human rights and social justice. A work like mine is not a substitute for concrete action. And yet, it is still born of the same desire for social justice as all these other demonstrations. So maybe I am slowly growing into an activist, in my own way. Maybe I am one of the seeds to which the protest slogan refers.

Acknowledgments

Somewhat naively I expected that writing and publishing a first book of cultural analysis would serve as a valuable road map for a second endeavour. Not quite. I am beyond grateful to each and every person who challenged me, supported me, and cared for me over the last six years – often in spite of my own wishes. This time the research proved more emotionally draining than anything I had ever attempted previously. I have never been closely attuned to my own emotions, often claiming I did not have any; however, examining the portrayal of youth murders and feminicides in Mexican visual culture opened deep pits of despair within me, but also big cracks through which the sun shone.

I am aware that I speak from a place of considerable privilege when I say that the first year of the pandemic came almost as a blessing for me. The forced pause and the extra time to think were great gifts offered under not-so-great circumstances. For the first time since embarking on this research in November 2017, I had time – lots of it in fact – to think, to ponder, to listen to the silence, to stare into the void, to scrutinize a single poster for days on end. More importantly, this unanticipated hiatus allowed me to reset, to step back, and to remember why this research mattered to me. I am not proud of it, but in the turmoil of teaching and researching and writing – rinse and repeat – I might have lost sight of the fact that while to me it was a manuscript with a due date looming, my research topic was for many Mexicans a lived, and even haunting, ever-present experience.

As the pandemic persisted, there was an increase in the number of cases of feminicide in Mexico, in Canada, and in my home province of Quebec. Every time a woman was killed in Quebec, I listened to the outrage in the news coverage and, while I shared it, I could not help but think each and every time, "And that's ten women in Mexico today." The least I could do was to keep writing about the activists who seek to restore some dignity to these women, and to do it to the absolute best of my ability. Which in this case meant taking a lot more time than I had planned to finalize the manuscript of *Pasting Up Protest.*

Thank you to McGill-Queen's University Press for allowing me a few extra years to complete this book. Working with the editorial team at McGill-Queen's was a wonderful experience. I am particularly indebted to my editors, Richard Ratzlaff and Marie-Claude Felton, who guided me through the past years, pushed my thinking forward, and responded to my many queries with precision and grace. Thank you to Kathleen Fraser and Elena Goranescu, who helped me capture the essence of this project with the perfect cover design. I was fortunate to benefit once again from Ryan Perks's meticulous copyediting of the text; his expertise sharpened my prose, enhancing the clarity of my work, and his comments about the content made the process quite enjoyable! Finally, I extend my sincere gratitude to Timothy Pearson for his technical support in the last years of this project and for organizing the book's index.

This book has been published with the help of a grant from the Federation for the Humanities and Social Sciences, through the Awards to Scholarly Publications Program, using funds provided by the Social Sciences and Humanities Research Council of Canada.

Publication of this book has also been aided by the College Art Association through its Wyeth Foundation for American Art Publication Grant.

Several institutions provided funds to make this research and writing possible. *Pasting Up Protest* is supported by a Seed Grant (2018–19) from the University of Waterloo and an Insight Development Grant (2019–22) from the Social Sciences and Humanities Research Council of Canada. My field trips to Oaxaca and Mexico City with research assistants would not have happened without this funding. Indeed, travelling to Mexico with students has been one of the most enjoyable aspects of this project.

Two different sets of eyes are always better than one, and my students' diverse backgrounds and rich reflections informed my own thinking and propelled my ideas forward.

Angela Roorda (formerly arts research development officer at the University of Waterloo) and Ruth Knechtel (formerly senior manager, fund agencies and non-profit sponsors at the University of Waterloo) deserve more praise than words can convey. Both were instrumental in helping me think through and refine the grant proposal that launched this study.

A special thank-you to Dr Monica Leoni, chair of the Department of Spanish and Latin American Studies at the University of Waterloo, who understood early on that far from taking time away from my teaching responsibilities, research keeps me attuned to the world our students inhabit and feeds my pedagogy.

To my wonderful colleagues at the Centre for Teaching Excellence at the University of Waterloo, thank you for helping me reconcile the many facets of my professional identity and encouraging me to find balance. To Brianna and Mark, thank you for urging me to carve out time and mental space for my research. Your flexibility means the world.

I would also like to extend my thanks to the anonymous reviewers for their astute and thoughtful comments. *Pasting Up Protest* is stronger because of their thorough reading of the manuscript and many useful suggestions. While it is always challenging to read evaluators' reports, never have I been more grateful for peer review than after reading the anonymous reviewers' reports, each of whom provided me with a critical but kind take on the manuscript.

This investigation would not have happened without direct access to the artists I study. They all opened their doors and were very generous with their time and thoughts. A very special thank-you to the members of ASARO, URT-Arte, and ARMARTE for meeting with me multiple times over the years, and for always being willing to answer my many, many questions. I am particularly indebted to Shannon Sheppard for allowing me to reproduce photographs of artworks by URT-Arte and ARMARTE; to the Center for Southwest Research, part of the University of New Mexico Libraries, for letting me reproduce prints by ASARO; and to the members of ARMARTE for going through their own archives to send me the best images possible to illustrate this book.

To my wonderful team of research assistants, I am not exaggerating when I say that this book would not exist without you and the countless hours you have dedicated to it. Thank you for helping me become a (hopefully good) team leader. The funny thing about the humanities is that most of our work is single-authored, and as such no one teaches you how to lead a team. And since I did not really know what I was getting into when I embarked on this path, I could not really tell you where it was headed … And yet, you were all more than happy to travel with me on this journey and help me shape and expand this project. When given an unfiltered look at how messy my research process is, you accepted this "behind the scenes" access with grace. To all of you, thank you for letting me treat you more as collaborators than assistants.

Ariane, your wealth of knowledge across disciplines and your artistic expertise still intimidate me to this day (in a good way!). Many of the thoughts laid out in this book stem from our conversations. Working alongside such a talented artist helped me to refine my position on the role artists play in society and to start seeing the world through the eyes of a creator.

Anushka, you have a knack for turning the most mundane tasks into adventures. "Stalking artists" sounds a lot more exciting than "creating and updating a pictorial database" even if it was also a lot more awkward to explain when we were caught using that expression. Our short trip to Oaxaca in October 2019, in the weeks leading up the Día de Muertos celebrations, remains a highlight of this adventure. Eating *pan de muerto* "for research"? Check. I am happy you graduated and finally went from "sometimes friend" to "full-time friend."

Hannah, research assistant extraordinaire on three projects, co-author, you are an exceptional woman who taught me boundaries. Thank you for encouraging me to take up climbing and gifting me the first house plant I have yet to kill, and above all for holding me accountable and letting me hold you accountable about resting and taking time off. Two strong, shall I say stubborn women forcing each other *not* to work makes for an interesting work dynamic. And yet, ours is by far the most enriching "work" relationship of my career to date.

Rafael, thank you for helping me select the images that are reproduced in the book, and for bridging this project with the next.

Clara, merci de m'avoir ouvert les portes d'une nouvelle discipline et de m'avoir patiemment expliqué toutes les nuances entre les différents régimes de pratique. Ton aide a été inestimable à la rédaction de la deuxième et de la troisième partie du livre. Je garde un excellent souvenir de l'été passé ensemble au Mexique, où chaque murale sur laquelle nous tombions ou chaque musée que nous visitions nourrissait de longues conversations.

This book was written on a steady musical diet of Alexandra Stréliski, Jean-Michel Blais, and Half Moon Run. Thank you for making music that I can write to, from which I can take something new from every time I listen, and that reminds me that beauty still exists in this world. For some obscure reason, the mental images of the myriad ways of destroying a human body never stuck to your songs the way they did to other artists' music, and that makes me so very happy.

I am indebted to the generosity of the following individuals, who have provided comments and advice at various stages of my career.

For affirming my voice and offering guidance and moral support over the years, thanks to Nadine Fladd. You are a highly skilled communication specialist, and an even better human being. Our meetings are the highlight of my week; you lend me words when I lack the right ones, you endure my half-baked ideas and roughest drafts without judgment, and you expand the boundaries of my intellectual world. I admire your kindness and sharp thinking: You showed me that there is no academia without kindness, and that I was not "flawed" for caring more about people than deliverables. I will always owe you more than I can express. I know you will say that I am the one who did the work, and while there is no denying that, you have unreservedly contributed a great deal to my growth – as a writer, obviously, but also as a teacher, team leader, co-author, person. I want to be like you when I grow up.

Jorge Carlos Guerrero, never have I been more grateful for all the lessons you imparted during my PhD years than when I started revising this manuscript. After a thorough freak-out – some things will never change – I went back to my notes from the summer of 2016, and there it was waiting for me: a system. Even if we do not work as closely anymore, sometimes I still hear your voice in my head, making a suggestion or two.

I am grateful to my friends, who either urged and reminded me to take breaks, or sent me memes and pictures of hedgehogs, alpacas, and penguins. You also listened to me rant and complain about the state of the world and helped me think through my ideas.

Murals, stencils, and tags consistently catch my eye when I travel. Wherever I go, I return with hundreds, sometimes thousands of pictures of graffiti and street art. Anyone who has travelled with me can attest to the fact that I am obsessed, stopping every other minute to snap a picture. Thank you to everyone who is still willing to travel with me, and nice enough to always let me stop – yes, again – just to take one more quick shot.

Julien, thank you for convincing me to take up photography more than a decade ago. I never thought it would be (the best) part of my research, and yet here we are. I am grateful for all the pictures of tags and murals you email me from around the world.

Noah, putting *Getting Up for the People* in my hands changed the course of my research. I am still not as much of an activist as I would want to be. At least now I write about it. Baby steps.

Jesse, thank you for being the best sounding board I could dream of, for calling me out on my biases with so much love and compassion, for reading early drafts of this book, and for sharing your wealth of knowledge of Latin America and visual culture. Our Friday afternoon accountability sessions are the best way to end the week.

Nicole, merci de m'avoir inculqué (imposé?) le 9 à 5, le repos dominical et la minutie du cannage. Je ne suis pas tout à fait saine d'esprit, mais certainement davantage qu'auparavant, et définitivement plus grâce aux fins de semaine passées ensemble.

Alice, merci de m'avoir enseigné que "pain is just an information." Ma santé à la fois physique et mentale t'en sera éternellement reconnaissante.

À mes parents, Férial et Réjane, merci de ne pas trop vous inquiéter quand je suis au Mexique ... ou au moins de ne pas trop me le dire. Votre appui inconditionnel m'est extrêmement précieux.

These acknowledgments would not bear my signature if I did not get a bit cheeky toward the end. I have been lucky to avoid heated conversations and needless insults despite the feminist underpinnings of this investigation, and I know from talking to feminist colleagues that this is truly a special gift.

To everyone (I am too polite to write "To all the men," but yes, they were all men) who commented that I "should work on something more uplifting," I ask, What could be more uplifting than studying artists who are actively trying to change the world? (I know you mean "stop working on violence." I will not.)

Many people who believed I should change the focus of my research were eager to share their favourite artists with me. Thank you for sending me the social media accounts of street artists and activists you believed I should know about. You contributed to expanding my network and, more often than not, helped me discover artists I would not have heard about otherwise.

To all those who said at some point something along the lines of "What's happening in Mexico is so sad" with pity in their voice, I say the following: Yes, it is, but we Canadians, North Americans, the West, indeed the entire world are not faring much better. Our nations, too, face an epidemic of gender-based violence. I highly recommend that you take the time to explore the website of the Canadian Femicide Observatory for Justice and Accountability (femicideincanada.ca/). While it is unlikely to make your day better, it might help you understand that gendered violence is not a "Mexican issue."

After hearing me talk about the high number of feminicides perpetrated in Canada, people generally respond with something like, "Here, at least we don't disappear students." No, we do not. We have not in a while, anyway. As I was finishing the manuscript, news of mass graves located on the grounds of former residential schools in both Alberta and British Columbia started to circulate. The circumstances may be different, but at the core, this is also about how societies hierarchize the value of human life.

We all need to do better.

Abbreviations

AMLO	Andrés Manuel López Obrador (president of Mexico, December 2018–September 2024)
APPO	Asamblea Popular de los Pueblos de Oaxaca (Popular Assembly of the Peoples of Oaxaca)
ARMARTE	Alianza Revolucionaria de Mujeres Haciendo Arte (Revolutionary Alliance of Women Making Art)
ASARO	Asamblea de Artistas Revolucionarios de Oaxaca (Assembly of Revolutionary Artists of Oaxaca)
CNDH	Comisión Nacional de los Derechos Humanos (National Human Rights Commission)
CNTE	Coordinadora Nacional de los Trabajadores de la Educación (National Coordination of Education Workers)
EZLN	Ejército Zapatista de Liberación Nacional (Zapatista Army of National Liberation)
GIEI	Grupo Interdisciplinario de Expertos Independientes (Interdisciplinary Group of Independent Experts)
IAGO	Instituto de Artes Gráficas de Oaxaca (Institute of Graphic Arts of Oaxaca)
TGP	Taller de Gráfica Popular (People's Graphic Workshop)
LEAR	Liga de Escritores y Artistas Revolucionarios (League of Revolutionary Writers and Artists)
MUGRe	Mujeres Grabando Resistencias (Women Engraving Resistances)

PDLP Partido de los Pobres (Party of the Poor)
PGR Procuraduría General de la República (Office of the Attorney General)
PRI Partido Revolucionario Institucional (Institutional Revolutionary Party)
SEDENA Secretaría de la Defensa Nacional (Secretariat of National Defence)
TAC Taller de Arte Comunitario (Workshop for Community Art)
UNESCO United Nations Educational, Scientific and Cultural Organization
UPVA Unión Popular de Vendedores Ambulantes 28 de Octubre (Popular Union of Street Vendors 28 October)
URT-Arte Unión Revolucionaria de Trabajadores del Arte (Revolutionary Union of Art Workers)

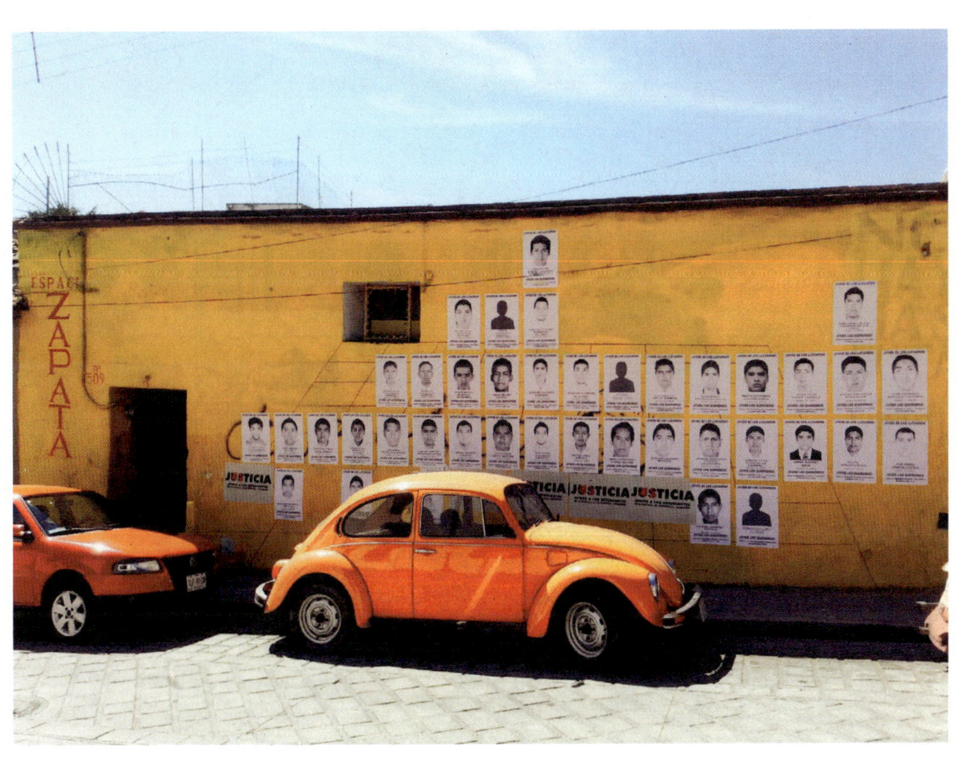

Plate 1
Facade of Espacio Zapata in October 2014, with a billboard-like installation made up of the forty-three Ayotzinapa students' "missing" posters.

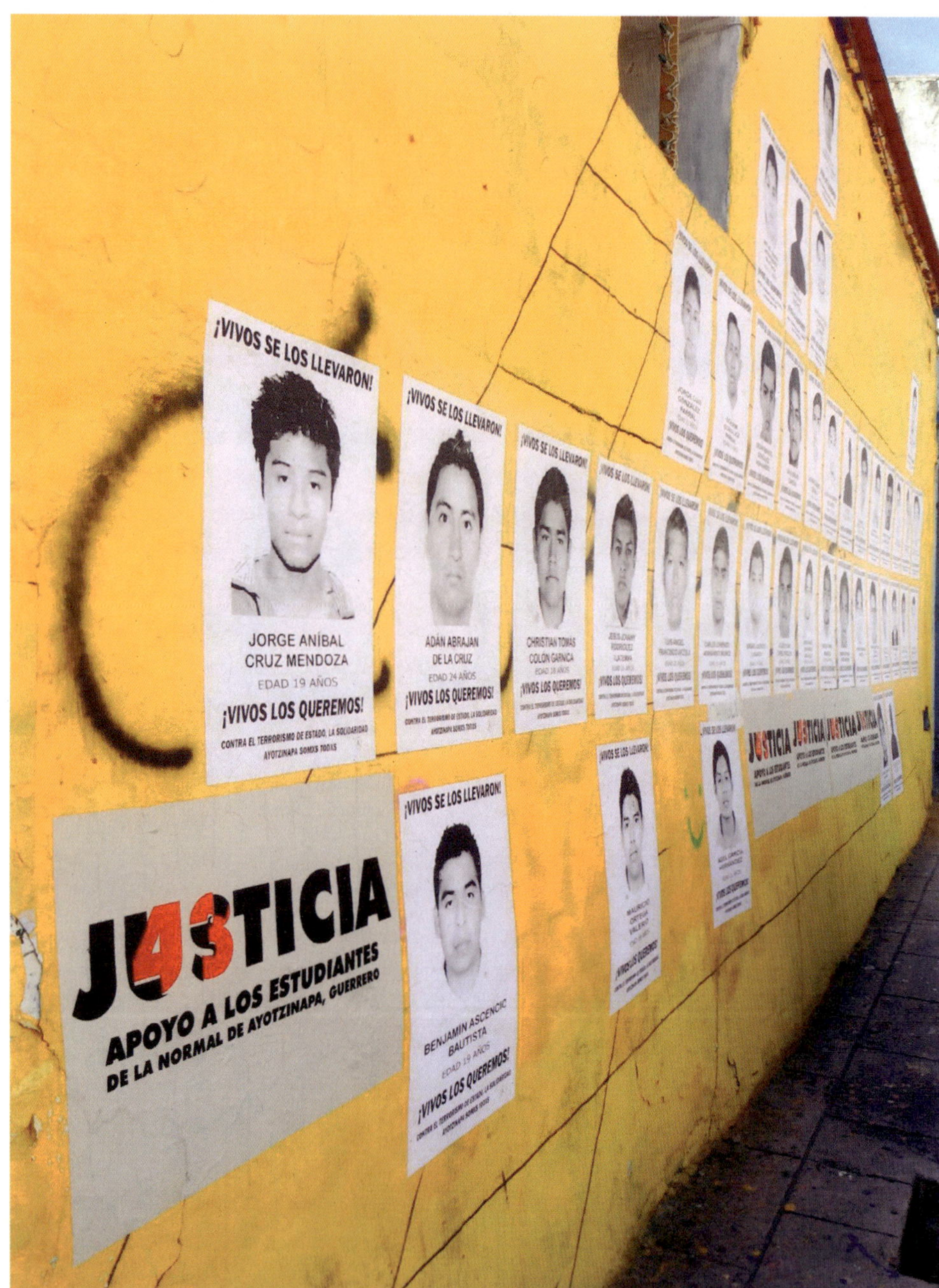

¡VIVOS SE LOS LLEVARON!
JORGE ANÍBAL CRUZ MENDOZA
EDAD 19 AÑOS
¡VIVOS LOS QUEREMOS!
CONTRA EL TERRORISMO DE ESTADO, LA SOLIDARIDAD
AYOTZINAPA SOMXS TODXS
¡VIVOS SE LOS LLEVARON!
ADÁN ABRAJAN DE LA CRUZ
EDAD 24 AÑOS
¡VIVOS LOS QUEREMOS!
¡VIVOS SE LOS LLEVARON!
CHRISTIAN TOMÁS COLÓN GARNICA
¡VIVOS LOS QUEREMOS!
¡VIVOS SE LOS LLEVARON!
BENJAMIN ASCENCIO BAUTISTA
EDAD 19 AÑOS
¡VIVOS LOS QUEREMOS!
JU43TICIA
APOYO A LOS ESTUDIANTES
DE LA NORMAL DE AYOTZINAPA, GUERRERO

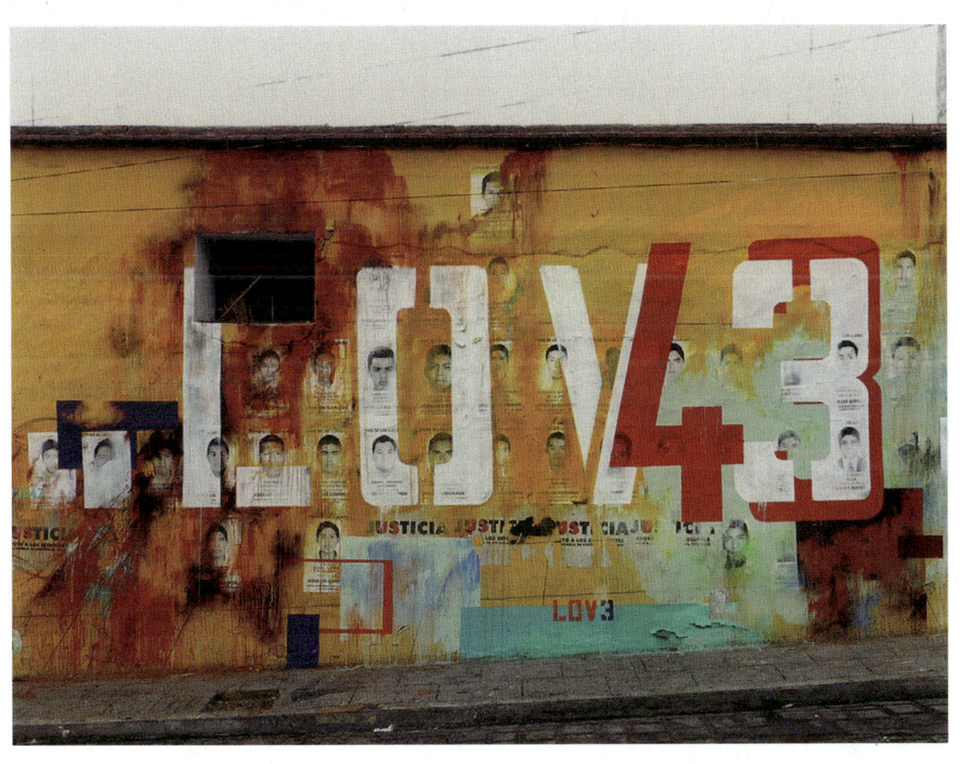

Plate 2 Opposite
Close-up of the "missing" posters installation with a poster that reads, "Justicia 43" (Justice 43).

Plate 3 Above
Evolution of the billboard-like installation made up of the forty-three Ayotzinapa students' "missing" posters, now reading "LOVE 43."

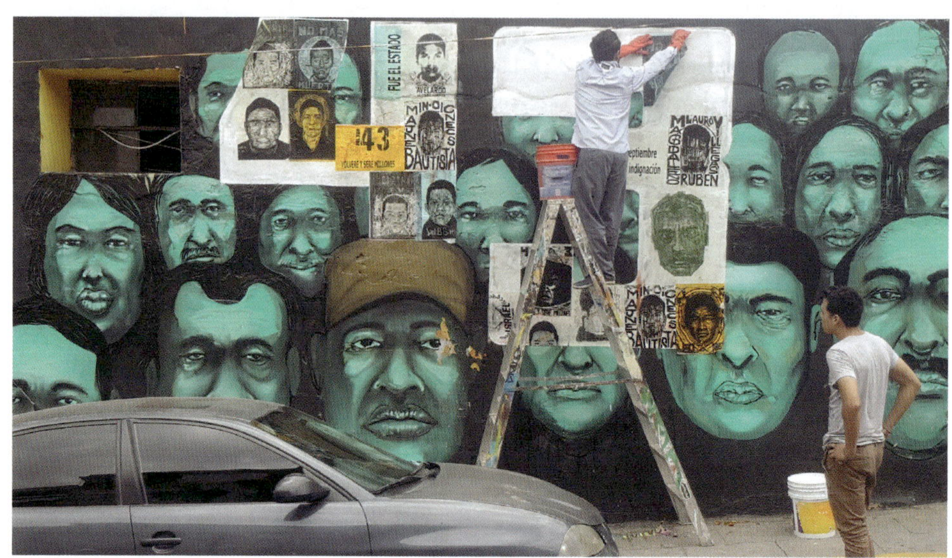

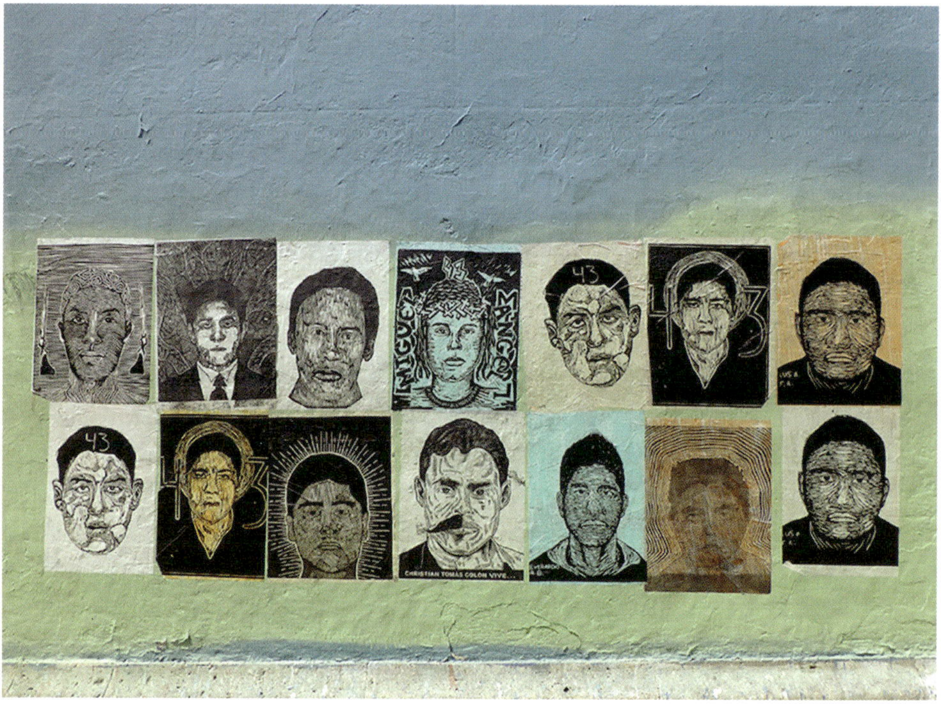

Plate 4 Top
Installation in progress, with the number 43 filled in with wheat paste posters portraying the forty-three missing students.

Plate 5 Bottom
Wheat paste posters depicting some of the forty-three missing students.

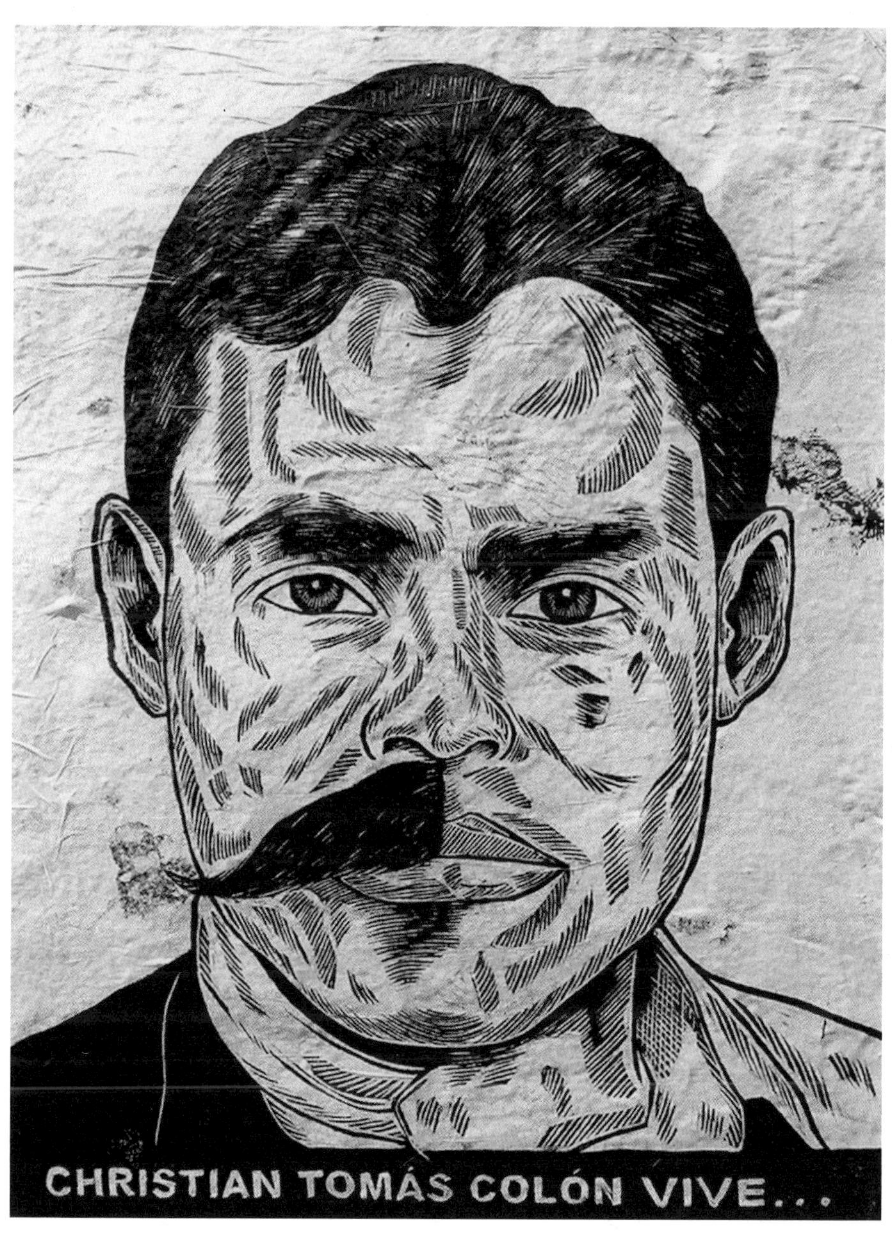

Plate 6
Wheat paste poster depicting Christian Tomás Colón in the likeness of Emiliano Zapata. The poster reads, "Tomás Colón vive" (Tomás Colón lives).

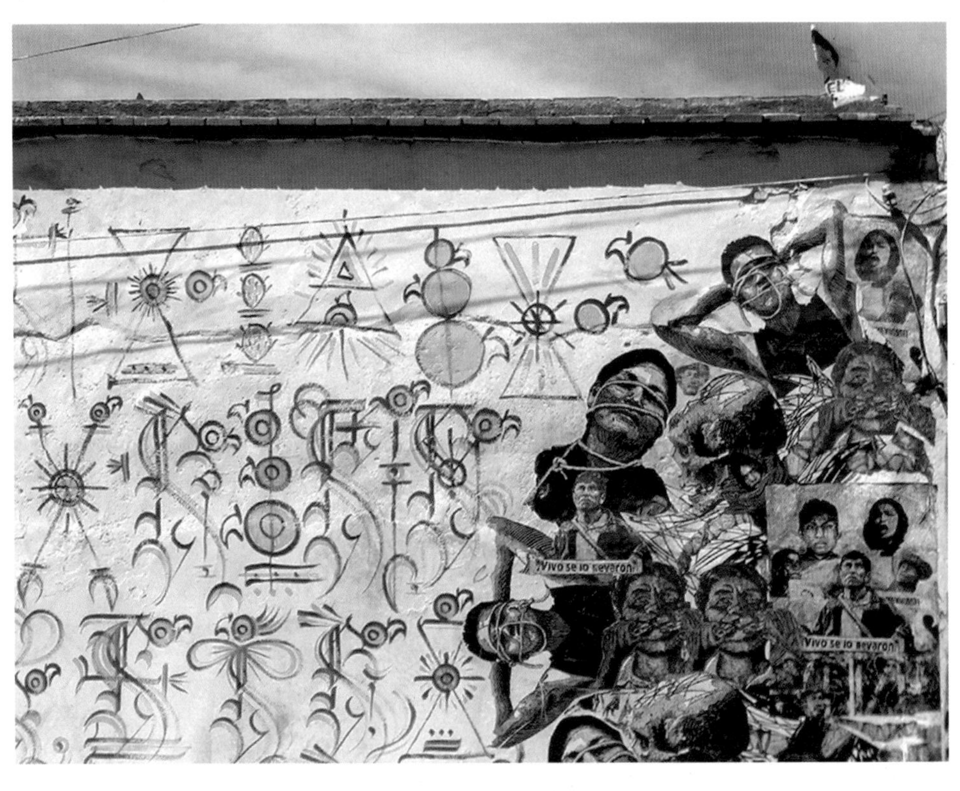

Plate 7 Above
Mural installation on the facade of Espacio Zapata.

Plate 8 Opposite
Poster showing political leader Lucio Cabañas Barrientos holding a placard that reads, "#43."

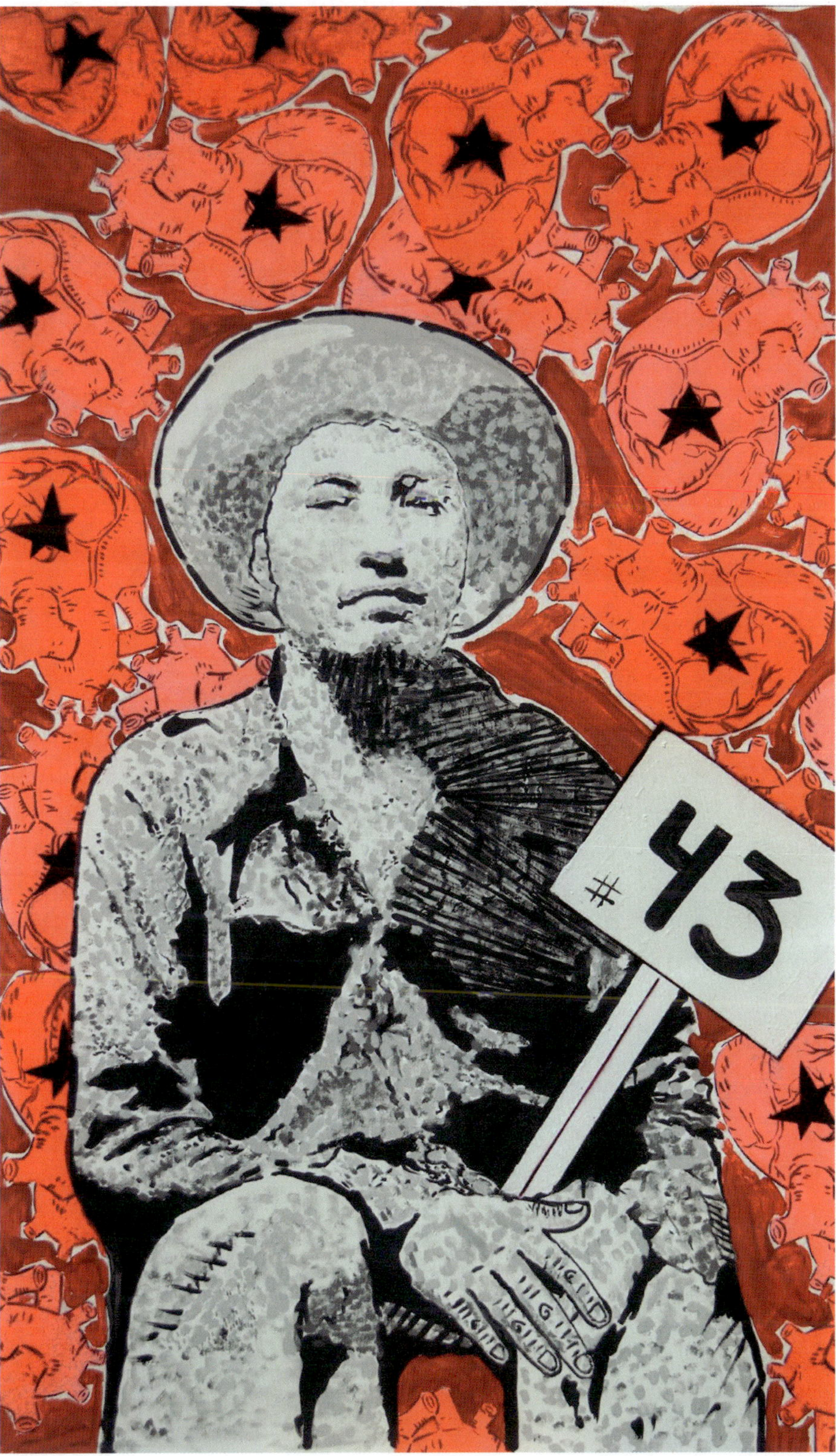
#43

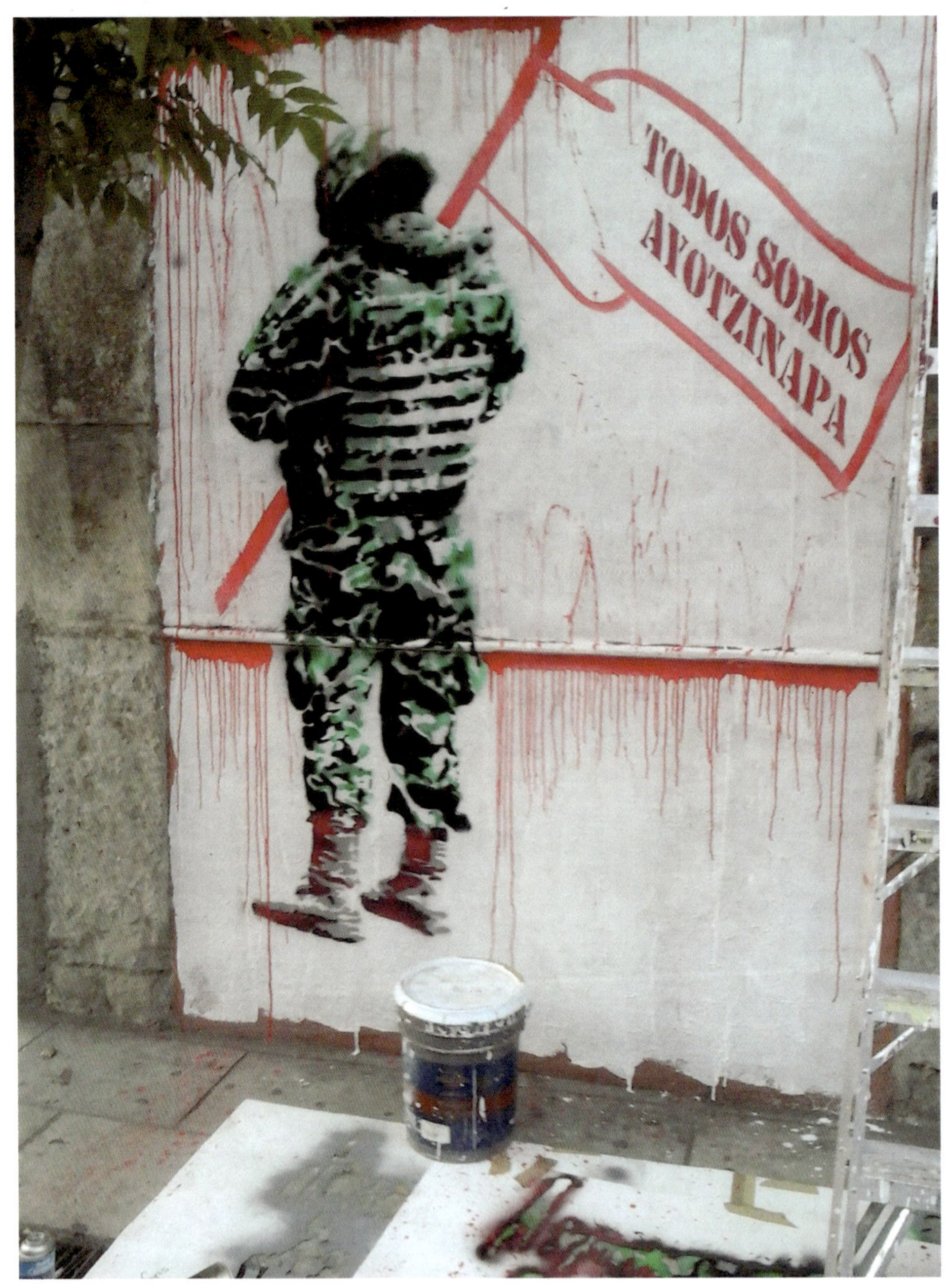
TODOS SOMOS
AYOTZINAPA

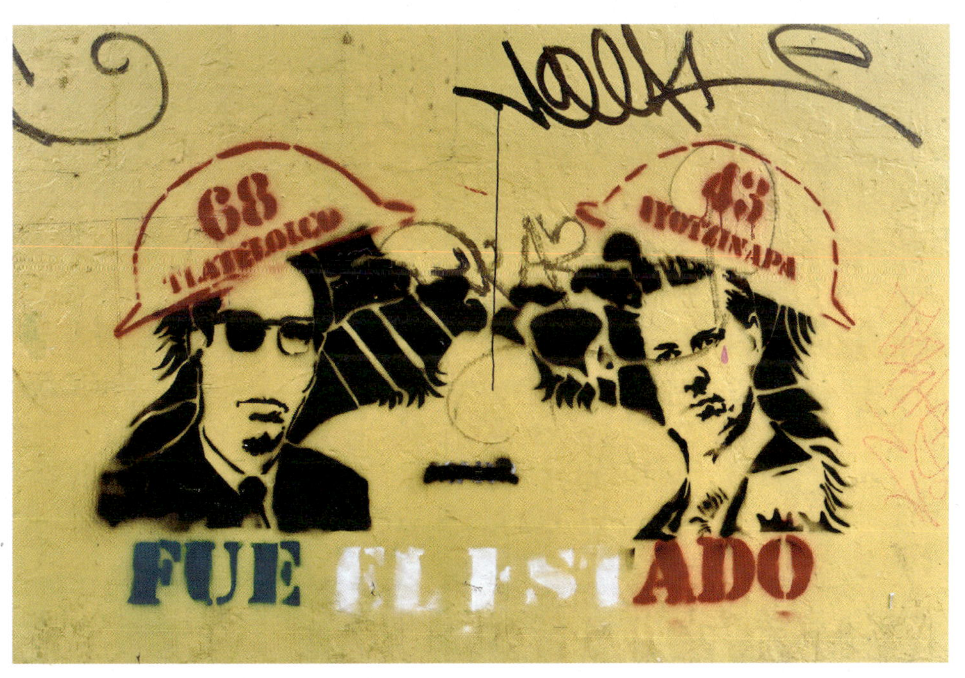

Plate 9 Opposite
Stencil of a soldier holding a banner that reads, "Todos somos Ayotzinapa" (We are all Ayotzinapa).

Plate 10 Above
Stencil linking the 1968 Tlatelolco massacre to the 2014 mass disappearance of the forty-three students.

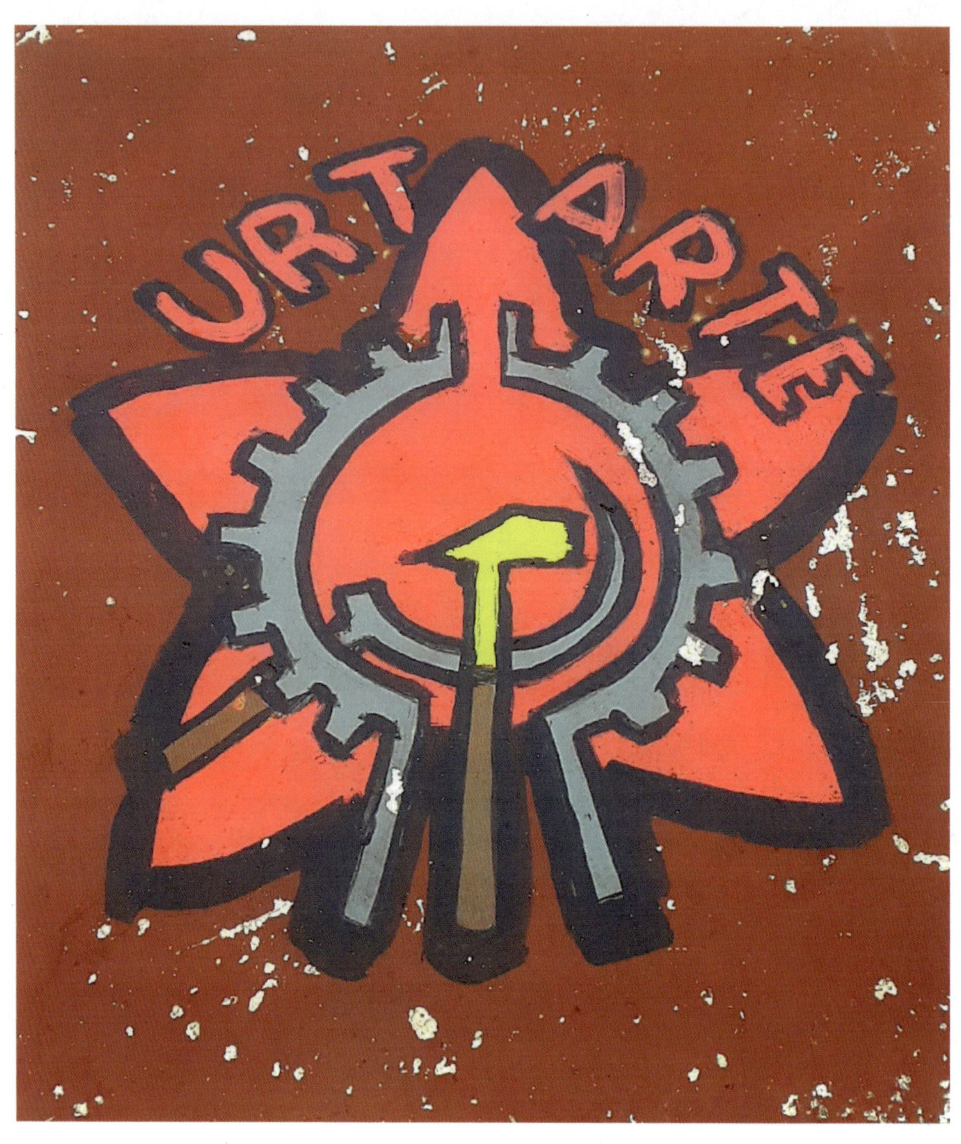

Plate 11
URT-Arte logo hand-painted on the facade of the Taller de Arte Comunitario on Calle Porfirio Díaz in Oaxaca.

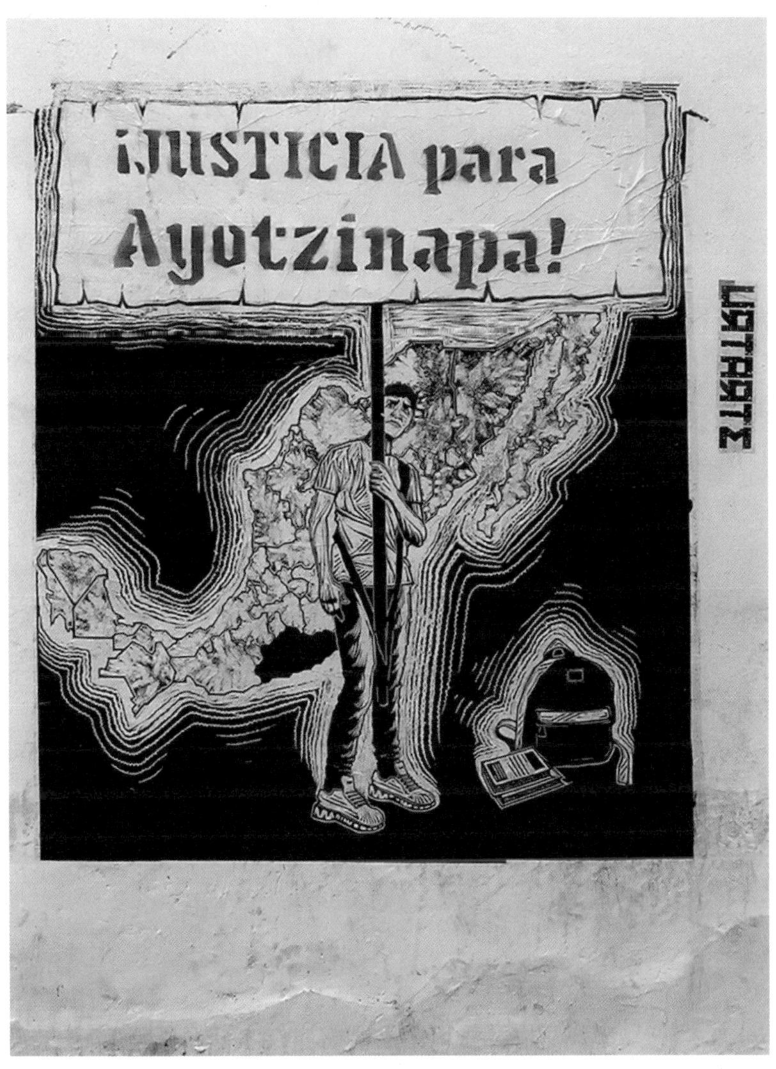

Plate 12
Wheat paste poster showing a student standing in front of a map of Mexico and holding a poster that reads, "Justicia para Ayotzinapa" (Justice for Ayotzinapa).

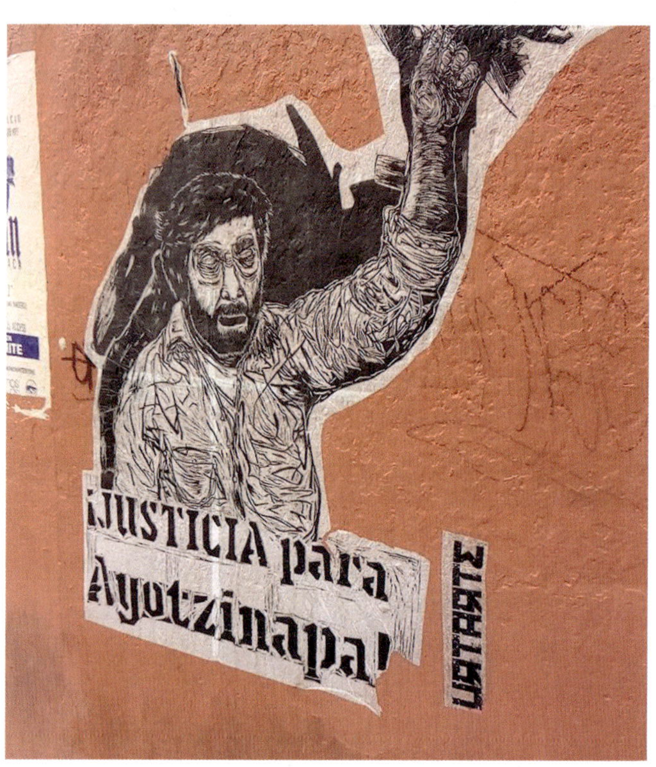
¡JUSTICIA para
Ayotzinapa!
URTARTE

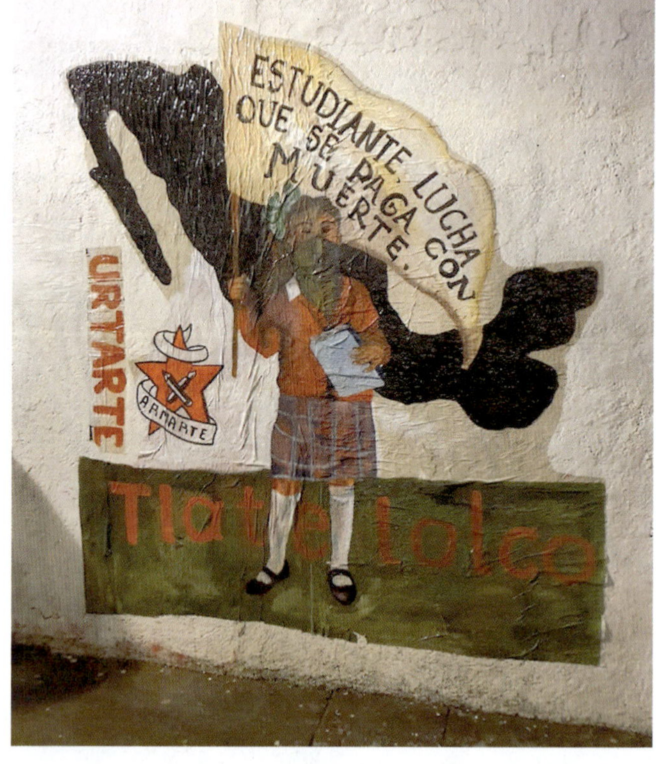
ESTUDIANTE LUCHA
QUE SE PAGA CON
MUERTE.
URTARTE
ARMARTE
Tlatelolco

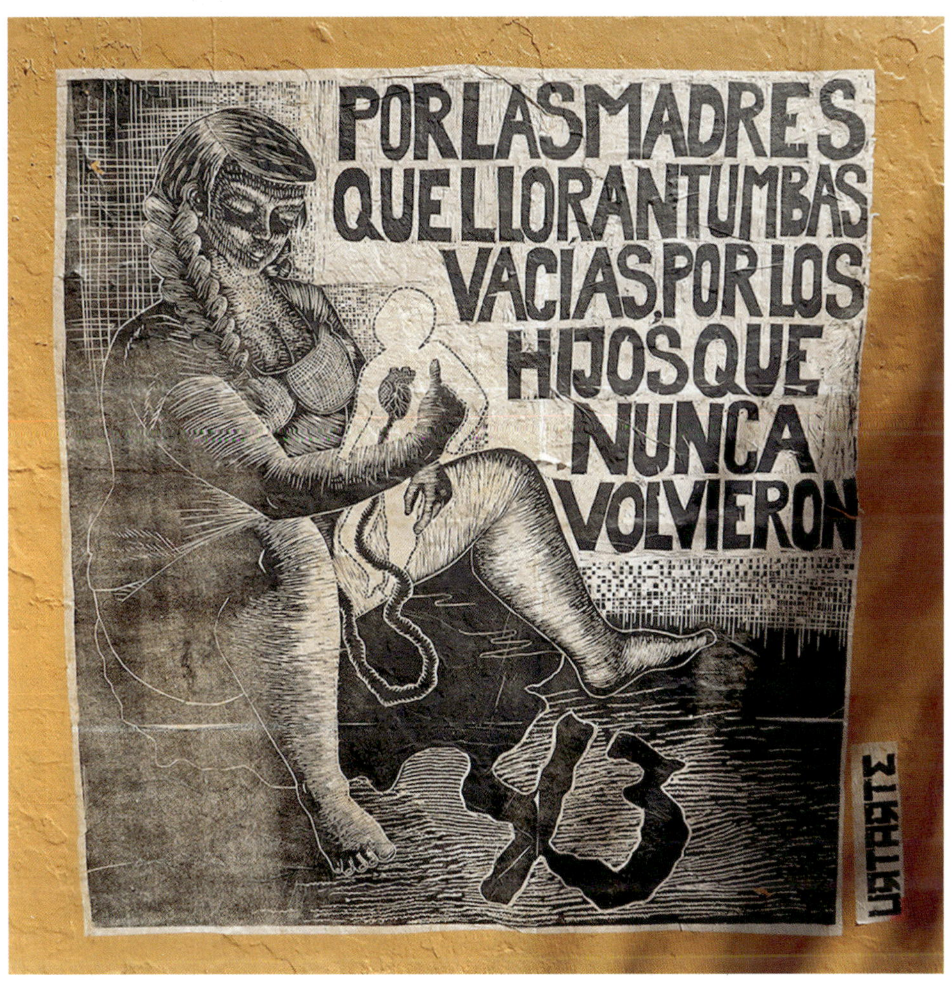

Plate 13 Opposite top
Wheat paste poster showing a teacher protesting. The caption below reads, "¡Justicia para Ayotzinapa!" (Justice for Ayotzinapa!).

Plate 14 Opposite bottom
Hand-painted poster of a female student protesting. She holds a banner that reads, "Estudiante que lucha que se paga con la muerte" (Students who fight pay with their lives).

Plate 15 Above
Wheat paste poster showing a mother holding her dead son. The tagline reads, "Por las madres que lloran tumbas vacias por los hijos que nunca volvieron" (For the mothers who cry empty tombs for children who never came back).

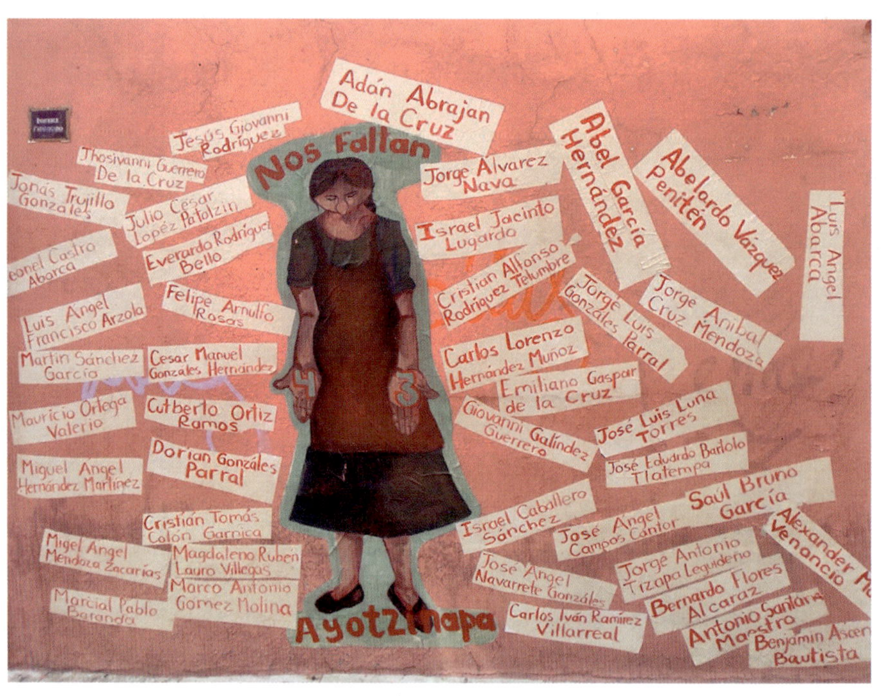

Plate 16
Installation consisting of a hand-painted poster of a woman surrounded by the names of the forty-three missing students.

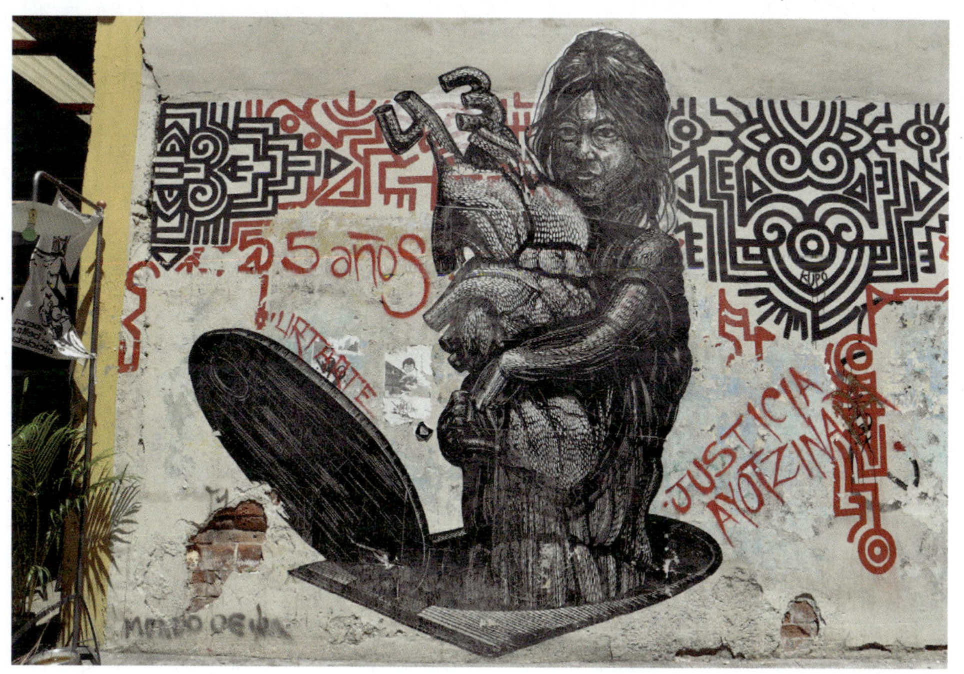

Plate 17
Monumental-sized wheat paste poster commemorating the fifth anniversary of the students' disappearance and showing a young woman holding a heart and emerging from a manhole.

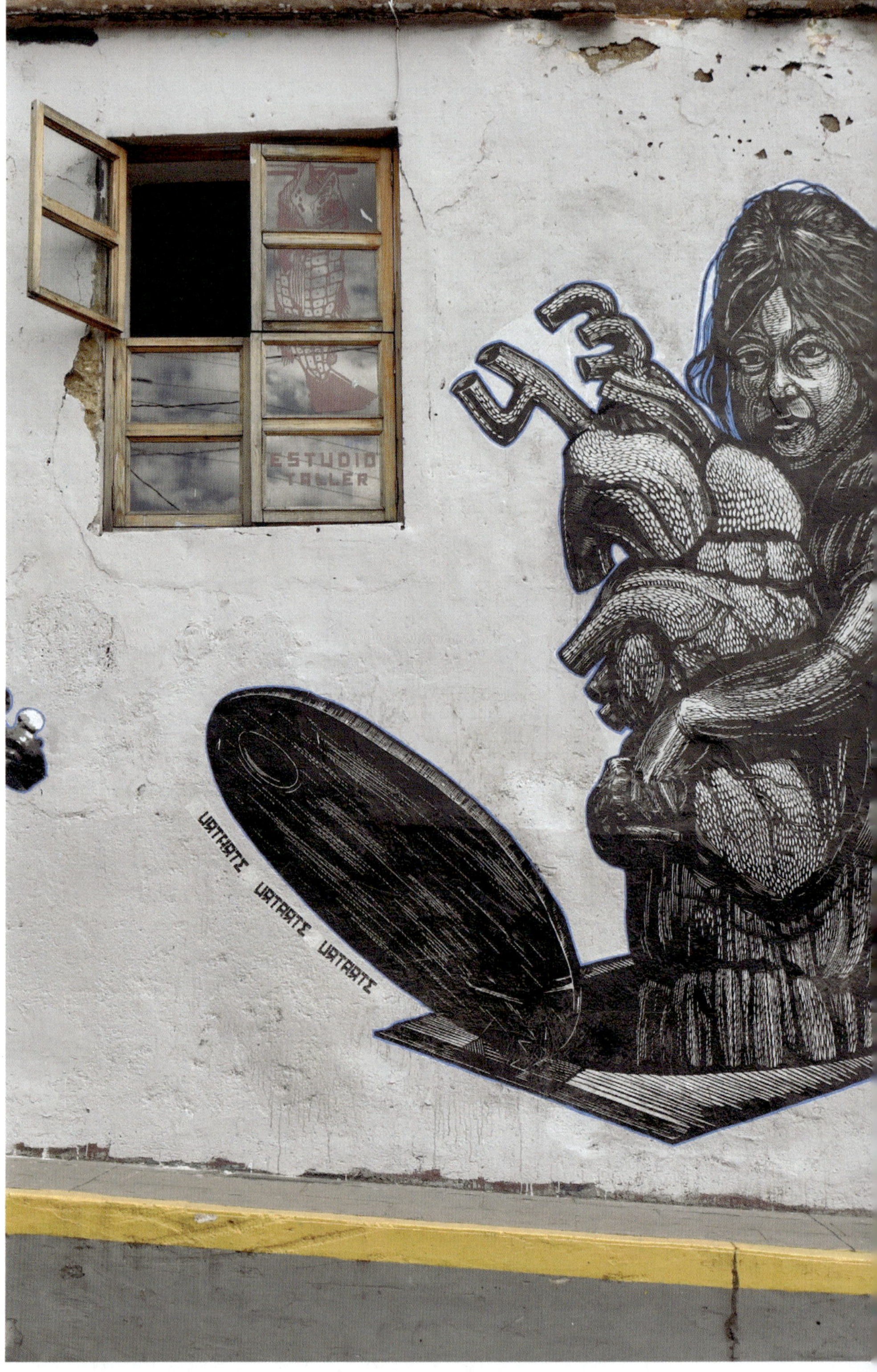
ESTUDIO
TALLER
URTARTE URTARTE URTARTE

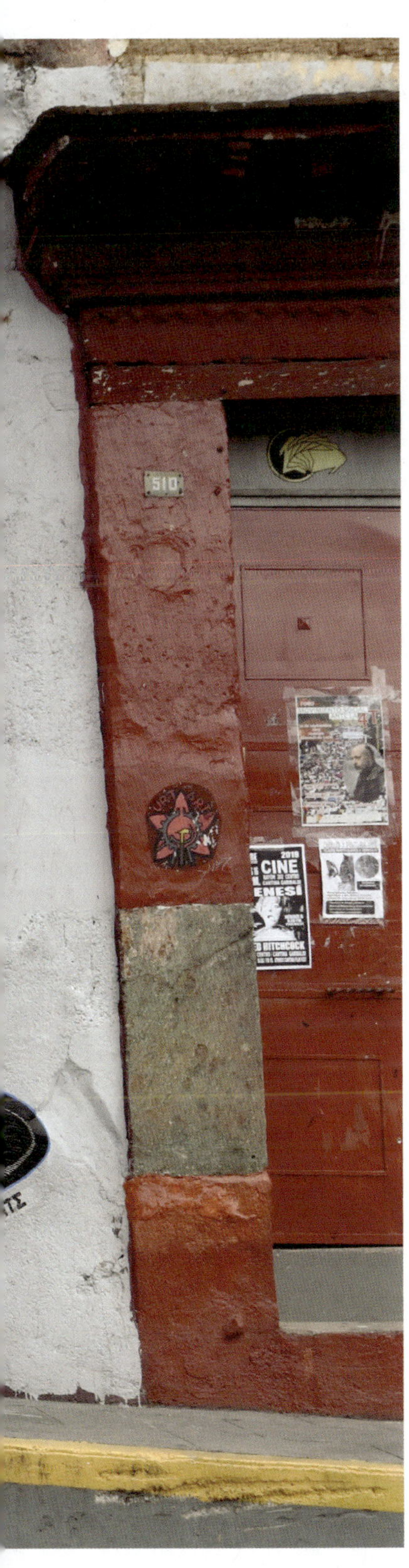

Plate 18
Monumental-sized wheat paste poster of a young woman holding a heart and emerging from a manhole.

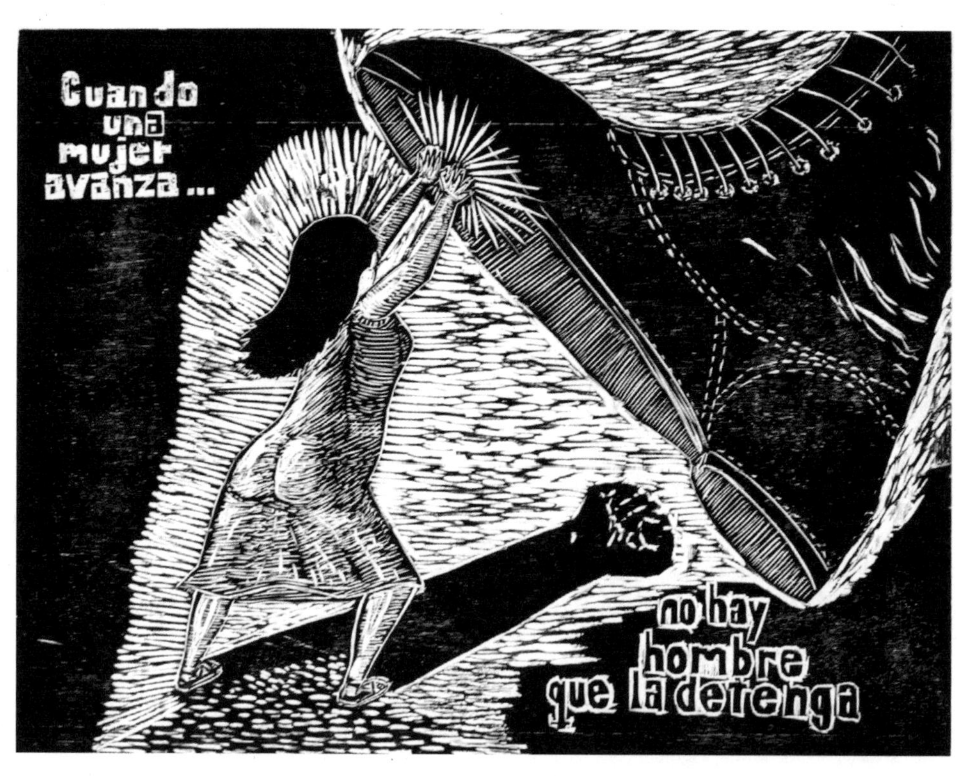

Plate 19 Above
"Cuando una mujer avanza … no hay hombre que la detenga"
(When a woman advances, no man can stop her).

Plate 20 Opposite
"Alto a la violencia contra las mujeres" (Stop violence against women).

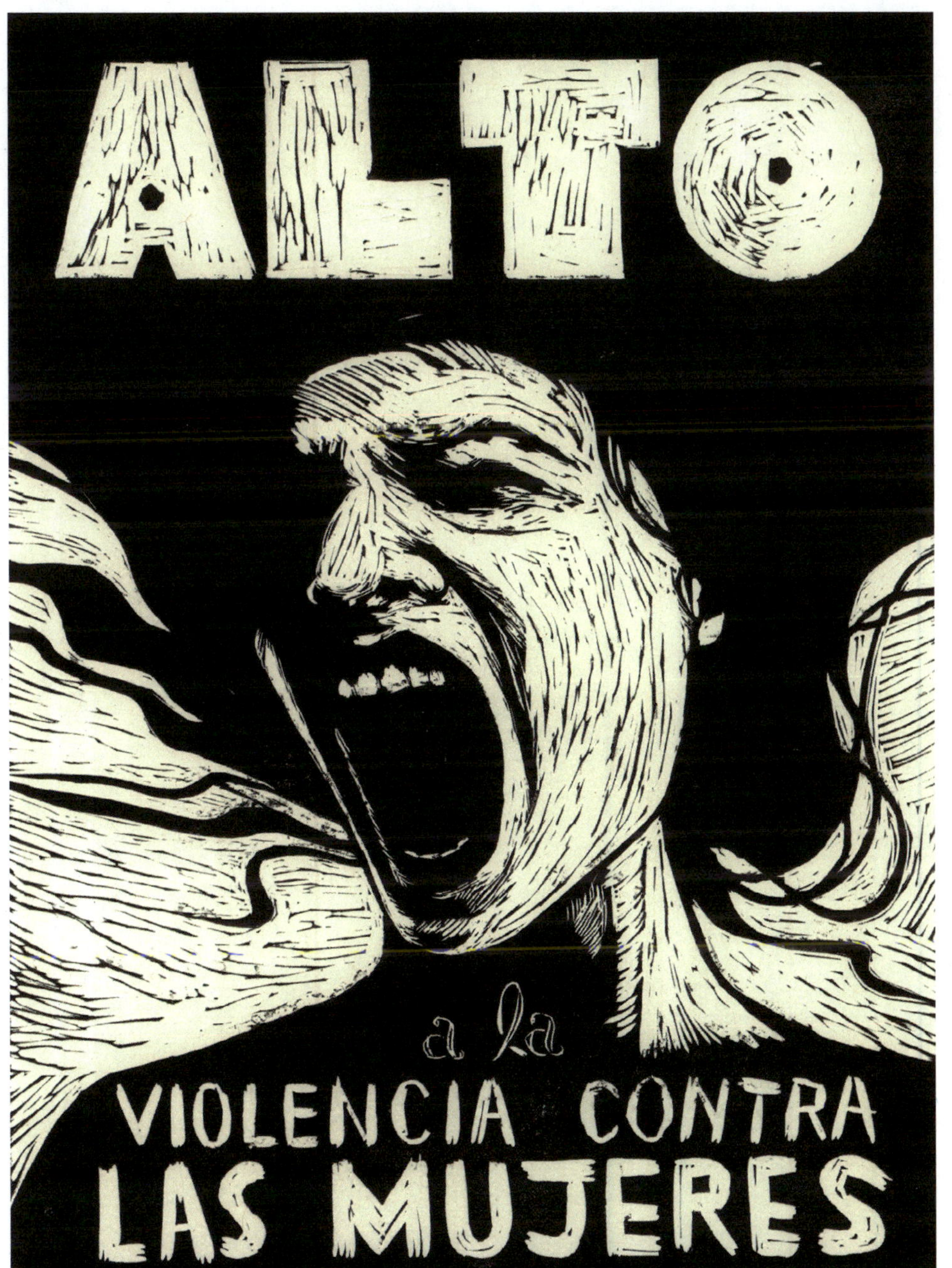
ALTO
a la
VIOLENCIA CONTRA
LAS MUJERES

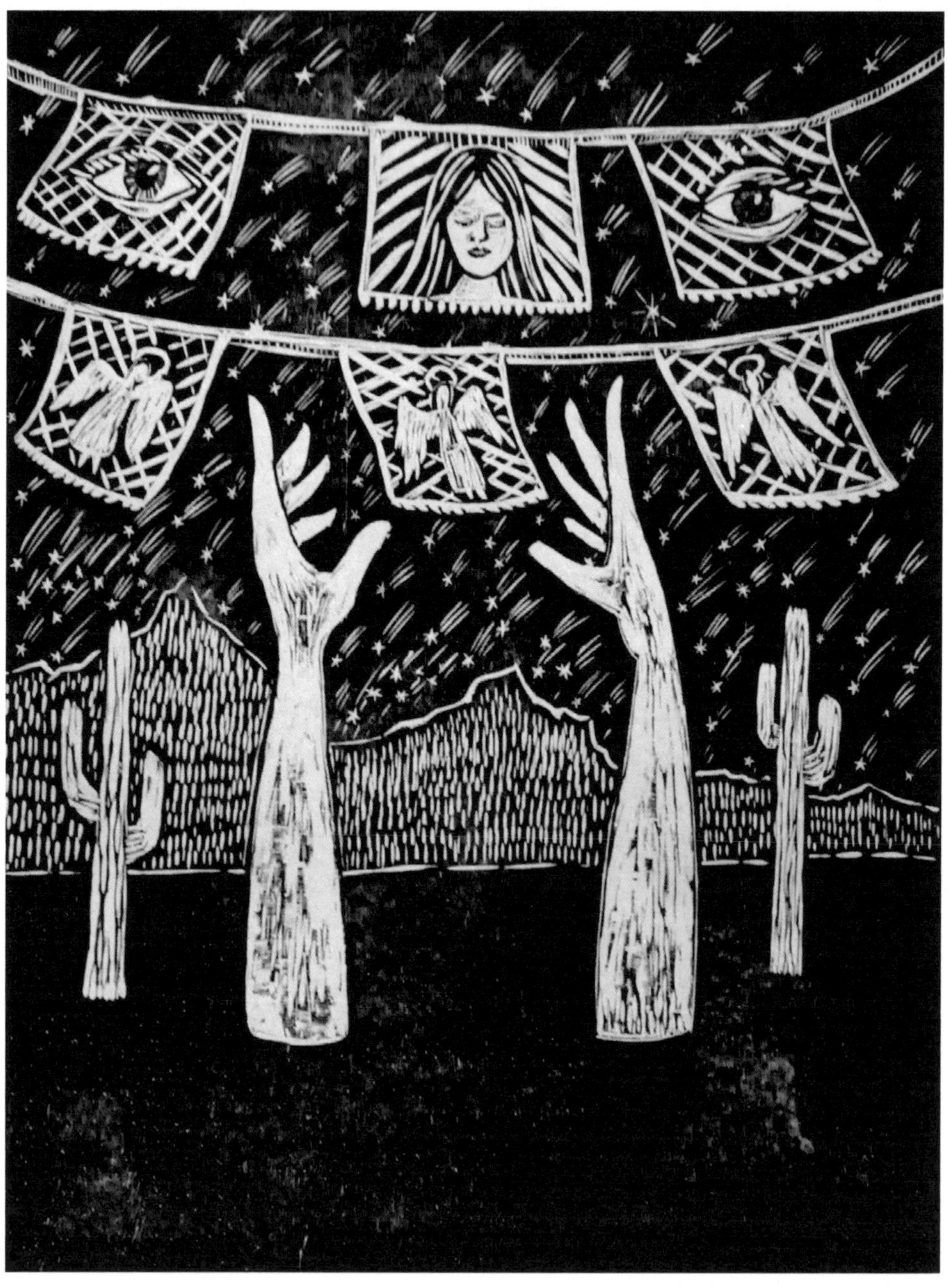

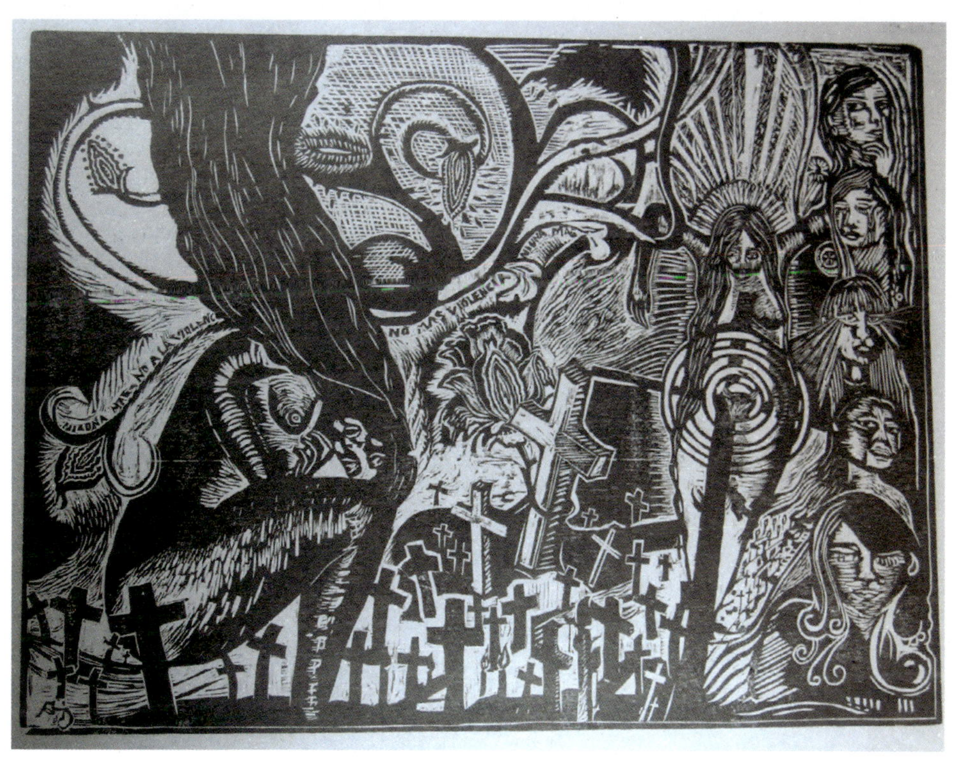

Plate 21 Above
Print showing a buried woman with outstretched arms reaching above the ground.

Plate 22 Opposite
"No a la violencia. Ni una más" (No to violence. Not one woman more).

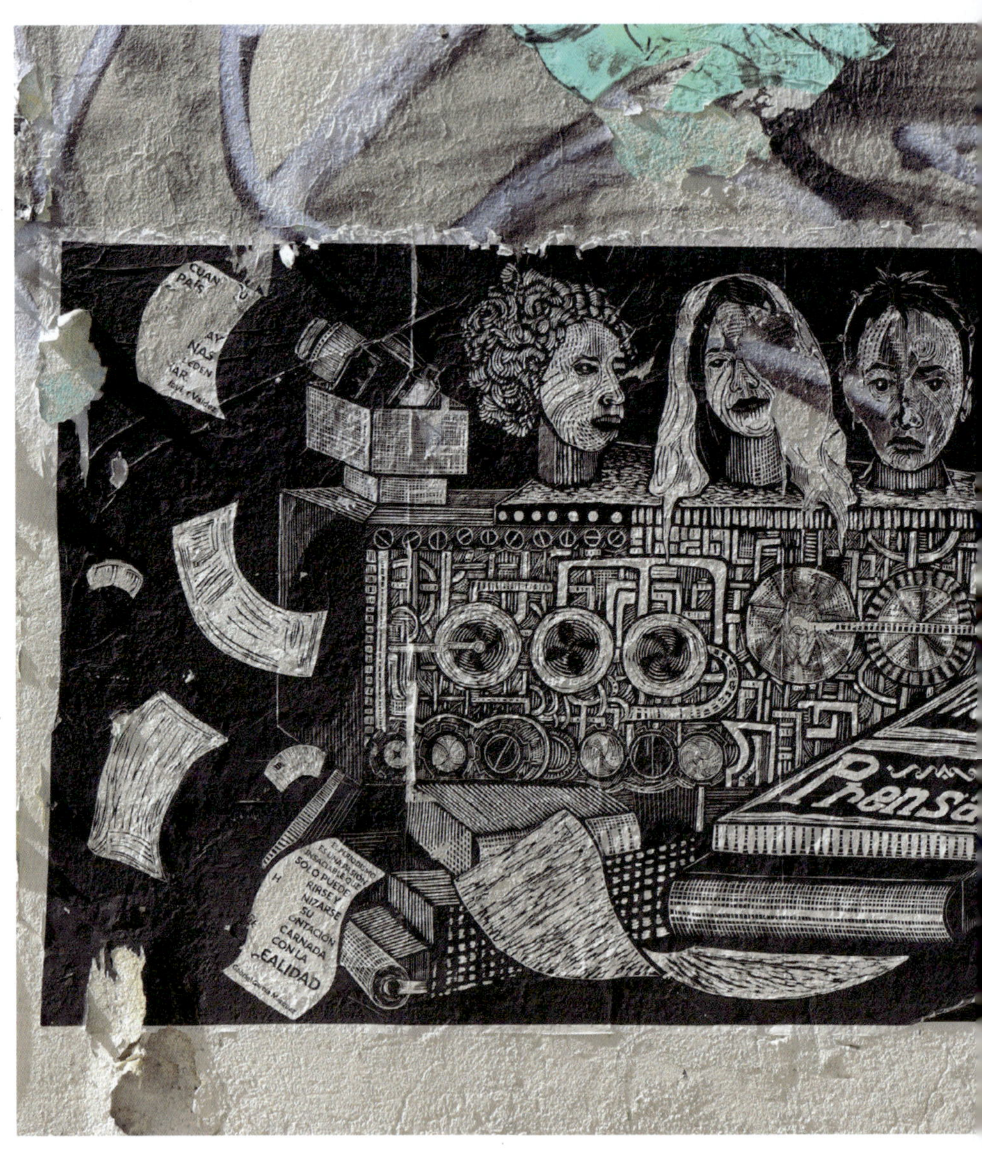

Plate 23
Wheat paste poster depicting women's heads on a printing press becoming news headlines.

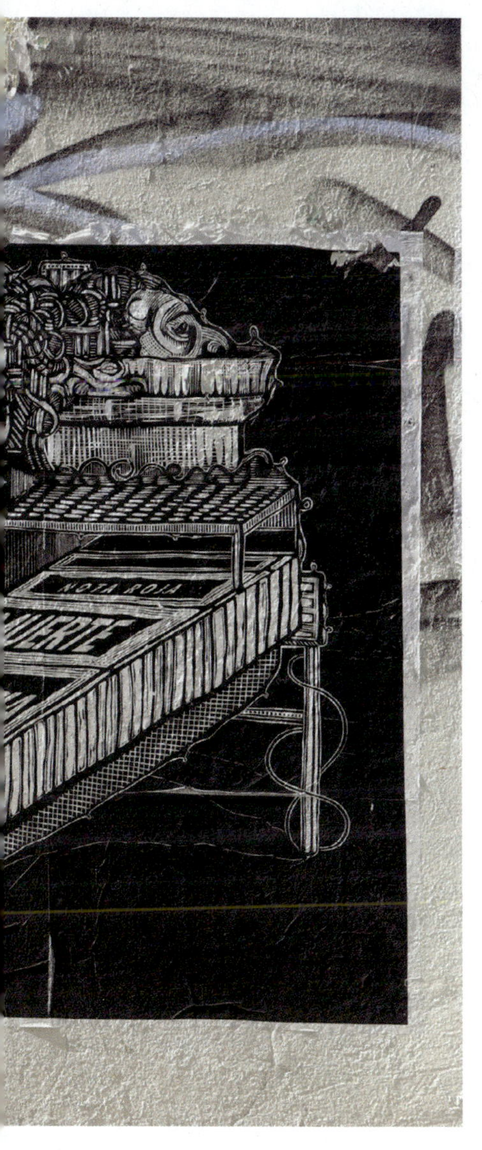

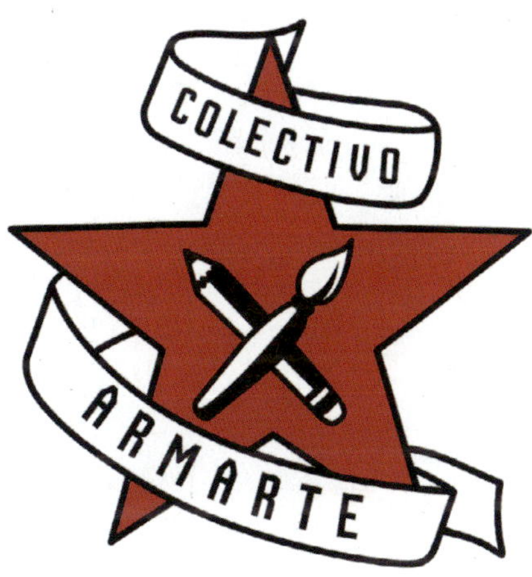

Plate 24
ARMARTE's logo.

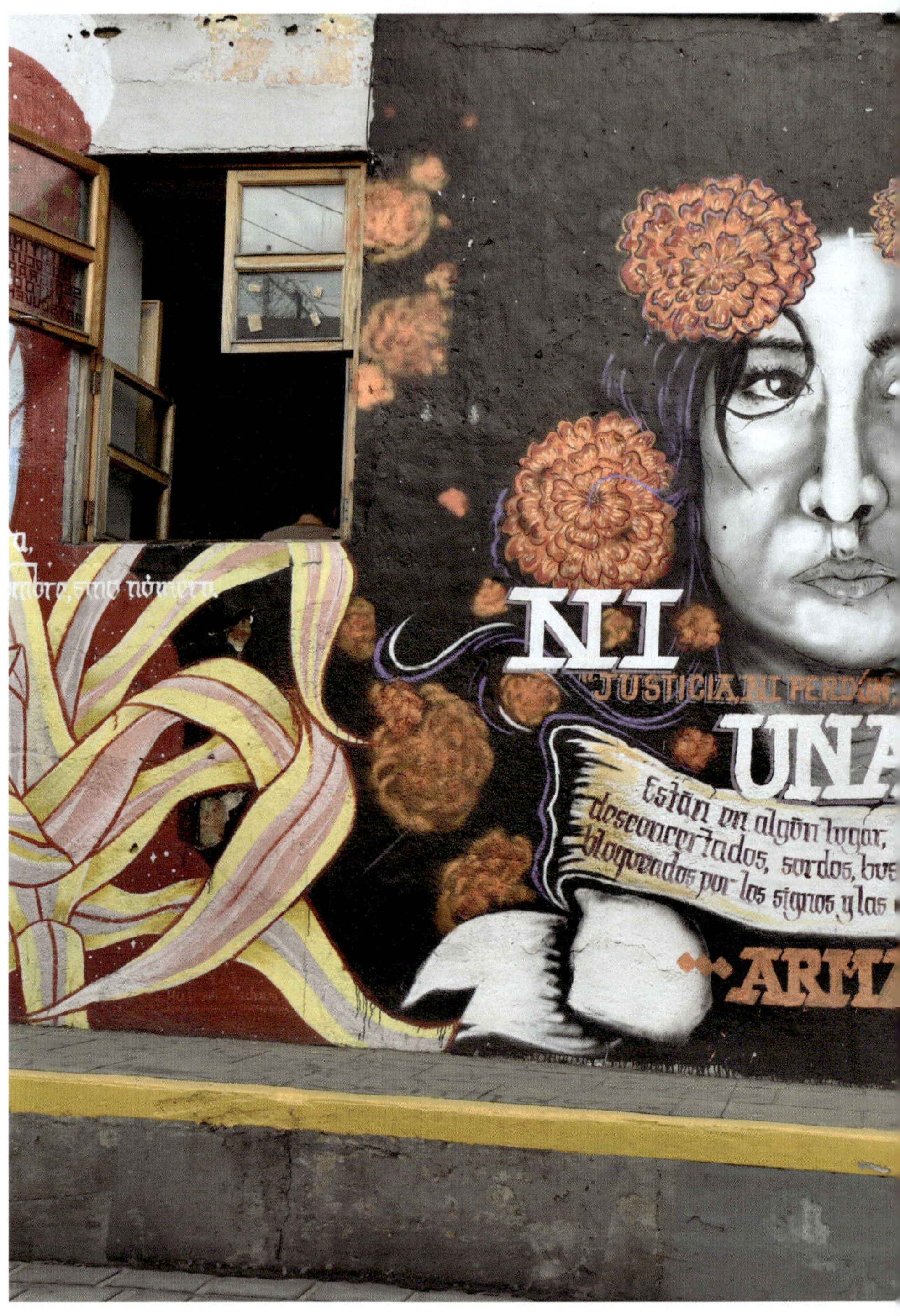

Plate 25
Mural on the facade of the Taller de Arte Comunitario on Calle Porfirio Díaz in Oaxaca.

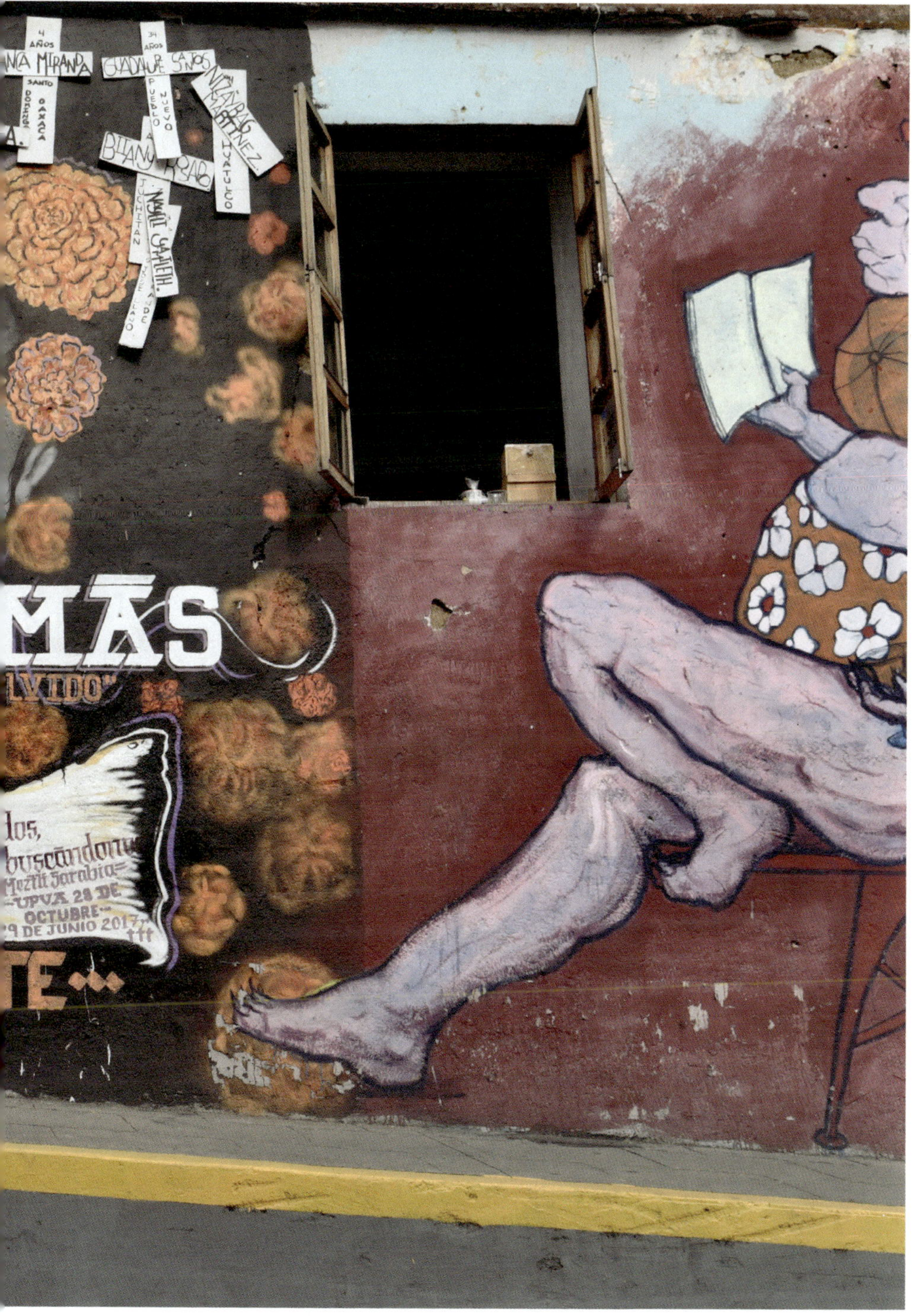
4 AÑOS
SANTO DOMINGO
OAXACA
PUEBLO
NUEVO
HUATULCO
MÁS
UPVA 28 DE
OCTUBRE
29 DE JUNIO 2017

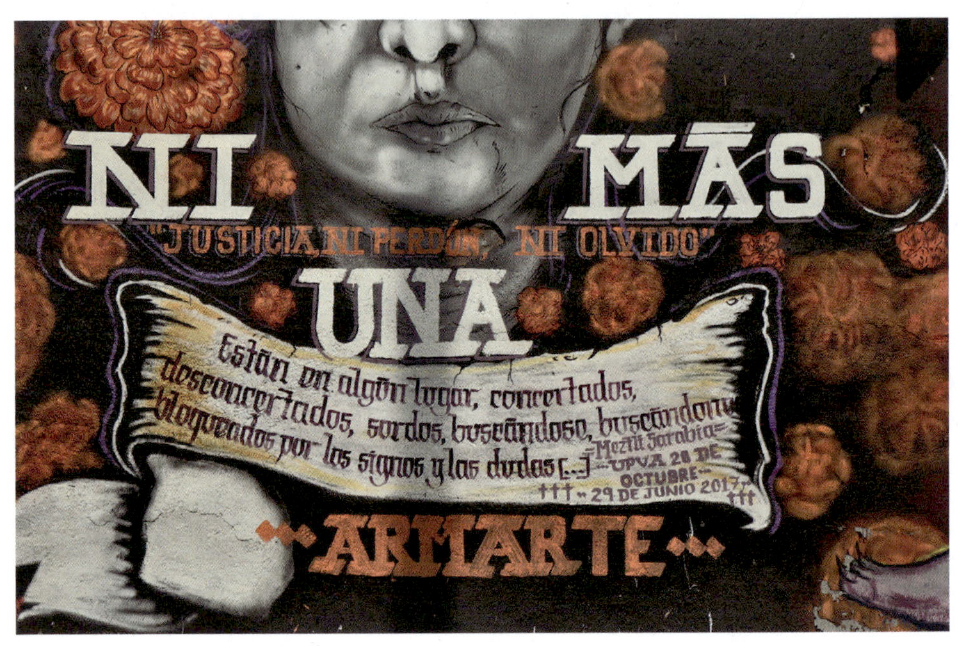

Plate 26
Close-up view of the inscription on the mural in plate 25.

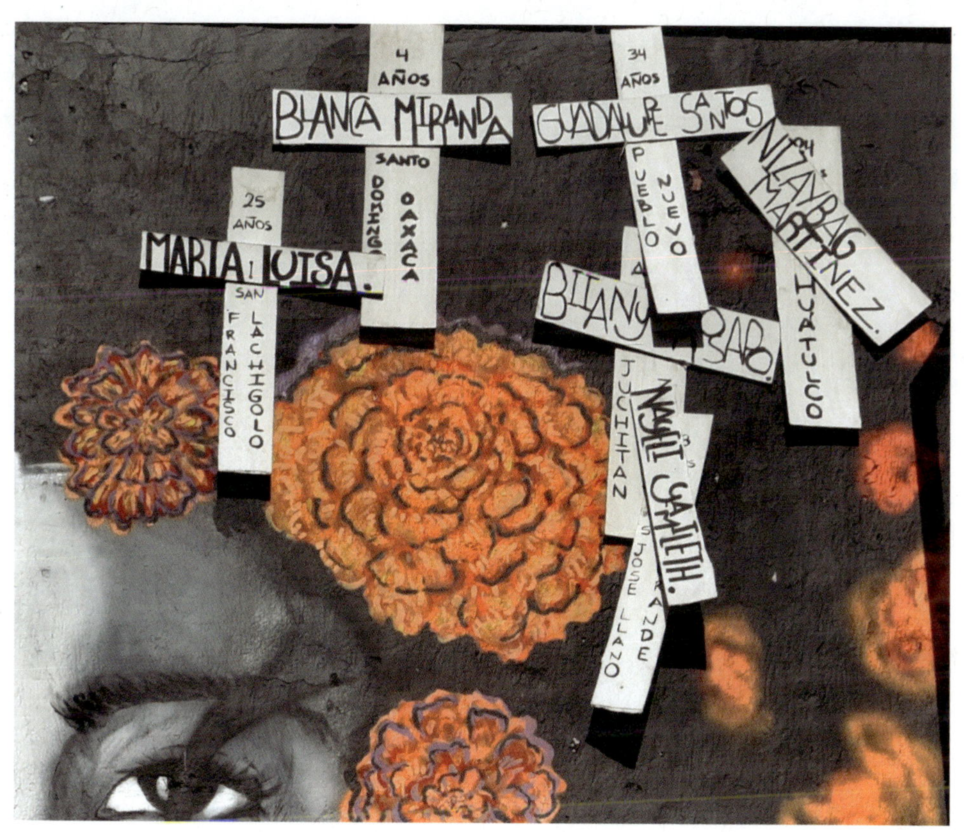

Plate 27
Close-up view of the white crosses, each bearing the name of a victim of feminicide, in the mural from plate 25.

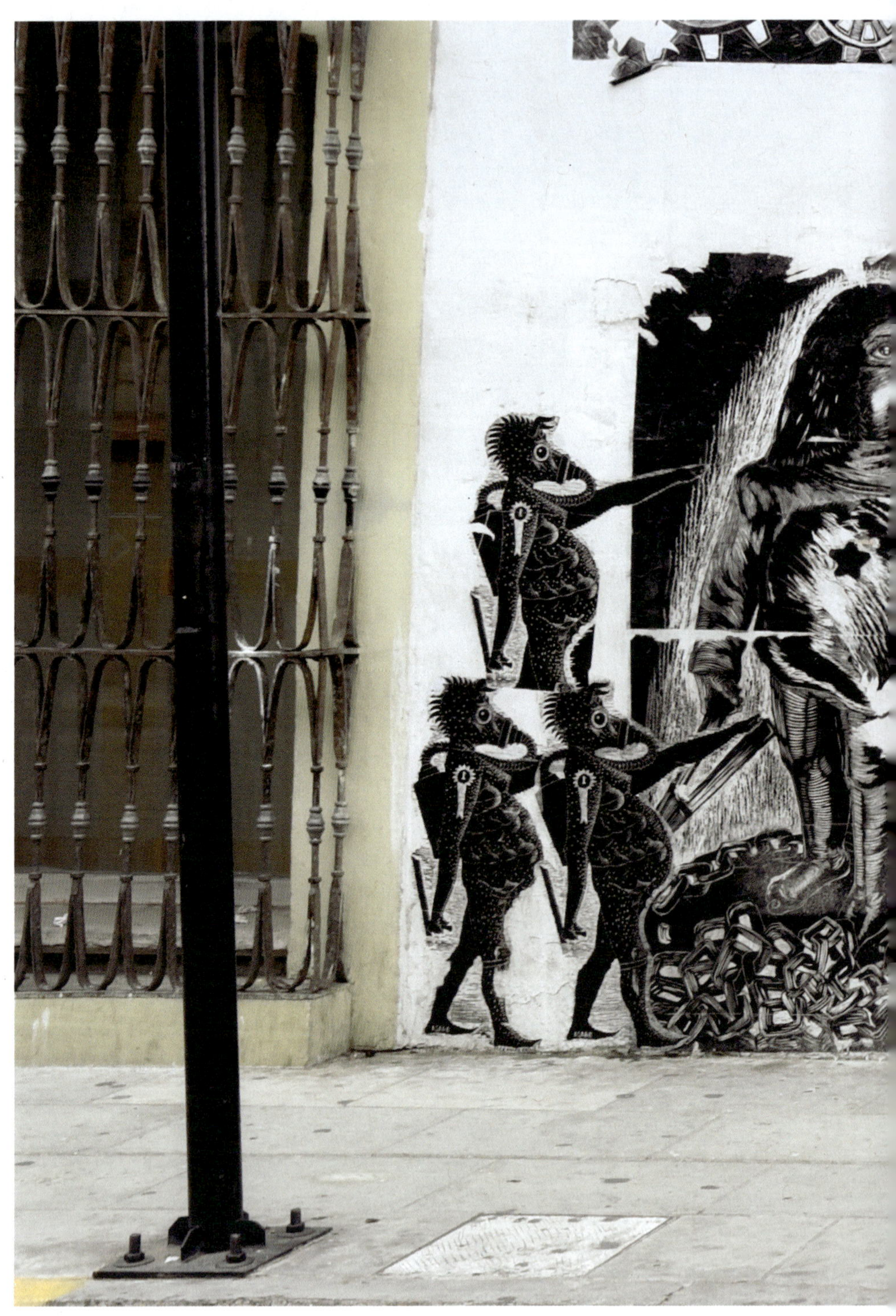

Plate 28
Wheat paste poster showing a woman with bolt cutters surrounded by chains.

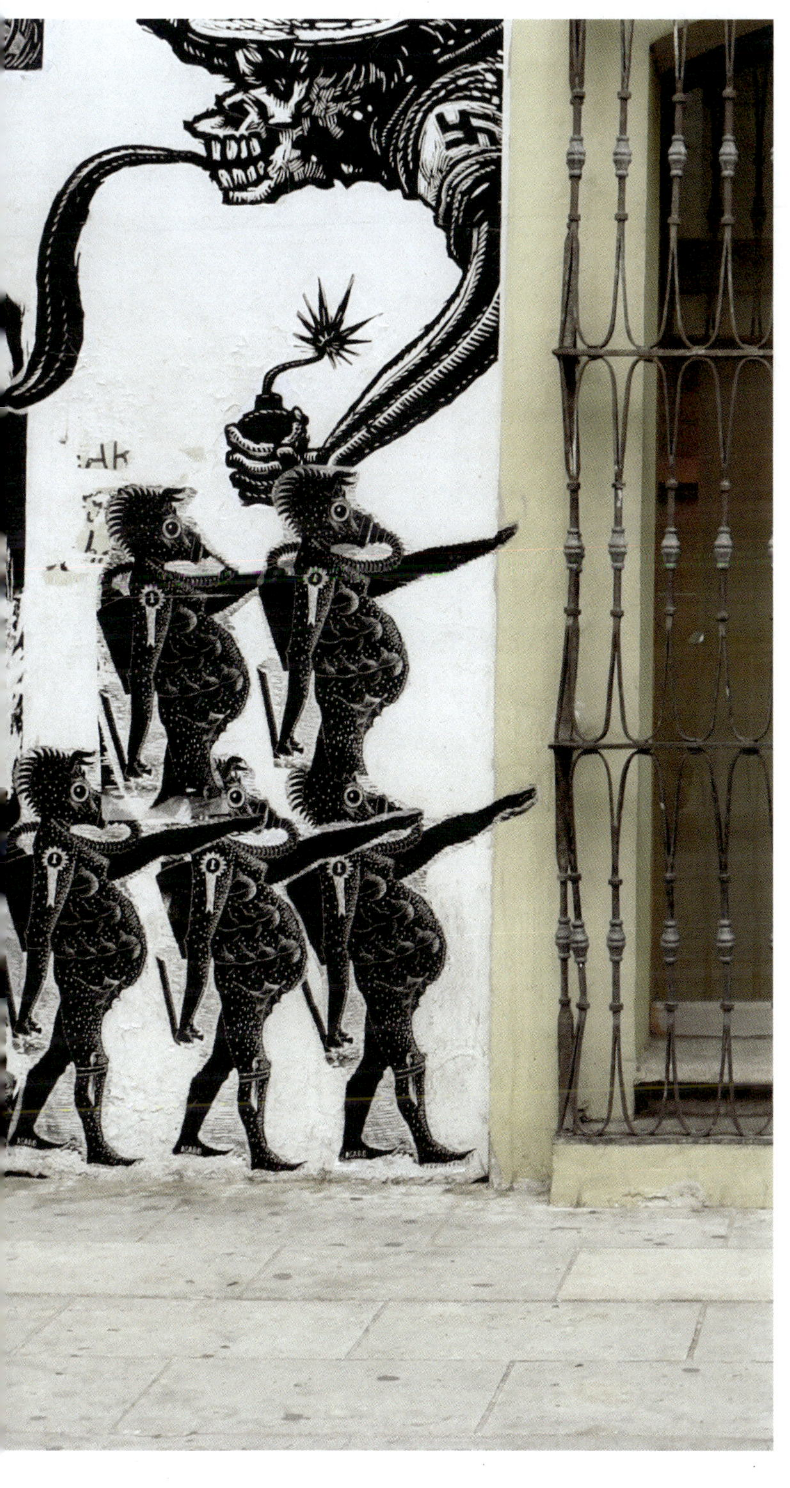

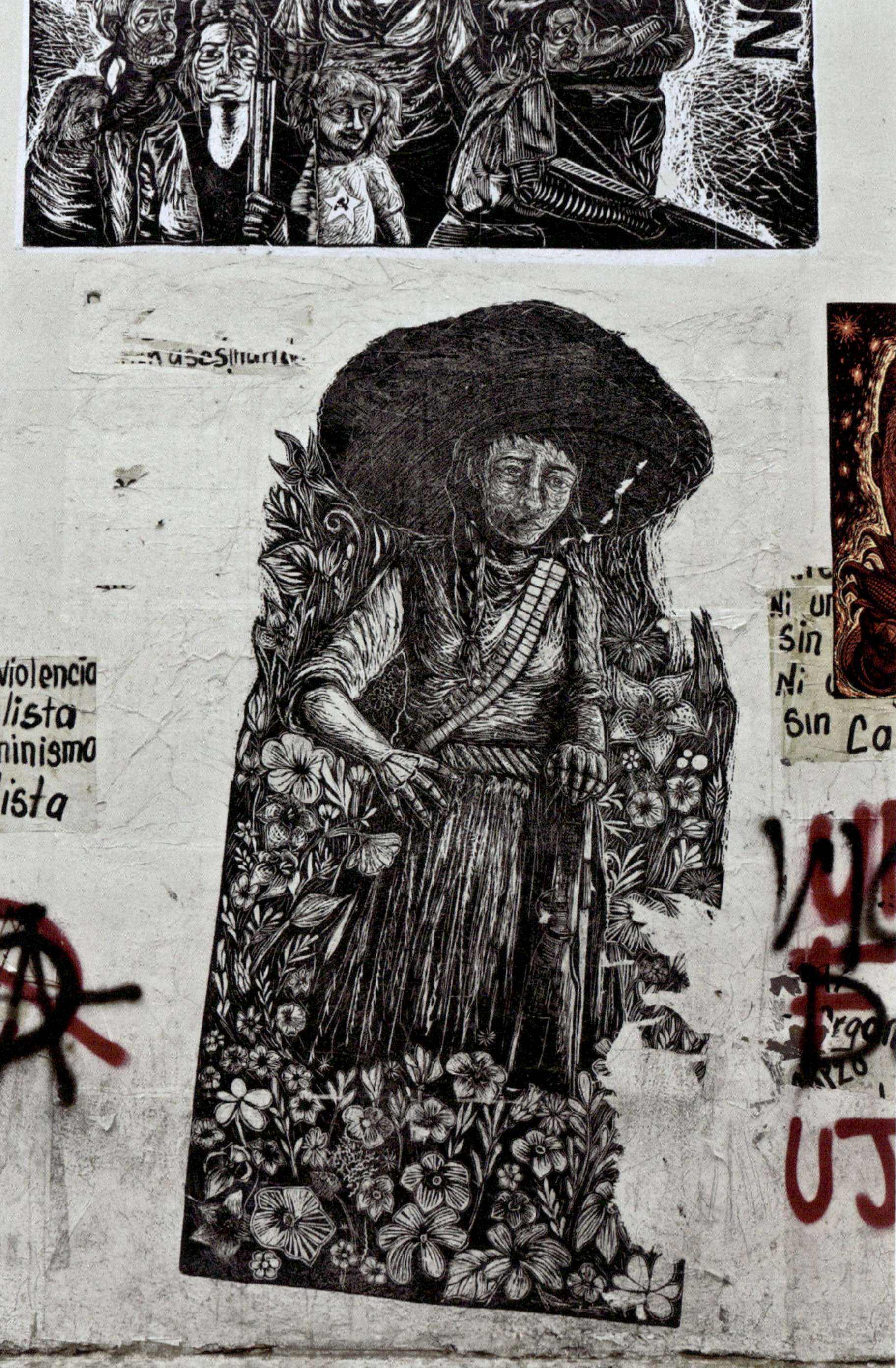
Violencia
alista
minismo
alista
Sin
Ni
Sin

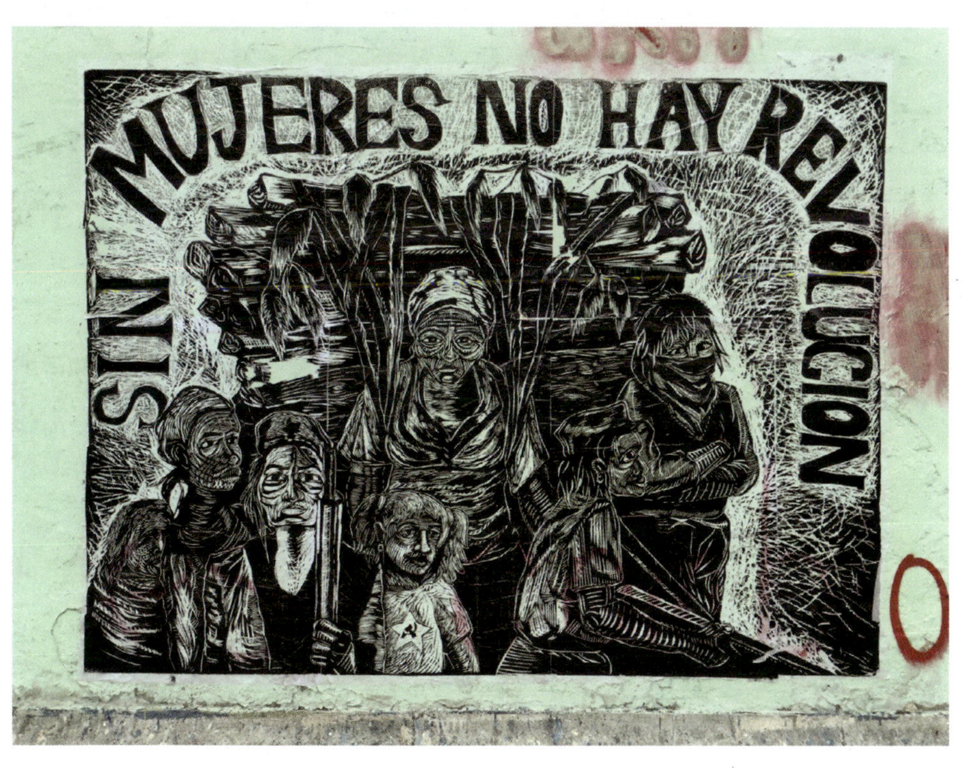

Plate 29 Opposite
Wheat paste poster showing a Mexican *soldadera* surrounded by handwritten taglines.

Plate 30 Above
"Sin mujeres no hay revolución" (Without women there is no revolution).

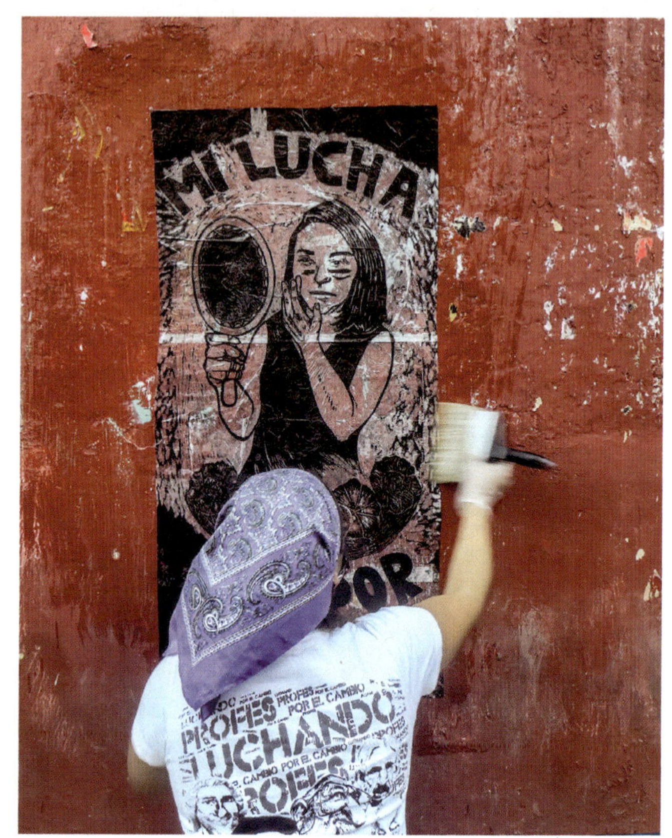

Plate 31 Top
A member of ARMARTE pasting a wheat paste poster. It reads, "Mi lucha es por vivir" (My struggle is to live), and includes ARMARTE's signature stencilled in black spray paint.

Plate 32 Bottom
"Somos el grito de las que no están" (We are the scream of those who are not here anymore). ARMARTE's signature is stencilled in red spray paint.

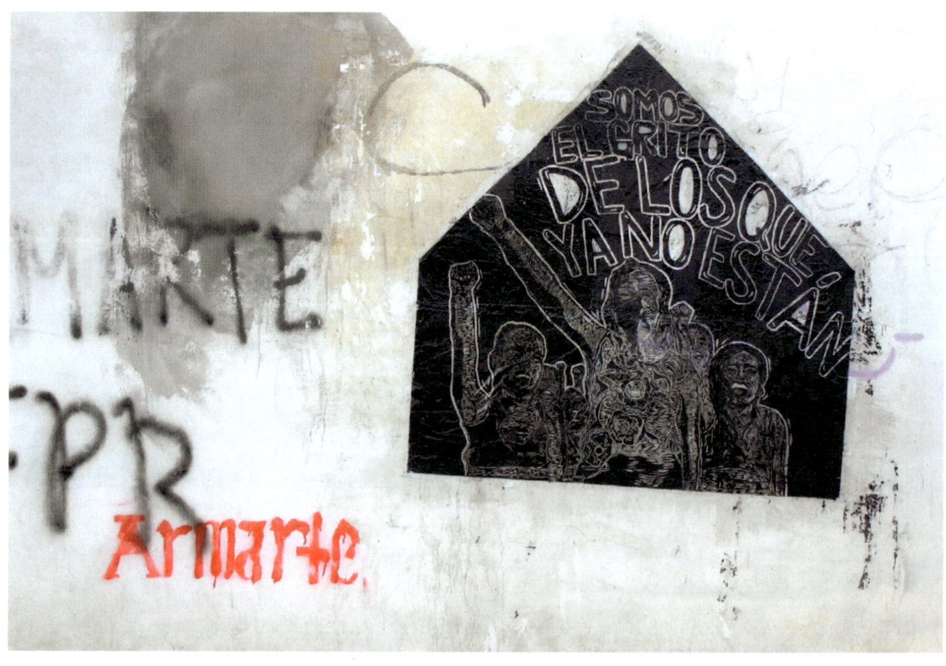

Pasting Up Protest

CHAPTER 1

The Duty to Remember: Artistic Strategies for Resistance

In Mexico we walk on a carpet of old bones, and others more recent.
– Elena Poniatowska[1]

There are currently more than 100,000 missing or disappeared individuals in Mexico (OHCHR 2022). It is a number that is hard to fathom, and yet it keeps mounting every day.[2] According to the Registro Nacional de Datos de Personas Extraviadas o Desaparecidas (National Registry of Disappeared and Missing People) there are nearly three times more women missing than men (Martínez Arellano 2018). Across Mexico, *los desaparecidos* – the missing – are often cold statistics without a face. For the authorities and the media, most of the victims, particularly youth and women, are even held responsible for the violence they experience.[3]

Since the 1970s, writers and artists have represented the issue of disappearances in their work in an attempt to process trauma and give a voice to citizens, who are often ignored equally by the state and by political parties. In *The Work of Art in the World: Civic Agency and Public Humanities*, Doris Sommer (2014, 29) refers to these types of artistic protests when she claims that "Resistance to abuse uses art." These five simple words sum up the praxis of the artists I study in *Pasting Up Protest: The Art of Memorializing Violence in Mexican Printmaking*. Across Mexico, human rights abuses take many shapes and forms, as do the strategies designed to denounce and resist them. The technique of choice adopted by ASARO, URT-Arte, MUGRE, and ARMARTE, the four groups I examine here, is political street art – artistic interventions displayed or performed on the street to actively engage citizens politically and critically (Ryan 2017, 5). The three Oaxaca-based groups – ASARO (Asamblea de Artistas Revolucionarios de Oaxaca, or the Assembly of Revolutionary Artists of Oaxaca), URT-Arte (Unión Revolucionaria de Trabajadores del Arte, or the Revolutionary Union of Art Workers), and ARMARTE (Alianza Revolucionaria de Mujeres Haciendo Arte, or the Revolutionary Alliance of Women Making Art) – as well as the Mexico City–based MUGRE (Mujeres Grabando Resistencias, or Women Engraving Resistances / Women Recording Resistances)[4] use their art and the street itself to challenge the Mexican government to respond to ongoing systemic violence against the *pueblo*, the people, to whom the members of the collectives belong. Their street art interventions also incite their fellow citizens – who are often disenchanted with the state of politics – to surmount their apathy and help empower disenfranchised sectors of society. While the four collectives advocate for justice for all marginalized people, in this study I concentrate on two case studies: the artists' depiction of young people and women, and their attempts to bring to light the high numbers of forced disappearances, juvenicides, and feminicides.[5]

Despite persistent government apathy and the cone of silence that surrounds the disappearances of young people and women, some sectors of civil society refuse to be silent. Activists and artists are instrumental in voicing the concerns of these sectors, as they consciously incorporate the disappeared and the missing into a national narrative of violence and loss, thereby drawing them into collective memory. *Pasting Up Protest* focuses on the work of these four collectives of street artists and activists that, in street art slang, are "getting up" for their people,[6] plastering their cities with the faces of the disappeared as well as political slogans. These artists are motivated by a driving desire to construct an alternative Mexican history that carves out a visible place for marginalized sectors of society, highlights injustice, and urges reform. To ensure their message is not misconstrued, they employ evocative visual imagery such as crying mothers, hearts ripped out of rib cages, or protesters in chains. In short, their pieces are an attempt at restoring the human dignity of overlooked victims. Their artistic praxis seeks to empower citizens through art and move people to action. Theirs is protest art, a demand for justice; it shows the crude, unaltered reality of living and surviving in Mexico, the enduring social inequalities, the poverty, and the forced disappearances, as well as the systemic impunity that protects local, state, and federal officials.

Corpus and Claims

Pasting Up Protest analyzes a corpus of images and presents a series of semi-structured interviews with members of Mexican art collectives since August 2018. My corpus of wheat paste posters, stencils, murals, social media posts – each type of work will be defined in due course, when relevant – and manifestos comprises about two thousand artworks produced by these four Mexican collectives. Despite the similarity in their strong social commitment and activism, ASARO, URT-Arte, ARMARTE, and MUGRe have never been studied together.

The principal claim I advance in this book is as follows: By blending street art and political activism the collectives become alternative producers of cultural memory. The members of ASARO, URT-Arte, ARMARTE, and MUGRe are thus memory activists, since their political project revolves around the recognition of past wrongs, and the integration of these occurrences into Mexican collective memory. I go one step further and posit that they are in fact memory *artivists*. These artists have been moved to act in the world by the emotional hold of a variety of artworks depicting past state violence, and by violent events they have sometimes experienced or witnessed themselves. These experiences have shaped their trajectory as artists. Through installations, workshops, and paste-ups, the members of the collectives now seek to transmit this emotional hold to others. To achieve this, they deploy a range of well-designed artworks and resistance strategies. As activists whose main resource is art, they are artivists, and since they use art to bring past wrongs to light so that authorities acknowledge them, they are memory artivists.

I read the collectives' artivistic practice as one of arousing or conscientization – that is, "assisting oppressed people to recognize their position and to build on their strengths as a basis for seeking to improve their lives" (Freire in Harris and White 2013, 111). For the members of the collectives, creating solidarity and building bridges, and encouraging others to do the same, is a concrete political project that blends art and activism with resistance strategies and memory work. This need for action shapes the whole of their artistic practice, and for some of them, it is more than a praxis – it becomes an "art de vivre" (Lemoine and Ouardi 2010), making art to live, and imagining and showing others a better life through art.

For these groups of artists, two main factors influence their selection of printmaking as their medium of choice: Prints are generally inexpensive to produce, and they have a potential for large-scale reproducibility.[7] These features make them ideal for disseminating political ideas. The long-standing Mexican tradition of printmaking for political purposes also means that contemporary audiences already possess the aesthetic literacy needed to understand the works and can therefore immediately recognize the resistance purposes of posters.

In the pages that follow, I make three key arguments. First, I maintain that by occupying a space that is at once concrete and virtual, the collectives' highly reproducible prints and social media posts subvert the traditional understanding that we have of street art.[8] It is no longer consumed solely on the streets, nor, for that reason, is it ephemeral in nature, bound to disappear as soon as passersby interact with it or deteriorate due to the passage of time and the effects of weather. Neither is it destined only to be experienced locally. Indeed, by being posted, promoted, and shared on social media platforms such as Instagram and Facebook, some artworks and installations acquire a state of permanency, becoming objects of memory that underline the state violence the collectives denounce.

By documenting their own production as part of a duty to remember, the collectives undertake a twofold process: producing an alternative historical *and* cultural memory. Street art scholar and feminist activist Jessica Pabón-Colón (2018, 38) proposes the concept of "transephemerality" to describe "the ontological condition of an ephemeral art form that remains present in the digital world." While the art itself is conceived with the street in mind and seeks to "broadens the public sphere(s)" (Costa et al. 2017, 15) to include new actors, it becomes a "transephemeral" political artifact that remains accessible online even after the original has been lost. This online circulation prolongs or "elongates" the life of the artwork itself or the particular protest for which it was designed (Ferrell 2004; Geoffray 2013), thus expanding its reach and its impact.

Building on the concept of transephemerality, I hold that, unlike other street artists who document their own production for promotion and marketing purposes, the collectives are attempting to embed an alternative historical and cultural memory (Taylor 2003). Given the political tensions inherent in portraying and seeking justice for disappeared individuals, depiction itself is a bold and even dangerous move, as is the collectives' efforts to effectively document, disseminate, and archive their production online. In a nation that erases people, representing them is a statement that the collectives dare to make repeatedly, installation after installation.

In the face of violent events whose very existence is systematically disputed by the Mexican authorities, the state cannot legitimately act as a guardian of cultural memory. The authorities influence collective memory by shining a light on historical and cultural events and figures that contribute to "institutionaliz[ing] a narrative of the past" (Jelin 2003, 23) that suits their purpose. Ultimately, while it is not the state's responsibility to guard cultural memory, state authorities certainly contribute to a nation's cultural memory by proposing their vision of it. However, the fact that these occurrences of violence are not recognized at the higher levels of the state apparatus does not make them any less real for many sectors of civil society. The 2014 Iguala massacre, in which the Mexican military allegedly played a direct role, and the waves of feminicides that have been plaguing the country since the 1990s are cases in point. Officials have consistently refused to acknowledge the importance of these crimes, or even, in some instances, to recognize them as "crimes"; yet these non-events are included among those that have set off the most visceral reactions in civil society, spurring demonstrations, acts of dissidence, hashtag activism campaigns, and other forms of protest. By producing artworks and organizing gatherings intended to commemorate victims of these acts of violence, the collectives open a space and encourage citizens to remember and process the trauma caused by these experiences.

Second, by seeking to create an alternative collective memory, the artists make state-sanctioned and state-ignored violence visible to a wide audience. Their works, through the depiction of real victims and a reliance on highly reproducible media such as stencils and prints, honour and commemorate victims of state violence; victims who, due to the deliberate and wilful lack of official recognition, would likely have been mourned only by their immediate families and friends, on a small scale and at the local level. Much like the effects of documenting their own production, the collectives endow this outrage with a global reach. Even as the authorities strive to silence divergent voices, the memory of violent events lives on and keeps feeding the groups' political demands. By inscribing these crimes into "official" Mexican history, the artworks make violence visible and function as an archive. Resorting to alternative means – either by reaching out to other nations or supranational organizations like the United Nations or the Inter-American Court of Human Rights or using records like social media posts – further reinforces their objective of increasing awareness of human rights abuses in Mexico on a global scale.

Finally, by seeking to empower citizens to speak up against state violence, these artists engage with society at its base. Their prints address citizens directly, encouraging them to take part in protests and denounce the authorities or the patriarchy. In reaching out to civil society through their workshops, where citizens can learn about artistic practices, and by hosting various activities such as art camps and reading circles, the collectives articulate very clearly their role in the recruitment and training of new revolutionaries. Part of their praxis is to host youth workshops, through which they openly seek to create more revolutionaries. Street art becomes utilitarian, a tool to foster a revolution, and the creation of highly reproducible artworks raises awareness about past and current struggles, links them in a historical narrative of resistance and resilience, commemorates historical events as well as famous leaders and victims of state violence, and ultimately empowers citizens through art.

By studying collectives of street artists whose works keep the large number of forced disappearances in Mexico in the public eye, *Pasting Up Protest* assesses the relationship between street art, social mobilization, and memory building. Ultimately, in revealing this double process of identification – through pride for the popular tradition of printmaking and empathy for victims – I elucidate how the artists keep the state's crimes alive in collective memory and turn citizens into political agents. Through a close examination of specific manifestations of street art created and disseminated since 2014, I probe how visual culture can shape social movements, and how contemporary social movements can in turn give shape to visual culture in contemporary Mexico, more specifically those movements related to systemic violence against post-secondary student activists and women. Although I focus on juvenicide and feminicide through an examination of violence carried out on the disappeared, *Pasting Up Protest* is not an in-depth political analysis of these phenomena. Rather, I draw attention to how the issues of feminicide and juvenicide intersect with street art, and how street art turns into a resistance strategy that helps counter official narratives that overlook these crimes. In profiling citizens and showcasing stories that the national narrative ignores, the collectives participate in the development of new community narratives and a new sense of community identity. In order to make these social issues visible and advocate in favour of better law enforcement, police investigations, and legislation, contemporary artists call on and repurpose the long-standing tradition of Mexican printmaking, thus communicating with their audience by way of an already familiar visual vocabulary.

Along similar lines, I conclude that street art affords artists a new and welcome opportunity by adding divergent voices and counter-histories – namely, of women and LGBTQ+ individuals – to Mexican collective memory and telling stories that those wielding power, whether political or patriarchal (the two are often one and the same), work to silence. While earlier generations of activists were as militant, they were often denied opportunities to emphasize these divergent voices explicitly due to the conservative nature of Mexican society. Given that those generations fought to create spaces where marginal voices could be heard, thus encouraging minds to change, new voices and memories can build on this base to draw a more accurate portrait of past struggles. The collectives are articulating themselves alongside these earlier generations as a claim to legitimacy. As such, the street art interventions designed by ASARO, URT-Arte, ARMARTE, and MUGRE act both as memory work and as resistance work. It is a form of artistic activism that seeks to share in the dynamics of inclusion and exclusion of memories (Feldman 2021), a sphere where the authorities are often the gatekeepers. The cultural producers studied here keep an ear to the ground, are often at one with their communities, and sometimes experience – or have experienced – some of the abuses, inequalities, and struggles they denounce. Being a part of the groups whose conditions they strive to alter or improve awards the collectives a particularly rich vantage point from which to expose abuses and the resulting trauma, and to denounce them.

My interest in these particular artists was sparked by their involvement in their respective communities. Each of the four collectives has an acute understanding of where it fits in a long line of politicized Mexican artists and of their struggle with power and its structures. The works of these street artists and engravers build on the legacy of the likes of Diego Rivera and Leopoldo Méndez, and they draw openly from these masters. But there is one major difference. Whereas these earlier muralists were part of a state-funded elite, they maintained a sometimes ironic acquaintance with power, and their works represented but were not truly accessible to the *pueblo* itself, the artists analyzed here are very closely involved in their respective communities, they are themselves members of the *pueblo* for which they fight, and their art is a way to concretely empower the people of their community. In some cases, artist-survivors have experienced the violence they denounce, and turn to art to work through their own trauma.

While the proliferation of graffiti and street art is a relatively new part of the struggle for social justice – in fact it only dates back to the 1990s – the challenges that the Mexican people face, and that artists and activists denounce, can be traced back to the conquest (1519–21) and colonization of Mexico (1521–1821), and more recently to President Porfirio Díaz's years in power (1876–1911) and the Mexican Revolution (1910–20). By raising social issues in their artworks and linking them to past uprisings and historical traumas, the collectives that form the basis of my investigation forge an ongoing dialogue with citizens and passersby, both on and off the walls, about human rights abuses. Their art draws from the past to condemn the flaws of the present, in the hope of shaping a better future.

In fact, ASARO, URT-Arte, MUGRE, and ARMARTE's work falls on a continuum of resistance in Mexico. Ways to challenge state actors and their decisions – or often the lack thereof – abound, whether we think, for example, of formal or spontaneous political demonstrations on the Paseo de la Reforma, Mexico City's most famous avenue, that often attract citizens by the tens of thousands, or of the myriad forms of artistic protest that weave explicit political messages into Mexican folk art – *corridos* or textile arts, for instance. Together, these strategies form a rich tapestry of denunciations that share common objectives: to name injustices faced by the *pueblo*, to put a face to individual tragedies, to commemorate and memorialize lives lost due to systemic violence, and, finally, to inscribe these lives into a broader narrative of state-enacted violence. Ultimately, the purpose of these political and artistic manifestations is to process trauma at both the individual and the collective level and to create a space to acknowledge losses ignored or minimized by state actors. In their political work and their artistic production, the collectives "collectivize grief" (Morbiato 2017, 141), thus opening a space for civil society to process the trauma of disappearances.

To understand the centrality of activism to these groups' praxis, we must begin with the start of the Oaxaca street art scene as we know it today. In 2006, the annual Oaxaca teachers' sit-in, at which teachers demand better salaries and infrastructure, turned violent. The protests lasted from May to early December of that year and led to the creation of a temporary autonomous zone – a space of freedom outside the rule of municipal, state, or national authorities, and which serves to disrupt existing power structures (Wilson 1991). However, more importantly for my research, the protests centred the role of street artists, and of art more broadly, in the dissemination and enduring nature of the demonstrations themselves. Many of these artists who are still active today established their repertoire of symbols back then, building on previous graffiti writing and stencil work.

What started off as a protest by teachers ended up involving many sectors of the citizenry (Bolos and Saavedra 2013; Sotelo Marbán 2008). Many factions organized under the Asamblea Popular de los Pueblos de Oaxaca, with the aim of making Governor Ulises Ruiz Ortiz resign from office. During the 2006 protests, ASARO produced art "in conflict and conceived as a fighting instrument" (Bolos and Saavedra 2013, 141), and the walls were turned into alternative spaces of communication and expression for disenfranchised sectors of the population.

The impact of the Comuna de Oaxaca (Oaxaca Commune) is instrumental to understanding three of the four collectives under investigation here, and I explore it in more detail in chapter 2. After the teachers' protests ended, most ASARO members went on to establish new collectives, while also continuing as members of ASARO. Born in the wake of the 2006 events, URT-Arte tends to be more politically inclined than ASARO. The third Oaxaca collective, ARMARTE, was formed at the end of 2018 as a direct response to the lack of women in the Oaxacan street art scene. This collective is ideologically aligned with URT-Arte, with whom it also shares members. Finally, while Mexico City–based MUGRe dates to 2014, the umbrella workshop to which it belongs, the Escuela de Cultura Popular Mártires del 68 (School of Popular Culture 1968 Martyrs), was founded in 1968 as a response to the Tlatelolco massacre, where the army opened fire on unarmed students demonstrating against the Olympics.

I selected these four groups because they offer coherent bodies of work, are very active on the streets of their respective cities, have been in existence for several years, and have maintained an organized and streamlined level of output. These two last points are of particular relevance when examining street art collectives. Indeed, most activism-oriented collectives emerge as part of a specific social movement and tend to disband once the issue disappears from the public eye – or protests are harshly repressed. ASARO and URT-Arte, dating back to 2006 and 2007, respectively, can thus be viewed as anomalies in the world of street art collectives. Over a period of more than fifteen years they have built up extensive bodies of work, another important aspect worth considering when mapping the evolution of the visual treatment and representation of social issues like disappearances and systemic violence. While ARMARTE and MUGRe were founded more recently, they compensate for their short production span with a prolific output.

The four groups also adhere to clearly defined ideologies, both in their prints and in their manifestos: ASARO is anti-capitalist, URT-Arte and ARMARTE are Marxist-Leninist, and MUGRe is feminist.[9] While ASARO and URT-Arte are mixed-gender groups, ARMARTE and MUGRe are women-only. ARMARTE is also linked to URT-Arte, allowing for an interesting comparative discussion of the extent to which ARMARTE's production differs from that of URT-Arte.

My analysis of the collectives' work is predicated on the notion that their members are *artivists* – artists who use activism and act with an explicit political objective in mind. Indeed, my analysis demonstrates that the collectives dialogue with the past to effect political change in the present, and ultimately to create a better future. This desire to disrupt the social order is overt in the work of all four groups. The four collectives share the stated intention of engaging citizens and persuading them to become involved in changing the existing political structures and environment. By blending art and activism in their daily practice, the members of each collective engage the citizenry either as co-creators – in witnessing the work, viewers complete it – or as participants who experience their work (Lemoine and Ouardi 2010).

Art to Deal with Trauma

The notion of commitment to their community extends to the very people the collectives portray in their work. The focus on real victims is of primary importance to the analysis in *Pasting Up Protest*. Unlike what is found in most works of fiction, the art that I examine often depicts real victims and real survivors in order to awaken a stronger emotional response and build solidarity with viewers. While in past decades there was "a domination of fictional accounts" to document and process the trauma that results from state violence (Volk and Schlotterbeck 2007, 112), the collectives studied here often select actual victims in an attempt to elicit empathy and compassion in the viewer.[10] These two emotions are major drivers to incite viewers to identify with the represented victims and to act on those feelings. This process of identification is akin to Martha Nussbaum's (1998) concept of "narrative imagination," which claims that narratives encourage viewers not only to conjure up a story but also to put themselves in other people's shoes (44–5). Works of art can initiate a similar process. By experiencing art that portrays real-life victims, viewers can better relate to victims' lives and circumstances and be moved to develop solidarity and take concrete steps toward ending the depicted forms of violence. For Cynthia Milton (2014), "art break[s] down the barriers between formal politics and political production" (16) and can then serve as a more accessible point of entry into grappling with difficult topics than can factual reports or even novels.

Indeed, images often exercise an "emotional hold" (Möller 2016, 8) on viewers, since "the[ir] social-relational content … is not simply descriptive-historical, but affective and empathic" (Roberts 2014, 4; see also Bennett 2005). This affect often spurs a desire to convert a feeling into action. As Stephen Duncombe (2016) explains, "Before we act in the world, we must be moved to act" (119). Works of art hold just such a power to move an audience. Being exposed to art can be the catalyst to becoming committed to the world and building solidarity with new communities. Duncombe adds that "the ability of artists to create worlds and move people … is what makes art so powerful as a form of activism" (116). As human beings, we understand the world and the lives of others through stories and symbols. Nussbaum's (1998) concept of "narrative imagination" (44), as well as Anthony Kwame Appiah's (2010) claim that "our modern solidarity derives from stories in which we participate through synecdoche" (245), explain why the "emotional hold" of images can often propel viewers to want to provoke changes in the world. Audiences see themselves reflected in other people's stories: They not only empathize with their plight but begin to seek ways to build solidarity with others whom they do not even know or might never meet.

That being said, it must be acknowledged that most audience members tend to simply view an artwork without necessarily acting on their initial urge to change the world. It might also be that, as Duncombe and Lambert (2021) claim, our understanding of activism is too "restrictive" (5) and should be broadened to include everyday forms of activism, actions that generally occur on a small scale, such as engaging our peers in a debate or lobbying city council for a change that will have a positive impact on the community around us. Feeling driven to act is also acknowledging power and power relations, as well as their role in shaping our world, and attempting to disrupt them.[11] There are myriad small ways to resist and undermine power: signing a petition, attending a march or a protest, donating to a cause, etc. For Vinthagen (2019), resistance is an "activity in a dynamic interaction with opposition to power" (2), one that is "integrated into social life and … part of normality" (4). Incorporating art into these acts of resistance further lowers the barriers to entry. By handing viewers the tools to "face life" (Aladro-Vico et al. 2018, 15), art can make them act to improve the world.

While street art in and of itself does not reduce systemic violence against youth and women, posters and inscriptions that speak directly to people – emboldening them to confront either street harassment or domestic and police violence – do plant seeds that lead to a small-scale change, and arguably where they matter most: in these citizens' everyday lives. In this context of "politics by other means," change is brought about by politically committed cultural producers (Kerkvliet 2018). Indeed, "to be political is not just to express political opinions but rather to be oriented toward society and to engage with its variegated terrains of power" (Ryan 2017, 5). I understand the artivists' "politics of the street" (Butler 2020) as a "talk back mechanism" (Ryan 2017, 4) that empowers citizens to both take control of and to re-semanticize this space where capitalism and neoliberalism have historically harmed them (Friedman and Tabbush 2016).

The current political climate, in Mexico and globally, underscores the need to identify, discuss, develop, and apply alternative ways of becoming politically involved, and to share strategies to promote these alternative modes of engagement. Indeed, protest movements have been emerging across the globe for the past decade or more, whether it be the 2011 Occupy movement, the 2010–12 Arab Spring, the 2017 #MeToo or #SayHerName movements, or the Dakota Access Pipeline protests in Standing Rock, North Dakota (also 2017), in addition to the Black Lives Matter protests that took place in 2020,[12] and the Wet'suwet'en railway blockades that started in British Columbia and spread across Canada in the same year. Similar protest movements have also surfaced in Latin America (Munck and Sankey 2020). For instance, in Chile students staged massive protests between 2011 and 2013 to demand a better education system, one that would be more accessible to students from less privileged socio-economic backgrounds. Less than a decade later, the *estallido social* (social uprising, 2019–21) erupted and eventually led to the creation of a constitutional assembly. A group of 155 delegates

– 78 men and 77 women – drafted a new national constitution to replace the one promulgated under Augusto Pinochet in 1980. The assembly was divided, and the new constitutional proposal was rejected in a national referendum in September 2022 (Bell 2022). New delegates went back to the drawing board (Reuters 2022) and tabled a second proposal in 2023 that was also defeated (Montes 2023). Another example is the *Marea verde* (Green Tide) that lobbies for the decriminalization of abortion and better access to reproductive health care. After its resounding start in Argentina in 2018, it has swept across the continent, with countries like Chile and Mexico slowly decriminalizing abortion in the early stages of pregnancy. Finally, in Mexico, the 2012 movement #YoSoy132 – dubbed the Mexican Spring – was launched by 131 university student protesters who insisted on greater freedom of expression during the election campaign that led to former President Enrique Peña Nieto's *sexenio* (six-year term in office). By using the hashtag #YoSoy132, each participant proclaimed their status as the 132nd member of the group and indicated their support for its demands. Unlike most of the movements noted here, #YoSoy132 was not as successful in reaching its objective.

All these movements, which indicate that citizens want to be heard by their governments, call attention to a systemic lack of representation in spheres where decisions that affect them are made. Even in democracies, legal ways to be politically involved and effect change, such as running for office, are not open to everyone. Democratic participation is even harder for sectors of the community that have historically been disenfranchised, let alone whose participation or inclusion in the political sphere is not welcomed by political parties. Above all, traditional means of political involvement are not accessible to the people who most need a change in policies.

This exclusion from sanctioned political involvement leads citizens and groups to design alternative paths outside the regular political arena. For instance, the artists and activists I examine in *Pasting Up Protest* do not believe in the political system they are combatting; instead, their main objective is often to overthrow it. For them, working toward alternatives and empowering citizens through street art offers a back door to political involvement. The collectives are, in fact, engaging in politics by other means (Kerkvliet 2018).

The contemporary significance of street art as an alternative manner of engaging politically and of creating memory and heritage is widely recognized in Latin America (Pabón-Colón 2018; Ryan 2017). However, the role it plays in Mexico is still routinely overlooked by the scholarly community. This is problematic, particularly considering the long national tradition in Mexico of artist protests and other means of raising political issues. The fact that best practices do not circulate among protesters presents a further obstacle. As a rule, most resistance movements are spontaneous and decentralized. As a result, participants do not share lessons learned, either among themselves or with other groups. Many resistance movements in North America and across the globe would benefit from adopting strategies that were successful in making gains elsewhere. The artists that form my corpus have not yet attained the reach outside Mexico that the Zapatista Army of National Liberation (Ejército Zapatista de Liberación Nacional, or EZLN) has achieved since rising in the state of Chiapas in 1994,[13] but the collectives do propose productive ways to concretely engage their fellow citizens and transform them into political agents through street art. Their success at disseminating their techniques and strategies to other Mexican cities and beyond to some other Latin American nations hints at the fact that a broader network of protesters sharing strategies and techniques is possible, even desirable. In other words, these activists would gain from building solidarity across borders.

Methodological Approach

My study sits at the disciplinary boundaries between street art studies, visual culture studies, visual anthropology, and art history more broadly, in addition to memory and resistance studies. Whereas most explorations of street art centre on the political involvement of collectives and artists and focus on discerning how artists dialogue with power, *Pasting Up Protest*, while it identifies collectives that do express political views, concentrates more specifically on the works they produce by providing an artistic and semiotic analysis.

This visual analysis involves a two-step process in which I analyze both individual works of art and the corpus as a whole. I apply Erwin Panofsky's (1955) three-part framework to identify, analyze, and interpret the artworks that I have selected. I look at context, content, and form. It is thus both an iconographical and iconological analysis of the corpus. In the first phase, I describe what an image shows and create an inventory of elements and symbols used (or "literal meaning": What are we seeing?). Then, in the second phase I concentrate on denotational meaning ("conventional meaning": What does it mean?), to focus, ultimately, in the third and final phase on the connotational meaning ("symbolic meaning": What does it mean ideologically or symbolically? What is the cultural and social significance?). I also draw on intertextual and intervisual connections to illuminate the symbolic meaning of the works, which enables me to situate the interpretation of the visual texts in their socio-cultural and political contexts (Panofsky 1955, 59).

Aligned with Foss (2004), I also identify the visual grammar of the corpus by looking at its symbolic qualities, human interaction, and presentation to the audience (when, where, how) (167), and search for coherent discourse across multiple sites. I point out commonalities within the corpus, but I also highlight differences when I compare the artworks produced after the Ayotzinapa disappearances with art centred on gender-based violence and the feminicide crisis. Following Rose (2012), I also note absences (229). Finally, borrowing from Mitchell (2010), I ask the images in my corpus a series of questions:

> What does the picture want from me or from "us" or from "them" or from whomever? Who or what is the target of the demand/desire/need expressed by the picture? … What does this picture lack; what does it leave out? What is its area of erasure? Its blind spot? Its anamorphic blur? What does the frame or boundary exclude? What does its angle of representation prevent us from seeing and prevent it from showing? What does it need or demand from the beholder to complete its work? (49–50)

Through the images, I identify how these groups document the past (historical narrative), which narrative about the past and the present they choose (the representations), and how the past and the present can or could inform the future (the changes). I pay close attention to how they depict violence, to what aim, what type(s) of future they propose, and how they propose to shift mindsets.

Graffiti and Street Art

The artworks produced by the collectives integrate elements of graffiti, street art, political art, and artivism. Our initial topic of discussion will centre around graffiti and street art, followed by an examination of political art and artivism.

The world of graffiti and street art is riddled with misconceptions. While graffiti often carries a stigma that conjures up images of inscriptions spray-painted ad nauseam on urban furniture, street art is praised for its aesthetic qualities. These rigid categorizations hinder our understanding of each artistic regime and the role they play for practitioners.[14]

The resurgence of what we now call "graffiti" dates to the 1970s and '80s, and most Western scholarship identifies Philadelphia and New York City as its birthplaces.[15] There exists, however, long and diverse traditions of graffiti and political street art in Latin America and other locations in the post-colonial and non-Western world, in locales as varied as Egypt, India, South Africa, and Turkey. Many of these traditions developed organically over the course of the twentieth century, in relative isolation from the hip hop movement of the late 1970s, and in many cases predating it. In all these national contexts, however, the notion of individual identity – building it, affirming it, and leaving traces of it – lies at the core of graffiti.[16]

Graffiti writers[17] produce "words, figures, and images that [are] written, drawn and/or painted on, and/or etched into or on surfaces where the owner of the property has NOT given permission" (Ross 2016, 476; emphasis in original). The best-known of these illegal textual inscriptions is perhaps the tag; Anna Wacławek (2008, 14) calls it a "visual demonstration of existence." Tags are monochromatic, self-referential signatures that are quick to execute and directed at other writers. The more often graffiti writers reproduce their signatures, the more exposure they gain. Unlike street art practitioners, who generally seek to be understood, graffiti writers do not attempt to dialogue with a broader audience. Besides, most viewers outside the graffiti community – myself included – do not possess the aesthetic literacy needed to read graffiti, which often leads to people lamenting its lack of aesthetic value.[18]

Graffiti's disrepute spread when some New York City–based gangs incorporated graffiti writers and had them literally mark their territory with their tags.[19] The relationship between gangs and graffiti led "moral entrepreneurs" (Becker 1963, 147–53) to condemn graffiti as an illegal, aggressive, and dangerous practice related to crime – a misconception that persists to this day. Much like crime, graffiti was seen as an epidemic to be contained.[20] Despite being a lost battle, many cities still erase graffiti; white squares on dark walls indicate both that a tag was covered up and that a new one is about to appear.

The expansion of graffiti quickly gave rise to a diversification process that integrated regional cultural elements, as images, styles, techniques, and artists circulated beyond the subculture. Its diffusion – through hip hop culture, media coverage, magazines, websites, and social networks – escaped its practitioners, and resulted in aesthetic and social exchanges, as well as in its absorption into traditional art channels such as galleries or marketing.[21]

In Mexico, "without accepting that there is a single and exclusive itinerary for graffiti ... it is possible to affirm that there was a dominant route: Los Angeles–San Diego–Tijuana–Guadalajara" (Zapiain et al. 2007).[22] Mexican citizens, returning to Mexico from the United States, brought elements of the subculture with them and introduced it, first to smaller cities, then to the Mexican capital, while also integrating elements specific to their own culture.

According to Itandehui Franco Ortiz (2011, 74), specifically in relation to the city of Oaxaca, graffiti culture travelled from the United States via *cholismo* – gangs that controlled specific neighbourhoods. This mode of organization can be interpreted as a resistance strategy against power holders seeking to transform peripheral urban sectors – those often removed from the city centre, and thus with higher rates of poverty – into what elites would consider "proper" spaces (70). Much as gangs in New York City did in the 1970s, leading to graffiti being equated with vandalism and marginality, cholos[23] painted their neighbourhoods, thus converting them into active spaces of free speech (70–1). While in New York the technique of choice was tagging, in Oaxaca cholos appropriated the muralist tradition from Chicano artists (74), used Old English lettering, and drew heavily from an established repertoire of symbols, depicting figures like the Virgin of Guadalupe, Emiliano Zapata, and Francisco Villa (83) as a way to link directly to their historic roots and generate Mexican pride.[24]

Around the same time, as cholo writing was growing, the number of *graffiteros* – graffiti writers, almost all male – was increasing in Oaxaca.[25] Unlike cholo writing that started in poorer areas, the graffiti crews often came from less marginalized and more economically stable areas (Franco Ortiz 2011, 89), and moved across artistic regimes, often including stencils along with their graffiti work. Societal reactions to the graffiti boom did not take long to materialize, and with them generational "ruptures"; some adults saw it as vandalism and a transgression of the values of the dominant culture (91). And yet, it was common for *graffiteros* to master the codes of this dominant culture, as many were architecture, fine arts, or graphic design students (93). In short, they were using the codes of the dominant culture to mock it. This educational background is not unlike that of many members of the collectives under investigation.[26] The works stencilled in the years leading up to 2006 paved the way to using public space to spread an alternative political message, ensuring that people experiencing the work could join a wider social network.

As graffiti writing spread across countries and its popularity increased, practitioners began experimenting with and integrating new techniques and forms of media into their works. These additions challenged some purists' understanding of graffiti, leading to the creation of the moniker "street art." The definition of that word has been in constant evolution since 1985, when it became preferred over the less palatable "graffiti" (Wacławek 2011).[27] Street art is exposed in and to the street, just like graffiti, but uses a different visual vocabulary, one that is often more accessible than graffiti writing.[28]

Defining street art involves discussing its legality, the types of interventions the term encompasses, and the role the "street" plays in the creation and display of interventions. Numerous scholars conclude that the legal/illegal debate has become moot over time, especially now that street art is more widely accepted. However, for some artists the illegal aspect remains paramount. Street art purists argue against off-site designs, considering only on-site interventions authentic.[29] Similarly, for some, performances or happenings cannot be considered street art, since they do not include interventions on walls.[30]

Street art is an inclusive art form that engages citizens politically and socially, whose production and display are related to the street. In line with Olivier Dabène's *Street Art and Democracy in Latin America* (2020), I understand street art as a "broad category that includes all forms of expressions displayed on city walls, including graffiti" (6), political messages, and inscriptions written for and during marches and demonstrations, as well as installations and performances.[31]

My definition of street art includes both legal and illegal production. Illegality is a defining factor of these Mexican artists' production. The members of the collectives are activists who lobby against various levels of government. Illegality is thus central to their artistic practice and activism, and to the public perception of them.

I am also aligned with Eva Holly Ryan's (2017) loose definition of "political street art," in which she includes any form of artistic intervention that is created in and for the street and that aims "not just to express political opinions but rather to be oriented toward society and to engage with its variegated terrains of power" (5). For instance, an outdoor performance can be classified as political street art under Ryan's definition, even if it is not technically "displayed on city walls" (Dabène 2020, 6). If it is art made "for" the street and displayed in it, it is street art. It becomes *political* street art when the artists actively engage politically and socially with their milieu. This active community engagement is akin to artivism, which I develop later.

My working definition of *political street art* thus blends Dabène's and Ryan's definitions. I understand political street art as all forms of expression displayed on city walls or performed in the streets that critically engage with society, usually from the bottom up. With this, I also line up with Riggle (2010, 245), who claims that "an artwork is street art if, and only if, its material use of the street is internal to its meaning"; in other words, I would add, if the street is needed for its creation and/or display.

Since they display posters and murals on city walls, I consider the work of the four Mexican collectives street art. As mentioned above, the collectives have, like many institutions or artists before them, made printmaking their technique of choice; this often political decision is also related to very down-to-earth considerations, such as the availability and price of the materials used. Both print and poster are the result of the engraving process. When examining a print, the audience is looking at the "negative" of the plaque that the artist used to create the artwork. There are two main engraving techniques – intaglio and relief printing; both are printed as stamps. Their main differences lie in the materials used and in the impression processes.

Intaglio[32] and relief printing use the same impression process: A surface is soaked with ink and then stamped on any material. By applying pressure, a printing press helps spread the ink uniformly and allows for fine and intricate designs. The pressure level of the machine is adjusted depending on the medium, its thickness, and the desired effects.

Unlike intaglio, which is often practised on copper, relief printing generally relies on less expensive materials, such as wood and linoleum, and is the technique of choice for most of the collectives I examine. It works on the opposite principle of intaglio: Artists must dig out everything they do not want to appear on the printed output, using a gouge or knife. It is the relief, uncut, that will appear on the printed output. The four collectives use it for its affordability and relative ease of application. Once they have a matrix, they can produce both high-quality prints – which are sold in their workshops – and wheat paste posters to paste up on the streets.

Street artists also select relief print techniques in the production of wheat paste posters or paste-ups. Like graffiti, wheat pasting is a direct-action technique used by activists around the world. Choosing wheat paste posters follows a cost-benefit rationale. Once the etching or the woodcut is designed, posters are easy and cheap to mass-produce.[33] Their off-site creation also minimizes the risk of being caught in the act, a good way for political activists to participate without undue risk. In this type of production, printing presses are particularly advantageous when artists want to create large-format pieces, which electronic printers produce less easily.

Groups that do wheat pasting work like a well-oiled machine: The first person holds the poster to the wall, the second applies the glue using a mixture of water and flour, and a third one watches for the police. In the case of a police intervention, the material can be abandoned as it is both cheap and easy to obtain, and the posters quick to reproduce. As we will see in chapters 2 and 3, wheat paste posters are ubiquitous in Mexico. Collectives like ASARO and URT-Arte have even developed printing presses that enable them to print monumental-sized posters, thus blending the monumentality of twentieth-century Mexican muralism with printmaking.[34]

Political Art and Activism

While all the art discussed in *Pasting Up Protest* is political, the artworks can be read either as political art or artivism, depending on the setting in which they are deployed.[35] In my understanding, political art exists on a continuum, from theoretically impossible apolitical art (González-Torres in Rollins 1993), to political art, to artivism (Duncombe 2016; Lemoine and Ouardi 2010).[36] I discuss these concepts in this order, which corresponds to the degree of involvement expected of the audience – namely, in the form of intellectual engagement in the case of political art, and often an intellectual, physical, and spatial involvement for artivism.[37]

In *Aesthetics, Disinterestedness, and Effectiveness in Political Art* (2018), Maria Alina Asavei proposes dividing "political art" into two main categories: propaganda – "deficiently political" (2) as it lacks an autonomous critical posture – and critical-political art. She claims that "one of the main positions for art to be considered critical and political is to manifest varying degrees of both *autonomy* and *opposition* towards the status quo" (14; my emphasis). To be deemed critical-political, then, an artist must possess a certain degree of self-awareness, be autonomous from institutions, and exhibit a desire to participate in a critical dialogue with power, often in opposition to it. Asavei emphasizes that these characteristics exist to "varying degrees" (14), implying that critical-political art itself falls on a spectrum. In her view, critical-political art "gives a voice to those who are marginal, forgotten, and excluded. *Political art is art that critically intervenes in relations of power and … does not merely reflect on them.* In its narrow, critical sense, political art is not merely a container of political messages (as propaganda is), but politically polyvalent in its criticality" (2; my emphasis). Critical-political art "is not only about politics," depicting a political situation, "but it also appeals to the viewer as a political being too, in possession of the faculties needed for genuine political evaluation and participation" (2). When they encounter critical-political art, audience members become political agents who must interact with politically loaded content and challenge it if they are to come to their own conclusions.[38]

Much like memory work – which I explore shortly – critical-political art is future-oriented. Indeed, Chantal Mouffe points out that one of its main objectives is to disrupt the current socio-political order and establish a new one by "re-articulating the situation in a new configuration" (2008). Critical-political art does not merely denounce a situation; it advances concrete or action-oriented solutions to remedy it and presents new ways of being or acting. This disarticulation and re-articulation of a political situation begins with an active engagement with the future, since it underscores the "yet unrealized … potentialities of what could be" (Möller 2016, 2). In other words, political art "can contribute to unsettling the dominant hegemony" (Mouffe 2013, 91) by "bringing to the fore the existence of alternatives to the current post-political order" (92–3), by showing "what could be" (Möller 2016, 2), and by expanding the realm of possibilities and citizens' world views.[39]

To enlist more citizens in imagining a different future, Möller (2016) proposes to replace "creating empathy" as a goal of political art with "creating solidarity" (12). While empathy can lead to pity – and is therefore more focused on the present than on the future – solidarity and engagement with the situation depicted look forward and can induce concrete change. Solidarity is a call to action, the actual impulse that moves the viewer from a passive to an active political role.

Since it often requires physical engagement with a work, artivism is sometimes conceived of as a more embodied or hands-on form of political art. Duncombe (2016) proposes a relatively straightforward theorization: The first constitutive element of artivism is activism, which he describes as various activities that (aim to) create an "effect," and the other is art, which creates an "affect," indescribable and almost impossible to measure empirically. Artivism, then, combines the effect of activism and the affect of art in "a practice aimed at generating Æffect: emotionally resonant experiences that lead to measurable shifts in power" (Duncombe and Lambert 2018). These changes, however, are sometimes hard to quantify. How can shifts in power be measured? Is artivism only effective when there is a change in government or when new laws are adopted? Attitudes and outlooks are slow to change, but any individual who is touched by artivism and changes their mind as a result represents a small shift in the balance of power, even if this shift is not visible on a larger scale. In *Pasting Up Protest,* I understand artivism as a form of resistance, and I side with Vinthagen (2019), who claims that with resistance practices, "no particular effect or outcome should be mandatory; only the potential of undermining power" (18). In the case of the collectives, their resistance to hegemony through the conscientization work they perform and their growing numbers slowly undermine power. Much like resistance, artivism is an ongoing practice, not an outcome or an end goal, that must integrate as many participants as possible if it is to reach its full potential.

Artivism has been theorized principally by two scholars: Beverly Naidus (2009) and Stephen Duncombe (2016). Each have elaborated lists of criteria for artivism (see table 1.1). As the table indicates, some criteria overlap, intersect, or are conceptually similar.

It is worth underscoring that, much like memory work and memory activism, artivism acknowledges the ills of both the past and the present in an effort to envision a better future. On art and memory studies, Dominick LaCapra (2004, 43) argues that "art, in its specific (often highly mediated, indirect, darkly playful, powerful but other than nar-

Table 1.1
Aims of artivism

Naidus (2009)	Duncombe (2016)
Process or document an experience	Foster dialogue
Question or offer solutions	Build community
Foster dialogue	Make a place
Awaken those who are numb or in denial	Invite participation
Compensate for social amnesia	Transform environment and experience
Heal the maker	Reveal reality
Make the invisible visible	Alter perception
Express outrage	Create disruption
Stretch the mind	Inspire dreaming
Envision a different reality or a better future	Provide utility
Find other like-minded individuals	Political expression
Make the most beautiful thing	Encourage experimentation
	Maintain hegemony
	Make nothing happen

Sources: Duncombe (2016); Naidus (2009).

rowly documentary or informational) forms of bearing witness or testifying to that [traumatic] past, might assist in partially working that past over and through, thereby making more available other possibilities in the present and future." With artivism, artists are doing more than imagining the possibilities; they also actively taking part in creating this potential future by planting seeds – by engaging citizens, fostering critical reflection, and expanding "what we consider normal, possible, or even conceivable" (Duncombe and Lambert 2018), and thereby offering alternatives. In short, they "critically intervene in relations of power" (Asavei 2018, 2) and focus on "what could be" (Möller 2016, 2) by engaging citizens as political beings.

Finally, both Duncombe and Naidus identify "fostering dialogue" as a main objective of artivism. This dialogue may reduce political distance between the authorities and citizens – and other artists. Another important aspect of artivism, one shared with memory activism, is the need for audience interaction. Art can be about art, but a praxis that seeks to have a concrete impact on the world must also involve audiences. Indeed, as more people are "æffected" (to return to Duncombe's term) by the work, the more concrete a change can be.[40]

Much like "political street art," political art and artivism both aim to confront the public and make it reflect critically. They also elicit an emotional response in the viewer. These responses can range from anger at the authorities to empathy and compassion for victims; all of them contribute to building solidarity between artists and audiences in order to tackle socio-political issues. In both political art and artivism, the audience must be receptive to the artist's work and the ideas it conveys for solidarity building to take root. Both are no less political if an audience is either not responsive to or rejects the premise of an artwork or an intervention. The refusal to become politically or socially engaged is, after all, a political posture.

Artivism goes one step beyond political art by using social and/or political art in a very active way to tackle an issue identified by the artists; it is a form of direct action and often used as a resistance strategy, and in that way it has a lot in common with graffiti and street art. I agree with Gilles Deleuze when he states that "L'art n'est pas une notion mais un mouvement. L'important n'est pas ce qu'il *est* mais ce qu'il *fait*" (Art is not a notion but a movement. What is important is not what it *is*, but what it *does*) (quoted in Lemoine and Ouardi 2010, 187; my emphasis). This movement can either be toward people – physically reducing the distance between artivists and audience members – or toward the future; and often it is both. In my view, both political artworks and artivistic interventions can create this movement toward the Other and contribute to building bridges toward a better future; in this they align with memory work. This reaching out toward an audience is more explicit with artivism than with political art, since viewers are either engaged by the work or are needed to complete it. In other words, both political art and artivism aim to reduce the distance – "the increased 'social space' between different individuals" – between stakeholders, but only artivism strives to collapse the social distance – their individual position with respect to others (Hatuka 2018, 14) – between artists and audience members, and between individual audience members.[41]

For the four collectives, this movement toward the Other is explicitly political. The artivistic practice they deploy in the street, using street art staples such as wheat paste posters and stencils, is tied to their objective of embedding events into Mexican collective memory so as to disarticulate and re-articulate it (Mouffe 2013). Integrating elements that contribute to creating a counternarrative to the one presented by the Mexican authorities is inherently political. The collectives use their art both to protest and to create a new cultural memory. Their blending of political protest art and memory work spurs a political change on a small scale, challenging more people to participate in their actions.

Despite the importance of challenging current historical narratives to re-articulate collective memory, these actions can lead to violence. As with most scholarship on the topic, Naidus and Duncombe focus on the Global North. Indeed, most of the literature on the subject discusses French, British, and American artists. This is an oversight as it is impossible to accept that there are no artivists in the Global South. Subcomandante Marcos and the EZLN, known for their 1994 uprising in Chiapas, are generally the only group examined in the literature (e.g., Lemoine and Ouardi 2010). While they might be the best known, they are by no means the only ones. One of my hypotheses – one that could form the basis for future investigation – is that artists from the periphery tend to be labelled as "political artists" rather than as "artivists," because the periphery, due to its history of coloniality, is always perceived as political.

Indeed, decolonial scholars argue that any intellectual or artistic endeavours coming out of a position of subalternity are inherently political (Dussel 1995; Mignolo 2007). This raises several questions: For nations that were once colonized, is there even a way out of political art? And when the subaltern speaks (Spivak 1988), even to another subaltern, is it always political? In the specific case of Mexico, some thinkers claim that intellectual work is always political (Volpi 2000); creators are either close to power, and benefit from it, or raise questions and strongly oppose it.

Another source of tension with current definitions is the claim that artivism does not promote violence (Duncombe 2016; Tate Gallery, n.d.). This poses a challenge when we examine some artists from the Global

South, as both their material and social conditions can often be violent. Sometimes, their artworks even promote violence against the authorities, as activists see such action as the only way to achieve political and social gains. More specifically the works of three of the collectives featured in *Pasting Up Protest* were born out of the violence experienced during the 2006 siege of Oaxaca, and for all of them, there is still a violent potential to the work – both artistically and within their community – as the members can be arrested, jailed, or in the worst-case scenario, disappeared.[42] While I neither encourage nor condone violence, I do not believe the potential for violence in the Global South should disqualify these artists' works from being called "artivism." They engage their community, are future-oriented, and want to create a better world by blending art and activism. Ultimately, I believe the artists' positionality and geographical location might add useful nuance to the argument about non-violence.

The importance of non-violence in Duncombe's (2016) theorization of artivism also erases the major contribution the EZLN made. That being said, while his analysis might take into consideration the work of Zapatista artists, it does not explicitly refer to them, which is a problem in itself and warrants being pointed out. We need to clarify this history and codify the connection between artivism and the Global South and remedy the erasure of Zapatismo in theorizations of artivism. Despite the potential violence inherent in their subjectivity and positionality, the collectives should not be erased from current and future theorizations of artivism.

The collectives' artwork both share similarities with and are starkly different from our general understanding of street art and artivism, because the artists infuse it with traditional Mexican engraving techniques, themes, and semiotics, and with their own memory activism. In other words, the collectives take the reproducibility of graffiti, the desire to establish a dialogue with an audience, and the techniques and visual repertoire of Mexican engraving to create artworks that challenge, move, and inform audiences. Their work is political street artivism developed at the periphery (Mignolo 2007), for peripheral audiences, whom it engages both socially and politically (Ryan 2017) so as to awaken their conscience and equip them to fight for a better future.

Memory Artivism

Indeed, the collectives I study focus on a traumatic past – one in which they and their fellow citizens experienced violence – and its repercussions in the present, and work toward shedding light on one of the enduring consequences of systemic violence in Mexico: disappearances, missing people, and missing and murdered girls and women. Memory activism is thus at the core of their work. According to Yifat Gutman and Jenny Wüstenberg (2022, 2), memory activists are "actors (individual or collective), who engage in the strategic commemoration of the past in order to achieve or prevent change in public memory by working outside state channels."

My analysis reveals that, by becoming producers of cultural memory, the four collectives are celebrating sectors of society that have historically been ignored in state commemorations. According to Eduardo Bautista Martínez (2008), the 1968 Tlatelolco massacre, the 1994 Acteal massacre, and the 2006 violent dismantling of the Oaxaca Commune by police – and I would add to this list the ongoing wave of feminicides in Ciudad Juárez that started to be documented in 1993 and the unresolved 2014 Ayotzinapa massacre – are symptoms of the disintegration of the Mexican political regime. By interacting with, challenging, and contributing to Mexican collective memory, street art collectives are active in illuminating this dissolution and its effects on Mexican citizens, and work toward the creation of competing social narratives about the past and of different regimes of memory where their struggles are acknowledged.

The workings of memory and its representations have come to greater prominence since the 1990s (Hodgkin and Radstone 2011; Olick et al. 2011), leading scholars across disciplines to privilege memory as a primary constitutive element of human experience and subjectivity. In simple terms, memory studies explore how the past informs the present, and how this knowledge can contribute to creating a better future.

For scholars like Boido (2018) and Milton (2011), fiction and art are accessible sites for observing memory at work, since the reader or the viewer can experience the events being remembered. Despite their importance, truth and reconciliation reports are more formal points of entry into the memory of an event and how individuals lived it. Whereas the complexity of these reports can repel readers or viewers, fictional narratives and artworks are, for lack of a better expression, "more approachable." Nussbaum's (1998) "narrative imagination" comes into play here as well; as fiction engulfs the reader or the viewer, they can picture themselves as the protagonist.

At the heart of memory lies the notion of identity, which is experienced individually as well as collectively; both types shape identity. Individual memories contribute to collective memory, and collective memory in turn nurtures individual memory. These narratives share in a constant dialogue, feeding off each other, and at the same time opposing and responding to each other. Collective memory – "the distribution throughout society of beliefs, feelings, moral judgements and knowledge about the past – is associated with a given group's identity" (Schwartz 2016). The past, or an interpretation of it, affects the group's identity and binds its members together. This knowledge of the past comes in two forms: history and memory. While history is based on generally agreed-upon facts, memory is shaped by the elements that social groups choose to remember about these historical facts and their surrounding narratives; both facts and narratives contribute to cementing the group's identity (Jelin 2003). My analysis of the collectives' artistic production and the ways they depict collective memory is informed by the tense relationship between history and memory. Sociologist Michel Wieviorka argues that when certain social groups like these collectives set out to re-articulate a past in which they have been denied a role, the collective memory they introduce is generally at odds with the accepted historical consensus, one that is generally highly political and politicized. In a way, these social groups go against accepted history and the agreed-upon narrative(s). Wieviorka also posits that by becoming a mobilization tool, memory acquires a double function. On the one hand, it becomes "scientific" as it attempts to add information to existing historical knowledge (the discipline of history); on the other, it becomes political or ideological as it seeks acknowledgment and reparation for the mistakes of the past (Wieviorka in Blais 2012, 27). By insisting that their version of history is accepted and folded into a broader collective narrative – in other words, that their lived experience is recognized – social groups not only disrupt the accepted collective memory but also the very political order out of which it emerged. In a way, social groups are affirming that the consensus is either a lie or that it is, at best, incomplete. These tacit negotiations of power can pit different social groups against each other, thus making memory highly political.

Related to the narratives embedded in memory are the regimes of truth under which a society operates. According to Michel Foucault, "Each society has its regime of truth, its 'general politics' of truth: that is, the types of discourse which it accepts and makes function as true; the mechanisms and instances which enable one to distinguish true and false statements, the means by which each is sanctioned; the techniques and procedures accorded value in the acquisition of truth; the status of those who are charged with saying what counts as true" (quoted in Rabinow 1991, 73). These regimes of truth, or agreed-upon narratives about the truth, participate in the creation of regimes of memory, defined as "institutionalized ways of setting and managing the supply and demand of remembrance in historical contexts. A regime of memory usually makes room for different, sometimes incoherent, even contradictory discourses on the past … memory deals with how the past is managed in the present" (Foucault in Rabinow 1991, 73). The two regimes are interconnected; one simply cannot exist without the other. Both the individual subject and society define themselves in relation to both regimes and by opposition to one of them. Regimes always provoke a response and are always in some sort of tension. Milton (2011) uses the expression "fractured past" to refer to two distinct "currents of memory," "attempts at dialogue and at closing down the conversation," which are "contrasting [endeavours] to rewrite the past" (192). These regimes of memory are political (what or who is included or excluded), whether institutional or not (official narrative, alternative story), and cohesive. As Elizabeth Jelin (2003, 3–4) points out, "In scenarios marked by struggle and confrontation, social agents develop narratives that contradict other interpretations, often to ward off oblivion and silences surrounding the past." These silences are highly political.

The political nature of memory is also underlined in Tzvetan Todorov's (1995) notion of *sélection*. In his short essay *Les abus de la mémoire* (The abuses of memory), Todorov is categorical: "la mémoire est sélection" (memory is selection) (15). Indeed, just as in the case of history, curation/selection (*sélection*, in the original French) is one of the main characteristics of memory (14). To remember, in the sense of creating a narrative about the past, as a community, is necessarily to sort and select the elements that are deemed to be worth remembering. Determining what is worthy of being preserved is a highly political process. Any curating of "happenings" can be ideological, as it is constrained by political demands and pressures, either implicit or explicit, and often both.

In stronger democracies, this selection can be challenged and rejected given the prevalence of multiple perspectives. However, in nations where dissidence is repressed, curating events often has negative outcomes for marginalized social groups. On the one hand, it erases past challenges to power in the hopes of consolidating collective memory. On the other, it silences victims and social groups who have been or are oppressed. This suggests that in the absence of social groups having risen in the past to oppose power in collective memory, current social groups cannot base their struggles on previous ones to solidify a shared identity in struggle. This lack of historical reference thus strengthens the powers that be. Not having a precedent can lead to memory activism, where memory is seen as a way to effect justice, often by seeking reparations for past misdeeds, and always by attempting to shed light on almost-forgotten stories. When tapped by marginalized sectors, memory activism is a means to "correct the past": "In some cases, the challenge from the point of view of memory is to put an end to the forgetfulness, or even the lies of history, to force it to amend itself, … to bring it to open itself up, to transform itself" (Wieviorka in Blais 2012, 47). This transformation can be as simple as folding the contested event(s) into recognized collective memory – for example, by having the state acknowledge it.

There is always pushback and resistance to the top-down imposition of events and memories, as a social narrative can never be shared by everyone. People and stories are necessarily excluded; it is impossible, after all, to remember everything and everyone (Jelin 2003, 4; Jelin 2021, 17). As long as most people agree on the narrative, the social fabric holds. Problems arise when authorities strive to maintain cohesion in spite of enough dissidence to provoke competing and often contradictory narratives. These multiple competing regimes reflect a fractured society and a fight for the imagination of the people; this struggle is inevitably political. Built around conflicting interpretations, these multiple memories (Raynaud in Blais 2012, 18–22) are problematic, since the main objective of collective memory is for society to coalesce around a common understanding of its past. It is generally easier to hold a group together when its members share strong ties and references to the past (Anderson 2016, 12; Hobsbawm and Ranger 2009). To create these strong bonds, it is sometimes necessary to suppress some less palatable events in the collective interest (Wieviorka in Blais 2012, 65).

The selection of historical events and figures both to celebrate and forget is not specific to Mexico. Every country performs a similar operation, and the process is politicized to varying degrees. The tensions between those sitting at the apex and those at the base of society can provoke an ideological fracture between social groups. In the case of Mexico, there is an ever-expanding fault line between the authorities and artists-activists. While the government strives to downplay occurrences of violence like feminicides and forced disappearances, activists and artists categorize them as tears in the social fabric; consequently, the nation's "master narrative" cannot hold (Jelin 2003, 27). These deaths, but more so the fact that they accumulate to form a pattern of violence sponsored by the state against its citizens, make them not only worth remembering but also worth exposing and embedding into the nation's collective memory. Being unacknowledged means that there can be no closure. More specifically, the artists under investigation here are trying to create an alternative or more complete collective memory than the one espoused by successive Mexican governments by etching these violent events – what Jelin calls the "wounds of memory" (2003, 17) – into the main social narrative. The collectives attempt to shed light on different chapters of Mexican history, on stories that have been ignored, neglected, or purposefully erased. As we will see in the following chapters, this re-articulation of the content of collective memory can lead to violence when opposing political forces confront each other. For the four artist collectives discussed here, this battle for memory is the "labour" (Jelin 2003) of their generation, one they hope will "transform the social world" (6).

Structure of the Book

Pasting Up Protest is organized around the analysis of two case studies that cover the last fifty years of Mexican history. More specifically, I examine how Mexican collectives deploy street art to represent and to re-semanticize the victims of the 2014 Iguala massacre – positioning it as one of the most recent occurrences in the ongoing state-sponsored violence perpetrated on post-secondary student activists – and the wave of feminicides documented since the 1990s. Although the ever-escalating feminicide crisis has been recorded over the past three decades, I begin the artistic analyses with Ayotzinapa, since the 2014 events acted as a catalyst for most subsequent movements in Mexico, including those related to gender-based violence, and prompted their re-articulation and expansion.

Chapter 2, "Commemorating Ayotzinapa," considers the representation of ongoing state violence against students, from the 1968 massacre and the 1971 *Halconazo* (the Corpus Christi massacre), both of which took place in Mexico City, to the 2014 Iguala mass disappearances. While 1968 is seen as the genesis of resistance and dissent by young protesters and students, 2014 marked a tipping point in social resistance emanating from all sectors of society. A close analysis of the corpus demonstrates that by explicitly linking these events in their murals, wheat paste posters, and stencils, Oaxaca-based ASARO and URT-Arte construct a narrative of the state-sponsored violence against student activists. I compare their production related to Ayotzinapa in terms of the political demands the collectives put forward and the chosen medium. I show that the scale of each collective's artworks meshes with the different political purposes they serve: First, to make the events visible; second, to honour the memory of the students; and third, to help recruit new members. I also examine how the two collectives integrate slogans related to the Ayotzinapa disappearances into their work or create their own, and how these protest writings position the collectives in the broader history of Mexican political art.[43]

The corpus of images I retain in chapter 2 comprises three murals and one installation made by ASARO and five wheat paste posters created by URT-Arte. I track the evolution of their production – from exposing, to protesting, and then commemorating the disappeared students. I compare how the two collectives integrate language related to the Ayotzinapa disappearances – "Todos somos Ayotzinapa" (We are all Ayotzinapa), "Vivos los llevaron, vivos los queremos" (They took them alive, we want them back alive), "Fue el Estado" (It was the state) – and how it inscribes their struggle in the long history of Mexican student movements.

The third chapter, "Women Empowering Women," analyzes how feminicides influence and inform the production of street art in Oaxaca and Mexico City. In *Pasting Up Protest*, I employ the term "feminicide" – instead of "femicide" – as it is most frequently used in Mexico to describe a form of gender-based violence that is more systemic than individual. Despite their similarities, the terms "femicide" and "femi*ni*cide" are not equivalent and do not describe the same reality. Journalist-activist Alice Driver (2015, 16), best known for her investigative work on the Ciudad Juárez murders, explains that "femicide refers more generally to gender-motivated violence, and feminicide has evolved to include an analysis of violence that results from … the power structures that create inequalities for women." These power structures are rooted in patriarchy and machismo. In short, feminicide encompasses a broader scope of systemic power inequalities that lead to women being murdered – the term is used "to identify and codify specific types of violence against women in a country [Mexico] that has a long history of ignoring violence against women from a legal, institutional, and political perspective" (2). In essence, in Mexico the responsibility of the government for the high rates of violence against women must be factored in when analyzing gendered violence, as inaction and impunity are contributing factors to its prevalence.

I argue that the ongoing waves of feminicides have spurred and continue to inspire an artistic production that, first, seeks to empower Mexican women; second, pays homage to and makes visible victims of gender violence; and third, fosters the development and promotion of other types of social mobilization campaigns. The female artists are thus concretely engaged with specific sectors of society. I also demonstrate that the representation of female-focused issues – such as domestic, gender-based violence and feminicide – has become more prominent in Mexican street art over the last decade. I believe that this is linked either to the

2007 adoption of the Ley General de Acceso de las Mujeres a una Vida Libre de Violencia (General Law on Women's Access to a Life Free of Violence), which included a legal definition of feminicide, and/or to the fact that more women street artists are joining historically masculine collectives. I pay close attention to how each group portrays these issues differently: For Oaxaca-based ASARO and URT-Arte, gender-based violence is but one of the many themes they tackle, whereas for women-only collectives like Oaxaca-based ARMARTE and Mexico City–based MUGRe, it is their principal theme. I highlight how these changes in legislation also provoked a shift in street art production and in activism by women for women. As women have become more visible in civil society, so has their representation in street art. Indeed, there is a shift from depicting the issue of *feminicidios* through the portrayal of faceless women – either buried or dismembered – to depicting women taking matters into their own hands, to directly calling on women to join in the struggle. This empowerment extends to the slogans, taglines, protest writings, and hashtags that the women-led groups espouse. Indeed, campaigns like MUGRe's #VivasNosQueremos (We want ourselves alive) are talk-back mechanisms directed at patriarchy itself.

The corpus of images in chapter 3 is formed by the thirty-five responses that MUGRe received as part of their two calls for images, titled #VivasNosQueremos, ARMARTE's mural on the facade of the Taller de Arte Comunitario (Workshop for Community Art) in Oaxaca, and the various wheat paste posters this second collective created for International Women's Day in 2018 and 2019. Unlike what transpired during the Ayotzinapa protests, which relied mostly on taglines that turned into hashtags, the artworks by MUGRe and ARMARTE featured hashtags from their inception. They are producing art that already has a foothold in the virtual world; they blend traditional engraving and social media culture. I also analyze how the slogans "Ni una más" (Not one woman more) and "Ni una menos" (Not one woman less) are integrated and how the two female collectives are positioning their work as part of a Latin American network of women-led groups, thus seeking to foster Pan-American sisterhood through their praxis.

At first sight, feminicides and the Ayotzinapa disappearances might appear to be unrelated. While both deal with missing persons and violence, the former is an ongoing, systemic issue, while the latter, for which there is yet no resolution, constitutes a single occurrence of violence, even if it reflects a culture of systemic violence in Mexico. In fact, they intersect on multiple fronts, both in terms of social activism and artistic creation. The strategies and styles deployed and the ideologies at play are similar. Both crises also provoked social movements that are still going strong, despite the passage of time.

Examining cases that cover a long period of time (1993–; 2014–) means that there exists a large body of cultural artifacts on which to draw. This extended time frame enables me to map and analyze any evolution (or lack thereof) in the artistic production. It is useful to delve not only into the art itself, but also to examine political tactics and strategies and how activists modify artistic forms to better fit their purposes. What works? Why? Do these movements feed on or learn from one another? Choosing well-known cases also means that an English-speaking audience might be more familiar with some of the relevant facts, since many readers are already aware of the ongoing violence in Mexico.

The artists and activists turn to street art for the same reasons: The state dismisses or minimizes troubling events and calls for action fall on deaf ears. The battle to inscribe the victims into history and collective memory arises from the people, from the bottom up, and is fuelled by a desire to construct an alternative history – dare I say a richer, more complex and complete history – one that includes marginalized sectors of society that are usually left behind and not commemorated or remembered. The authorities' lack of interest in finding missing citizens symbolically captures "the contempt and the demonstration that there are lives that have no value, whose corpses are erased and annulled" (Gutiérrez Castañeda 2018, 74). Mexican subjects are disposable, particularly if they occupy a position of marginality in society, be they women, poor, of Indigenous descent, journalists, or activists.

In both case studies, victims cannot tell their stories. They need someone else to do it for them; this is the role that activists and artists choose to play. They re-centre the narrative on each individual victim. Although each movement is motivated by a different ideology, the artifacts are meant to dismantle – or to try to, at least – power structures and systemic violence in Mexico. They seek to shift the balance of power and give silenced sectors of society a voice.

The protest surrounding the Ayotzinapa case triggered a renewal of feminist protests in Mexico. As Marcela A. Fuentes (2019) explains in "NiUnaMenos (#NotOneWomanLess) – Hashtag Performativity, Memory and Direct Action Against Gender Violence in Argentina," groups in Mexico and Argentina took up the hashtag #VivosLosQueremos (We want them alive) and transformed it into #VivasNosQueremos (We want ourselves alive). By using the pronoun *nos* (ourselves), the activists emphasized that the norms they were challenging affected them too; ultimately, they counted themselves among the many women for whom they were marching and protesting:

> By recycling #WeWantThemAlive into #WeWantOurselvesAlive, the movement against femicides fueled a digital spark and made an important feminist intervention. In the change of grammatical person, from "them" to "ourselves," *activists drew attention to the structural vulnerability that conditions women's lives.* This discursive intervention helped the movement address the situation of very specific bodies. *The hashtag also transformed mourning into vitality, into the desire to live, and it asserted a politics of self-care and autonomy that stood in contrast to previous activisms centered on women's naturalized role as mothers and caregivers.* (182; my emphasis)

By altering the grammatical person,[44] activists disrupted a narrative that claimed that victims of feminicides were somehow anomalies in the social fabric and focused instead on the notion that, much like in Ayotzinapa, everyone was at risk, since gendered violence is more systemic than specific. In the end, the social movements that coalesced around the forty-three disappeared students were not restricted to Ayotzinapa; they acted as a catalyst for a broader shift in several other social movements and expanded the scope of militancy.

Comparing these two cases allows me to demonstrate how these four groups adopt similar techniques and tactics successfully. By deploying a similar repertoire of contention – "the limited range of performances that present a regularity but are open to negotiation and innovation by the protesters" (Giacoman and Torres 2019, 3) – that is shaped by Mexican history and culture to depict the two types of human rights violations, they are able to bridge the gap between two seemingly disparate issues.

In the next chapter, dedicated to the Ayotzinapa disappearances, I explore ASARO and URT-Arte's depiction of juvenicides and how the collectives tie the 2014 atrocities to a broader narrative of Mexican government violence against student and teacher activists.

CHAPTER 2

"Pienso luego me desaparecen": Commemorating Ayotzinapa

Aquí en México … hay que defender nuestros derechos *en contra del* gobierno.
(Here in Mexico … we have to defend our rights *against* the government.)
– A parent of a missing Ayotzinapa student

No sabemos si duermen 43 pero despertamos millones.
(We do not know if forty-three are sleeping, but we have awakened millions.)
– Seen on a T-shirt during a protest in Mexico City

Introduction

Fue el Estado. It was the state. Since the 1960s these three words have appeared on innumerable posters across Mexico to denounce the government's role in human rights violations perpetrated against its own citizens. In September 2014, after forty-three teacher trainees from the Ayotzinapa rural school in the state of Guerrero were disappeared, #FueElEstado went viral on all major social media platforms, effectively blurring the lines between traditional street protests and their online counterparts.[1]

Starting in early October, demonstrators gathered everywhere: While many took to the Paseo de la Reforma in Mexico City with posters demanding that the students be brought back alive – chanting *¡Vivos los* *llevaron, vivos los queremos!* (They took them alive, we want them back alive) – many more assembled online to shift the focus away from the failings of President Enrique Peña Nieto's government and directly onto the victims.

The civilian population and activists have often been the targets of Mexico's persistent state-sponsored violence; whether we think of the Dirty War of previous decades or the more recent war on drugs launched by President Felipe Calderón in 2006, citizens regularly vanish without a trace, and the authorities are often reluctant to investigate. In spite of these decades of state-enacted violence, or perhaps because of them, the September 2014 police- and army-led mass disappearance of the forty-three Ayotzinapa students became a tipping point for Mexican public opinion (Taibo 2019; Volpi 2016).[2]

This chapter considers the artistic representation by Oaxacan collectives of the September 2014 forced disappearances of the forty-three students and situates it within broader representation by Mexican artists of ongoing state violence against student activists. As a reminder, on 26 September 2014, about one hundred first-year students from the Raúl Isidro Burgos Normal School in Ayotzinapa had travelled by bus to the city of Iguala – a four-and-a-half-hour drive – to raise funds and commandeer buses, in order to reach Mexico City, where they planned to participate in a demonstration on 2 October commemorating the 1968 Tlatelolco massacre.[3] Early in the evening, armed groups assaulted a number of these students; the attacks lasted through the night. By dawn the next day, three students had been executed,[4] three passersby had been killed,[5] twenty-five more people were injured, and forty-three students – aged seventeen to thirty-three – had been disappeared. The fact that the forcibly disappeared were students, teachers-in-training from poor rural communities, and that they were not abducted by criminals but allegedly taken by the very police forces meant to protect them sparked outrage in Mexico and abroad. The lies that the Mexican government concocted to cover the police and the military's role in the concerted offensive against the students and their subsequent disappearance only added fuel to the fire. The students' names and faces, as well as the numbers 1–43, quickly became their symbolic visual representation in weekly Ayotzinapa marches.

The disappearance of the forty-three students also highlights another cruel reality that many Mexicans face: Forced disappearances are the norm rather than the exception, and, much like the crisis of feminicides I discuss in chapter 3, they are rarely fully investigated. Similarities with investigations into feminicides are many: The groups that disappear citizens – be they composed of members of criminal gangs or military personnel, as is suspected in the Ayotzinapa case – generally benefit from impunity, evidence goes missing, witnesses are untraceable, or court cases are dismissed before they ever reach the judicial system. Now, almost ten years after the forty-three students were forcibly disappeared, the outcome in the Ayotzinapa case is no different. By May 2024, various reports had confirmed the role of the highest levels of the state apparatus in disappearing these students (COVAJ 2022; GIEI 2022b), but whether justice will ever be done, let alone be seen to be done, remains in question.

In "Commemorating Ayotzinapa," I argue that artistic representation of the September 2014 occurrences promotes the building of an alternative collective memory, one that seeks to mobilize citizens to act against ongoing injustices. I demonstrate that by disseminating this alternative collective memory, the groups that I examine empower citizens to fight back against a state narrative that criminalizes victims of forced disappearances and shames their families into silence. By "collectivizing grief" (Morbiato 2017) and representing the disappeared as part of their resistance practices, not only do the collectives inscribe the missing citizens into Mexico's national narrative – thus dispelling the myth of national cohesion that the government insists on – but they also open a space for civil society to grieve and regain its voice.

"Commemorating Ayotzinapa" is divided into two main sections: a historical and theoretical framework, followed by an analysis of street art production in Oaxaca. I begin the historical and theoretical section, entitled "A Rebel Tradition," with an overview of Mexico's wars against student movements, from the creation of the system of *escuelas normales rurales* (rural normal schools) in the 1920s to the present. Starting with the establishment of the schools in the wake of the Mexican Revolution (1910–20) enables me to highlight the century-long neglect these schools have endured, which contributed to transforming their students into active political agents. I then concentrate on the year 1968 and the 2 October

Tlatelolco massacre, as both remain watershed moments of student protest and a response culminating in state violence. The 1968 Plaza de las Tres Culturas shooting is considered the genesis of resistance and dissent by young protesters and students. The massacre also constitutes a prime example of the Mexican government's attempts at silencing dissent, and at covering up police and military intervention against the very population they are supposed to protect. In light of the 1968 events, the Ayotzinapa disappearances present an air of déjà vu. A close look at the repertoire of symbols, patterns, and slogans that activists used during the May–October 1968 protests is necessary, as many were woven into the 2014 artworks in a conscious and deliberate attempt to tie past cases of impunity to current ones.

A subsequent section, "*Pa'l pueblo* (For the People)," is dedicated to an analysis of Oaxacan street art that deals with the Ayotzinapa disappearances. I concentrate on the works of ASARO and URT-Arte and contrast the different purposes they serve. Although a lot of attention has been paid to ASARO's production, scholars have focused mostly on works created in 2006, during, or in the wake of, the Oaxaca uprising. These early works display the anti-capitalist position of the collective, and most of them highlight landlessness and agricultural issues. ASARO's latest body of work has yet to benefit from an analysis that takes into account the role new social problems play in its production. Moreover, despite URT-Arte's consistent production and clearly defined political project, the scholarly community has yet to study this collective. Even though artist and activist Mario Guzmán founded both collectives, comparing their production related to Ayotzinapa highlights stark ideological differences between the two groups.

I examine the artworks and installations of the two collectives chronologically, beginning with ASARO and continuing with URT-Arte. The corpus of images I analyze is novel and was selected from a group of between 125 and 150 artworks that circulated in and around Oaxaca between October 2014 and October 2022. More specifically, I concentrate on three murals, four stencils, and one installation that ASARO mounted between 2014 and 2017, and five wheat paste posters that URT-Arte designed between 2017 and 2022. These works were selected because they contribute to the development of a narrative protesting state-sponsored violence against student activists, thus adding counter-voices to official Mexican collective memory. All also actively engage citizens by challenging viewers to become agents of change themselves, to share in the demise of Mexico's politics of memory that is designed to erase student activism and forced disappearances.

I have identified three main purposes for these works of art. First, through depiction itself as well as repetition and reproduction, they shine a light on, honour, and pay homage to the forty-three disappeared students. The members of the two collectives do this in a context where they, too, could easily become victims. Indeed, given the political tensions inherent in depicting disappeared individuals, portrayal itself is a bold move, as is effectively documenting their production and posting it online for further dissemination. In a country that erases "undesirable" people, representing them is a daring political statement that the collectives make and repeat, installation after installation, poster after poster, leaving a ghost of the victims to follow in the footsteps of those responsible for their disappearances. By deploying an artivistic practice that reaches out to the Mexican people, and weaves past and future together, the two collectives dare to speak to sectors of the population that are not generally politicized.

Second, either implicitly or explicitly, both collectives seek to empower citizens to speak up in reaction to state-sponsored violence. In this, they align themselves with numerous activists who have denounced the lies and falsehoods surrounding the Ayotzinapa case. ASARO's interventions are quite ominous in theme and size; they represent violence and its aftermath, but do not address citizens directly. In contrast, URT-Arte deploys imagery to which everyone can relate – mothers sobbing or bleeding with empty wombs, peasants crying, or students demonstrating. These prints show a different approach to violence: the violence experienced by those left behind by the disappearances, which is ultimately a type of violence that can motivate people to turn to activism.

Finally, these works serve as a soft warning to the authorities; a reminder that although forty-three are missing, activists continue organizing. This is further highlighted by one of the movements' slogans – the very one I cited in the preface: Nos quisieron enterrar, pero no sabían que éramos semillas (They tried to bury us, not knowing we were seeds).

And indeed, the social movement that emerged in September 2014 planted, and keeps planting, many seeds. It has spurred hundreds of marches across Mexico, with protesters demanding that the students be brought back alive and denouncing the federal government's inaction and lies. More than ten years after the events, monthly marches still take place, reminding the authorities that the friends and families of the forty-three disappeared students will not be bullied into silence and will not accept lies.

I have elected to frame my two analyses of artworks produced by ASARO (2006–) and URT-Arte (2007–) around the notion of kinship – an affinity or similarity between groups – that often leads to solidarity. Given their previous activism and political artworks, ASARO and URT-Arte's interest in keeping the disappearance of the forty-three students in the public eye was only to be expected, especially in the city of Oaxaca. The kinship between the Oaxacan collectives and the Ayotzinapa students – the deceased, the survivors, and the student body more broadly – also extends beyond their shared activism. Indeed, the repression experienced by the Ayotzinapa students is not unlike that endured by protesters and artists during the 2006 Oaxaca protests, when many were also detained or forcibly disappeared. However, unlike the Ayotzinapa students, some of the Oaxacan artists were released and are now involved with ASARO and/or URT-Arte. It is probable that these graphic artists feel a kinship with the disappeared students: Much like some street artists and activists in 2006, the missing Ayotzinapa students were opposing a system that silences dissent and dissenters by repressing them and making them disappear. As such, one of the objectives of creating and disseminating images could be, in Naidus's (2009) artivism framework, to "heal the maker" (5), a way to process their own trauma.

These artists are actively engaged in empowering citizens. Comparing the collectives' street art production in terms of political demands, taglines and captions, and media enables me to demonstrate how the scale of each collective's art is aligned with their different political purposes. Much like their forebears in the Liga de Escritores y Artistas Revolucionarios (League of Revolutionary Writers and Artists)[6] and the Taller de Gráfica Popular (People's Graphic Workshop) of the 1930s and '40s, both groups resort to prints to keep the forced disappearances in the forefront, honour the memory of the students, and recruit new members. They also draw from post-revolutionary muralism. Whereas ASARO opts for monumental print installations and murals located on the facade of their workshop to memorialize the students, URT-Arte's choice of smaller, highly reproducible prints plastered all over the city serves to make the events visible and to recruit new members, as they often address the bystander directly.

I also examine how the two collectives integrate the protest slogans related to the Ayotzinapa disappearances – "Todos somos Ayotzinapa" (We are all Ayotzinapa), and "Vivos los llevaron, vivos los queremos" (They took them alive, we want them back alive) – or create their own. Their recourse to well-known taglines inscribes their struggle in the long history of Mexican social movements, and their visual language makes them part of the tradition of Mexican political art. Bringing this corpus together contributes to developing a more nuanced understanding of how Mexican artists and activists tackle the issue of forced disappearances in their works.

A close look at the works produced by ASARO and URT-Arte indicates how their production reflects the position of civil society at large. There is a progression from *visibilizar* (making visible) to *protestar* (protest and denouncement). This progression also tracks the grieving process of the Mexican population. At first, the art expressed support for the families and friends of the forty-three student teachers, with the artworks and installations representing the students and aimed at making their disappearance known to the broader public in Oaxaca. Then, as it was becoming clearer that in fact the students were not "missing" but had been disappeared, and likely murdered, the collectives – much like thousands of other Mexican citizens – started protesting the state's inaction with more militant artworks and slogans and various spray-painted inscriptions directly calling out the authorities. At that point, the artworks started to integrate or dialogue with previous protest art – such as that designed as part of the 1968 protests, or during the Dirty War – because the collectives moved from building awareness to condemning the government for repeating past transgressions.

Even if the two collectives ultimately commemorate the victims, they do it quite differently. Whereas ASARO fits along a continuum of visual representations of the massacre, using the names and faces of students, representing them individually but always as a group, works by URT-Arte attempt to reach other sectors of the citizenry, with the prints representing women grieving lost sons or citizens affected by the disappearance of the forty-three. ASARO's representations of the massacre itself commemorate and honour the memory of the students, while URT-Arte concentrates on "those who were left behind," and on people who can be empowered to combat state violence. URT-Arte's works also show that, ultimately, almost every citizen was affected by yet another outbreak of state-sponsored violence. Not only do the artworks create empathy in and solidarity with the viewer; the installations and prints also act as a subtle reminder that those protesting today could easily become tomorrow's disappeared.

Before moving to the analysis of ASARO's and URT-Arte's works, it is necessary to take a brief look at the history of systemic violence against student activists that culminated in the 2014 massacre. Born out of the promises of the Mexican Revolution, the social project of training strong, politically engaged students, who would become strong, politically engaged citizens, was designed and sponsored by the government itself; that is, until government authorities realized that, by training citizens to think critically, they would eventually start applying that critical thinking to the government's own failings, and then attempt to reform it.

Socio-Historical Context: A Rebel Tradition[7]

> Systematic forced disappearances constitute a social reality designed to haunt, to be both known and invisible.
>
> – Gibler (2017, 142)

The mass disappearance of the forty-three Ayotzinapa students in September 2014 is part of a larger pattern of state-sponsored violence against the students enrolled at the Raúl Isidro Burgos Normal School, and more broadly against student and peasant activism in the state of Guerrero. Three key moments shaped the context of the 2014 disappearances: the establishment of the *escuelas normales rurales* in the

1920s, the Dirty War (1960s–80s),[8] and the 2011 confrontation between Ayotzinapa students and police forces.

These three events illuminate the disregard, contempt, and lack of protection the authorities showed, and continue to show, the Ayotzinapa students. Indeed, for the authorities, the Ayotzinapa students are not "grievable subjects" (Butler 2016); they are not at all worthy of protection. Moreover, these abuses highlight why the reaction of both artists and activists, and of civil society more widely, was immediate and visceral. Indeed, after years of self-imposed silence for fear they would be the next to disappear, many Mexicans viewed Ayotzinapa as a tipping point.

The Escuelas Normales Rurales*: A Lifeline for Poor Communities*

The authorities are suspicious of *escuelas rurales normales*[9] and their students, perceiving them as a threat to the established order. At the time of their creation in the 1920s, the authorities envisioned these schools as community-oriented institutions with a high degree of autonomy (Civera-Cerecedo 2004, 4): On the one hand, being removed from Mexico City made oversight more challenging, while on the other, and perhaps more realistically, the student body was of less interest to the capital's governing elites. In the 1930s, the school curriculum took an explicitly socialist turn. This change in ideology led to tensions with the government – tensions that were still simmering during Enrique Peña Nieto's presidency (Hernández 2020). While the pupils of the *normales rurales* were always conceived of as future cultural, economic, and political leaders in their communities, the introduction of supposedly "socialist" topics led to more self-sustaining political initiatives both in and emerging from the *normales rurales* (Civera-Cerecedo 2004, 6). The schools not only trained students to become teachers but also transformed them into political agents. Intellectually, students from rural normal schools were, and indeed still are, perceived as "dangerous," as they refuse to settle down and rather continuously push for reforms.

Over time, the *normales rurales* have acquired a reputation for training revolutionaries and protesters. While learning to think critically aligns with the ideals set out by then–Secretary of Public Education José Vasconcelos, the various governments that followed the Obregón presidency (1921–24) developed, then fostered, mistrust of the student teachers, since they disrupted the top-down, centre-periphery social order to improve their social conditions and those of their pupils. Indeed, "The *normalista rural* is that thinking man from below who teaches those from below to think, and since to think is to stir up places, and since to be from below is to settle for the place of resignation, ignominy, despair, and lack of opportunity, this is a cultural contradiction in Mexico" (Abud Jaso et al. 2018, 83). The *normalista* is, then, a contradiction: He is simultaneously funded by the state to receive an education and thwarted in his attempts to improve his socio-economic condition when his actions do not align with state views. Since the 1940s, this contradiction has led to a steady decline in funding,[10] thus affirming the need for activism.

The Escuela Normal Rural de Ayotzinapa: A School for Political Activism

The Raúl Isidro Burgos Normal School is one of the seventeen *escuelas normales* left across Mexico. Best known as the Escuela Normal Rural de Ayotzinapa, the institution is a male-only, higher-level education centre in the state of Guerrero. Most of the students – 532 in 2018 – belong to families that earn a living by farming. Receiving formal training at the *normal* is often the only way to escape a future of subsistence farming. Most of the students receive a full scholarship that covers tuition with room and board; in exchange, they are expected to farm the school property and assist with maintaining the installations (Hernández 2020).

The Ayotzinapa *normal* is perhaps Mexico's best-known rural teachers' school, because of the 2014 forced disappearances, but also because, since the 1960s, it has been considered a hotbed for guerrilla movements and budding activists. Indeed, many revolutionaries active in leftist guerrilla movements during the second half of the twentieth century can be traced to Ayotzinapa. During the 1960s and well into the 1970s, major popular protests proliferated across Mexico – fuelled by endemic poverty, expanding commercialization of agriculture, foreign capital investment, a history of extreme institutional instability, and political corruption (Blacker 2009, 185) – leading to strong state repression. Starting in 1962, the Mexican government, aided by the United States, combatted and harshly repressed left-wing activism and student movements composed of teacher activists. For instance, Lucio Cabañas Barrientos, a former student leader who was trained at Ayotzinapa, created the Party of the Poor (Partido de los Pobres, or PDLP), a socialist party active from 1967 to 1974 that originated in the poorer communities of *campesinos* (peasants) in Guerrero and that campaigned in favour of an agrarian revolution based on the ideals of the 1917 constitution.[11] This, in turn, increased the repression of the *escuelas normales* (Villanueva 2020), peasants, and emerging social movements (Hernández 2020).

While social movements were emerging and spreading in the poorer states, most major marches and protests still occurred in Mexico City. Two watershed moments that have had an enduring impact on student and teacher activism are the 2 October 1968 massacre in Tlatelolco and the 1971 Corpus Christi massacre, both in the federal capital. The 1968 Tlatelolco massacre is a prime example of government-led repression.[12] In the decade leading up to the 1968 Olympics (12–27 October), successive governments had suppressed labour unions while spending millions of pesos to rebuild Mexico City into a new, modern metropolis. Following a march protesting the authorities' spending, about 5,000 people gathered at the Plaza de las Tres Culturas in Tlatelolco, a district lying slightly north of the historic centre of Mexico City. Under the orders of President Gustavo Díaz Ordaz, tanks surrounded the protesters and soldiers fired into the crowd. The Mexican government estimated the death toll at under 100, listing other participants as "missing"; however, activists tallied between 200 and 1,000 deaths. These individuals remain unaccounted for to this day.[13] Following 2 October, protesters added an image or a caricature to the "Mexico 1968" slogan, depicting the dove, another symbolic branding element of the Olympic movement, bleeding, with either bullet or knife wounds.[14]

Then, about three years later, on 10 June 1971, a paramilitary group known as the Falcons, affiliated with US military forces, attacked a group of about 10,000 demonstrators who were protesting in Mexico

City against the ongoing Dirty War. Some 120 students, aged fourteen to twenty-two, were killed during the *Halconazo* (literally "the attack of the Falcons"), President Luis Echeverría Alvarez's response to the first large-scale student protest since 1968 (Special Prosecutor's Office 2006; US Embassy Mexico 2002). And once again, the police turned a blind eye; no one from the paramilitary group or its supporters was arrested or jailed.[15]

Both these massacres led to the regrouping and reorganization of grassroots movements. The state of Guerrero – given its proximity to the capital – became the hub for urban radicals who were aiming to reignite the revolution after it fell dormant in the wake of these losses (Blacker 2009).[16]

The deaths of young activists and the ensuing lack of justice, as well as the trauma suffered by the citizens who were detained, tortured, and then released (McCormick 2017), have all had a major effect on rural populations ever since. Not only is there a severe distrust of government, but most people have internalized the need to remain silent, even when faced with oppression and human rights violations. "For the peasant communities, seeing their members disappear implied a grief impossible to imagine, but living in constant terror meant that fear became an integral part of their being, the result of installing silence as a device of collective discipline" (Echavarría Canto and Vázquez Carmona 2018, 113). Ultimately, the government succeeded in silencing activists, as well as deterring anyone from speaking out against its abuses, for fear of also being disappeared.

Peruvian author and intellectual Mario Vargas Llosa aptly described Mexico's low-intensity Dirty War as "the perfect dictatorship" (*El País* 1990): It tactically forced society into obedience through fear. Morbiato (2017) argues that, over the years, three main elements contributed to the current culture of silence in Mexico. Indeed, "a perpetual and unfinished mourning, an alarming anomie and the perfection of the use of fear as a privileged tool of social control" (140) all ensured that civil society would not break rank. But in the wake of the forty-three's disappearance, civil society did tear down the wall of silence surrounding state violence.

The 2011 Confrontation

Like most students enrolled in a rural normal school, the Ayotzinapa students are activists, and their first battleground is the school itself. Over the years, their main demand has not wavered: better funding from the state of Guerrero and the federal government in order to improve the school's facilities. The authorities' response is generally dismissive, which only leads to more demonstrations.

A more recent example of the authorities' refusal to respond to the students is the 2011 *Conflicto de Ayotzinapa* (Ayotzinapa Conflict). On 12 December, about five hundred students blocked Federal Highway 95 near Guerrero's capital, Chilpancingo, requesting an immediate meeting with the state governor to discuss conditions at the school. Governor Ángel Rivero Aguirre agreed to meet, but then cancelled four times, infuriating the student body (Ocampo Artista 2011).

Blocking Highway 95 is a sure way to get the attention of the authorities. Because it links Mexico City to Acapulco, an important tourist destination, maintaining a fluid traffic flow on the highway is essential to the economy. After state and federal police moved to dislodge the protesters, both sides resorted to violence. Students armed themselves with Molotov cocktails and rocks, while police officers carried guns. During the confrontations, 2 Ayotzinapa students were killed,[17] 7 protesters were wounded, and 24 others were detained "arbitrarily" (National Security Archive 2015). Of the 24 detainees, 23 were released the next day. This arbitrary detention, followed by a quick release, explains in part why the authorities did not pay much attention to 43 missing students in 2014; like their peers in 2011, they were expected to resurface once the situation had settled.

Hours after the altercation on Highway 95, the police strongly rejected the students' allegations that they had opened fire. Instead, the police claimed that they had only fired warning shots and that the students had not complied with orders to disperse. Camera footage of the supposed "warning shots" was soon released to the media, and while it was impossible to confirm visually that the police had indeed fired on the students, several state and federal police officers were seen physically assaulting them. The video clips quickly disproved the state attorney general's claim that the police officers acted peacefully despite the protesters being especially violent.[18] Mexico's Comisión Nacional de los Derechos Humanos (National Human Rights Commission) travelled to Guerrero to investigate and found government agents guilty of violating human rights. And yet, no one was charged or jailed, as the courts deemed the evidence insufficient to proceed (Hernández 2020).

This brief overview of altercations between student movements and police and other armed forces illuminates the contempt the Mexican power apparatus has for dissenters. Perpetrators of the 1968 and 1971 massacres were not held accountable, nor were the police officers charged with human rights violations in 2011.[19] This may explain why no one really expects a meaningful and honest resolution to the 2014 Ayotzinapa disappearances, and why political activists and artists are leading the charge against the authorities.

26 September 2014

The 2011 events, when students and police forces faced off, foreshadowed the abuses that unfolded on a much larger scale in 2014 – from extreme violence against students, to the destruction and planting of evidence, to special investigations that various organizations conducted afterwards.

Before moving to a historical overview, I must point out that it is impossible to do justice to the horrors the students experienced that night or the trauma of the survivors. Nor is this the objective of this overview. Many authors, writing in different genres, have produced detailed and compelling accounts of the students' experiences, which have shaped and informed my thinking about the case. Among them I recommend the works of novelist Tryno Maldonado (2015), journalist John Gibler (2017), and investigative reporter Anabel Hernández (2020). Based on countless hours of interviews with students and their families, their respective books provide invaluable insights into the events that took place on the night of 26 September 2014.[20]

Earlier that day, about one hundred first-year students travelled to the city of Iguala to raise funds and commandeer buses; this was a normal occurrence for the students of the Ayotzinapa normal rural school. While both practices are frowned on by the community and the authorities, they are nonetheless tolerated because everyone is aware of the school's lack of financial resources.[21] Over the month of September, the students had been raising funds in order to participate in a demonstration in Mexico City commemorating the Tlatelolco massacre on 2 October.

On 26 September the students travelled from Ayotzinapa on the two buses they had previously taken under their control and commandeered three others at the Iguala bus station.[22] According to Hernández (2020, 327), the forty-three students' fate was sealed the moment they took over the buses. Indeed, these buses are believed to have carried about US$2 million worth of heroin, which a drug lord had tasked the army with retrieving.

Around nine o'clock in the evening, only a few minutes after the unarmed students entered Iguala, municipal police officers opened fire on them at four different locations across the city.[23] Federal, state, and municipal police, as well as soldiers, witnessed the assaults and failed to protect the students.[24] Reports have since revealed that the police and the military were fully aware of the scope of the events as they unfolded, as they had been monitoring the students since they had left the school earlier that evening (Hernández 2020, 83, 88). Monitoring the students was standard practice, since, as I mentioned earlier, the authorities consider them "dangerous" and disruptive. At 11:30 p.m., students who had been attacked earlier held a media conference to denounce the assault and to show reporters bullet casings. They feared that once the authorities arrived, the crime scenes would be cleaned and their allegations disputed. In the middle of the media conference, students, teachers, and reporters were attacked again, spurring everyone to flee. Many hid in the hills surrounding Iguala or took shelter in the homes of Good Samaritans. Those who stayed in the city due to injuries sought medical attention but struggled to find any; hospitals had been warned not to treat them. Meanwhile, students who were riding on the three buses taken that night at the Iguala bus station vanished without a trace.

By dawn on 27 September, three students had been executed, three passersby had been killed, twenty-five more people were injured, and forty-three *normalistas* – aged seventeen to thirty-three – had been disappeared (Eber and Vázquez Carpizo 2015). These are their names:

Abel García Hernández
Abelardo Vázquez Peniten
Adán Abrajan de la Cruz
Alexander Mora Venancio[25]
Antonio Santana Maestro
Benjamín Ascencio Bautista
Bernardo Flores Alcaraz
Carlos Iván Ramírez Villarreal
Carlos Lorenzo Hernández Muñoz
César Manuel González Hernández
Christian Alfonso Rodríguez Telumbre
Christian Tomás Colón Garnica
Cutberto Ortiz Ramos
Doriam González Parral
Emiliano Alen Gaspar de la Cruz
Everardo Rodríguez Bello
Felipe Arnulfo Rosas
Giovanni Galindes Guerrero
Israel Caballero Sánchez
Israel Jacinto Lugardo
Jesús Jovany Rodríguez Tlatempa
Jonás Trujillo González
Jorge Álvarez Nava
Jorge Aníbal Cruz Mendoza
Jorge Antonio Tizapa Legideño
Jorge Luis González Parral
José Ángel Campos Cantor
José Ángel Navarrete González
José Eduardo Bartolo Tlatempa
José Luis Luna Torres
Jhosivani Guerrero de la Cruz
Julio César López Patolzin
Leonel Castro Abarca
Luis Ángel Abarca Carrillo
Luis Ángel Francisco Arzola
Magdaleno Rubén Lauro Villegas

Marcial Pablo Baranda
Marco Antonio Gómez Molina
Martín Getsemany Sánchez García
Mauricio Ortega Valerio
Miguel Ángel Hernández Martínez
Miguel Ángel Mendoza Zacarías
Saúl Bruno García

From the outset, the state of Guerrero and the Mexican federal government mishandled and minimized the significance of the disappearance of the forty-three students. In hindsight, now that the role the authorities played in the disappearances is widely known, it makes sense that they were reluctant to investigate their own actions. During the first forty-eight hours (27–28 September), authorities even claimed that the forty-three *normalistas* were not missing; no formal search was organized, despite those first hours being the most important ones in missing persons cases. The authorities believed that much like other students had done during the night of the twenty-sixth, the missing students were hiding in the hills and eventually would reappear. On 28 September, the students were officially reported missing by both their parents and the school. On 29 September, the authorities began searching for them. By then their parents had already been canvassing the surrounding areas for two days. On 30 September the official list of the missing forty-three was made public and distributed state- and nationwide.

The disappearance of the Ayotzinapa students became the biggest embarrassment of President Peña Nieto's time in office (2012–18). Early on, the president expressed little concern, and called for trust in the institutional resolution of the crisis. In a country with an extremely high impunity rate like Mexico – some studies mention up to 98 per cent (Ferri 2020) – faith in official investigations was a lot to demand from distressed parents and friends, even before allegations that it was a state crime gained traction. Trust in the authorities was further eroded when Attorney General Jesús Murillo Karam refused to answer any more questions in the now (in)famous 8 November 2014 news conference called to announce the students' supposed deaths; his offhanded comment, "Ya me cansé" (I am tired of answering questions), appalled both families and civil society (*Animal Político* 2014; Presidencia Enrique Peña Nieto 2014). The comment also encapsulates the contempt from and the lack of interest of the government in pursuing or resolving the case.

The federal government tried to claim that the students had been killed by the Guerreros Unidos (United Warriors) drug cartel and then incinerated in a Cocula garbage dump. According to this narrative, which Murillo Karam called the "verdad histórica" (historical truth), the students were handed over to the Guerreros Unidos by Iguala police officers after having disrupted a political event and were then taken to the Cocula garbage dump, a thirty-minute drive from Iguala (GIEI 2015). The Guerreros Unidos, then, presumably proceeded to kill the students and burn their bodies.[26] Ashes were recovered from the pits, transferred into garbage bags, and dropped into the Río San Juan, forty minutes from the Cocula dump. Subsequent investigations proved that evidence supporting this version of events had in fact been planted by investigators in the Office of the Mexican Attorney General (Procuraduría General de la República, or PGR) with the full knowledge of the head of the Criminal Investigation Agency (Agencia de Investigación Criminal), Tomás Zerón de Lucio.

In December 2014, aware that a significant proportion of the population was growing restless with the authorities' lack of response and did not believe that the students had died, Peña Nieto asked Mexican citizens to *superar* (move beyond) the disappearances and accept the "historical truth" – namely, that the deaths could be attributed to cartel activity: "I want to call you together so that with your capacity, with your commitment to your state, to your community, to your own families, we really make a collective effort to move forward and really *move beyond* this moment of pain" (*BBC News Mundo* 2014; my emphasis), highlighting once more how little the government cared.[27]

Some time later, in January 2015, the Inter-American Commission on Human Rights mandated the Interdisciplinary Group of Independent Experts (Grupo Interdisciplinario de Expertos Independientes, or GIEI) to investigate the events in Ayotzinapa. From the outset, these experts labelled the case a violation of human rights. Their first report, released in September 2015, concluded that the Mexican government had lied, that it was incompetent in leading the criminal investigations, and that it had resorted to torture to extract false confessions that aligned with the so-called historical truth (GIEI 2015).[28]

In their report, the GIEI experts cast severe doubt on the credibility of the federal government's narrative, which claimed that drug cartels had coordinated the events.[29] The experts also identified major mistakes and gaps in the investigation carried out at the state and federal levels,[30] and rejected the federal government's "historical truth" that the Guerreros Unidos had killed the students and then incinerated them in a Cocula garbage dump. The GIEI's first report was well-received by the international community; however, this was not so much the case in Mexico, where smear campaigns against the panel of experts emerged as soon as their conclusions were released. Yet, despite the criticism, the GIEI's mandate was renewed for a second term in November 2015, and they submitted a second report at the end of April 2016 (GIEI 2016). This report highlights the many roadblocks the GIEI encountered during its investigation, concluding that "there are certain sectors that are interested neither in uncovering the truth, nor in an effective collaborative relationship that really helps Mexico face the problems of human rights violations in the Ayotzinapa case that motivated the GIEI to come to the country" (10).[31] Ultimately, the government "expressed that it did not want the GIEI mandate renewed" (GIEI 2016, 2), effectively expelling the experts from the country.[32] It also proved the experts right: The Peña Nieto administration was manifestly not interested in the truth. This refusal to allow the experts to continue their work, and maybe even to find the missing students, reinforced the population's distrust of the authorities.

Despite the GIEI's expulsion in 2016, criminal cases have slowly made their way through the courts. Indeed, many of the falsely accused sued the PGR. In the midst of the last general election, on 4 June 2018, the Federal Judiciary Council announced that the First Collegiate Tribunal of the Nineteenth Circuit, based in Reynosa, Tamaulipas, had ordered that the Ayotzinapa case be reopened in light of severe irregularities identified in the handling of the investigation (Suarez-Enriquez 2018). The ruling concluded that "the PGR's investigation has not been timely, effective, independent, or impartial, and that it consistently violated the rights of the victims, including the forty-three students and their families as well as the accused persons" (Suarez-Enriquez 2018). The court concluded that only lines of investigation aligned with the PGR's pre-established narrative of events had been pursued, and determined that most of the confessions on which the case was built should not have been considered valid; 77 per cent of the supposed perpetrators – in some instances, members or affiliates of drug cartels, but oftentimes citizens who were not involved in crime at all – showed signs of having been tortured by PGR investigators (COVAJ 2022, 86) prior to confessing to the murders (paragraph 764). According to the Washington Office on Latin America,

> The ruling acknowledges how the PGR's lack of autonomy and its political ties to the executive branch can lead to the *obstruction of investigations into human rights violations involving members of the armed forces, the Federal Police, and other agencies dependent on the executive.* It calls attention to how criminal investigations can be manipulated in Mexico in order to protect political elites – at the expense of truth, justice, and human rights. In this regard, the ruling is an indicator of the importance of Mexico's transition from the PGR to a more independent National Prosecutor's Office (*Fiscalía General de la República*), which will be independent from the executive branch. (Suarez-Enriquez 2018; my emphasis)

The court also ordered the creation of a truth and reconciliation commission to review the investigation. The creation of the Commission for Truth and Access to Justice in the Ayotzinapa Case (Comisión para la Verdad y Acceso a la Justicia, or COVAJ) was President Andrés Manuel López Obrador's first official decree when he took office in December 2018 (Comisión Nacional de los Derechos Humanos 2019). The COVAJ, chaired by the subsecretary of human rights, population, and migration, Alejandro Encinas, began its work on 15 January 2019. AMLO, as López Obrador is often called, professed that there would be no impunity, and that all levels of the police forces would be investigated. On 8 May 2020, the Mexican government confirmed that GIEI experts would return for a third mandate.

Investigations duly resumed, and in August 2022, the commission released a report in which the GIEI investigators concluded that "the creation of the 'historical truth' was a concerted action of the organized apparatus of power from the highest level of government, one that concealed the truth of the events, altered the crime scenes, [and] concealed the relationships between the authorities and the criminal gang (Guerreros Unidos) and the participation of state agents, security forces and authorities responsible for the pursuit of justice in the disappearance of the students" (GIEI 2022a, 96). This report confirmed in writing what everyone already knew – namely, that the army and various police forces were involved in the disappearances and that their role had been covered up from the very beginning of the investigations in October 2014. The COVAJ also concluded that the "historical truth" disregarded human rights (93) and re-victimized and stigmatized the students (88). Following the release of the report, the federal government and the Fiscalía General de la República (National Prosecutor's Office) detained former Attorney General Jesús Murillo Karam, opened a criminal case against him, and issued eighty-three arrest warrants for military personnel and other officials.

In September 2022, the GIEI released a fourth report (GIEI 2022b), which summarizes their findings beginning in 2020. (The panel's third report had been released in February 2022, though only to the commission members, so as not to impede ongoing investigations.) The experts highlight the role of the United States in obtaining phone records that helped to prove that police forces and the military were in contact with Guerreros Unidos to coordinate the whereabouts and the disposal of the bodies of the forty-three students (7, 15, 17). A fifth report (GIEI 2023a), summarizing the findings of the previous eight years, was made public in 2022. Finally, in July 2023, the GIEI withdrew completely from the case, citing the armed forces' refusal to fully disclose all relevant information pertaining to the events. In its sixth and final report (GIEI 2023b), the GIEI concluded that the army and the navy were complicit in the forty-three's disappearance, exposed in detail SEDENA's (Secretaría de la Defensa Nacional / Secretariat of National Defence) failure to intervene to protect the students on 26 September 2014, and their ongoing efforts to withhold pertinent information and materials concerning the case and the conduct of its personnel (Brewer 2023). As long as SEDENA retains key information, it is unlikely that the case will be solved. Even if one of his first promises was to solve the case, AMLO admitted in March 2024 that this would not happen during his time in power (Oliveres Alonso 2024), adding that he did not trust the Inter-American Court of Human Rights (Arista 2024), effectively casting shade on the GIEI.[33] His successor, Claudia Sheinbaum, took office in November 2024, and has since declared that the investigation in the forty-three students' disappearance remained a priority, and that a new team of investigators was reviewing the case (MND Staff 2025).

Now that we have a better understanding of the political and ideological views that allowed the 2014 disappearances to transpire and then remain unacknowledged and unpunished, we can turn to how the events were denounced and depicted in various artistic media. In the next section, I concentrate on ASARO's and URT-Arte's print murals and woodcuts. My analysis shows that, whereas ASARO's murals seek to memorialize the disappeared, URT-Arte's woodcuts aim to elicit solidarity, and ultimately to encourage citizens to turn to activism. Through art, the collectives tap into this open wound and the unending state of mourning, to fight back against the politics of fear instilled by the power apparatus. They do this by recognizing – through depiction and repetition – that the disappeared are "grievable subjects" (Butler 2016), important members of their respective communities whose loss is still felt almost a decade after their forced disappearance.

Artistic Analyses: *Pa'l pueblo* (For the People)

Soon after the disappearances, the number 43, graffitied and stencilled, started to pop up on walls and urban furniture across Mexico. Its repetition made the disappearances inescapable in the public space. Wherever they looked, Mexicans were reminded that forty-three of their own were missing. As time passed, more elaborate murals or installations started cropping up, coexisting with more "spontaneous" expressions of solidarity.

This section analyzes the works of Oaxaca-based ASARO and URT-Arte. In a subsection below dedicated to ASARO, I examine two iterations of *Justicia 43*, a 2014–15 billboard-like installation; followed by the collective's participation in the September 2016 Día de la indignación, a pan-Mexican commemoration to mark the one-year anniversary of the disappearances; and finally a mural dedicated to torture assembled in 2017. A chronological analysis of ASARO's installations demonstrates that their interventions combine with a broader social movement related to the Iguala events. With these mural installations, the collective remembers the fallen students and ensures their continuing presence in the public space. I conclude the subsection with an analysis of four stencils created to respond to specific milestones in the investigation of the 26 September attacks. Indeed, whereas murals take longer to plan and execute, stencils can be more reactive. While ASARO's murals are dedicated to the fallen students, the stencils are aimed at the armed forces and criticize them quite openly, resorting to symbols that highlight reoccurrence, violence, and impunity. The focus on the students reinforces the notions of kinship and solidarity; I claim that for ASARO, the role the state apparatus played in the events of 26 September 2014 must not overshadow the lives of the forty-three Ayotzinapa students. At all times, the spotlight is projected onto the students.

Next, I examine five wheat paste posters URT-Arte designed and disseminated between 2017 and 2022. Unlike the murals and stencils created by ASARO, which draw on an established repertoire of symbols, most works by URT-Arte depict other victims of the September 2014 attacks – namely, those who were left behind. Other students, parents, protesters: all are Mexican citizens who could potentially play a role in the still-evolving situation surrounding the disappearances. I have divided the prints into two main categories: those calling on the notion of "protest" to catch viewers' attention and those using "affect" – in other words, emotions – to elicit the audience's empathy and encourage it to act in solidarity with the victims. URT-Arte's use of two different types of prints reinforces my claim that one of the purposes of these artworks is to draw new members into the collective, ultimately to create more designs, pertaining to more causes, and expand the scope of its advocacy.

Some of these works are explicitly critical of the authorities, openly tracing a history of student repression from 1968 to 2014. By creating elaborate mixed-media murals and numerous wheat paste posters, both in the wake of the events and in subsequent years, the collectives not only permeate urban space with the ghosts of the forty-three missing students, but also effectively inscribe them into collective memory.

Colectivos *and* Talleres

Despite their prevalence in Mexico, the very concept of the collective remains vague. In the world of art, they are groups of artists that pursue the same aesthetics, or similar social or political goals through various socio-artistic experiments.[34] For the groups I study, the notion of the collective is indissociable from the physical space in which their art is created, and from their internal mode of organization. To add to the accuracy of the definition of these groups, I propose to blend the notion of the collective with the concept of the *taller* (workshop).

The *taller* is both concrete and abstract. *Talleres* are the physical spaces where artists share the equipment and materials they need to create, especially expensive printing presses. From a sociological point of view, they quickly emerge as the epicentres of the Mexican engraving scene; they are spaces where artists learn, develop, network, and make a living. This means that the function of workshops is not limited to an actual physical space. Indeed, they also embody a particular social organization and constitute a whole system of values, revolving around democratization and accessibility to resources, that are at the core of collective ideals and of the collective's identity (Pérez Garci 2015, 12). The close collaboration through which learning takes place carries humanistic values, an ethic of collegiality, of openness to criticism, and the shared ideals of excellence and solidarity (Rojano Pérez 2015, 15). Moreover, the openness of the workshops, both physical – anyone is welcome to walk in – and symbolic – anyone who shares the same ideals is welcome to join – reflects a deep desire to democratize art and image (Flores 2015, 19). In this way, the spirit of the *talleres* is an integral aspect of the artworks themselves.

According to Mario Guzmán (interview with the author, 2018), founding member of both ASARO and URT-Arte, having their own space "was what unified our work permanently. We had a press, we had tables and something very important that we had and that we struggled a lot to have, which were the raw materials that was precisely the ink, the paper, the aerosol, paint, and all the material. Why? Because we think we need a workshop where this … will not limit the creation of the comrade because they did not have a piece of paper, paint and all this stuff." Having a workshop means that individual members' creativity is not stifled by their socio-economic background. The space itself is social, aligned with the political goals of the collectives, where anyone can have access to art, both for creating and for experiencing it. Having a space to call their own is also a recruitment tool for the collectives; any passerby can walk in, experience the hustle and bustle of groups working on a print together, or overhear a political conversation, all of which can pique their curiosity. As one member of URT-Arte, Israel Salcedo (interview with the author, 2018), put it, "the workspace is the tool that we use to act" as creators, political actors, and recruiters, echoing the Taller de Gráfica Popular's "Declaración de principios" (Declaration of principles), where the members affirmed that the workshop was a "center of collective work" (Williams 2006, 16). Without an actual *taller* from which to plan actions, the collectives' memory artivism would be almost impossible.

Facade

ASARO and URT-Arte have much in common: They are among the most militant artivist groups in Oaxaca, both were founded by artist Mario Guzmán (in 2006 and 2007, respectively), and both follow a specific ideological line. But more importantly for the dissemination of their political message, they also boast something that not all Oaxacan collectives can – their own workshops, the Espacio Zapata and the Taller de Arte Comunitario (TAC).[35] Their imposing facades and prime locations offer the chance to create and display murals or series of smaller scenes underlining their political demands. The artworks on these facades are generally murals or large wheat paste posters. They change every season or so and are usually commemorative in nature.[36] They also remain unblemished, an unusual feat in the urban and street art worlds.

When artists choose to display their work in public spaces, they implicitly accept the loss of power over the fate of their creations. They concede the artwork to the public domain, knowing that other artists might interact with it. These interactions can range from adding a tag (known as *tagging* or *slashing*) to a complete defacing of the work (known as *going over*). Street art is driven by competition and street credibility is built around visibility. The larger the piece the more credibility a collective or crew acquires. Surprisingly, over the years, both murals on the facades of ASARO and URT-Arte's respective workshops and their monumental interventions in the streets of Oaxaca have seldom been marred or destroyed. As I mentioned in chapter 1 in relation to *cholismo* writing, the respect paid to these works testifies to their credibility. Oaxacan artists demonstrate a lot of respect for ASARO's and URT-Arte's works, and I would argue that the commemorative nature of the murals makes people even less prone to touch them. In a month or a few years, it could be your own disappearance, or that of someone close to you, that they denounce.

In an interview, Israel Salcedo (2018) summarized the situation like this: Oaxacan street artists respect each other's works because "there is no competition between the workshops – the sun rises for everyone," adding that "there are many walls." While this might be true, few walls have as much visibility as the facades of the two workshops.

An important element that the facades offer the collectives is relative control over their creations and permanency, especially important when one of their explicit goals is to expose state-sponsored violence. During the teachers' protest in 2006, the artists used tags and stencils because they are quick to execute, and it did not matter very much if the authorities or citizens opposing the movement painted over them soon after. As long as the collectives had the stencil design and spray paint, they could repeat the same images an infinite number of times. But the mural installations that the collectives have been designing since 2007 are large and time-consuming to create. Placing them on their own walls affords them greater control and a degree of certainty, acquired over time, that they will not be defaced by the public or taken down by municipal workers.

Even public officials are reluctant to remove the collectives' works, which reveals a double regime of legitimacy at play in Oaxaca, or, as Salcedo put it, "a double standard." While there are enough "walls for everyone," most tags, inscriptions, and posters are removed monthly by the municipality (Municipio de Oaxaca 2021), which prides itself on the cleanliness of its walls. Citizens living in the Historic Centre of Oaxaca, a UNESCO World Heritage Site, must also obey strict rules when modifying their properties.[37]

And yet, despite these legal restrictions, the murals and other monumental installations on the streets of Oaxaca remain untouched. The collectives' workshops are located within the Historic Centre, on Calle Porfirio Díaz, which makes their work not just technically illegal – through the use of more than two colours and, for some installations, elements other than paint – but also overtly political, which means it can be deemed "propaganda" under these rules (Municipio de Oaxaca 2018, articles 40 and 42). Yet, the city allows the works to remain in place. This testifies to a noteworthy level of credibility, but also to a recognition by the municipality that these works are tourist attractions in their own right. Salcedo indicates that some stencils and wheat paste posters remain on the walls "not because it is necessary for people to become aware of the social problem, but because they attract attention and many tourists come and take a photo … And the boom in graphic arts currently in Oaxaca has encouraged more people to come."[38]

In short, there are tensions between the municipality's regulations and its need for and reliance on tourism, one that, ironically, ends up serving the collectives' objectives. Another member of a collective, who elected to remain anonymous, implied privately that it was less trouble for the city to ignore the murals and wheat paste posters than to have to deal with the uproar their removal would entail. This backlash would come from the local community that supports the collectives as well as the Mexican and international tourists who visit Oaxaca expressly to view its public art. To that effect, Salcedo also added that "we belong to a political organization with, shall we say, considerable weight and that also allows certain things to remain untouched." Even if the city judges them through a cost-benefit lens, disregarding both their artistic and political value, these artworks have much to offer. By correcting the distortion of history, they constitute a form of peaceful resistance, facilitating the politicization of their audience. The objectives of 2006 are still alive but conveyed differently.

Another reason the murals endure might also be tied to the audience they target. ASARO's and URT-Arte's murals and installations are on the streets for every citizen and passerby to view and absorb. They operate as a reflection of and on Mexico, where citizens can both see themselves mirrored and think critically about the state of their nation. Unlike sixteenth-century church murals – only visible to friars and priests – and twentieth-century post-revolutionary murals – painted almost exclusively inside government buildings despite the stated intention of democratizing art and making it accessible to everyone – the collectives' works blend the ethos of street art with what muralism was intended to be, a pedagogical art that included all sectors of society. They are accessible to everyone, and anyone can contribute to their meaning by adding, removing, or remixing elements. In this, the Oaxacan collectives take from Zapatista muralism, which I will introduce shortly. ASARO shares the Zapatistas' ethos that history is in flux, and that murals can be reworked to account for its reinterpretation. These artworks, exhibited in the public space, prove the existence of an active opposition and break the complicity of silence from which the authorities traditionally benefit.

The Asamblea de Artistas Revolucionarios de Oaxaca, 2006–Present[39]

As ASARO is the longest-running of the four collectives I study, it makes sense to introduce it first. A lot has been published already about this group, but I wanted to meet the artists and hear their story in their own words. Over the summer of 2018, I interviewed Mario Guzmán in his current workshop, URT-Arte's TAC space, and two members of ASARO at Espacio Zapata. Guzmán is one of the only members of the four collectives to whom I refer by name. As with all interviewees, I offered him full anonymity, but as he told me, he is well-known on the local and national printmaking scenes, so even if I anonymized his words, readers would likely recognize him. At the founding of the collective, too, most artists in ASARO chose to remain anonymous, as it was safer to sign under the name of the collective than their own. Now, almost twenty years after the 2006 crisis, most members have established a streamlined production under their own name, while also remaining members of ASARO.

ASARO, the Asamblea de Artistas Revolucionarios de Oaxaca (Assembly of Revolutionary Artists of Oaxaca), was formed in 2006 as part of the teachers' protest in Oaxaca. The collective was the artistic arm of APPO (the Asamblea Popular de los Pueblos de Oaxaca, or Popular Assembly of the Peoples of Oaxaca),[40] and the artists were charged with covering city walls with political slogans, demands, and calls to action. To fully understand ASARO, it is worth going back to 2006.

As I already mentioned in chapter 1, graffiti culture travelled from the United States to Oaxaca via cholo writing (Magaña 2020, 141),[41] a style that draws heavily from Chicano muralism and Mexican symbols like the Virgin of Guadalupe, Emiliano Zapata, and Francisco Villa (Franco Ortiz 2011, 83). Around the same time, the number of *graffiteros* – graffiti writers, almost all male – was increasing in Oaxaca. (The first generation emerged in the 1990s, the second in the early 2000s and continues to the present.) Their educational background led some graffiti writers to move toward using stencils to convey their messages. The stencil is a hybrid of two traditions, street graffiti and graphic art, in which it is valued for its reproducibility, its use of public wall spaces, and its pluralist technique associated with graphic design (113).[42] Stencil graffiti is generally figurative and consists of recognizable people and/or legible messages, which means it can be used decoratively but also for propaganda or resistance purposes by a variety of social movements. Combined with its reproducibility, this makes the stencil a strong visual and political weapon (115). In 2002–03, groups of youths started forming collectives whose primary technique was the stencil, despite all of them having roots in graffiti culture. These collectives used provocative images – like George Bush with Mickey Mouse ears, or a Ronald McDonald suit and a weapon – influenced by global graphics circulating on the Internet. They also started producing stickers and posters that they would plaster on walls (116). Their use of stencils, serigraphy, and stickers facilitated diverse forms of communication, with stickers proving particularly helpful for multireproduction (117). Some stencils and stickers tackled the situation in Mexico and Oaxaca directly, criticizing the political system and its failure to improve the social conditions of Indigenous peoples, women, and children (117–18; Magaña 2020, 147–8).[43] While these works made issues visible and exposed the authorities' inaction, full identification with the works would only come about during and after the 2006 movement (Franco Ortiz 2011, 123). Nevertheless, works from the years leading up to 2006 paved the way to using the public space to spread an alternative political message, ensuring that people experiencing the work could join a wider social network.

The social network triggered by these political artworks expanded exponentially in the summer of 2006. In the state of Oaxaca – one of Mexico's three poorest states, along with Guerrero and Chiapas – teachers, more educated than most of the population, are often at the forefront of social change. They are also often the voices of the marginalized, holding a variety of positions in political organizations. In 1979, teachers in Oaxaca left the Sindicato Nacional de Trabajadores de la Educación (National Educational Workers Union), which they perceived as corrupt, to form the Coordinadora Nacional de los Trabajadores de la Educación (CNTE, or National Coordination of Education Workers), a self-proclaimed dissident group within the national union; they later left the national body entirely and stood as a distinct union. The CNTE is known for the one- to two-week *plantón* (sit-in) it organizes in the centre of Oaxaca every year to ask for better infrastructure in rural zones and better working conditions.

In 2006, the CNTE held its annual sit-in, listing sixteen demands, including that Oaxaca be recognized as "a high-cost-of-living entity" (Bautista Martínez 2016, 122), making it hard for teachers to fulfil their duties. The sit-in started on 22 May, and on 14 June the state governor at the time, Ulises Ruiz Ortiz (URO as he is commonly known), ordered the police to disband the protest with tear gas and rubber bullets.[44] A harsh repression of the protests was to be expected. Indeed, when he was elected in 2004, Ruiz Ortiz promised that there would not be any more sit-ins during his term. Many irregularities plagued his election (Sotelo Marbán 2008, 31), and indeed many citizens already distrusted him. Early on, he established a politics of repression (47–62), and some scholars go as far as to say that his tenure as governor was authoritarian (Martínez Vázquez 2007).[45] All movements against him were crushed (Sotelo Marbán 2008, 62) in what Martínez Vázquez (2008, 55; 2007) calls state terrorism. URO was particularly terrible during the Comuna de Oaxaca, cautioning police brutality and arbitrary detentions, and ignoring forced disappearances.[46]

Around 4:00 a.m. on 14 June, police attacked the sleeping teachers in their camps, on the ground with attack dogs and from the air with tear gas grenades. The teachers managed to force the police officers to retreat by throwing rocks and grenades back at them, and by 9:00 a.m. they were back in control of downtown Oaxaca (Gibler 2009, 140–3). Many sectors of civil society – outraged that the authorities had resorted to lethal force to dismantle the sit-in, and their anger fuelled by the siege of Atenco months before, the contested presidential elections, and the EZLN's Otra campaña (Magaña 2014, 71) – got involved and later established a self-governing anarchist community, the Comuna de Oaxaca, that lasted until the end of November. The movement has been called the first insurrection of the twenty-first century (Osorno 2007). Many factions organized under the APPO, which "agreed to the single demand of Ulises Ruiz's ouster" (Gibler 2009, 147). According to Bautista Martínez (2016, 123),

> Although the popular movement began with specific union-type demands by the Oaxacan teachers, the repressive response of the local government provoked and garnered solidarity from other social groups with the protesters, who found a way within the APPO to reject the authoritarian exercise of public power, articulating a collective "enough is enough," and opening the public space for channelling age-old economic, political, and social demands, never resolved.

Gibler (2009) concurs, adding that "tens of thousands of people who had never felt as if they belonged in the world of politics" joined the APPO, in addition to "founding entirely new organizations" (147), with over three hundred such groups banding together to contribute to Ulises Ruiz's political demise (Magaña 2014, 67). The APPO and various organizations besieged the city of Oaxaca, organizing daily marches and seven mega-marches that each drew millions of people. They also took control of radio and TV stations, publicizing their demands on the airwaves, on television screens, and on the walls.[47] During that time, in one APPO member's words, these groups served as "el brazo cultural de la APPO," the cultural arm of the APPO (quoted in Estrada Saavedra 2012, 138). During the 2006 protests, ASARO's work was "art produced in conflict and conceived as a fighting instrument" (141), and the city's walls were turned into alternative spaces of communication and expression for disenfranchised sectors of the population.

The installation of barricades in late August – to close off the city to death squads doing drive-by shootings (Gibler 2009, 161–3) – transformed the once open transit space into a territorialized one. However, with this territorialization came a liberation of the space, particularly with the newly acquired freedom to fill these barricades with political paintings (Franco Ortiz 2011, 135). The protest images – such as closed fists with the slogan "Oaxaca resiste" (Oaxaca resists) or "La Virgen de las Barricadas" (The Virgin of the barricades), the latter a play on the iconic Virgin of Guadalupe – were powerful because they attacked and weakened the symbolic apparatus of the state government. The stencils became a form of constant rebellion, and a symbolic resistance through the images in the streets and the variety of ways it was expressed by different people and artists demonstrated the diversity of ideologies found within the APPO and how different social sectors came together in the movement (149). Franco Ortiz aptly points out that although many of the visuals produced during the Oaxaca uprising reflect the struggle of the time, they were also part of an accumulation of past struggles through which there has persisted a lasting resistant and symbolic collective (157). In her view, and taking into consideration Asavei's (2018) framework, the fact that these images are politically and ideologically charged, but also impossible to separate from their aesthetic and sensory nature, means that they lend themselves to becoming propaganda (174) and thus losing aspects of their critical-political nature. Indeed, while the artists aimed at intervening critically in power relations, with the ultimate objective of disrupting them to the point of destruction, the social context of reception – an ideological confrontation between two strongly held, diametrically opposed positions – might turn them into propaganda, even if the goal of generating individual awareness of their history of oppression is achieved (174).

Graffiti writing was still seen as vandalism, since it was done on private properties (Lache Bolaños 2009, 215). Over time, it became accepted as one of the movement's emblematic protest forms. ASARO, who designed some of the movement's most influential works, was created in October 2006. During the 2006 teachers' crisis, the collective made stencils and prints with a great sense of urgency (Franco Ortiz 2011).[48] Once the Partido Revolucionario Institucional (PRI) government forcibly and violently ended the sit-in and dismantled the barricades in Oaxaca's city centre starting on 25 November, the collective started producing several series of prints and wheat paste posters around themes that were central to the APPO movement, while also developing ad hoc stencil work to attract attention to timely issues, like resource exploitation, land ownership, and agriculture.[49] Direct contact with the people is at the centre of their artistic vision.

ASARO's exposure, as well as its growing popularity and recognition following the 2006 uprising, gave them a platform from which to advocate for any social cause of their choosing. From 2006 to 2010, the collective mostly created prints and stencils that denounced government corruption at all levels. For instance, they emphasized issues around energy production with prints such as *Petroleum Drinkers* (2010), which shows ugly, monstruous humanoid figures fighting each other to drink from an oil drum – a jab at national elites' in-fighting to make the most profit from Mexican oil – and *¡Pueblo! ¡Defiende tu petróleo!* (People! Defend your oil!, 2010), which portrays an Indigenous man in an Uncle Sam pose urging Mexicans to defend the country's natural resources. Both these artworks drew attention to various oil spills and the inaction of the state-owned Petróleos Mexicanos. ASARO also tackled agricultural issues, and the proliferation of genetically modified organisms with prints such as *No país sin maíz* (No country without corn, 2006), and *Transgénico* (Transgenic, 2010), focusing on the overall negative impacts of such technology on the Mexican people. *La tierra es de quien la trabaja* (The land belongs to its workers, 2006) tackled landlessness among agricultural workers, an issue that can be traced back to the early days of independence and led to the Mexican Revolution.

Like many collectives, ASARO's name is straightforward: It first presents their mode of organization – the assembly – and then focuses on the media used to promote social change – revolutionary art. ASARO is "a gathering of artists from various artistic disciplines which creates public art for the purpose of restoring social order" (Graham de la Rosa and Schadl 2014, 1). The assembly provides a horizontal mode of organization where meetings are held during which every member has the same right to speak and to weigh in on decisions: "We resumed the model of the assembly, because we believe in the possibility of recovery of force in the art community and because the assembly is the way we dialogue and make decisions based on the collective interests" (44). Much like artivism, the assembly invites collaboration and dialogue, both from inside and outside the collective. According to Yesca, another founding member of ASARO, "assemblies are a good way to form relationships and organize, and revolutionary because we experiment with art to create consciousness and be driven by the people" (quoted in Nevaer 2009, 58).

Unsurprisingly, political affiliations are at the core of most collectives in Oaxaca. During our conversation, Guzmán highlighted that unlike his current collective, URT-Arte, ASARO was a coalition of people representing various ideologies, which could make internal discussions complex at times: "The diversity of thoughts had to be respected; this part was vital because, well, we knew that there were comrades from half-anarchist tendencies or with anarchist influence or comrades … [who] perhaps had neither anarchist nor revolutionary thoughts but considered it important to participate because something unfair was happening." To avoid factions and internal struggles, "we took up the assembly as an organizational body to reach an agreement, and also to reach a consensus because we knew that … groups or positions were going to develop within" (interview with the author, 2018). They followed collective decision making and consensus as their ideological line, and most members shared anti-capitalist core beliefs. Bolos and Estrada Saavedra (2013, 124) point out that, despite the absence of a clear ideology, through Guzmán ASARO was fairly close to the Frente Revolucionario Popular (Popular Revolutionary Front) and their youth organization, the Juventudes Revolucionarias Universitarias (Revolutionary University Youths), giving the group – or part of the group – a Stalinist leaning with which not all members were comfortable.

The model of the assembly also enabled the collective to establish an organized process of designing graphics and pasting them on the streets at regular intervals, and ensured that everyone participated, not only the members who were the most technically skilled. ASARO wanted to avoid becoming a "sectarian, *caudillista*" group, where only "the four, five companions who were … the best technically" (Guzmán interview, 2018) would design prints. Ultimately, ideas mattered more than technique, and as Guzmán explained, they were hoping to do things differently from previous collectives: "This is what we were trying to break, and in the case of ASARO, because we proposed that everyone could speak, everyone could participate and propose, and at some point also make decisions … they felt that a collective was being built, collectively."

Over the years, the number of members in ASARO has fluctuated. While there were only thirteen members at the beginning, the numbers rose steadily following the 2006 crisis – up to thirty-five toward the end of 2007. According to Guzmán, ASARO peaked in 2007–08 – with an output of about ten prints per week – and then in 2009 numbers started to dwindle. He estimates that during his ten years with the collective, there was always a gender imbalance, with 90 per cent of members being male. Guzmán left ASARO in 2016 to concentrate on URT-Arte, the collective I introduce next.

Following Guzmán's departure, ASARO's production began to slow. According to the members I interviewed in 2018, ASARO has entered a new phase, *de memoria*, which I call a phase of memorialization, in which the remaining members are not as active on the street but want to make their archives available to the public. It is under this new approach that I was able to access materials they had not yet shared with the public (clips of demonstrations, of pasting up posters on the street), consult their archives of prints and posters, and take photographs for dissemination. ASARO still host exhibits in Espacio Zapata, but it is no longer as active on social media as it once was.

Since the group's inception, ASARO's works have been both in the streets and on gallery walls. Early on, in 2007, famous artist Francisco Toledo invited them to showcase their work at the IAGO (Instituto de Artes Gráficas de Oaxaca / Institute of Graphic Arts of Oaxaca).[50] *Graffiteros al paredón* (Graffiti writers/artists to the wall) debuted in February 2007. To ensure the artists' anonymity, at a time when URO was still in power, members of ASARO executed their works while IAGO was closed (Nevaer 2009, 65). While this enraged the authorities, Toledo basically consecrated ASARO's work by comparing it to Rivera's muralism (Velez Ascencio 2007).

For Bolos and Estrada (2013), the role played by art collectives in 2006 was instrumental in conveying the APPO's message, since they depicted reality from the latter's perspective (140), allowed it to reflect both the conflict and its political project, spurred identification with the social movement, contributed to preserving collective memory related to it (141), and embedded historical narratives and figures into the conflict, further highlighting historical continuity between the APPO's struggle and that of its forefathers (141–2).

Creating a Space to Mourn

In this section, I analyze chronologically the murals and installations that ASARO has dedicated to the Ayotzinapa disappearances since 2014. The chronological analysis of these works demonstrates that ASARO's interventions closely follow Mexican society's reactions to the events that occurred in Iguala. With these interventions, ASARO became quite literally the "voice of the *pueblo*." I also demonstrate that, by reactivating the repertoire of symbols established by student and peasant activism in the 1960s, ASARO ensures that historical human rights crimes, such as the Tlatelolco massacre, are embedded in the discourse surrounding more contemporary human rights violations like Ayotzinapa. The accumulation of historical anger informs the reaction of both the artists and the public, as the latter is already familiar with the symbolic matrix and possesses the aesthetic and historical literacy to understand the message conveyed by the works.

***Justicia 43*: Making the Disappearances Visible** About a month after the September 2014 events, ASARO unveiled its first installation related to the Ayotzinapa students on the facade of Espacio Zapata (see plate 1). Unlike some major interventions that would come later, this one was not commemorative in nature, as it appeared in late October 2014, when there was still hope that the students might be found alive. The mural installation consists of forty-three missing person posters. Each poster adopts the same structure: Moving from top to bottom, the posters read, "¡Vivos se los llevaron!" (They took them alive), followed by a picture of a missing student, his name and age, the inscription "¡Vivos los queremos!" (We want them alive), and finally, "Contra el terrorismo de estado, la solidaridad. Ayotzinapa somxs todxs" (Against state terrorism, solidarity. We are all Ayotzinapa). Echoing Möller's (2016, 12) comment that a goal of political art is "creating solidarity," by saying "Ayotzinapa somxs todxs" ASARO calls out passersby and attempts to make them critically reflect on and engage with the disappearances. The installation also features four posters that read, "Justicia 43 Apoyo a los estudiantes de la normal de Ayotzinapa, Guerrero" (Justice 43 support for the students of the Ayotzinapa normal, Guerrero). The number 43 is spray-painted in red over the letter *v* in *Vivos* and the *s* in the word *Justicia* (see plate 2).

With this addition, the poster installation also highlights another series of victims rarely considered in the fall of 2014: the "other" Ayotzinapa students, both those who escaped the massacre and those who did not travel to Iguala to commandeer buses. While it is expected that search efforts would focus on the missing, about sixty students survived the night of 26 September, and they, too, need *apoyo* (support), as do the other four hundred students who were not in Iguala, but who may have experienced police repression and suffered from post-traumatic stress disorder (Hernández 2020).

The three juxtaposed phrases displayed on the posters link the events of Ayotzinapa to the broader Mexican context and also seek to create a sense of solidarity across all walks of life. Although the events occurred in the state of Guerrero, the whole of Mexico – "Todos somos Ayotzinapa" (We are all Ayotzinapa) – subsequently rose up. These words highlight the universality of the case; ultimately, any protester in Mexico could be disappeared. Even worse, any citizen could suffer the same fate. However, despite all citizens being at risk, Echavarría Canto and Vásquez Carmona (2018, 115) argue that "Todos somos Ayotzinapa" further "points out the fact that this extermination has centred on students opposed to the system." Anyone who opposes the system, whether the official state authorities or the para-system enforced by the drug cartels and tolerated by the police – often one and the same (Hernández 2020) – could be disappeared and their bodies obliterated. As we have already seen, in the specific case of the students of the Raúl Isidro Burgos Normal School these disappearances can be traced back to the late 1960s and '70s.

Moreover, the phrase "Todos somos Ayotzinapa" encompasses other disappearances and crimes based on social status and marginality: "it is the only universal possible in our country, since it names not only the Iguala massacre, but also feminicides, inequality, hunger, lack of opportunity, all the injustices that occur to those born between the Río Bravo and Suchiate" (Abud Jaso et al. 2019, 92). The wording highlights Mexico's inequalities. A lot of Mexicans felt compelled to adopt the phrase "Todos somos Ayotzinapa," because many suffer from poverty, are despised by what they refer to as *el sistema*, which I understand to mean the *mal gobierno* (bad government) and patriarchal structures, and see themselves as potential victims. Across Mexico, the slogan appeared in marches, on posters and T-shirts, and even became a trending hashtag on Twitter and Instagram.

ASARO adapted the seminal slogan as "Ayotzinapa somxs todxs." This gender-neutral version of the phrase, where *x* replaces *o*, made the cry even more all-encompassing by highlighting the intersectional nature of violence. In Spanish, nouns as well as many adjectives and articles are gendered either masculine (generally ending with an *o*) or feminine (generally ending with an *a*). This grammatical binary is problematic, as it does not account for non-binarity when addressing groups of people. The way that the language has adapted to account for this challenge has been to replace the *o* or the *a* with an *x* to remove the allocation of gender from the term. For instance, the word for "all," *todo-toda*, becomes *todx*.[51] Implicit in the *x* is the understanding that individuals who are marginalized are more susceptible to experiencing acts of violence, and that these violences intersect and accumulate.

Despite its importance as one of the first major installations representing the missing Ayotzinapa students in Oaxaca, the missing person poster piece (plates 1 and 2) is not meant to be figurative. Unlike most of ASARO's works, the traditional technique of engraving was not retained in the making of each poster. The installation as a whole functions as art, but also as a billboard for forty-three missing persons. It blends artistic representation and activism on a very basic level: In October 2014, the public had to be made aware of the disappearances. Using actual missing person posters reinforces ASARO's intention and at the same time makes the event more real for viewers by putting forty-three names and faces to the abstraction of the disappearances. Moreover, for anyone familiar with ASARO's work, the mere fact that they tackled the subject meant the authorities were somehow to blame. The collective could allow their first installation to focus on the missing students and their peers without directly criticizing the various levels of authority. Indeed, the reputation and credibility the collective had established over the previous eight years meant that the latter message was implicit.

This installation is part of a continuum in terms of the visual expressions selected to convey the disappearances of the missing forty-three and draws from the repertoire of symbols adopted by artists in the wake of Tlatelolco and by other activists in Ciudad Juárez. Like many other artists and activists over the years, ASARO built on the photographs that circulated right after the disappearances. These were in fact the most recent photos of the *normalistas*, taken when they arrived at the school just a few weeks before they were disappeared. For some students, it was the only photo taken of them. The fact that the installation consists of forty-three missing person posters reinforces my argument that this first major intervention is about making visible an event that to that point had been downplayed by the Mexican authorities, and which had yet to receive the media coverage it has since garnered.

Despite the hope many still held in the months following the disappearances, the longer the billboard stayed up, the more it could be perceived as a collective shrine, with ASARO inviting a wider public to mourn the loss of the forty-three student teachers. As Alba Griffin (2023) argues, "The vernacular appropriation of the public space as a site for mourning and remembrance … links the personal tragedy to a wider message" – namely, that state violence is an ongoing problem in Mexico. By interrupting the "audience's routines as they move around the city" (69), the work forces viewers to reflect on both power structures and the struggles of activists.

Another form of interruption of the "audience's routines" (69) was ASARO's periodic remixing of the billboard. Indeed, ASARO kept on adding to and modifying the original installation, which evolved from a billboard meant to publicize the disappearances into a message of support and love as hope of finding the students alive began to wane. This sense that history is in constant flux, and that consequently artworks must evolve to reflect new knowledge, is taken from the Zapatista muralism that arose in the 1980s.[52] This change in ethos is articulated in the evolution of the tagline on the installation, from "Justicia 43" to "Love 43" (see plate 3). The word "love" is painted in white, with the letter *e* flipped so that it resembles the 3 in "43," painted in red. The motif is reminiscent of the blending of "Justicia" and "43" in the mural's previous iteration. The English language was likely chosen for design purposes; indeed, the word "amor" does not offer the same design flexibility, since the number 43 can more easily be blended into the inverted *e* in "love."

Two major modifications were made to the original installation. A shadow of red paint that resembles a trail of blood was applied on top of the installation, while the word "love" and the number 43 were painted over some of the missing person posters. While the red paint covers some of the students' faces, almost making them disappear, where the letters of the word "love" are painted over the face of a missing student, the wheat paste poster was redone, so that it becomes part of the letter's design. This generates a tension: While the red paint, representing violence, hides the missing person posters, the word "love" highlights them, as if to say that, unlike the state, ASARO will not erase the memory of the missing students. And yet, the physical appearance of the original wheat paste posters – greyish and faded – reinforces the waning hope of finding the students alive.

The evolution of this billboard installation aligns philosophically with Zapatista muralism, which considers murals living artifacts. If the visual content becomes outdated or is the object of valid criticism, the works are altered. For Zapatistas – and, I would add, for ASARO – the murals act as vehicles for the expression of collective memory and its transmission, teaching both history itself and the fact that it is not static: "Murals are thus the space to forget, to remember, to cover up, to erase – to create or destruct history; spaces, in short, that rethink myths and genealogies and redefine political agendas" (Vargas-Santiago 2015, under "Transformative Spaces"). They embody the ever-evolving cultural and collective memory. According to the 2013 Junta de Buen Gobierno

(Zapatista Boards of Good Government): "A mural is very important to the Zapatista communities … [it allows us to] learn something about those who are often forgotten today or tomorrow, and remain unseen. For us the communal paintings are like a mirror, reminding us to act politically, to never forget our history, to remind us of our heroines and heroes of yesterday and today; and to tell our dreams, so that future generations will know about them" (Sánchez Contreras 2024).

For Zapatistas, "Murals, therefore, affirm the existence of an alternative political project" (Vargas-Santiago 2015, under "Origins: Visual Genealogies"). For ASARO, the evolution of their works as more evidence surfaced about the Ayotzinapa disappearances affirms the existence of an alternative political project – one that arguably might not be as developed as that of the EZLN. ASARO's alternative political project is to speak up against violence, and to demonstrate to Mexicans that, once again, the authorities have been complicit in human rights abuses.

The faces were repurposed once again in December 2014 when ASARO and Espacio Zapata launched a call for faces (*convocatoria de rostros*) on Facebook (ASARO 2014). The post itself shows the face of a missing *normalista* and calls on "jóvenes artist@s … democráticos, progresistas, revolucionarios" (young, democratic, progressive, revolutionary artists – note the @ in the original, another way to remove grammatical gender) to paint the faces of the missing students on a two-metre-high canvas. To ensure maximum participation, and in conjunction with its goal to work with and for the local community, ASARO opened its doors and invited artists to paint at Espacio Zapata, also offering them painting materials. The resulting artworks were posted around Oaxaca in January 2015 with the inscriptions "Faltan 43" (Forty-three are missing), "Fuera Peña" (Out with Peña), and "La APPO somos todos" (We are all APPO), an attempt to reactivate the wording used in 2006. By reproducing the students' faces yet again, albeit in a more artistic fashion this time around, ASARO communicated that they were refusing to let the missing students' faces disappear from the public space. ASARO undertook a similar activity in March 2015, this time with paint rather than wheat paste posters, to keep the students in the public conscience, and again in the summer of 2018, when they painted the number 43 on the facade of Espacio Zapata and superimposed the posters created for the Día de la indignación, an activity I examine below, to "fill" the number 43 (see plate 4).

The monumentality of the faces serves multiple purposes. First, the fact that they are so big means that viewers cannot escape the posters; they occupy viewers' full field of vision. The faces, and the images of torture they conjure, are unavoidable and inescapable. Second, the faces are so big that the eyes of the painted figures are often at viewers' own eye level. The eyes, and the pull they exert on viewers, become inescapable. According to French Lithuanian philosopher Emmanuel Levinas (1969), the face and the eyes confront viewers with the completeness of the Other. By seeing the face and the eyes of the Other, he becomes my responsibility, someone I need to take care of. This *rapport de face à face* (face-to-face relation) shapes the responsibility that I, as a viewer, feel toward the person – or the representation, in this case – in front of me. Basically, the viewer becomes subordinated to the image (the face) and must take responsibility for it. This is the pull of artivism. The mural does not work if the viewer is not "affected," and the face and the eyes tug at the emotions of viewers, because they see more than the face – they can imagine what the face (and the body attached to it) suffered.

Día de la Indignación On 26 September 2015, to mark the first anniversary of the disappearance of the students, multiple marches were held all over Mexico in what activists called the Día de la indignación, or Day of Indignation. As they marched, protesters chanted, "El cielo está llorando porque nos faltan 43 y miles de desaparecidos" (The sky is crying because we are missing forty-three people and thousands of disappeared), thus highlighting that the forty-three are only the tip of the iceberg. They drew attention because forty-three people going missing at once is inconceivable, even if Mexican citizens go missing one at a time every day without receiving as much media coverage or artistic exposure. The Día de la indignación marches took these disappearances into account by naming other disappearances.

ASARO took part in the Día de la indignación by creating another major installation, this time in downtown Oaxaca. This one is similar to the one produced in 2006 for the Día de Muertos (Day of the Dead) celebrations during the city lockdown, to honour the fallen members of the APPO. They printed the faces of the *normalistas* on china paper and then created banners with them. These banners were hung over Oaxaca's Andador Turístico, the city's main tourist pedestrian street, and on Calle Independencia in front of government buildings.

Papel picado, or perforated paper, is a staple of Mexican folk art generally associated with the Day of the Dead celebrations. It is also used for both religious and secular celebrations. Leading up to the Day of the Dead, on 2 November, Mexicans from all walks of life build altars to honour family members who have died. These altars generally include a picture of the loved one, objects they held dear, flowers, and banners of *papel picado*, intended both to mark their memory and entice their souls to return for the celebrations. The relationship between memory, honouring the departed, and *papel picado* is an obvious one: Any Mexican seeing the installation would understand that it is intended to pay homage to the people represented on each piece of *papel picado*. Indigenous beliefs suggest that the paper acts as a conduit between life and death. In ancient Mesoamerica, the *amate* paper, used for codices and similar to today's *papel picado*, was seen as a sacred material bestowed by the gods. Indeed, the tree from which *amate* is derived is closely related to the underworld, and it was believed that through the perforations in a sheet of *amate* paper viewers could see from the world of the living to the world of the dead. Today, *papel picado* fulfills that function in the offering.

By tapping into Day of the Dead iconography, ASARO acknowledged that the students were dead, and that after the protests, another "period" of mourning was beginning. The Day of the Dead is a way not only to reflect on the past, in a community setting – in short, a duty to remember – but also to develop strength and resilience in the face of the inevitability of death; indeed, "the act of remembering allows us to transcend the loss, grieving, and our fear of death" (hooks and Mesa-Bains 2018, 121). hooks and Amalia Mesa-Bains uses the expression "politicizing spirituality" to refer to the development of "skills that allow us to face the acute conditions and challenges that might decimate others" (hooks and Mesa-Bains 2018, 121). One year after the disappearances, those coping skills were being put to the test.

Day of the Dead iconography also taps into Indigenous resistance and emphasizes that "our traditions around death and dying ... have always been tied to resistance and struggle" (122). hooks and Mesa-Bains duly point out that "this tradition of spirituality and sacrifice is also part of art's power to transform moments of struggle into a language that creates meaning and understanding" (123). Acting collectively – collectivizing grief, to use Morbiato's (2017) wording – draws a seemingly private matter into the public sphere, helping Mexicans to process their pain.

Much like their previous *Justicia 43* installation, the Día de la indignación installation of *papel picado* posters over the city's main street can be read as both political and apolitical, walking a thin line between honouring and protesting. ASARO's Day of Indignation installation is political inasmuch as it was created specifically for a day that remembered forcibly disappeared students, and the collective's commitment is explicit on individual posters. That being said, even someone who does not share ASARO's political positions could engage with and appreciate the installation, as it both recognizes and protests the students' deaths. It is a moderate installation that resorts to traditional symbols to convey its message that society should come together to mourn the loss of forty-three young lives; that suffering is an experience that builds collective memory. This drawing on symbolism that is both commemorative and celebratory is a staple of the second wave of memory activism, where memory activists "employ a new vocabulary to address ... violence – disruptive, ludic, or celebratory" (Mandolessi 2023, 297). While the iconography of the Day of the Dead is not new, mobilizing it to honour the Ayotzinapa disappearances was a way to bring the students back into public discourse by highlighting life and death, and the limbo where the families are left. By leveraging it in a celebration about Ayotzinapa, ASARO also indirectly answers a criticism often levelled at Mexico – namely, that it is a country "without memory" (Allier-Montaño and Crenzel 2015). Honouring Ayotzinapa using the Day of the Dead was not only a demonstration of remembrance, it was also a display of memory as resistance and the memory of resistance.

The installation can be analyzed as "an installation," but the posters can equally be studied individually (see plate 5). Like the first ASARO mural installation, the visual motif follows a regular pattern: On most posters, the name and the face of a missing student appears. As in their school photographs, later circulated on missing person posters, the students look straight at the viewer with their eyes wide open. Once again, viewers are forced to acknowledge their emotional and ethical duty toward the victims.

Moreover, the faces of the *normalistas* are again meant to dominate the public space. There is a slight emphasis on the humble origins of the students. While some of them are portrayed dressed in peasant garb, with wide-brimmed hats, others are depicted standing in a field among corn stalks. This is reinforced by the recurring figure of Indigenous leader Emiliano Zapata, as is the notion of activism through education. Zapata was from the state of Morelos, close to Mexico City. Like the politicized students and teachers, he became a role model for his community. While he did not have a high level of education, he was more educated than most (Brunk 2007; Krauze 1987) and was able to rally people to his movement. He also embodies the centre/periphery paradigm as an outsider to the metropolis who sought to change the status quo by fighting for the people of Morelos, not for himself. Nonetheless, the leaders in Mexico City could not be convinced. In addition, like the students being trained in Ayotzinapa, he worked toward the "emancipation of the rural masses" (Brunk 2007). Unsurprisingly, Zapata is a staple of ASARO's prints, whether we think of the early stencils in which he is depicted as a punk figure or the 2019 mural on the facade of Espacio Zapata that celebrates the centenary of the end of the Mexican Revolution.

On the *papel picado* prints, Zapata either appears as a "guardian angel" positioned over the left shoulder of a *normalista* or is subtly alluded to by a *normalista* sporting half of the famous revolutionary's legendary mustache. Indeed, the depiction of student Christian Tomás Colón actually comprises only half the image (see plate 6). The print is divided in two parts: on the left is Zapata's face, and on the right, Colón's. Even the left eye and the clothing belong to Zapata, as any photograph of the leader will attest. This physical merging of Zapata and Colón highlights the continuity of historical struggles; Zapata perhaps inspired Colón, who will in turn influence another generation of activists. The inscription "Zapata vive" (Zapata lives) – a phrase that most activist groups fighting for the recognition of Indigenous rights use – is updated to "Christián Tomás Colón vive" to show that while ASARO is drawing from a familiar visual repertoire, the focus ought to be on the missing student. Leveraging the figure of Zapata also offers implicit recognition that the struggle is still ongoing, more than a century after the beginning of the Mexican Revolution.

The posters seen in the Día de la indignación intervention can be categorized according to the symbols they contain. While doves, halos, and crosses emphasize the fate of the students, raised fists remind the viewer of both the students' activism in life and the public activism that their disappearance spurred. Despite the violence perpetrated against the victims, the posters themselves tend to eschew violence; only one shows a handgun and refers to the brutality enacted on the students. The firearm is a not-so-subtle hint at the role of the armed forces. Other taglines inscribed on the posters include "Ayotzinapa vive" (Ayotzinapa lives) and "No más muertos" (No more dead). The form "X-Y-Z vive" is a recurring one in protests, meant to emphasize that while important figures might have died, their legacy lives on. Likewise, "Ayotzinapa vive" is saying that the *pueblo* will never forget and will ensure that the memory of these youths endures. "No más muertos" is a demand made to the authorities to stop the recurring massacres of innocent people.

Some of the posters designed for the Día de la indignación introduce a new slogan in ASARO's production: "Faltan 43 – Volveré y seré millones" (Forty-three are missing – I will be back and I will be millions). While this phrasing is not deployed as often as "Todos somos Ayotzinapa" or "Fue el Estado," it still emphasizes the collective nature of any revolutionary movement. Even if one activist dies, his demise has the potential to ignite a movement. By placing this inscription under the drawing of an Indigenous peasant, ASARO is positioning Ayotzinapa as part of the history Indigenous rebellions, and the ongoing extermination of Indigenous leaders by the state. By doing so, the collective highlights the continuity in the community's historic battles to secure basic human rights.

Indeed, the phrase "Volveré y seré millones"[53] is believed to have been uttered for the first time by Indigenous military leader Túpac Katari, an Aymara who led an insurrection in 1781 against Spanish colonial authorities in what is today Bolivia. During the insurrection, Katari recruited mestizos, mulattos, and Black people – in short, those belonging to the lower echelons of society – to fight the *peninsulares* and *criollos* (Acre 2013) who deprived them of their humanity. The 1781 uprising was a down-top rebellion crushed from above. Invoking it reinforces the continuity of the fight against an imposed power dynamic that seeks to annihilate anyone who opposes it. Once again, we return to the idea of sowing seeds, to which I first alluded in the preface. While one protester or activist might die, he will be replaced by many, and furthermore, his death will encourage the multitude to fight in his place and in his memory.

A History of Repression in Mexico The facade of Espacio Zapata was altered once again in the summer of 2016, this time to create a more subtle, but no less striking, mural (see plate 7). I have been unable to confirm with ASARO if they formally title their murals, but, inspired by Diego Rivera's iconic mural *History of Mexico*, I choose to refer to this one as *A History of Repression in Mexico*. There is a tension in the print, which portrays the unending cycle of being silenced and speaking up.

The mural comprises a variety of elements: a young man (appearing twice); a woman (appearing once in full and a second time the top half only); an older-looking man (appearing twice); a reproduction of Adolfo Mexiac's *Libertad de expresión* print (appearing three times); the face of an Ayotzinapa student (appearing once); two young female activists; and Ayotzinapa alumnus Lucio Cabaña Barrientos (appearing three times). All these figures are dressed in black. The mural installation consists of various wheat paste posters assembled to create a larger image.

The young man appears to be gagged. There is a rope over his mouth, he is blindfolded, and his arms are held behind his head in a scene that hints at torture or police detention. The pose of this young male recalls Mexiac's *Libertad de expresión* print, although here the figure is restrained by a rope and not by actual chains. The woman shares similar characteristics, though the rope is wound around her neck, as if she were about to be hung or dragged. Both the young man and the woman have their eyes closed. The older adult male, a parent maybe, holds a sign that says, "Vivos se los llevaron," a reproduction of the signs Ayotzinapa parents carried during marches. Mexiac's *Libertad de expresión* print is reproduced three times in this installation. Mexiac, a member of the Taller de Gráfica Popular (TGP), created the image in 1954 in support of Indigenous communities in Chiapas, in the TGP's realist and expressive style. We also see one of the posters crafted in 2015 in the Día de Muertos–like celebration with *papel picado*. The young activists are both women: one of them is screaming, maybe in a demonstration; the other may be about to cover her face with a scarf, similar to what we see in some of the 2006 prints, with activists concealing their faces during protests when exposed to tear gas. Finally, to the uninitiated eye, the peasant is not easily linked to Ayotzinapa. This is in fact Lucio Cabaña Barrientos. The wheat paste poster incorporated into the installation is a re-articulation of a painting on cloth that is openly about Ayotzinapa: It shows Cabaña sitting down, holding a sign with "#43" on it and superimposed on a background of red hearts with a black star at the centre (see plate 8).[54]

The 2016 mural is both directly and indirectly about Ayotzinapa. There are, for example, very clear elements that indicate that it refers to Ayotzinapa, such as the sign held up by parents and the missing students; but it is also more broadly about repression and silence, about being silenced in Mexico. Invoking Mexiac is an unmistakable allusion to the many strikes that occurred in the 1950s (namely, by the railway and teachers' union movements), and to the TGP's support for the Indigenous community – the original purpose of the print.[55] The print was also reactivated during the 1968 student protests. This particular work carries a lot of history and conjures up ideas of resistance to abuse and denunciation.

Yet, there are also elements that represent the opposite of being silenced: One activist is screaming, and the other is preparing for a fight with the authorities – covering her face either because of tear gas or to avoid being identified. The older adult figure, even if he might not seem to be as forceful as the young activist, brandishes a sign that conveys his discontent and criticism of the Mexican government. And this is one of the major changes brought about by the events of September 2014: Across all walks of life, people who were afraid of speaking up for fear of violent reprisals began raising their voices to condemn the state's abuses.

Reflecting on ASARO's Body of Work

Since ASARO began in 2006 by designing stencils, it seems fitting to conclude here by briefly examining four that deal with the subject of Ayotzinapa; all were disseminated in 2015. Whereas the murals and installations relied heavily on the images of the missing students – emphasizing their group identity either as "missing," departed people to be remembered, or as activists who entered the collective memory of student activism – the stencils do not emphasize this representational matrix at all. Instead, akin to those produced during the 2006 protests, these stencils are highly critical of the government and the military as institutions and leave little room for interpretation or nuance.

ASARO circulated two stencils in February and one in September of 2015 (ASARO 2015a, 2015b). As a reminder, in February 2015 Attorney General Murillo Karam's days in office were numbered, as the "historical truth" that the forty-three students had been incinerated in a garbage dump became increasingly untenable and scientifically improbable by the day (Goldman 2015). Indeed, the Argentine Forensic Anthropology Team (Equipo Argentino de Antropología Forense), summoned to examine where the students' remains had supposedly been discarded, concluded on 9 February that there was no scientific evidence to support Karam and the PGR's conclusion that drug cartels were responsible for the students' deaths. With this, the military's probable role in disappearing the students emerged even more forcefully, as very few other groups had the resources necessary to make forty-three bodies disappear overnight.

These two stencils represent different facets of the military: the individual soldier – whose depiction adds nuance to ASARO's generally black-and-white positions with respect to the Mexican authorities – and the military as an opaque institution. The first stencil (see plate 9) depicts a soldier wearing green military garb, his head bowed in respect, holding up a banner that reads, "Todos somos Ayotzinapa," indicating that he, too, supports the victims and their families. It is an interesting take for ASARO that separates the individual from the institution. While the army might have disappeared and massacred the students, individual soldiers can still take a stance against the actions of the institution they serve, a stance that could well cause them problems with their superiors. By depicting a soldier speaking out against the narrative upheld by the state and the army, ASARO emphasizes that small acts of courage can be a starting point for the development of a more expansive consciousness.

The second stencil is not as nuanced as the first one. It shows a black tank rolling over a pile of skulls and bones, with the inscription "#Fue ElEstado 43!!" (#It was the state 43!!) calligraphed above it. The tank advances over the pile of bones, hypothetically moving in the direction of further massacres. The tank transforming the bones of the massacred into a launching pad reinforces the lack of accountability shown by the military, as well as the contempt the institution holds for the disappeared. This artwork does not leave any possible doubt about ASARO's position: The army and the state apparatus are to blame for the forced disappearance of the Ayotzinapa students.

A third stencil, which circulated on social media in September 2015 after Karam's resignation, portrays the former attorney general wearing the typical black-and-yellow uniform donned by street sweepers in Mexico as he steps on and sweeps away a human skeleton. The meaning is straightforward: For ASARO, Karam is responsible for the disappearances. Even if he did not disappear the students himself, by sweeping away the truth and covering up the military's actions, he is a full accessory to the crime.

Finally, a last, undated, stencil (see plate 10) explicitly links the Tlatelolco massacre and the Ayotzinapa forced disappearances by depicting the presidents in office at the time; Gustavo Díaz Ordaz wears a military helmet with "68 Tlatelolco" inscribed on it, while Enrique Peña Nieto's hat, similar in style, reads, "43 Ayotzinapa." Under the images of the two former presidents, the words "Fue el Estado" are spray-painted in the colours of the Mexican flag, tying together the two events and emphasizing that state violence is still prevalent, almost fifty years after the Plaza de las Tres Culturas massacre, and that past massacres – and the state's indifference – fuel current human rights violations.

Examining the murals and installations that ASARO has dedicated to the Ayotzinapa disappearances since 2014 in chronological order allows me to demonstrate that the collective's interventions closely follow Mexican society's reactions to the events that occurred in Iguala on 26 September 2014. Each mural denotes a step in the evolution of collective and social grief. *Justicia 43* (2014) serves a dual purpose, expressing the shock of the collective and the broader Mexican population and making the disappearances visible. It also conveys solidarity with the broader Ayotzinapa community. Then, the modifications made in 2015 communicate that hope is waning, but that the students are still present in Mexican citizens' hearts and minds. By resorting to Day of the Dead imagery, the 2015 Día de la indignación installation acknowledges that the students are likely dead; they are depicted as loved ones to be mourned. The prints on china paper also emphasize the students' Indigenous ancestry and their activism by picturing them in the company of Indigenous leader Emiliano Zapata. Finally, the 2016–17 mural that concentrates on torture and activism registers the students in the collective memory of student activism by reviving imagery from 1968 Tlatelolco massacre and showing them alongside fellow Ayotzinapa student and Indigenous leader Lucio Cabaña Barrientos, who has been influential in peasant and student activism since the 1970s.

By reviving symbols associated with student and peasant activism in previous decades, ASARO establishes a narrative of state violence. In the end, the collective demonstrates that historical human rights crimes, such as the Tlatelolco massacre and the many atrocities perpetrated during the Dirty War, have helped to shape more contemporary human rights violations like the Ayotzinapa disappearances.

In the next section, we will see that URT-Arte calls on different symbolism to denounce the Ayotzinapa disappearances and that their work targets a different audience. Whereas ASARO honours the memory of the students who were sacrificed due to the state's disinterest in the forced disappearances of marginalized citizens, URT-Arte seeks to recruit artists and activists who want to play an active role in challenging this same state.

Marxist-Leninist Continuity: The Unión Revolucionaria de Trabajadores del Arte, 2014–2022[56]

In this section, I examine nine works – primarily wheat paste posters – designed and circulated by URT-Arte from 2014 to 2022. Unlike ASARO, which also released stencils to mark milestones in the investigation, URT-Arte commemorates the 2014 disappearances only once a year in September. For analytical purposes, I divide their prints into those focused on "protest" and those focused on "affect." While the protest prints depict the protesters themselves, the prints calling forth affect generally highlight mothers. These prints are designed to elicit different feelings in the viewer – protest versus empathy and solidarity – but both suggest a pathway to activism.

Unlike ASARO, URT-Arte did not begin to disseminate images about Ayotzinapa when the events were first reported in October 2014, likely because Guzmán was still a member of ASARO at that time. URT-Arte's first mention of the Iguala massacre is found in a reposting of ASARO's December 2014 call for faces. In response to the call, URT-Arte contributed a portrayal of student Jorge Luis González Parral with a red star on his forehead (Urtarte 2015). This red star highlights URT-Arte's ideological position, and thus the poster stands out in a series of posters that were not particularly ideological. It is also one of the rare times the group chose the traditional matrix of representation of the *normalistas*, with the faces and the number 43. URT-Arte tends to avoid well-known symbols and slogans, such as "Todos somos Ayotzinapa." Instead, it seeks to show that citizens from every walk of life *are* Ayotzinapa, without having to proclaim it on their posters.

URT-Arte was formed in 2007 by Mario Guzmán as a parallel project to ASARO, one that is explicitly Marxist-Leninist, ideologically homogeneous, and organized vertically. Guzmán was then part of two collectives at the same time. In its beginnings, URT-Arte consisted of eight political engravers; it now boasts a membership of about thirty artivists. During my stay in Oaxaca, I interviewed five members (three men and two women) and spent many hours watching everyone work in the TAC.

Despite being founded in 2007, URT-Arte only established a regular posting pattern in 2012, and then picked up the pace in 2016–17 as ASARO's activities were winding down.[57] Most of URT-Arte's production denounces the inequalities that most Mexican citizens experience. To inspire them to fight against the *mal gobierno* (bad government), a lot of URT-Arte's artworks depict well-known revolutionary figures, such as Karl Marx, Vladimir Lenin, Josef Stalin, Emiliano Zapata, and at times Pancho Villa, Che Guevara, Samir Flores – an environmental activist killed in 2019 – and the fictional V from the comic book *V for Vendetta*. In URT-Arte's visual repertoire, these figures are treated as symbols of resistance to governments and the elite, or as leftist intellectual leaders whom the *pueblo* should emulate. URT-Arte also portrays political figures – such as former presidents Carlos Salinas de Gortari, Enrique Peña Nieto, and even Donald Trump – to criticize them and their policies.

Unlike ASARO, whose members are all graphic artists or painters, URT-Arte is a gathering of artists from various backgrounds ranging from visual artists to musicians. Little is known about URT-Arte's artistic, community, and social work. According to their Blogspot site – which used to serve, alongside their Facebook page, as their official website – URT-Arte seeks to organize all creators who hold progressive, democratic, or revolutionary ideals. They see artistic expression as "a tool to raise awareness among the working class of the countryside and the city (workers, peasants, students, teachers, etc.)" (Urtarte, n.d.).

The name of the collective – Unión Revolucionaria de Trabajadores del Arte – is fairly descriptive. The word *unión* stresses the notion of a group; unlike in English, it does not always mean "labour union" or "syndicate." The word *revolucionaria* refers to the nature of their political project, and finally, *trabajadores del arte* refers both to the media through which the revolution will happen and Marxism; all the members are workers. Their logo (see plate 11) encapsulates all the elements of their political position: both the red star and the hammer and sickle underscore Marxism-Leninism, while the wheel highlights the ongoing process of the revolution and the collective nature of the struggle.

Once again, political affiliations are at the core of the collective, dictating its very mode of organization. Unlike ASARO and its horizontal assembly, URT-Arte has a vertical organization: "Vertical? And why vertical? Because we believe that the most experienced, most determined colleagues should be higher up" (Guzmán interview, 2018). This experience is both artistic – the best artists train the newer members – and political – the older members train the younger ones during reading circles. For the members of URT-Arte, verticality does not contradict the principles of collective organization.

Working for the benefit of the community is perhaps the most important of URT-Arte's goals. Guzmán is aware that leading a Marxist-Leninist project in 2023 comes with challenges and can sometimes open the group to ridicule:

> Many of my colleagues criticize me, assuming that I am a communist or a political activist because, well … someone almost forced me, right? They do not see that many people sometimes assume that attitude due to very specific experiences. It's not because … I'm romanticizing the struggles … It's just … I think I belong to a social class and then I need to leave something to it. So everything that I am today, well, I owe it to [that social class]. That's why a lot of what I do is directed at the places that exploit us … And I know that it might not be easy to sell [the group's particular message] right now. Maybe after I die, I don't know. The important thing is to contribute, and change the things that are wrong … from what we are, from what we do and all this, right? (Guzmán interview, 2018)

For Guzmán, giving back to his community takes many forms; printmaking is only the most visible of them. Not unlike the Liga de Escritores y Artistas Revolucionarios in the 1930s, members of URT-Arte also travel to smaller communities around Oaxaca to work with young people, either giving them art classes or organizing summer camps, or participating in *tequios*, chores such as cleaning or painting that arise periodically.

The vertical mode of organization and its strict ideological position influence URT-Arte's artistic production: Its designs are generally of high quality and display a high degree of artistry. This means that URT-Arte can sell them as artworks in their workshop, which in turn helps the collective finance various projects. Ultimately, the art created always has the *pueblo* in mind, either to alert it to various crises on the street or to teach it various artistic techniques; both facets of URT-Arte's work promote reaching out to the Other and collaborating.

Protest

The posters I categorize under "protest" depict sectors of the citizenry that one might expect to see, such as students, but also new ones, like fathers and young schoolgirls, whose inclusion I read as a desire to show the future of protest.

The 2017 print shown in figure 2.1 embodies the very ethos of Ayotzinapa: A student holds up a sign and appears to be participating in a

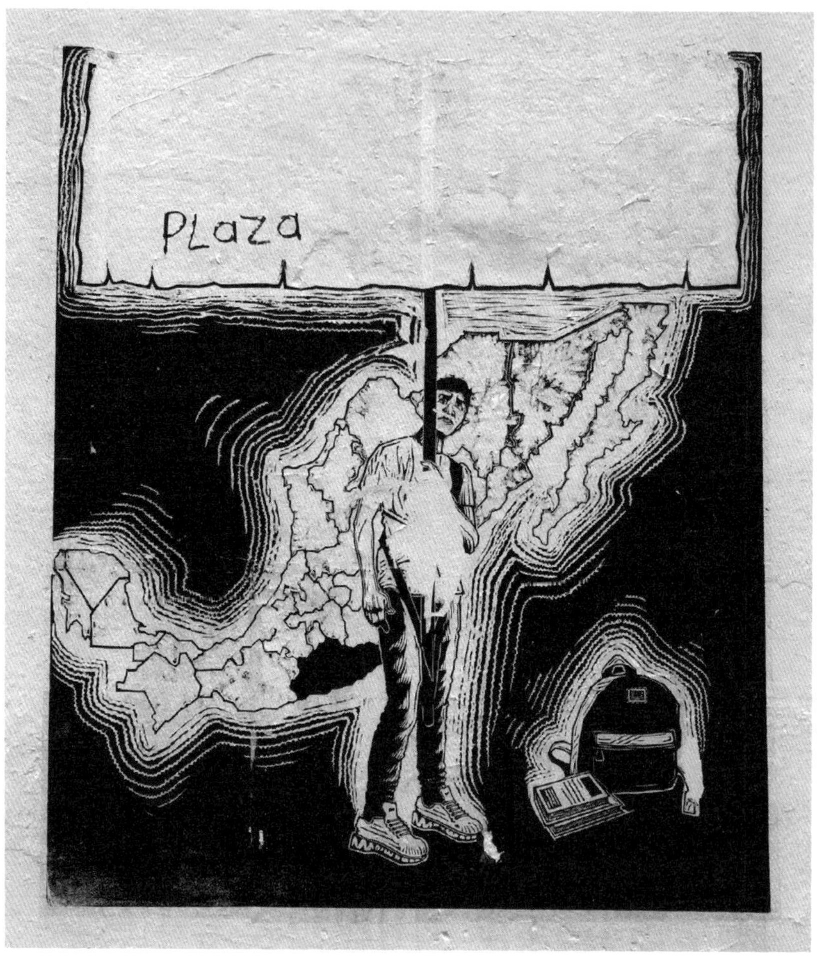

Figure 2.1
Wheat paste poster showing a student standing in front of a map of Mexico and holding a poster; the poster is blank: a tagline has yet to be written.

protest. Upon closer inspection, we notice that while the poster depicting the student protester was printed mechanically, the inscription is meant to be inserted by hand, increasing the poster's versatility.[58] This transposition is easily performed since the sign the student holds up is blank on the matrix. Because the words are not part of the print – they are not engraved but added later by hand – the poster can be adapted to other situations. This flexibility permits a more targeted use of the print and broader dissemination across Oaxacan neighbourhoods. As figure 2.1 demonstrates, the tagline can even be ripped off by passersby who likely disagree with its message, without removing the poster completely.

The version shown in plate 12 reads "Justicia para Ayotzinapa," a message most Mexican citizens rallied behind, which is perhaps why the tagline was not removed. A third version (not reproduced here) reads, "Vivos los llevaron, vivos los queremos" (They took them alive, we want them back alive). It is the only print by URT-Arte that repeats this well-known phrase. Interestingly, this slogan was also popular among the mothers of the disappeared during the Mexican Dirty War; its invocation here thus further ties the events of Ayotzinapa to the broader history of state-sponsored violence against students who openly oppose the Mexican authorities.

There are at least two separate but interrelated readings of this print. For anyone familiar with the map of Mexico, the fact that the state of Guerrero is shown in black makes explicit that the print is about Ayotzinapa. If the viewer is not well versed in geography, the poster condemns the crushing of student activism in Mexico more broadly. Finally, even if "Todos somos Ayotzinapa" is not part of the poster, by standing in front of a map of Mexico, the student further reinforces the national dimension of the case. The print was also produced with the protest slogan "La lucha es de todos" (It's everyone's fight), highlighting the collective aspect of the struggle and calling on every viewer to consider their role in it.

Also from 2017, the print shown in plate 13, which reads, "¡Justicia para Ayotzinapa!" (Justice for Ayotzinapa), follows the same logic. It depicts a male teacher dressed in work clothes seemingly protesting the disappearances and demanding that justice be done.[59] The fact that the print portrays a male figure is relevant; indeed, many fathers of the dead students led, and are still leading, the fight against the inefficiency of the authorities and their reluctance to investigate the crime. The depiction of a father is a slight departure from the portrayals of many social movements revolving around forced disappearances. Most social movements dealing with murdered and/or missing persons are led by women, whether we think of the Madres de la Plaza de Mayo in Argentina – who from 1977 onward demanded that their children, and then their grandchildren, be returned to them – or the mothers still fighting for better police investigations and laws around feminicides. This is not to say that men are not active in social movements around forced disappearances, human rights, or political violence. However, the figure of the mother is more common in artistic depictions, as it elicits compassion in viewers. The depiction of a male protester further reinforces my contention that URT-Arte is targeting specific sectors of the Mexican population that have historically not been portrayed protesting human rights abuses, despite their active involvement in these social causes.

The large wheat paste poster *Estudiante, lucha que se paga con muerte* (Student, a fight paid for with death; plate 14)[60] also deviates from traditional representation. This 2021 collaboration between URT-Arte and its sister collective ARMARTE – which I discuss in chapter 3 – portrays a young girl in her school uniform waving a banner on which the tagline is written. The appearance of colour on the poster is a departure from most of URT-Arte's works and can be attributed to the collaboration with ARMARTE. The *paliacate*, the scarf that the young girl wears over her mouth, is likely intended to avoid the fumes of tear gas following a police attack. She represents militancy, innocence, and righteousness, which is further highlighted by her school uniform. She is standing in front of a map of Mexico and the word "Tlatelolco," which connects past struggles and present events. In the matrix of representation around the Ayotzinapa disappearances and subsequent protests, it is particularly relevant that the protestor is a young girl, and not an older male student. She represents the future of protest, the people the collective hopes will take on the fight, and her presence hints at the fact that for URT-Arte, it is imperative to raise the conscience of youth early; this is a task they perform in their art youth camps in the villages around Oaxaca.

With these two last prints, URT-Arte inverts the matrix of representation of movements protesting the forced disappearances of the forty-three Ayotzinapa students.

Affect

Unlike the prints I categorized under the heading "protest," those that tap into "affect" rely on a more traditional matrix of representation.

For instance, *Por las madres que lloran tumbas vacías por los hijos que nunca volvieron* (For the mothers who cry on empty tombs for the sons who never returned) (see plate 15), a 2018 print, depicts a mother holding a child. Mother and child are linked by the umbilical cord, and the mother is "bleeding" the number 43. The white outline of the baby with the inscription "nunca volvieron" explicitly references the absence of the child. The white child can symbolize both innocence, the fact that there is no blood left in the dead body – a comment on the fate of the missing students – and the universality of the case; it could be any child who has been forcibly disappeared. This print also highlights a particularly insidious characteristic of forced disappearances: the uncertainty they generate for those left behind. The disappeared, as long as they are not located, exist in an in-between state that is not quite life, but also not quite death. This leaves society in a limbo of sorts, and the absence of a body to grieve means there is room for hope, however faint, that maybe, and against all odds, a loved one has survived. Ultimately, this print deals with the lack of closure that both the families and the Mexican population feel.

Similarly, a 2021 wheat paste assemblage portrays a woman wearing an apron and standing with her palms up, the numbers 4 and 3 written on her right and left hands, respectively (see plate 16). Her head is bowed down, as in grief, and she is surrounded by the names of the forty-three missing students. The notion of loss is indicated by the words "Nos faltan" (We are missing), which can be read in two different ways: "Nos faltan 43" considers the forty-three Ayotzinapa students as a group, but their names, written by hand, also take into account their individuality.

Whether they depict young students protesting or maternal figures in pain, the prints portray the types of Mexican citizens who are likely to come across them on the streets: the worker, the maid, the citizen of Indigenous descent. This choice is deliberate on the part of URT-Arte, whose members are acutely aware of the field of the viewers' gaze. As Salcedo explained, they want people to see themselves reflected in the works: "We are not looking for this canon or this archetype, let's say Europeanized, no, or Caucasian, but to talk about local people. I am sure that the local people identify because they can tell that that woman who is there comes from that community because there is that traditional scarf or skirt, or motif in the fabric" (interview, 2018). Seeing themselves reflected in the work might influence citizens to build solidarity with the victims portrayed in the prints, while also encouraging a desire to fight.

Protest and Affect

Finally, let us examine a print that blends protest and affect (see plates 17 and 18). URT-Arte has repeated this print multiple times, modifying the phrases they plaster around it, which attests to its versatility and its power to move audiences. The print depicts a young woman dressed in peasant clothing from mid-thigh up and emerging from an open manhole. Her face bears a severe expression as she looks straight at the observer, almost as if challenging us to argue with her. Her arms are wrapped around an oversized human heart that is almost as large as she is, while arteries and veins at the top form the shape of the number 43, thus linking the print unequivocally to the Ayotzinapa disappearances.

A small version of the print was disseminated in 2015 around the Historic Centre of Oaxaca bearing the tagline "Justicia o revolución violenta" (Justice or violent revolution). Later, on the fifth anniversary of the disappearance of the forty-three students, URT-Arte installed reproductions of a large-format print (approximately ten feet by feet feet) around the city, each bearing a different wording. This placement aligned with the political purpose the prints serve: In the Historic Centre, prints are generally commemorative in nature and designed to attract the attention of both tourists and citizens, whereas in the suburbs they are meant primarily for the eyes of Oaxacan. In the latter case, the wording is more political in nature and encourages citizens to join the ranks of URT-Arte. During a field trip in October 2019, I identified three monumental versions of this print: on the façade of the Taller de Arte Comunitario – without a caption – next to the Santo Domingo Cathedral – with the wording "5 años – Justicia para Ayotzinapa" (Five years – justice for Ayotzinapa) – and in the suburbs – with such captions as "#Fue el Estado" and "#Fue el ejército" (It was the state, It was the military). This last one was unveiled as part of a recruitment event hosted by URT-Arte.[61]

The image of the young woman embracing the heart is at once an image of mourning (affect) and of defiance (protest). In keeping with the lengthy tradition of public art in Mexico, the print lends a voice to "an underdog," the young peasant or woman worker who, in an urban setting, emerges from the underbelly of the city to raise her call for justice and remind the public that a full five years after the fact, forty-three individuals were still missing, the circumstances of their disappearance shrouded in mystery, because authorities were unwilling or unable to investigate.

This wheat paste poster is larger than the other prints examined above. The possibility of creating large wheat paste posters emerged shortly after the 2006 teachers' protest, when ASARO built a larger printing press. ASARO and URT-Arte, thanks to Guzmán's resourcefulness, can now undertake *gráfica monumental* (monumental printmaking), mixing traditional printmaking and muralism. This blending of techniques blurs boundaries in representation; indeed, while printmaking has generally been used to portray the *pueblo*, muralism has a certain aura of elitism attached to it.[62] The larger printing press allows for the portrayal of the *pueblo* in monumental size. In doing so, URT-Arte "restore[s] the social sense" (Guzmán interview, 2018) of printmaking, but uses the monumentality of muralism to attract new audiences:

> Taking it to large dimensions … [allows people to] see the print from afar, not like the work that we see in a closed space, inching closer to it one metre to see the detail … but rather [we created] it so that any citizen who drives by in a car can see the print and that … at first sight, they get the idea, no? It was also about visibility. In fact, right now, part of what we are proposing is to take a print to a monumentality of six, eight plates [of ten feet by five feet]. Take it to gigantic dimensions, no? Let's say, the type of murals that Mexican muralists make, large dimensions, but also have the sense of reproducibility because that is not only on a wall if we allow it to be sent anywhere and that people can install it.

This new technique thus blends the reproducibility of prints with the visual impact of murals, furthering URT-Arte's goal of recruiting more members into the collective by conscientizing them about an imminent revolution.

Reflecting on URT-Arte's Body of Work

In their production, URT-Arte opts for images either of people who have been left behind or of citizens demanding justice; unlike in ASARO's works, the forty-three missing students are themselves rarely portrayed. An image of a lonely student or a crying mother with an empty womb awakens a sentiment of empathy in the viewer, a feeling that can ultimately build up to solidarity. Viewers see themselves reflected in the print; it is a visual demonstration of "Todos somos Ayotzinapa." This "todos" refers to and addresses the people who felt these disappearances the most – namely, Mexican citizens who are at risk of disappearing too. As noted previously, in a country like Mexico almost every citizen can lose someone to state terrorism, almost anyone can identify with a variation of "Todos somos Ayotzinapa." The posters denounce this situation, but also seek to create emotional attachment, empathy, and solidarity in viewers. The prints act as a form of mirror: In these images, each audience member sees someone who looks just like them; who could in fact be them. From there, it is only a short step to seeing yourself as a protester, to thinking that you should be out demonstrating too.

In terms of content, URT-Arte's artworks are quite different from both ASARO's and most other artistic creations involving Ayotzinapa. Instead of depicting the missing students, they seek to reach other sectors of the citizenry, the people they refer to as *el pueblo* (the people): mothers, fathers, students, workers, activists; people who are usually ignored by those in power, who were either affected by the disappearances of the forty-three, or who, in line with URT-Arte's Marxist-Leninist beliefs, could be convinced to join in a revolution against the state and be empowered to fight for better living conditions or access to justice. URT-Arte's posters are either about "protest" – showing protesters demanding change – or about "affect" – portraying grieving figures that elicit empathy and solidarity. Both types of prints aim to ignite a spark in viewers, to push them to accept artistic activism as a means of fighting for change. This representational matrix in which lay citizens are the focus of the prints also offers a stark contrast to the most common artistic practice developed to handle the issue of missing people. Whether we think of the Argentinean *Siluetazo* of 1983 or the actual Ayotzinapa protests, artists generally show the missing people themselves, so as to visualize their absence and restore their place in the world (García Navarro 2008, 351), if only through visual representation. Ultimately, URT-Arte inverts the symbolic matrix of representation to involve citizens in its activism.

This desire to involve citizens also extends to prints and posters. Indeed, while ASARO's installations are generally larger and more elaborate, URT-Arte favours smaller and easily reproducible wheat paste posters, which facilitate broad circulation. Smaller posters might not have the same visual impact as a full-wall mural, but easy and cheap reproduction means they can be plastered around the city. Repetition then becomes a means to greater impact in more areas of the city. Making posters with a banner that can then be filled in by hand – as we see, for example, in plate 12 and figure 2.1 from 2017 – also ensures that a specific type of audience can be targeted. While the image is the same, the message it conveys can be adapted to different neighbourhoods, thus reaching more people more efficiently.

Conclusion

This chapter examined ASARO's and URT-Arte's artistic representations of the September 2014 forced disappearances of the forty-three Ayotzinapa students, concluding that the artworks the collectives designed and displayed in the years that followed the mass disappearances served three main purposes. First, by recognizing the forty-three lives lost, they transformed the disappeared students into "grievable subjects" (Butler 2016) despite the Mexican authorities' refusal to do so. Second, they encouraged citizens to speak up against state-sponsored violence. Finally, the artworks' easy reproducibility – and thus the high number of prints in circulation – turned them into a soft warning to the authorities, a reminder that forty-three individuals lost their lives needlessly and activists are still working to counter the narrative of silence imposed by the authorities and the state's dehumanization of Mexican citizens.

Ultimately, this artistic production attacked the phenomenon of activist-shaming, further reinforcing the right of Mexican citizens to denounce the actions of the authorities. In order to mobilize citizens to condemn their political leaders, ASARO's and URT-Arte's murals and posters portray protesters who look like the *pueblo* – students, peasants, housewives, and workers. In so doing, these artworks actively rally citizens politically by challenging them to become agents of change themselves.

Having analyzed the two groups side by side, I conclude that the dissemination of this alternative collective memory is intended to inspire citizens to fight back against a state and a broader social narrative that both criminalizes victims of forced disappearances and shames their families into silence. By refusing the accepted narrative that the disappeared are themselves to blame – and that therefore their families should be ashamed and grieve in private – and by using the public space to mourn, the collectives inscribe the missing citizens into Mexico's national narrative, thus dispelling the myth of national cohesion on which the government insists. Despite the authorities' posture, the forty-three students are not anomalies. Depicting the disappeared as part of their resistance practices, and grieving for them as fallen comrades, allows the members of the collectives to model behaviours that they encourage the rest of society to adopt: in short, being political and opposing the status quo.

While there is no denying that the events of September 2014 are about the Ayotzinapa students who were killed or forcibly disappeared, one type of victim is completely absent from the work of both collectives: individuals who were arrested under false pretenses, tortured by government officials, jailed, sometimes even convicted, then released without having their names cleared (Hernández 2020). They, too, were victimized by the state, but are notably absent from the collectives' commemorative work. This absence is hard to understand, as generally both collectives take a strong stand against state violence and any wrongdoing on the part of the authorities.

There is a missed opportunity here. While there is no denying that the portrayal of mothers crying or peasants and students protesting is inevitable, citizens arrested in relation to the original crime, who were tortured for no other reason than to extract a forced confession that would help the government close the case as quickly as possible, are also part of the Ayotzinapa disappearances. The events of 26 September 2014 resulted in more than forty-three victims, and all should be given equal importance, especially in highlighting the state's mistakes. These "other" victims, such as drug dealers and *sicarios*, are sometimes less palatable to the general public, but, ultimately, they are victims. Unlike the forty-three students, or the women and children, these other victims do not have a righteous claim to innocence; they had, after all, previously been convicted of all sorts of crimes (Hernández 2020). By not representing them, the collectives choose to show only one side of the event, the one that is the most likely to fit their narrative of repeated state abuse of innocent people. While this perpetuates a form of social shaming, where only some victims are worthy of compassion and depiction, pragmatically, in movements where the objective is to have people empathize with victims so they become engaged and committed to enacting change, representing criminals might be counterproductive.

Pasting Up Protest is premised on the assertion that the members of these collectives are artivists. By way of conclusion, let us examine some ways in which both ASARO and URT-Arte deploy artivist strategies. As I discussed in chapter 1, Naidus (2009) and Duncombe (2016) have set out a useful list of criteria (refer to page 27 for table 1.1) While some criteria concern the art maker, and others the intended audience, all of them reach out to citizens as political subjects.

Indeed, artivism is at once social and political engagement. By creating these artworks to express their outrage at the forty-three's disappearance, and more broadly at the systemic injustices affecting Mexican citizens, the two collectives participate in a broader discussion about what it means to be political in Mexico. They seek to "process" or "document the experience" (Naidus 2009, 5) of the latest occurrence of state-sponsored violence. It is possible to imagine that by expressing a sense of kinship with the students, the members can work through or capture their own lived experience of having been disappeared in 2006, and potentially even "heal" as makers (5).

The collectives attempt to "compensate for [society's] amnesia" (Naidus 2009, 5), "foster dialogue" with Mexicans (Duncombe 2016, 121), and "alter the perception" (122) of society. All these goals are obviously political: The collectives aim at awakening more minds to the numbing reality of life in Mexico, and to encourage Mexicans to join in their struggle to change it for the better. While a first reading might reveal that ASARO and URT-Arte work primarily toward raising Mexican citizens' consciousness around these events, a stencil like ASARO's lone soldier with a banner that reads, "Todos somos Ayotzinapa" (figure 2.12) highlights that objectives such as attempting to "awaken those who are numb or in denial" by "mak[ing] the events visible" (Naidus 2009, 5), or "fostering dialogue" (Duncombe 2016, 121), can also target state officials, citizens who do not constitute ASARO's primary audience.

By trying to empower students and citizens to raise their voices, the ultimate objective of the collectives is to alter the way the Mexican government operates, and to force the authorities to listen to the people. Through their memory activism – embedding new events into Mexico's cultural memory – they "envision a different reality or a better future" (Naidus 2009, 5) and "inspire dreaming" (Duncombe 2016, 122). They do so by questioning the workings of the government, and of society more broadly, and by "offering solutions" (Naidus 2009, 5) to both the population and its leaders. In my view, they do not simply question the government and its actions; they openly defy it and call for a complete overhaul of the governing bodies, which is hardly conceivable.

For some readers, the collectives' open criticism of the government and their goal of completely dismantling Mexico's political system might seem hard to reconcile with artivism's emphasis on dialogue. In my view, this might be how artivism in the Global North differs from that practised in the Global South. As I explained in chapter 1, the material and social conditions of artists in the Global South can often be marked by violence, and so are some of the solutions they propose, as violence may offer the only way to achieve political and social gains. As Mario Guzmán told me during our interview, he fully expects – and is prepared for – the fight for a better Mexico to turn violent in the future.

As this section concludes, one outstanding question remains: What is the "invisible" that the collectives are working toward "mak[ing] visible" (Naidus 2009, 5)? Since Ayotzinapa, forced or mass disappearances are no longer invisible. Indeed, dozens of mass graves have been discovered in Mexico. The reality the collectives are revealing (Duncombe 2016, 122) is multi-faceted, as are the perceptions they hope to alter (122). There is the reality of systemic injustices, but also the reality that some people are actually fighting back, and both contribute to altering Mexicans' perceptions. Citizens are not bullied into silence anymore.

In the end, both collectives strive to achieve an "ultimate cultural change" (Duncombe 2016, 124) ("culture" understood here in the broadest of senses) in Mexico; the goal is to put an end to the culture of violence, of silence, of shaming activists. They contribute to this change – which will undoubtedly take time to materialize – by having an "imminent material impact" through their works. Having more citizens speak up against the authorities in a society known to silence dissent is a cultural shift, notwithstanding the slow pace at which it plays out. Slowly but surely, as the number of participants involved in protests and in artistic workshops grows, the state can no longer resort to "fear as a privileged tool of social control" (Morbiato 2017, 140), and more Mexican citizens are overcoming silence as a device of collective discipline (Echavarría Canto and Vásquez Carmona 2018, 113).

Unlike several other Latin American countries, Mexico was never ruled by a military dictatorship, nor did it face an internal or civil war with a defined beginning and end point (De Vecchi Gerli 2018, 25; Délano Alonso and Nienass 2021, 355). Nevertheless, one-party rule between 1919 and the 2000 election, the first time a party other than the Partido Revolucionario Institucional or its immediate predecessors gained power since the end of the revolution, shares some characteristics of dictatorships, prompting some scholars to designate Mexico as a failed state (Derwich 2015). This in-betweenness – not quite a democracy, yet not quite a dictatorship – makes it all the more complex to recognize crimes committed by the state. After what De Vecchi Gerli calls "the first wave of disappearances" (2018, 15) during the 1970s, part of the Dirty War, the government and the military were never forced to answer for their transgressions against citizens, and the "never again" ethos, present in most nations where truth and reconciliation commissions were established or where the body politic underwent a transition to democracy, did not become part of the Mexican government's policy or vocabulary. Nor did it happen during the "second wave of disappearances" (15) that began with President Felipe Calderón's war on drugs. In truth, the Mexican government never really had to make "amends to the victims and promis[e] a better future" (Sodaro in Feldman 2021, 18). The collectives' perspectives are expressed in their artworks: Despite an acknowledgment of the past, the present remains problematic. No lessons were learned, and the unequal social structures remain. Their art serves, first, to contest the barbarity of the past and its enduring presence, second, to teach current generations about their history, so that they can bring about the social and political change they deem necessary, and third, to mourn individual victims.

In the next chapter, "Women Empowering Women," I examine how the 2014 Ayotzinapa disappearances contributed to expanding activism against gender-based violence, and how two female-only collectives contributed to this culture shift, this time in response to everyday sexism and toxic masculinity.

CHAPTER 3

Women Empowering Women

Introduction

In 1993, young women, most of them factory workers, started disappearing at an alarming rate in Ciudad Juárez (Chihuahua), a city on the Mexico-US border. Or to be more precise, human rights activist Esther Chávez Cano began tracking feminicides in the city. However, feminicides, as the murder of women simply for being women is termed in Mexico, did not begin in 1993, nor, more broadly, did structural gender-based violence. Rooted in patriarchy, particularly the cultures of machismo[1] and *marianismo*, gendered violence has an enduring history in Mexico, one that dates to the imposition of Spanish cultural norms during the conquest (1519–21). Machismo and *marianismo* are two sides of the same coin: While the former exults the dominance of a strong masculinity celebrated in the public sphere, the latter emphasizes women's similarity to the accepted image of the Virgin Mary, chaste and relegated to the home.

This surge in feminicides in Mexico correlated directly with the passage of the North American Free Trade Agreement in 1994, which facilitated the establishment of factories called *maquiladoras* at the US-Mexico border, often in isolated industrial zones in the desert.[2] Maquiladoras were primarily staffed by young women with low levels of formal education; women who could be easily labelled as prostitutes. Indeed, according to Lozano (2019), women who work are often viewed at the same level as sex workers because they are seen to be selling their physical bodies to corporations. Because of this, "the virgin/whore dichotomy cannot be transcended – both subject positions lead to the inevitability of disposable capital" (59). Unsurprisingly then, the state mostly ignored the disappearances in Ciudad Juárez. And when the authorities eventually started paying attention, they used what today we would consider "slut-shaming" – victim-blaming gendered narratives – to pin these women's deaths on issues unrelated to gender-based violence, further stripping them of their dignity. In the view of the authorities, these women led "double lives"; they were perhaps prostitutes, active gang members, or involved in drug cartels. The victims' mothers were shamed for raising "bad daughters" who dared to leave the home to make a living. Women, both the dead and their surviving family members, were continually re-victimized.

To fight this perception and humanize the victims, activists "put them back" into traditional gender roles, constructs by which some sectors of Mexican society still abide. As Melissa Wright (2011) explains, political activists from Coordinadora de Organizaciones No Gubernamentales en Pro de la Mujer (Coalition of Non-Governmental Organizations for Women) successfully introduced the victims to the public as "daughters" rather than "factory workers":

> Activists flipped the sexist discourse of "public women" on its head by declaring that the victims were in public space for private reasons: they were augmenting their family income by working outside of the home. It was their duty. Therefore, the violence that threatened these "daughters" was a violence that threatened the very foundation of Mexican society: the patriarchal family that taught its daughters to put family obligations first, even if that meant working outside the home. (715)

In other words, activists were able to restore victims' worth by placing them back into the private sphere, where they belonged – at least according to more conservative sectors of society.

Their mothers, however, had to walk a reverse path, from the private sphere to the public one. By tapping into maternal and family activism, the Coordinadora altered public perceptions for the better and gained broader support for its various campaigns. Indeed, these women, whom Cynthia Bejarano (2002, 126) dubs "mother-activists," have successfully "transfer[ed] empowerment from the private sphere of citizenship reserved for mothers and housewives to the public sphere"; by deploying a range of protest tactics, they restored their daughters' dignity, all while challenging the authorities (Szymanek 2022, 61).

Across the state of Chihuahua, hundreds of citizens have coalesced around the issue of systemic gender-based violence since the 1990s. While too many of these crimes remain either unsolved or unpunished, the victims' mothers have continued searching for their daughters' killers, raising their voices in opposition to the authorities.[3] In the process, they were instrumental in the creation of one of the first concerted movements to combat gendered violence in Mexico. Under the slogan "Ni una más" (Not one woman more), they not only protested their daughters' killings to the municipal, state, and federal authorities, and attempted to restore their dignity,[4] but also spearheaded the creation of various women's collectives to lobby the government to search for the missing women and to give families and relatives a space to grieve. Much like Argentinean mothers did in the late 1970s and early 1980s, Mexican maternal activists turned their losses into action.[5] The mothers involved in the movement selected "dominant counterhegemonic strategies" to create a visual identity for their cause – namely, pink crosses, which they used both as memory production and protest (Lozano 2014, 69), and the victims' faces, either seen on *pesquisas* – missing person flyers – or in murals. By turning to smaller, more private initiatives to resist the government's narrative that the murders and disappearances never happened, these activists were able to memorialize their loved ones and make their absence visible in public space.

Since the 1990s, activism centred on gendered violence has grown from grassroots, physical organizations mostly led by mothers searching for their missing daughters, to the current decentralized online activism headed by feminist activists who seek equality for all. This women-led activism attests to the fact that when formal mechanisms fail – for instance, when the police do not investigate, or botch investigations, leading to few arrests, let alone convictions, or when the government refuses to acknowledge a social issue – grassroots collective organizations challenge government inaction and demand change. Even if activist groups have secured major legal gains – such as the inclusion of feminicide as a specific type of homicide in the penal code in 2003 – the root causes of gender-based violence are still not being addressed. Patriarchy, systemic sexism, and machismo still run rampant in Mexico. By now, every Mexican citizen has witnessed how the state fails victims and their families: Perpetrators are unlikely to be brought to justice; many crimes are not properly tallied as feminicides; or police lose or mishandle evidence (Lozano 2019, 24). This incompetence and the impunity it affords perpetrators have led many families to resort to small-scale demonstrations to challenge the government and make visible the loss of a loved one.

As Alice Driver (2015, 12) aptly points out, "families and victims [need to] regain authority over the narrative of their own lives … rebutting official rhetoric that tends to blame women for the violence they experience." Many families turn to artistic initiatives to regain their voice and to restore their loved one's dignity. Artistic depictions of victims of gender-based violence act as a double protest: On a micro level they challenge the authorities' inaction in the specific case of their loved one, and on a macro-level with respect to the broader crisis.

In "Women Empowering Women," I analyze the evolution of the portrayal of gender-based violence in activist Mexican printmaking from 2006 to 2021, drawing on a selection of posters and prints designed by three collectives: ASARO, MUGRE, and ARMARTE. The analysis of this corpus reveals a shift away from representations of feminicide through depictions of faceless women – either buried or dismembered – in the mid-2000s, and toward the portrayal of activist figures who directly address women, demanding that they, too, become part of the struggle against structural violence, starting around 2017 at the height of the #MiPrimerAcoso (My first assault) and #MeToo movements (Rivera-Garza 2016). This evolution from only showing the victims to depicting activists who push back against patriarchal norms parallels changing attitudes and social awareness around the question of gender-based violence in Mexico.

This evolution is also evident in how the artists choose to portray women – as either passive or active – and in terms of militancy – the slogans used and the calls for action. Whereas a male-dominated collective like ASARO designed prints depicting mostly dead, faceless, and nameless women in the mid-2000s, the female-only collectives MUGRE and ARMARTE currently display militant artworks in which women lead the fight to increase awareness of gendered violence and counter it on a smaller and more immediate scale. Most of the women on ASARO's prints appear dead and positioned as victims of a crime, in line with the ethos prevalent in Mexico during the mid-2000s, when the Special Commission on Feminicide contributed to bringing the urgency of the issue to the forefront of public attention. Mid-2000s culture and activism emphasized physical harm and violence often resulting in death, and the lack of government or official response. I read these prints as portraying women as lacking agency, as victims who quite literally "suffer" the violence enacted on them and do not talk back. In contrast, a close reading of MUGRE's and ARMARTE's works reveals a more nuanced understanding of violence against women. By exploring the notions of gender and feminicides, as well as the private/public dichotomy, in their artistic production, these female collectives re-appropriate the public space, a space where women feel threatened and from which they have been historically excluded as agents (Federici 2022, 65; see also Butler 2020; Ryan 2017).

I also identify a shift in the repertoires of contention – the symbols deployed and actualized – of the female-identified Mexican activists, who went from presenting victims of gender violence as "daughters" to presenting them as "one of us." Whereas in the 1990s and early 2000s many activists were mothers of victims, in the past decade or so a new generation of activists has emerged. And, by concentrating on the spectrum of gender-based violence rather than solely on feminicides, they emphasize that it could – and in fact often does – happen to most women on multiple occasions throughout their lifetime. As I mentioned in chapter 1 and 2, this repositioning is closely tied to the social movements that coalesced around the disappearance of the forty-three Ayotzinapa students in 2014.

The evolution of the representation of structural gendered violence in Mexican street art over recent decades is the result of four interconnected factors. By proposing a legal definition of feminicide in 2007, the

Ley General de Acceso de las Mujeres a una Vida Libre de Violencia (General Law on Women's Access to a Life Free of Violence) not only codified feminicide but also launched a reflection on structural violence by making it more visible, and thus public, in a society that historically deals with this type of contentious issue in private. Around the same time, more women street artists started joining historically masculine collectives. As mentioned in chapter 2, in the wake of the 2006 events in Oaxaca, collectives of artists started expanding the scope of their activism to include gender-based violence. Then, 2013 marked yet another turning point in Mexico, as the United Nations published a report that shed a negative light on the country (UN Women 2013). The mapping of gender-based violence from 1985 onward led nineteen of the thirty-one Mexican states to add feminicide as a special category in their penal codes. Although changes in mentality are hard to quantify, these progressive developments in Mexican legislation also brought about an affective change in street art production and women-led activism aimed specifically at women. Finally, two viral campaigns, #MiPrimerAcoso (My first assault) and #MeToo, gave more exposure to the national epidemic, ensuring that conversations around gendered violence would not end. Overall, these key moments contributed to creating greater awareness of the feminicide and structural violence crises.

This started a positive feedback loop: The initial mid-2000s artistic reactions to the rise of feminicides brought more awareness to the extent of the crisis, which in turn generated more artistic projects that kept expanding the scope of activism, thus attracting more and more interested participants. This suggests that this artistic and activist production serves three main purposes: First, it makes the issue of gender-based violence visible in the public space, a space that allows women to realize how prevalent their lived experience is; second, it pays homage and gives visibility to victims of gendered violence; and third, it makes room for the development and promotion of other types of broad social mobilization campaigns on issues that concern and affect women.

This third point is particularly relevant for the analysis of the work of the two female-only collectives, MUGRE and ARMARTE. Indeed, their artistic production seeks to empower Mexican women in pragmatic ways through workshops, lectures, and reading circles, and they engage with women and with victims' families and encourage them to denounce all experiences of gendered violence. By lending this constituency a political and an artistic voice, these artists are active in creating change. My analysis shows that these artivistic works "express outrage" (Naidus 2009, 5), but they also seek to force a new form of dialogue on Mexicans generally (Duncombe 2016, 121) by disrupting accepted narratives around women's responsibility for the violence they experience. Following on my discussion of Duncombe's theorization in chapter 1, I demonstrate that, through their artworks, ASARO, URT-Arte, ARMARTE, and MUGRe demand an "imminent cultural [and social] shift." In Mexico, the road to empowerment has been lengthy and rough, and the work of recognizing the active role women can and should play in all sectors of society is mirrored in artistic production. Indeed, the Mexican art world has historically been dominated by men creating artworks reflecting on situations that resonated with them. Moreover, as I will discuss, when issues affecting women are portrayed, it is often through a male gaze (Mulvey 1975), one that lacks the awareness afforded by a lived experience. And yet, while this shift may take time to materialize, the gains made since 1993 show that the wheels are in motion.

"Women Empowering Women" begins with a theoretical and historical overview. By examining the relationship between coloniality and gender, "Theorizing and Memorializing the Spanish American Matrix of Suffering" highlights the challenges of combatting epistemic injustices in Mexico. I then apply this theoretical framework to three case studies, brought together by the slogan "Autodefensa o fosa" (Self-defence or unmarked grave). I conclude by comparing the three case studies, and by reflecting on how each collective's work contributes to Mexican print artivism.

I have elected to frame the artistic analyses of works produced by ASARO (2006–), MUGRe (2014–), and ARMARTE (2018–) under the slogan "Autodefensa o fosa" for the way it embodies contemporary calls for action made by activist groups who target gender-based violence and encapsulates the evolution of its portrayal in Mexican posters and prints. "Autodefensa o fosa," which loosely translates to "self-defence or unmarked grave," is often reproduced on physical items – posters and prints, stickers and buttons – but also taken up as a hashtag on social media. It describes rather provocatively the two options seemingly available to Mexican women, who are disproportionately at risk of experiencing various forms of violence due to their gender. This violence exists on a continuum: from attitudes and beliefs often described as a "boys will be boys" mentality, like slut-shaming, body-shaming, gendered stereotypes, and rape culture, to the normalization of violence in behaviours like wolf whistles, catcalling, and street and online harassment, to physical expressions of violence like sexual assault, rape, or feminicides (the "pyramid of sexual violence" [It's Time Edmonton 2019]).

While it is true that gendered violence too often culminates in women's deaths, most women regularly experience milder forms of this specific type of violence, which is generally tolerated by society. And yet, this "boys will be boys" attitude puts the onus on women to both police themselves to prevent acts of aggression and to learn to defend themselves against them when they inevitably occur. By recognizing that most women will experience gendered violence at some point in their lives, "Autodefensa o fosa" is a call to empowerment, a rallying cry to change women's perspectives on these daily offensive and crude interactions. While women recognize that these behaviours ought to be condemned, they are often afraid to speak up, or believe it is useless to do so. An attempt at *autodefensa*, or learning to defend oneself, can also be a first foray into activism. The call for empowerment is, then, both present- and future-oriented (Duncombe 2016).

I also read the slogan as a warning: Women ought to develop reflexes to combat gender-based violence, or the consequences could be dire and even fatal. The slogan thus operates similarly to the pink crosses erected where a disappeared woman was last seen; it shows that failing to act could lead to the grave. The slogan takes it one step further by emphasizing that empowering women is essential in the fight against all forms of gender-based violence.

An approach that puts the responsibility fully on women's shoulders might appear dubious to most North American readers. Instead of teaching women how to defend themselves against harassment, should men not be taught not to harass and rape? Without a doubt. But teaching self-defence techniques – either verbal or physical – is a tried-and-true strategy of numerous groups seeking to empower women. There is no reason why both cannot be done, for as long as gender-based violence remains pervasive, women will need strategies to defuse conflicts.[6] While women continue to exist in a position of vulnerability, expanding their tool kits offers a means to "talk back" (Ryan 2017, 4).

My analysis shines a light on a novel artistic corpus that has never been studied as a whole. While many studies have investigated the representation of feminicides in fiction, either in novels or in movies (Driver 2015; Finnegan 2021; Lozano 2019; Szymanek 2022), the literature on its representation in the visual arts, let alone in street or urban art, is extremely limited. This could be explained by the fact that these groups, despite their constant production, are not well-known outside of Latin America. Bringing this corpus together thus contributes to developing a more nuanced understanding of how Mexican artists and activists tackle this subject. Studying ASARO, MUGRE, and ARMARTE under a single rubric also allows me to chart the evolution of the portrayal of women, from victims to active agents of change.

Realistically, a single protest will not put an end to patriarchy and machismo in Mexico; neither would a protest for every victim of feminicide, or a thousand. These two social constructs go back to the colonial period and are deeply rooted in Roman Catholicism, and thus deeply ingrained in the Mexican psyche. "Dismantling patriarchy" is a noble goal, but it will not happen in the foreseeable future. So why protest? This takes us back to the notion of "seeds" that I introduced in the preface. For the collectives, every viewer offers an opportunity to challenge systemic violence. Small changes at a local level might be more effective than the authorities' efforts – or lack thereof – to curb gender-based violence. As one might expect, the message the collectives convey in their art and their performances are quite different from the various government awareness campaigns. Although both are directed at women, they could not operate in a more divergent fashion. Unlike official campaigns, the collectives do not tell women to be careful, to dress appropriately, or to police themselves around men. On the contrary, they exhort women to fight back and implicitly warn men that they ought to cease some of their behaviours. Ultimately, posters that address women as potential agents of change, in order to embolden them to speak up about street harassment or domestic violence, plant seeds that prompt changes on a small scale, and arguably where it matters most: in women's daily lives. *Autodefensa* might spare them the *fosa*.

Before moving to an analysis of the collectives' production, it is necessary to take a closer look at the history of systemic gender-based violence in Mexico, as well as the various measures that have been adopted to mitigate it. As we will see, gender-based violence is a multi-faceted issue that is extremely difficult to tackle, even more so when those in power refuse to acknowledge its very existence, let alone its highly systemic nature and its pervasive socio-cultural ramifications.

Theorizing and Memorializing the Spanish American Matrix of Suffering

Since the reactivation of the concept of "femicide" (Russell 1976) and the coining of the neologism "feminicide" to account for the specificity of the situation in Mexico (Bejarano 2002; Lagarde 1997; Mónarrez Fragoso et al. 2019), there have been myriad theoretical debates around these terms and what they entail. Simply put, "femicide" and "feminicide" both "describe the mortal violence that is committed by men on women," as well as the "structural dimensions of violence." More importantly, these words describe a specific form of violence by avoiding "gender neutral terms like homicides … and crimes of passion" (Monárrez Fragoso et al. 2019, 913). A criticism levelled at both terms, and one that I seek to invalidate from the outset, is their supposed uselessness given that the crime of homicide – the murder of a human being – already exists and is sanctioned in penal codes around the world. The term "homicide" erases the gender of the victim, as well as the systemic violence that often leads to feminicide. It also undermines the fact that gender-based violence is a specific type of violence, one that must be clearly named in order to be acknowledged and remedied.

Despite slight differences in their meaning, the terms "femicide" and "feminicide" are sometimes used interchangeably, and coexist in activist circles, the media, and academia. And yet, they are fundamentally not equivalent terms. The main difference between them lies in the roles that societal and legal structures play in reacting to these crimes. Journalist, activist, and scholar Alice Driver, best known for her investigative work on the Ciudad Juárez murders, explains that "*femicide* refers more generally to gender-motivated violence, and *feminicide* has evolved to include an analysis of violence that results from … the power structures that create inequalities for women" (2015, 16). In Spanish America, these power structures are rooted in what María Lugones (2008, 75) calls the "coloniality of gender," the intersection of gender, class, race, and sexuality, embodied by patriarchy. Patriarchy, the "social arrangements that privilege males, where men as a group dominate women as a group, both structurally and ideologically – hierarchical arrangements that manifest in varieties across history and social space" (Hunnicut 2009, 557) – is one of the principal legacies of colonialism in Mexico. As Hunnicut explains, patriarchy permeates all sectors of society: "There are patriarchal systems at the macro level (bureaucracies, government, law, market, religion), and there are patriarchal relations at the micro level (interactions, families, organizations, patterned behavior between intimates)" (557). In Mexico, as in most countries, patriarchy is present in both the private and public spheres, both of which shape gendered violence. The term "feminicide" speaks to a broader scope of systemic power inequalities that lead to women being murdered, used as it is "to identify and codify specific types of violence against women in a country [Mexico] that has a long history of ignoring violence against women from a legal, institutional, and political perspective" (Driver 2015, 2).

It is this intersection of the coloniality of gender and gender-based violence that Monárrez Fragoso and colleagues (2019, 915) call a "matrix of suffering" specific to Mexico, where the authorities accept the "official effacement" (918) of women. This explains why the official and legal treatment of feminicide over the past thirty years has become a main target for activist groups. In essence, the inaction of governments in response to the high rates of violence against women rests on socio-historical roots that must be considered when analyzing gender-based violence.

Although it is important to understand the origins of this concept and its various layers of meaning, the objective of *Pasting Up Protest* is not to find the best term to describe the phenomenon of women being murdered due to their gender. I use *feminicidio*, translated as "feminicide," as it is the word used both in Mexico and by the artists whose works form my corpus. Were a group I study to use *femicidio*, I would use that term instead, as the selection of one word over another is a political decision, one that informs artistic action.

Despite the many debates around terminology, most theorists and scholars agree that, with or without the extra syllable, both terms refer to women being murdered for being women, often by men with whom they are in a relationship, either personal or professional, of unequal power. These discussions related to the conceptual nature of femicide and feminicide allow for a deeper understanding of the issue at hand, underscoring both the complex relationship most societies have with gender-based violence and the ever-increasing understanding of its root causes. These debates also highlight researchers' positionality and how they expect their societies to react to the murder of a woman for gendered reasons. This last point is of particular relevance in the exchanges between Russell and Lagarde, whose perspectives on the role that authorities and the justice system play in gender-based violence are diametrically opposed. Although gender-based violence is, sadly, universal, Lagarde argues that Spanish America's specific history shapes our understanding of the concept.[7]

In 1976, feminist and scholar-activist Diana Russell employed the word "femicide" to describe the murder of women due to their gender during her testimony at the International Tribunal on Crimes Against Women (Brussels, Belgium).[8] Since then, she has dedicated her career to expanding and refining her definition with new layers of complexity and specificity. In 1990, Russell and Jane Caputi defined femicide as "the murder of women by men motivated by hatred, contempt, pleasure, or a sense of ownership of women" (34), emphasizing a perpetrator's motives for killing.[9] Then, in 1992, Russell and Jill Radford defined it as "the misogynistic killing of women by men" (3) and emphasized that femicide is the end point of the sexual violence spectrum. Finally, in 2001, along with Roberta Harmes, Russell amended the definition to "the killing of females by males *because they are females*" (27; my emphasis), this time emphasizing male domination and unequal power structures in a relationship.[10] While Russell's groundbreaking work is of the utmost importance in bringing femicide to public attention, her definitions provide a Eurocentric view, whereby citizens and authorities are expected to acknowledge the issue and adopt remedial measures. She identifies the perpetrators as responsible for murder – which legally they are – but these definitions do not consider the authorities as a second perpetrator due to their systematic inaction, and the broader society as a third perpetrator due to apathy. In brief, for Russell, femicide is not necessarily a "state crime."

In Mexico, activist and anthropologist Marcela Lagarde y de los Ríos, along with scholars Julia Monárrez Fragoso and Cynthia Bejarano, have been at the forefront of activism against gender-based violence since the early 1990s.[11] Lagarde not only reworked Russell's definition of femicide to embed ingrained misogyny and machismo as root causes of female killings in Mexico; she expanded it to take into consideration the impunity with which these crimes are usually met across Latin America. Her definition of feminicide, put forward in 2003, thus considers systemic and institutionalized violence to which the authorities turn a blind eye. This expanded definition highlights the lack of state response, thus contributing to the mapping of power dynamics rooted in gender. The same definition was retained by the Special Commission on Feminicide, created by the Mexican Chamber of Deputies in 2003 to investigate the murders in Ciudad Juárez, and for which Lagarde acted as government representative and chair. She described feminicide as "a crime of the state which *tolerates the murders of women* and neither vigorously investigates the crimes nor holds the killers accountable … feminicide is when the state offers women no guarantees and creates no conditions of security for their lives in the community, at home, not even in work or recreational areas. Even worse, authorities do not even do their job efficiently" (quoted in Staudt 2008, 5).

Lagarde likened lack of official action in preventing or stopping feminicides to an acceptance of these murders as a fact of life, a normal occurrence, which in turn often leads to a denial of justice for victims and their families. This is especially true when victims are perceived to exist "outside the norm" of traditional gender roles. Lagarde's emphasis on the government's "tolerance" for feminicides highlights women's status as citizens who cannot expect protection from the state (Agamben 1998) and whose loss need not be grieved on a societal level (Butler 2016).

In her scholarship, Lagarde (2010) also stresses that feminicide "is constituted by the whole set of violent misogynist acts against women that involve a violation of their human rights, represent an attack on their safety, and endanger their lives" (xxiii). Lagarde's definition corresponds to a violence that is more systemic than specific, in which the state plays an active role through its deliberate inaction.[12] To recall, this helpful nuance is absent from Russell's definitions.[13]

Lagarde's activist definition of feminicide, and more specifically her focus on the systemic nature of the violence enacted on a group perceived as "less deserving" of security, resonates with Giorgio Agamben's theory of the *homo sacer* (1998), the sacred man,[14] and with his feminine counterpart, the *femina sacra* (Lentin 2006; Masters 2009; Ruxton 2017). Agamben's theory stipulates that, to those in power, politically or socially, some lives are intrinsically less valuable than others. Due to her gender and her intrinsic "impurity" (Lentin 2006), the *femina sacra* is treated with even less respect than the *homo sacer*. The *femina sacra* – "she who cannot be sacrificed but can be raped or killed with impunity" (Ruxton 2017, 450) – becomes an outcast and is punished for challenging the status quo, questioning "the dominant tropes and cultural norms" (451), and is often threatened with sexual violence (Masters 2009) when she refuses to conform to these norms. In Mexico specifically, the coloniality of gender also informs society's treatment of the *femina sacra*. Indeed, significant inequalities are inescapable in a system that hierarchizes the value of a life.

Whether someone's life is recognized or dismissed – either *homo sacer* or *femina sacra* – depends on social status, which also informs how they are treated in death. As Judith Butler explains in "Precarious Life, Grievable Life" (2016), though these victims "can be apprehended as 'living,' [their existence] is not always recognized as a life. In fact, a living figure *outside the norms of life* not only becomes the problem to be managed by normativity but seems to be that which normativity is bound to reproduce: it is living, but not a life" (8; my emphasis).

Concretely, in the case of Mexico, women who are perceived to be "rejecting traditional gender roles," often by working outside the home, live "outside the norms of life" (Butler 2016) established by their conservative society. They are stripped of their social and political lives, in that the authorities do not grant them any form of protection whatsoever; pre-existing biases rooted in the coloniality of gender, such as race and class, inform the value of each life.

Ultimately, the concepts of *homo sacer* and *femina sacra* imply that a person can be murdered with no reaction from authorities. The "sacredness" of life, or whether an individual is considered sacred enough that violence committed against them might elicit a reaction, is determined by societal and political views (Zebadúa-Yañez 2005). In Mexico, these views converge to illustrate that most often a woman's life is not considered sacred. The authorities do not see, or rather choose not to see, what is happening, which leads to political invisibility and the erosion of safety on several fronts.

As this overview of the evolution of the theories around femicide and feminicide shows, in Mexico the term "feminicide" is not purely descriptive; it also carries political weight and demands that there be an end to gender-based violence, and to an extent symbolizes empowerment, as it allows women to name a lived experience that often goes unrecognized. "Feminicide" draws attention to the crisis as a whole and creates a platform from which action can be demanded (Bueno-Hansen 2010), even if changes are slow in coming.

With this background in mind, in the next three sections, my analysis demonstrates the power art has to challenge society's apathy and its ingrained biases, as it invites viewers to feel compassion for the dead and their families, helps build solidarity, and encourages action against abuse. ASARO, MUGRE, and ARMARTE all draw from the repertoire of symbols created by early activism in Ciudad Juárez and perpetuate the various processes of memorialization and memory building put in place by the families of victims of feminicide starting in the 1990s, whether in concrete physical spaces or online. By forcing private issues into the public sphere, this early activism paved the way for the street artists I study.

I first examine prints by ASARO (2006–), then concentrate on MUGRE's (2014–) and ARMARTE's (2018–) wheat paste posters. Examining the works chronologically enables me to map an evolution in the representation of gender issues. Considering ASARO's prints first also allows me to draw a comparison between male-dominated and female-only groups.

In the section "ASARO's 'Muertas de Juárez,'" dedicated to ASARO, I analyze some early prints depicting gender-based violence before I focus on a selection of later prints (2016–18).

"#VivasNosQueremos" considers MUGRE's artworks, especially a fanzine created in 2014 with sixteen prints, as well as the collective's three #VivasNosQueremos campaigns (2015–20). The following section, "Making a Place," concentrates on ARMARTE's 2018 Día de Muertas mural on the facade of the Taller de Arte Comunitario in Oaxaca, and three #8M series of prints created for International Women's Day in 2019, 2020, and 2021. I conclude by comparing the three collectives' artistic production.

Rapidly evolving social and political circumstances, both in Mexico and in the Western world generally, as well as the fact that today most societies have a better understanding of the workings of gendered violence, allow both MUGRE's and ARMARTE's prints not only to present a continuum of gender-based violence – from street harassment to feminicides – but also to communicate with women directly by telling them that even those forms of gender violence historically deemed "more benign" matter and should be targeted and eradicated. This change in mindset evidently aligned with the ethos of the mid-2010s. By speaking to women directly, female collectives show that they can take matters into their own hands, whether by talking back or saying "No." Their prints show role models, examples to follow, and constitute calls to action for women to challenge forms of violence that affect them on a personal and intimate level. Essentially, whereas ASARO exposes the violence without giving women the means to end it, MUGRE and ARMARTE lobby for women to join in the struggle against the specific forms of violence they endure, and through their imagery, offer strategies and tactics for doing so.

The protest writings selected by each group align with these depictions. Indeed, while ASARO's are generally descriptive, proffering sympathy and standing in solidarity with the victims, their families, the state of Chihuahua, and Ciudad Juárez, both MUGRE's and ARMARTE's address their calls for action specifically to women who are still very much alive. Where male-dominated collectives portray *fosas*, female-led ones choose *autodefensa*.

Artistic Analyses: "Autodefensa o Fosa"

In this section, I analyze a selection of nine prints created by the Asamblea de Artistas Revolucionarios de Oaxaca between 2006 and 2016. I selected these specific prints because they explicitly call into question violence against women and feminicide. I also refer to other prints to complement my analysis and situate the selected corpus within ASARO's larger body of production. Using ASARO's works as a starting point to chart the evolution of representations of gender-based violence and feminicides in Mexican printmaking is only logical; ASARO is one of the longest-standing artist collectives in Oaxaca, and one of the first to confront gender-based violence. For the purpose of my analysis, I have divided ASARO's prints into three broad categories: prints portraying men, either ridiculing or elevating them; prints where men and women are cooperating and fighting alongside one another; and prints where a woman is the protagonist.

Many of ASARO's prints only depict men. Only a few portray women or issues specifically pertaining to women, and when women appear, they often stand with men together against the state, mirroring what happened during the Oaxaca rising (or Comuna de Oaxaca) in 2006. This mode of representation aligns with the collective's political views and internal history. It represents how members understand the struggle to gain dignity and respect from the Mexican authorities. For them, this struggle is shaped by ethnic background and social class, rather than by gender.

For Schadl and Graham de la Rosa (2014), two of the first scholars to study ASARO, starting in 2007, "Depictions memorializing assertive women in public protest document female participation in social movements while also challenging normative discursive structures equating … women with limited visibility and power" (62). Representing women as leaders, such as in the prints *Resiste* (Resist, 2010) and *Libertarias* (Libertarians, 2010), and plastering them in the public domain, implicitly and explicitly "situates women front and center in the rebellion" and ensures that their participation is recognized by the public (62). Theoretically, it also encourages more women to join collectives and/or to participate in other social movements, as they see themselves playing an active part in the fight – as they have always had done, to be sure, only history has erased them. Indeed, whether we think back to the Revolutionary Law of Women of 1994, to the Dirty War (1960s–80s), to the Adelitas during the Mexican Revolution (1910–20), or to the Indigenous women who helped deceive Hernán Cortés in Cholula in 1519, women and the roles they have played are neither named nor sufficiently remembered because they were not considered important.

ASARO's "Muertas de Juárez"

Since their beginning, ASARO has challenged the historical and artistic erasure of women. As mentioned, Francisco Toledo was the first to exhibit ASARO's work in Oaxaca, and unlike many other collectives, ASARO has enjoyed a wide circulation of its work outside Mexico, primarily in the United States.[15] Schadl and Graham de la Rosa (2014) have been instrumental in the dissemination of the collective's prints. In their exhibit *Getting Up Pa'l Pueblo: Tagging* ASAR*-Oaxaca Prints and Stencils* (2014), they dedicated one section – the very last one – to ASARO's portrayal of women, writing that "ASARO's works often depict articulate, powerful and socially effective female subjects, actively advocating for themselves and their communities. Whether the topic is political (the failed promises of the revolution); economic (disputing the benefits of globalization in agriculture and oil extraction); social (education and mass media); or a combination of these three, women appear front and center." The importance of portraying women cannot be overstated. However, even when depicted as agents of change, women are always fighting for a greater purpose, for a change that would benefit every member of society. These depictions fail to take into consideration the fact that, even within marginalized groups, individuals can face discrimination due to race, gender, or sexual orientation.

Strong women standing up for themselves have been a staple of ASARO's production since the Oaxaca uprising in 2006. The block print entitled *Cuando una mujer avanza … no hay hombre que la detenga* (When a woman steps forward … no man stops her, shown in plate 19) is one such example, a variation of the popular APPO phrase, "¡Cuando una mujer se avanza no hay hombre que retroceda!" (When a woman steps forward, no man backs down), itself taken from the EZLN's "Cuando una mujer avanza, no hay hombre que retrocede" (When a woman steps forward, no man loses/goes back) (Gahman 2016; Samarrilleres, n.d.). The title of the work highlights the equality of men and women in the revolutionary fight, showing that women are daring to take steps toward change. Women do not want to be spared the fight – they will participate just like men, and as their equals. A close examination of the verb mood of the dependent clause provides illuminating readings. In Spanish, the indicative is used for factual statements and verifiable actions, and the subjunctive for wishes, desires, or actions that have yet to be completed. By featuring the indicative, "Cuando una mujer avanza, no hay hombre que retrocede" states a fact: that when women gain more power, no one loses. It puts women and men on the same level, furthering the idea that notions of machismo and strict gender roles ought to be condemned. By contrast, the subjunctive in "Cuando una mujer avanza … no hay hombre que la detenga" centres the woman's role in pushing forward in spite of challenge. The struggle is far from over, but women will not be stopped.

The print shows a woman from the back, pushing against a man's combat boot, which is about to crush her. The boot symbolizes the fight of the people against the military as it tried to take back Oaxaca in 2006. Like most of ASARO's prints, it is black and white, but in this particular case, this choice also affects the light and the shade, providing a metaphor of light and darkness. The woman stands in the light, pushing back against the darkness and the shadows with which the boot is attempting to trample her. If she were to let go, she would be crushed under the boot, and the whole print would turn black. To the initiated viewer, the man's boot symbolizes male domination writ large; the message conveyed by the print is not necessarily specific to Mexico. The woman is strong enough to push back, emphasizing that women are not only active members of society but an important part of the revolution. They have agency and are agents of resistance.

The print ALTO *a la violencia contra las mujeres* (STOP violence against women) (see plate 20), from 2010, depicts a young woman shouting.[16] It is one of very few prints to tackle the subject of violence against women without emphasizing feminicides. In 2018 and 2019, it was used as a stamp in Oaxaca's Pasaporte Gráfico (Graphic Passport), a tour of twelve artistic workshops in the city.[17] In the case of collectives with a political vocation, like ASARO, the Pasaporte Gráfico opens a valuable window of political opportunity; they benefit from additional access to an uninitiated audience. This initiative gave *ALTO* a lot of exposure and put ASARO's stance on gender-based violence front and centre among the issues they are known to combat, at least for visitors to Oaxaca.

Now that the depiction of women in ASARO's body of work has been briefly highlighted, we can turn our attention to the prints specifically dealing with the topic of feminicide. All the prints discussed below have one element in common: they portray gender-based violence's final form – feminicide. Even if many violent events generally precede a woman's death, these earlier occurrences rarely appear in ASARO's prints. The vast majority of the women portrayed are nameless and faceless, which I read as ASARO's chosen strategy to universalize the issue: Any woman could fall victim to gender-based violence. However, when compared to other women depicted in ASARO's corpus, these women-victims appear to lack agency. ASARO shows them as victims who have lost the fight. Bluntly put, ASARO focuses on dead women, and through its protest writings tells viewers that it is up to them to fight against the state to restore the dignity of these women-victims. The victims themselves do not wield any power over their fate. While the namelessness and facelessness of the women emphasize the universality of the crime, the images fail to recognize the individuality and uniqueness of each woman – a strategy that has been employed since 1993.

This depiction underscores a grim dichotomy in ASARO's body of work, in which women are assigned two starkly opposing roles: They are either alive as leaders in their communities, or dead as victims to memorialize, whose dignity and worth must be restored by a third party. While there is no middle ground between life and death, the women in ASARO's corpus are either dead and passive or alive and actively against capitalism and neoliberalism. No one appears leading the fight against gender-based violence. Another problematic aspect of these prints is the fact that, while they tackle feminicides, they do so as an issue intertwined with others, whether immigration, militarization, or the inaction of the Mexican authorities. This view aligns with ASARO's bigger purpose, but raises a fundamental question: Why can it not be only about women?

The topic of feminicides and the disappearance of women is easily identifiable in *Denunciar la complicidad del gobierno de México* (Denouncing the complicity of the Mexican government, 2006) (figure 3.1). The print shows a body that appears to have been buried hurriedly in a shallow grave, or dumped, allowing wild animals to devour the remains. It is divided into three sections. At the top, a wild animal, either a wolf or a coyote, appears to be dragging the remains of a woman's body by a piece of cloth, perhaps used to wrap the body for burial, or a piece of clothing. If it is an item of clothing, the animal is re-victimizing the woman by undressing her in death. In the middle section we read "Denunciar la complicidad del gobierno de México." The title reveals that, while the print portrays a murdered woman, it is framed through ASARO's overarching denunciation of government corruption and complicity in these events. It highlights that the government is ignoring the systemic violence against women that ultimately caused the death of this woman. This notion of *complicidad* aligns with Lagarde's findings in the 2006 commission report, which conclude that government inaction is responsible for this systemic violence.

The middle section of the print occupies the most space. I read this pitch-black burial ground as symbolizing the unknown number of missing and murdered women across the country. It is a dark pit with space for more bodies. The pitch-black colour also references the fact that families are often left in the dark about the fates of their loved ones. Indeed, as of June 2022, there were at least 100,000 missing people in Mexico (*Economist* 2022), of which 25 per cent are women and girls (Suarez-Enríquez 2018).

While the print exposes the responsibility of the authorities for knowingly allowing feminicides to continue without consequences, the presence of the canine figure expands the scope of this culpability. The canine is a subtle allusion to immigration to the United States, and how so many of these trips end in tragedy for the migrants involved, given the number of Central Americans and Mexicans who travel north hoping to find better living conditions. When analyzed as a coyote rather than

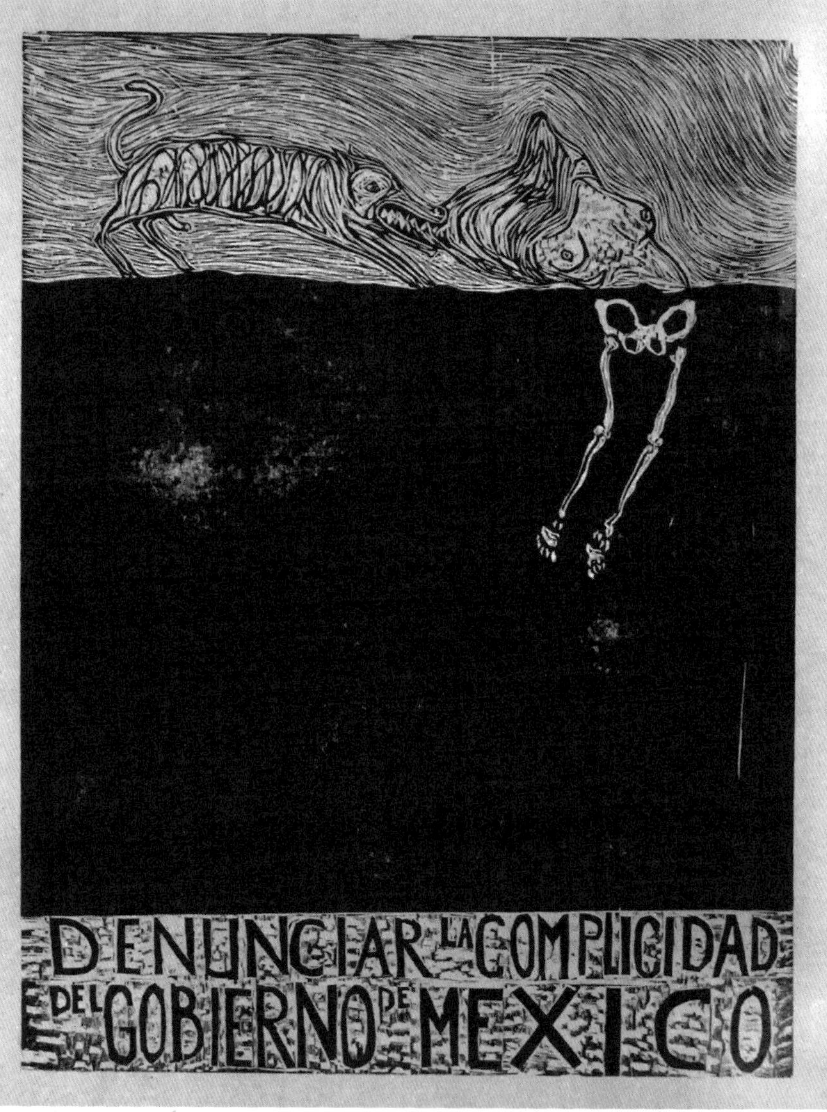

Figure 3.1
"Denunciar la complicidad del gobierno de México" (Denouncing the complicity of the Mexican government).

a wolf or a dog, the wild animal alludes to people smuggling across the Mexico–United States border, since smugglers are nicknamed "coyotes." Thematically, feminicides and migration intersect, and weaving the themes together highlights that most dead migrants – both men and women – generally fade into oblivion. Many studies have demonstrated how quickly "the desert eats away the dead" (De León 2015), and quite literally makes the problem disappear. This reinforces the notion of intersectionality and increased vulnerability at play in many feminicides, as socio-economic vulnerability, sometimes reinforced by illegal migratory status, makes individuals more susceptible to violence.

Buried Woman with Outstretched Hands Above the Ground (see plate 21) focuses on the hands of an unknown female figure reaching up toward a starry sky. Two delicate hands are reaching out and up from the ground to grasp *papel picado* – a staple of the Day of the Dead festival, a Mexican and Central American commemoration held from 31 October to 2 November that honours the dead, which ASARO also mobilized during the Día de la indignación in 2015. The two banners are made of *papel picado*: On the lower one, three angels appear, and on the upper one, we can see two eyes on either side of the face of a woman, whose eyes are closed. The viewer can infer that the open eyes in the centre on the *papel picado* belong to the buried woman. The eyes stare straight out at the viewer. This frontal gaze is disconcerting, as there seems to be a disconnect between the eyes and the face of the dead woman; the open eyes call on the viewer to bear witness to her tragic fate. I read *Buried Woman with Outstretched Hands Above the Ground* as honouring the disappeared and acknowledging that they are still part of the social fabric. The print also emphasizes the need to give the disappeared a face again, thus restoring their dignity.

Just like *Denunciar la complicidad del gobierno de México* (figure 3.1), this print can be read as a comment on immigration, crossing the desert to reach the United States border, and the violence many migrants experience in the process. The two saguaro cacti in the background further reinforce that this print might be set close to the border, as the saguaro is native to Arizona (United States) and Sonora (Mexico). Unlike the image shown in plate 22, though, which is explicitly graphic and violent, the violence illustrated in *Buried Woman with Outstretched Hands Above the Ground* is more subtle. Much as the open and closed eyes create discomfort in the viewer, there is a dissonance between the background – a dark sky with shooting stars, universal symbols of hope – and the foreground of the print with the dead woman. The Medusa effect – in this case, making eye contact with the person on the print – is disrupted; rather than mesmerized, the viewer is uncomfortable.

In *Getting Up for the People*, Schadl and Graham de la Rosa (2014) concentrate their analysis on the figure's outstretched hands. They argue that "this action [of reaching toward the sky] is further intensified by the eyes framing the face and staring forward ... As the woman raises herself out of the earth, the eyes crafted in the paper and propelled by the breeze invite the spectator to get up ... and help pull this figure out of her unmarked grave" (92). They read the print as an invitation to help this particular woman extract herself from her burial ground. That is to say, the woman has agency in that she wishes to escape the grave and make her passing known, perhaps offering some closure to her loved ones. The viewer is invited to complete the cycle of artivism and act upon the call. However, unlike other prints I analyze below, this invitation is not explicit; the print does not contain any protest writings and does not directly address the viewer.

Instead, the two prints examined above (plates 21 and 22) link the issue of feminicide to another major and long-standing issue, that of immigration. Tying these two societal problems together perpetuates the notion, prevalent in the 2000s, that feminicides were either random acts of violence and/or caused by migration, and not necessarily a systemic form of violence. The repeated image of the desert alludes to remoteness and isolation, hinting that feminicides are committed far away from the viewer, away from home. The desert is not life sustaining, but instead an infertile environment, which underscores the consequences of feminicides. The prints I discuss next, by contrast, show that this violence happens in very specific locations in Mexico.

I consider the next five prints together as they all depict a different aspect of feminicides: *Dignidad ni una más* (figure 3.2) reveals women's resiliency and strength, while *Ni una muerta más en la ciudad frontera* (figure 3.3), *No a la violencia. Ni una más* (plate 22), *Two Nudes Surrounded by Crosses and Barbed Wire* (figure 3.4), and *Mi cuerpo ha desaparecido* (figure

3.5) all illustrate both memorialization and the destruction of womanhood. Additionally, unlike in *Denunciar la complicidad del gobierno de México* (figure 3.1) and *Buried Woman with Outstretched Hands Above the Ground* (plate 21), in these five prints, the issue of feminicide does not intersect with any other social issue.

In *Dignidad ni una más* (Dignity, not one woman more) (figure 3.2), an older female figure – perhaps a "mother-activist" (Bejarano 2002) – looks straight out at the viewer with a stern face.[18] In this work, dignity is synonymous with strength. Numerous black-and-white crosses surround the woman, some superimposed on her clothing. The words "Ciudad Juárez" and "Oaxaca" also appear on her clothing, linking the two state capitals. This is a small acknowledgment that feminicide is a national issue. On the figure, the crosses under the word "ni" are shaped like rifles, a not-so-subtle hint at the militarization of Ciudad Juárez under President Felipe Calderón (2006–12). In 2006, Calderón launched a war against drug trafficking in Mexico and dispatched thousands of military personnel to border states like Chihuahua and Sonora. According to Lozano (2019), during this period an increase in feminicides was directly linked to the militarization of the state for three main reasons. First, the violence incited many to flee by attempting to cross the northern border, described by Gloria Anzaldúa as a "1,950 mile long open wound," a "thin edge of barbed wire," and even more figuratively as "*una herida abierta* where the Third World grates against the first and bleeds" (1987, 25). Second, external investigations into feminicides were halted, as outsiders could not enter Ciudad Juárez since it was deemed too dangerous. This in turn led to a rise in the number of feminicides. Finally, the military focused on eradicating petty crime rather than high-level drug trafficking or organized crime. This militarization turned into an attack on the socially underprivileged, women, and immigrant workers. Many were executed, raped, and tortured by the military, which proceeded to blame their crimes on gangs (Lozano 2019). In short, the militarization of the state created a rise in the numbers of feminicides, all the while making them invisible in the sea of deaths. Most of these women were young and worked outside the home, leaving their families – portrayed in the form of an older woman in the ASARO print – to mourn them.

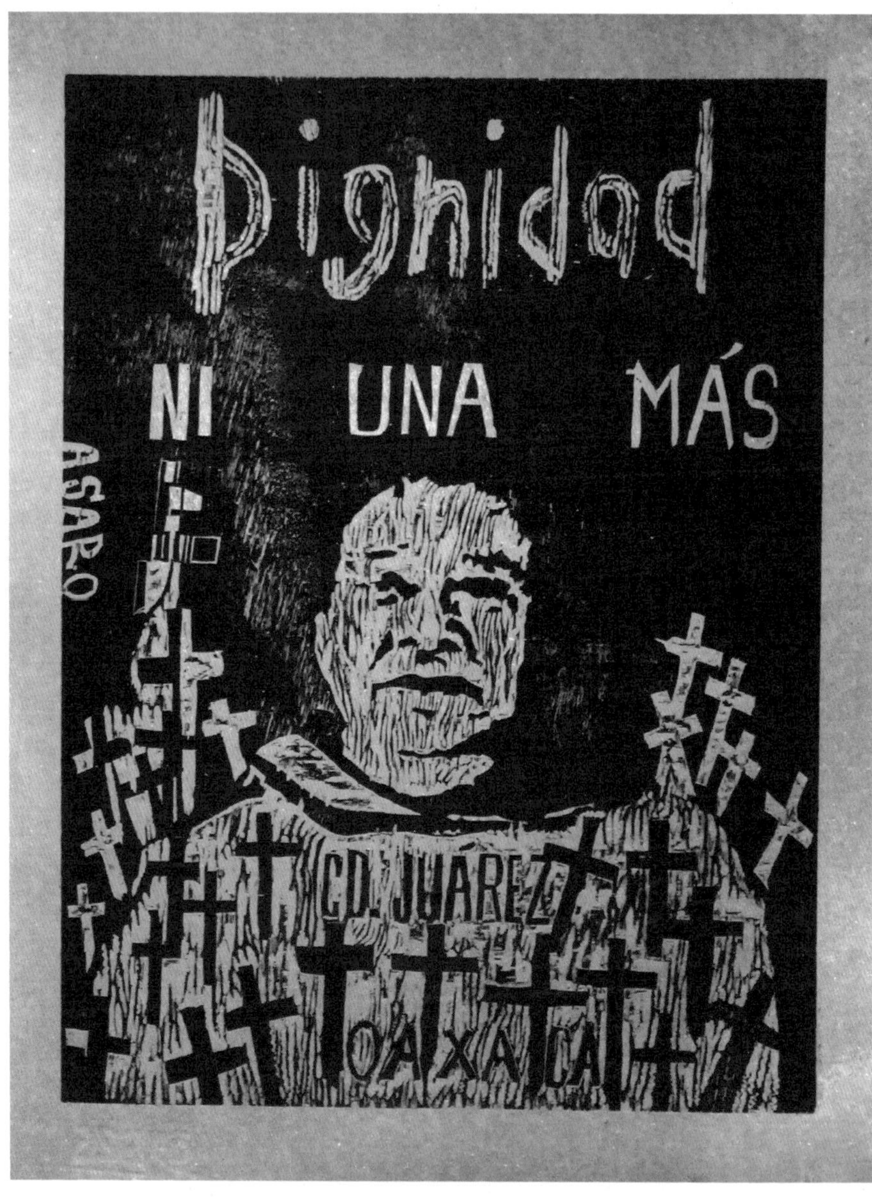

Figure 3.2
"Dignidad ni una más" (Dignity, not one woman more).

With its many crosses, this print also portrays the first form of memorializing the Juárez murders. "Memorials and memory projects in public space" (Driver 2015, 25), such as a pink cross marking the site where a woman disappeared or her remains were found, or posters with her face plastered on walls, are ways families' and activists' voices continue to echo in the public space. They play a dual role by both memorializing victims and warning potential new victims. Indeed, these visual markers serve as memory sites, but they also "create a system of visual symbols that seek to remind women of the danger they face in public spaces" (Driver 2015, 11) – a way to remind women that it could be their names on the crosses, or their faces posted on the walls. These informal sites of memory create a visual representation of the violence that was experienced at those very spots by drawing attention to the issue of feminicide.[19] Orozco-Mendoza (2017) refers to this phenomenon as the "funeralization of the city," a "peculiar repertoire of protest that operates through the public display of memorial objects, like pink crosses, monuments, graffiti, victims' photographs, and others, [and] extends the activists' struggle to make feminicide visible amid widespread attempts to conceal it" (351). Much like the wheat paste posters in Ayotzinapa, by "nam[ing], resist[ing], and redress[ing] violence," the pink crosses and visual depictions of victims serve as transephemeral objects whose voices keep echoing long after a demonstration is over. Contemporary artists continue to draw on this original repertoire of symbols, actualizing and remixing it, but still with the same intent of "build[ing] democracy from below" (352).

The next print, *Ni una muerta más en la ciudad frontera* (Never again another dead woman in the border city) (figure 3.3), is a triptych. Its three distinct scenes form a complete story presented from left to right: On the left, the face of a woman in pain appears to be clutched by a hand that is reaching in from outside the frame; in the middle, a hooded woman kneels over and holds another woman; and on the right, three white crosses, seemingly erected in the desert, appear to be caught in the headlights of a car. Both the slogans "Ni una (muerta) más" and "la ciudad frontera" clearly reference Ciudad Juárez. Indeed, as I mentioned earlier, "Ni una más" was first used there.

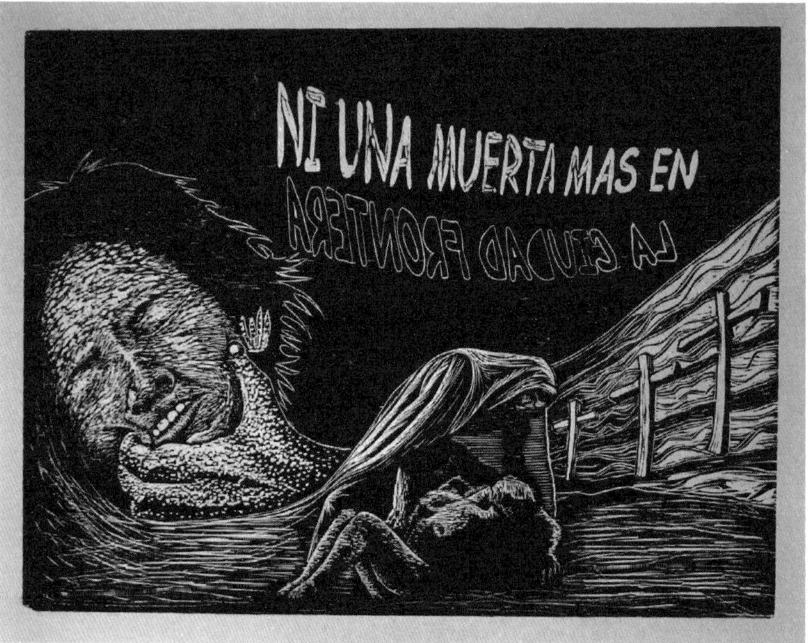

Figure 3.3
"Ni una muerta más en la ciudad frontera" (Not one more dead woman in the border city).

Tellingly, *Ni una muerta más en la ciudad frontera* is the only print in my corpus that depicts gender-based violence as a cycle, as each scene depicts a different step along the continuum. First, the woman is assaulted, then she is killed and laid to rest by a *Pietà*-like figure (Bénaud and Schadl 2013), and then her life is memorialized by the erection of a cross. It is not clear if the hooded figure laying the woman to rest represents a Madonna-like figure or death itself. Either way, the hooded figure is not menacing and appears to be handling the woman with great care.

Each cross stands for a single victim of feminicide and represents the memorialization process that takes place after each and every woman goes missing. The pink crosses also counter the lack of government statistics, the flaws in the justice system, and the false media reports. While nothing can replace reliable statistics, these informal sites of memory effectively create a visual representation of the violence that transpired on

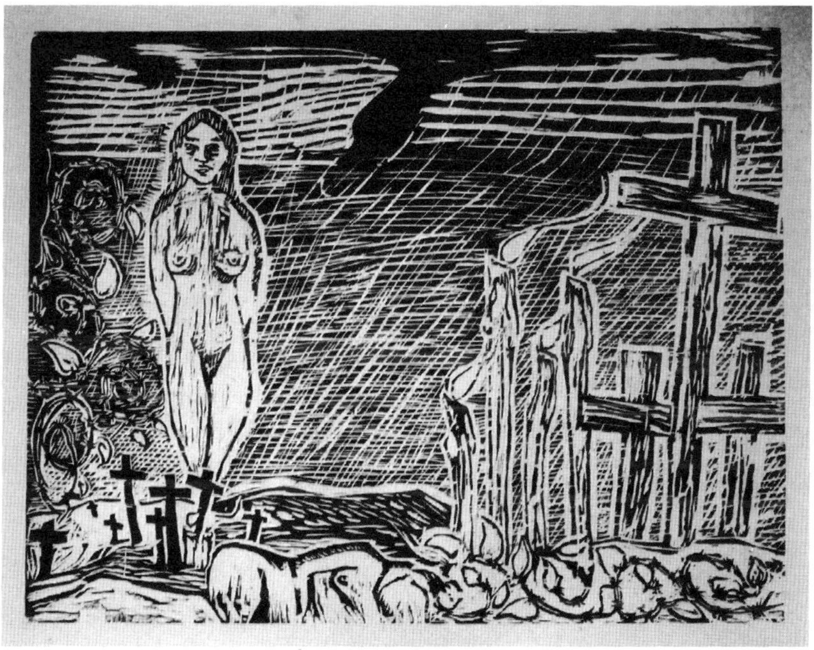

Figure 3.4
Print showing two naked women surrounded by crosses and barbed wire.

these very spots and draw attention to the issues of feminicide and violence. The public space is thus permeated with reminders of gender-based violence. Using crosses on prints, where they serve a symbolic function rather than as site-specific grave markers, reinforces the notion of warning and universality; feminicidal violence could affect anyone. There are no safe spaces anywhere.

Much like *Ni una muerta más en la ciudad frontera, Two Nudes Surrounded by Crosses and Barbed Wire* (figure 3.4) depicts a desert scene: Two naked women, one standing and one lying down, are seen in a barren field of crosses, with candles and flowers shaped like barbed wire surrounding them. The flames of the candles have the same shape as the leaves on the stems of the flowers. The wavering flames represent women's lives – one gust of wind and they are extinguished. Bénaud and Schadl (2013) read the women's nakedness as reminders of "female vulnerability, especially within the harsh physical environment" (29). This analysis stands in stark contrast to Schadl's earlier views on the representation of strong women (Schadl and Graham de la Rosa 2014).

Another print that draws on flowers is *No a la violencia. Ni una más* (plate 22). Unlike *Dignidad* (figure 3.2) and *Ni una muerta más en la ciudad frontera* (figure 3.3), which openly refer to Ciudad Juárez or Oaxaca, this image does not mention a specific location. Much like *Ni una muerta más en la ciudad frontera*, it presents a complex visual narrative that can be deciphered from left to right. On the far left, a woman with long, flowing hair is seen cradling herself, with her head on her knees. She is sitting in the middle of a field of crosses; their number highlights the appallingly high number of missing and disappeared women. Next to some crosses, burning candles emphasize both the mourning aspect and the remembrance nature of cross memorials.

The woman's long black hair floats into the sky, with flowers growing out of it. This whole section of the image evokes a woman's reproductive system. The branches in the shape of Fallopian tubes bear the text "Ni una más, no a la violencia, no más violencia, ni una más" (Not one woman more, no to violence, no more violence, not one woman more). The flowers themselves, blooming at the very tip of the branches that carry the poem, are shaped like vulvas that turn into carnivorous flowers, perhaps a subtle hint that women are building momentum to fight back.

On the right side of the print, another woman is pierced by one of the crosses, as if impaled on it, and two branches hold up her arms. It looks as though she has been crucified, with the rays of a halo over her head. The concentric circles over her midsection resemble a bull's eye, indicating that women are targets. In fact, the bull's eye or target imagery is a recurring theme in artistic production tackling gender-based violence and will be further explored when I examine ARMARTE's wheat paste posters. Finally, five women of different origins line up along the frame on the right. I read this both as an indication that no one is immune to violence and that intersectionality increases the risk of experiencing gendered violence.

Mi cuerpo ha desaparecido (figure 3.5), which depicts a naked woman lying on her back with her legs spread wide, shaped like the letter *m*, is reminiscent of Frida Kahlo's painting *My Birth* (1932). Unlike in other

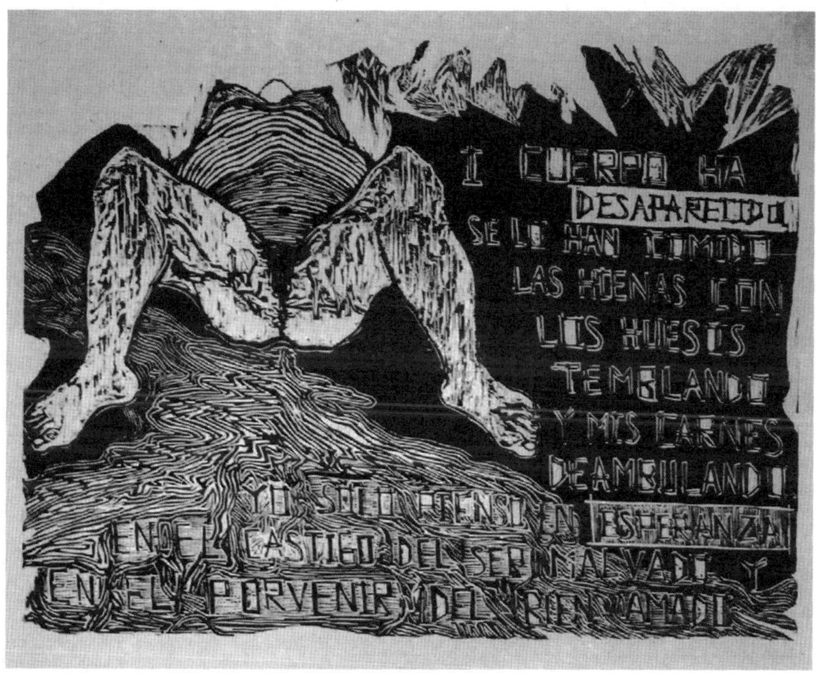

Figure 3.5
"Mi cuerpo ha desaparecido" (My body has disappeared).

prints by ASARO, the woman's head is turned away from the viewer. She lies in a position that is associated more with giving birth than with death, but her posture also alludes to sexual assault. A poem flows out of her body like a river of blood: "Mi cuerpo ha desaparecido. Se lo han comido las hienas con los huesos temblando y mis carnes deambulando. Yo solo pienso en esperanza en el castigo del ser malvado y en el porvenir del bien amado." (My body has disappeared. The hyenas ate it with my bones trembling and my flesh unravelling. I only think in hope of the punishment of the evil being and in the future of the beloved one.) The poem hints at revenge and at the possibility that her death will prompt a loved one to advocate against gender-based violence.

Taken together, these five prints paint a grim portrait of the situation of women in the mid-2000s; they show victims and family members who were left behind, and do not present any strong calls to action. They make the violence visible, but do not challenge its root causes. A wheat paste poster from 2018 (see plate 23), which I call *Women Making Headlines*, shows women reduced to fresh meat for the press. The print depicts a conveyor belt on which a series of three heads rest; a fourth is seen being processed through what looks like a meat grinder. The others follow as they move along the conveyor belt. The first head then exits, ground into newspaper headlines that read, from bottom to top, "Prensa," "Violencia," "Muerte," and "Nota roja." *Nota roja* (red note) journalism is a type of yellow journalism popular in Mexico that focuses on stories involving crime and gratuitous physical violence. *Nota roja* journalism is akin to slut-shaming, often uses gory images, and targets the lower echelons of society. Ultimately, ASARO's print comments on the treatment these women suffer at the hands of the press.

A few pages of the newspaper fly around: One features a quotation from Colombian author Gabriel García Márquez's 1996 speech to the General Assembly of the Sociedad Interamericana de Prensa (Inter American Press Association): "El periodismo es una pasión insaciable que solo puede digerirse y humanizarse por su confrontación descarnada con la realidad" (Journalism is an insatiable passion that can only be digested and humanized by its stark/crude confrontation with reality) (García Márquez 2007). This quotation presents some irony. What García Márquez means is that journalists are hungry for the truth and must be the voice of the people on whom they report. While *notas rojas* depict the crude reality he alludes to, they fail to humanize the constant appetite for stories on these gory crimes.

There is a second underlying layer of irony, this one involving the double meaning of the word *descarnada*, which can mean either "crude" or "flayed" (*des-carnar*, to remove the flesh, to skin). *Descarnada* refers to the treatment these women receive from the newspapers, where their every move is tracked and any deviation from the social norm becomes a cause for shaming. In *notas rojas*, women are still reduced to mere body parts and are still nameless.

One striking example of *notas rojas* is the media treatment of Ingrid Escamilla, a twenty-five-year-old woman who was murdered in Mexico City on Valentine's Day 2020. Her death provoked a national uproar, as crime scene photos of her dismembered body were leaked to the media. Some newspapers even printed them on their front page. The publication of the pictures acted as a second dehumanization, after the murder itself. Escamilla was reduced to meat for the press to devour, in both traditional and digital media. Online, her name became a trending hashtag. To prevent voyeurs from gorging on the pictures, activists started to post images of flowers, puppies, and seashores tagged with #IngridEscamilla. Instead of finding the gory images, searches of her name pulled up peaceful images. By tricking the algorithms, activists re-semanticized her in an attempt to restore her dignity.

Reflecting on "Muertas de Juárez"

ASARO has always represented women, but primarily in conjunction with other issues, such as their involvement in attempts to take down the military in 2006 (*Oaxaca libre, Zapata vive*, 2006), making these past- rather than future-oriented interventions. This raises a question: Was ASARO unable to conceptualize a future in which women lead the charge against feminicides? I do not believe this to be the case, since, as a reminder, in 2006 women were leaders of many protests, and ASARO's repertoire of historical figures contains many women fighters. In short, the collective only designs prints about women's lived experience of gender-based violence, but not about what society needs or would like to see – namely, the *pueblo* rising up against feminicides.

Since I first came to this research through ASARO's stencils and prints, identifying areas of weakness in their production poses some affective challenges for me. While it is true that the collective showcases feminicides in their production – with some major oversights – in a country like Mexico, where sectors of society still argue over the validity of even having a word to describe these murders, it must be acknowledged that, with these prints, ASARO is tackling the issue of feminicide, albeit imperfectly. The choice to depict the extreme end of the gendered violence continuum also aligns with the ethos of the 2000s.

That being said, their production related to feminicide reveals some areas of weakness. First, most of the prints analyzed in this section lack a concrete call to action. ASARO's message is generally clear, catchy, and concise, sometimes even constituting a call to take up arms, such as with *¡Pueblo! Defiende tu petróleo*. By contrast, most prints analyzed here do not contain what might be considered protest writing, and when they do it is a relatively tame, descriptive form of protest. Not a single one speaks to the *pueblo* directly, incites it to revolt, or to demand change. Although there is an acknowledgment of the phenomenon of feminicide, there is no compelling desire to tackle it.

I read the lack of agency of the women depicted in ASARO's early representation of feminicides as a metaphor for the way women from certain underprivileged sectors were often treated in Mexico in the 2000s: either as forgotten or objectified as body parts. Most of the women depicted in the prints are dead, positioned as victims, albeit stoic ones, their faces without expression. Their eyes look straight out at the viewer, but there is no cry for help; they seem to have accepted their fate. Missing from this selection of prints are women taking matters into their own hands or starting a revolution to help their sisters. This is in stark contrast to prints such as *Guerreras oaxaqueñas*, *Caserolas*, or *Libertarias*, where women lead the charge. The lack of representation of strong women is itself a critical comment on the social and political situation in the first decade of the 2000s, where people were not yet as militant about feminicides. But considering ASARO's stance on most other issues, this lack of militancy is surprising.

Moreover, the very manner in which most of the women are represented perpetuates harmful stereotypes. Except for the older woman portrayed in *Dignidad* (figure 3.2), all the women shown are young, in different stages of undress, and dead. Some of them are even dismembered or missing body parts, further reinforcing the very violence these prints are ostensibly denouncing. I say "ostensibly" because, as I claimed above, the prints do not have much of a denunciatory tone. They show feminicides, but it is left to the viewer to infer their militancy.

Another problematic aspect of ASARO's prints is that most focus only on the extreme end of the continuum of gender-based violence: death. Only *Ni una muerta más en la ciudad frontera* (figure 3.3) shows what I analyze as intimate-partner violence. There is no further recognition that feminicide constitutes only one of many forms of violence against women, albeit the ultimate one. Before they died, these "Muertas de

Juárez" endured significant violence, sometimes even torture, and that should also be pointed out.

Finally, the collective barely mentions that feminicide is not limited to the state of Chihuahua and Ciudad Juárez. Indeed, the civil society organization Consorcio Oaxaca indicates in its 2008–09 report that 594 women were murdered between 1999 and 2009 in the state of Oaxaca alone (Consorcio Oaxaca 2009, 15). Whether the collective was deliberately ignoring the crimes in their home state or not, it remains a lost opportunity to expand the conversation and the scope of their militancy. Is it too sensitive to point out that feminicide does not only happen in the remoteness of the US-Mexico border region?

Ultimately, compared to MUGRE, the female-led collective studied in the next section, ASARO mostly concentrates on the darker end of the gender violence spectrum – women's deaths – and oddly enough, their production has a less activist tone than that of their female counterparts. While they do represent and denounce feminicide, they do not call directly on the *pueblo* to take matters into their own hands and spearhead change. In recent years, there has been increased recognition that machismo and patriarchy also affect men negatively (Nuñez et al. 2015). If ASARO were to tackle gender-based violence today, there would be a way to present it as a battle that both women and men lead together.

MuGRe: Letting the Art Speak for Itself

Mujeres Grabando Resistencias is composed of about twenty women who work together in Mexico City with the primary objective of creating work that promotes social justice and sheds light on the experiences of women in public spaces. Their ultimate objective, however, is the re-appropriation of the public space, and they, too, have chosen the form of the *colectivo*, but unlike the other groups examined thus far, MUGRE extends invitations to international artists.

Little has been written about the collective. The North American Congress on Latin America profiled their work in 2018, but most of what we know comes from statements they release on social media (Mujeres Grabando Resistencias 2018). Despite repeated attempts to communicate with the members of the collective, I have been unable to interview any of them. Unlike ASARO, URT-Arte, or ARMARTE, MUGRE does not seem willing to talk to researchers or scholars; I do not know of any interviews conducted with them. MUGRE communicates with the public and their audience through their calls for prints and statements they release on their social media accounts, which are subsequently republished in other online publications with activist leanings.[20]

Mujeres Grabando Resistencias was formed in 2013, and they have had a steady, annual release of prints since 2014. They first created a fanzine dedicated to gender-based violence before starting the #VivasNosQueremos campaign. They have issued three calls for prints to date. These calls – in which they invite international artists to submit prints – are an important aspect of MUGRE's artistic and activist work, as they attempt to include other cultural producers in their series of prints. Labelling the series with the hashtag #VivasNosQueremos creates an even wider network of solidarity among women, as images of the prints often circulate on social media and reach new audiences.

The concepts of irony and subversive re-signification – turning an insult into a powerful linguistic tool to resist an oppressor – are critical to understanding MUGRE's body of work. The group's name, Mujeres Grabando Resistencias (Women Engraving Resistances or Women Recording Resistances), is descriptive, almost inoffensive; it emphasizes the artists' gender, the action they perform, and the main theme of their work. The verb *grabar* offers an interesting double interpretation, however, as it can either mean "to engrave," centring the medium used by the group, or "to record," emphasizing the memory work inherent to their work. Ultimately, MUGRE does both, using *grabados* as a means to record women's lived experience. Interestingly, the name invokes the plural *resistencias*, indicating multiple "resistances" – numerous ways to resist. That being said, *resistencias* is a broad concept, and MUGRE does not qualify these resistances in its chosen name. I contend that the pluralization of *resistencia* indicates that the collective understands resistance as intersectional, that there are as many *resistencias* as there are women with specific lived experiences. My interpretation is reinforced by the fact that the collective often issues broad calls for prints, to ensure that women who are not necessarily part of the collective, or even living in Mexico, can still engrave their resistance. Therefore, the very concept of resistance is manifold, and every woman who participates brings her own experience and reasons to resist.

Another reading, this time both ironic and subversive, emerges when considering the word formed by the abbreviation of the group's name. Had they selected the first letter of each word forming *M*ujeres *G*rabando *R*esistencias, the abbreviation would have been "MGR." The addition of two vowels not only makes the collective's name easier to pronounce; it also creates a double meaning, one that proves that the creation of an acronym was a conscious decision. In Spanish, *mugre* means "dirt," "filth," or a "greasy grime" that is often difficult to remove. In Mexico, it is also a colloquial term used to describe objects of little use or monetary value. Both these definitions of *mugre* indicate that Mujeres Grabando Resistencias is aware of how some sectors of society perceive their fight – useless and worthless, a blemish on cultural norms that ought to be eradicated – and that women fighting for a voice is not the norm in traditional Mexican society. In a way, they are dirty women. Far from rejecting the qualifier, these women embrace it, in parallel with women who participated in SlutWalks to reclaim the word "slut" in the early 2010s (SlutWalk Toronto, n.d.). MUGRE's very name also asserts loud and clear that, just like filth or grime, the women who form the collective are ubiquitous. Despite the double entendre and the criticism that the group levels at society, MUGRE is intended as a positive endeavour. Even with a name that can be read with a negative connotation, MUGRE wants its work to bring about positive change.

Even if I was not able to interview the members of MUGRE, their many online statements enable me to gain insight into the collective's political position. In their statement "Invisibilización y posicionamiento de mujeres en el arte" (Erasure and positioning of women in art) (Mujeres Grabando Resistencias 2015), they explain why they refuse to "put a face" to the collective. As with their name, there is a degree of irony in their posture, in that they perpetuate the very criticism that they level at art history. They contend that women are ignored as artistic producers: "If female artists claim to be producers of images, as women who have been able to express themselves, they are not recognized in the history of art." While this has been true historically, and still is to a certain extent, we must acknowledge that there has been an evolution of thinking in the field. Specifically in Mexican art history, the contributions of female artists like Nahui Olin (María del Carmen Mondragón, 1893–1978), María Izquierdo (1902–1955), Lola Álvarez Bravo (1903–1993), Frida Kahlo (1907–1954), Aurora Reyes (1908–1985), Remedios Varo (1908–1963), Leonora Carrington (1917–2011), Lilia Carrillo (1930–1974), Helen Escobedo (1934–2010), Graciela Iturbide (1942–), Monica Mayer (1954–), and more recently Betsabeé Romero (1963–), Teresa Margolles (1963–), Minerva Cuevas (1975–), Pia Camil (1980–), and María Fragoso (1995–) are both undeniable and celebrated. I thus interpret MUGRE's refusal to "put a face" to the collective as their way of re-signifying this erasure into a tool of empowerment, similar to choice made by the Guerrilla Girls, feminist artivists who wear gorilla masks and let their art speak for itself. More pragmatically, it also affords the collective some safety, since holding a feminist position can be contentious in Mexico. Either way, theirs is a blunt criticism of art history as a discipline. The lack of a spokesperson or visual icon with which the group could be identified puts their cause front and centre by ironically emphasizing and perpetuating the erasure of women. Ultimately, it shows that the work is not about its maker, but about the women it serves and helps.

In their manifesto, MUGRE also explains that their main goal is to reflect the many positions and various loci of enunciation that give the collective more than one voice:

> We drag into the light the different roles and positions of different women, beginning in our first work, *El fanzine*, making black women visible and the third root in Mexico, appropriating our bodies and sexuality, in the right to decide, in the role of social and political activists, like the Zapatista women, destroyer of an identity of Mexican and Latin women and betting on the multiplicity and differentiation of identities; as the corn woman, the migrant woman, the fire woman, as a woman appropriating the media technologies … emphasizing the struggle and resistance. (Mujeres Grabando Resistencia 2015)

The voices of Mujeres Grabando Resistencia are multiple and layered. First, there is the voice of the collective itself in their statements or calls for prints. Second, there is the individual voice of each contributor to a campaign, and third, the collective voice of the campaign. MUGRE is an accumulation of voices seeking to convey the breadth of experiences of being a woman in the contemporary world.

By refusing to be represented by a face or a specific icon, MUGRE frees the image from the author. They argue that the notions of "author" and "icon" are traditionally gendered masculine. More specifically, they claim that the history of social art "is framed by *caudillismo*, both in the image and in its production and symbolic reproduction. We think of the images of Che, Zapata, Francisco Villa or El Sub [i.e., Subcomandante Marcos] as recurrent icons in prints related to social protest, and we see reflected in these images that the participation of women in the struggle has been neither recognized nor represented" (Mujeres Grabando Resistencias 2015). Traditionally, women are only represented as the helpers or lovers of soldiers – like *La Adelita* – or as the wives, but never as combatants themselves.[21] This is an erasure from history, since *soldaderas* participated actively in the Mexican Revolution, and *comandantas* are numerous in the EZLN. MUGRE criticizes the fact that women are not portrayed as protagonists on the battlefield.

Their positioning is well considered, claiming as they do an explicit kinship to previous print artists, such as

> Rini Templeton, a TGP participant who takes many of the popular causes of Mexico from the 70s and 80s. Her images show her commitment and accompaniment in the social struggles in which she participated. Her way of working on-site is also noteworthy, in the marches, and it is possible to say that she is one of the first artists to liberate the image of the author: She did not sign what she did, she simply circulated her prints, on the spot. For all these [female] artists only their images remain, without knowing whose they are. (Mujeres Grabando Resistencias 2015)

Their decision to focus on the collective rather than on the individual is related to their working at the Escuela de Cultura Popular Mártires del 68 (School of Popular Culture 1968 Martyrs) in Mexico City, which shaped their world view and how they envisage their role (Mendoza and

ECPM68 2018, 6). This erasure of the artist and the desire for anonymity, coupled with a critique of North American scholars who approach the Global South as an "object of study," is probably why they chose not to speak to me.

Fanzine

Reviewing the fanzine, MUGRE's first creation, allows me to further pinpoint the ideological underpinnings of the group's positions. While the group collaborates with engravers from around the world, its calls for prints, statements, and the fanzine come from members of MUGRE only, which allows the voice of the fourteen founders to come through louder than in the print series.

The fanzine, consisting of fourteen black-and-white prints, and two illustrated covers (front and back), was released in 2014.[22] Each print highlights a different aspect of resistance or a different strategy to resist patriarchy. While the printed fanzine had limited distribution (like many activist publications in Mexico), and is currently out of print, the images are accessible on MUGRE's website as well as on their Facebook page.[23]

The front cover states the nature of the project: "Mujeres y resistencia" (Women and resistance). It shows the face of a woman staring straight at the viewer. Her face is split in two: The left side has darker skin, the right side lighter skin. I read this duality as synonymous with inclusivity, and as a way for MUGRE to emphasize from the viewer's very first contact with their visual work that they recognize and advocate for intersectionality in feminist struggles.

For its part, the back cover focuses on another important feature of MUGRE's fight: the lack of borders. It reads, "Mujeres Grabando Resistencias was born out of the initiative of 14 women who seek to capture the strength of our own struggles and protests, as well as those of other women who fight against the oppression of capitalism and patriarchy. As such we join with millions of women around the world. Even if they call you crazy for fighting, woman, fight!" (Mujeres Grabando Resistencias 2015).

Much like ASARO, MUGRE sees a link between capitalism and patriarchy; they even list the former first. Unlike ASARO, however, for MUGRE undoing patriarchy is not subordinated to the struggle against capitalism.

Moreover, it recognizes that the fight against gender-based violence is universal and cuts across cultures. The lack of borders in the battle against patriarchy is further reinforced by a print included in the fanzine. It depicts monarch butterflies that migrate from Canada to Mexico during the winter and reads, "Nuestras luchas no tienen fronteras" (Our fights do not stop at borders). This slogan, much like the wording on the fanzine's back cover, illuminates two important linguistic features that are staples of MUGRE's communications with its audience: the use of the feminine first-person plural *nosotras* (we), and the use of the imperative mood to connect with the viewers (*lucha*, fight). I analyze these two features later in this section.

The aesthetic of the back cover is relatively feminine: Roses and flowy lines frame the text. Although the fanzine is not street art per se, these prints could have been pasted up on the streets, and *la colectiva* – as MUGRE refers to itself – opens itself to the same sort of criticism levelled at street art created by women. According to their detractors, women street artists tend to have what they deem a "feminine style" – lace, flowers, and curves are more evident than in their male counterparts' style – somehow making their work less edgy than designs with straight lines. As with their name and acronym, I read MUGRE's use of flowers as another case of subversive re-signification, turning a negative comment on its head to make it a positive feature. The depiction of a so-called feminine symbol is also an indication that there is no contradiction between fighting and being a woman, even one who embraces some of – or all – the codes of femininity. I analyze the image of the rose as a subtle warning: While roses are delicate, feminine, and ephemeral, their thorns are prickly and can cause pain. Much like women, rose bushes are resilient. This resilience is underscored by another print in the fanzine, this time showing a hand holding a rose by the stem. Even though the thorns pierce the woman's palm, she does not let go of the flower, which emphasizes her strength and pain tolerance.[24] Indeed, MUGRE assigns a new meaning to the rose: The queen of flowers is transformed from beautiful and fragile to a symbol of endurance and power.

For analytical purposes, I organize the fanzine's images according to whether they display individual or group resistance. Each print offers a different way to resist either capitalism or patriarchy, often both. Since the prints are untitled, I am using the slogans or messages written on them as titles. All the prints I examine here are aimed at both Mexican audiences specifically – in that they address an issue that women experience in Mexico – and international audiences more broadly. While the prints portraying individual resistance show a different type of agency, the prints about group resistance highlight the kinship MUGRE has with other social movements.

Individual Resistance Six prints in the fanzine depict a lone woman and represent resistance, linguistic subversion, and re-appropriation, as well as female bodily autonomy. A first design shows a young-looking woman with a bob hairdo wearing pearls and a flowy dress; all these elements hint at a middle- or upper-class social status. She is holding a slingshot aimed at something or someone located outside the frame, and is surrounded by a halo, as if a spotlight were aimed at her. I read the fact that she is faceless and featureless as a way of ensuring that any young woman could project herself onto the character and take up resisting actions. This is similar to URT-Arte's prints about Ayotzinapa, where any viewer can imagine themselves as the protesting students and mothers and consider joining the fight. More than empathy with respect to an issue, these prints create an effect of solidarity and embody a call to action where the viewer can turn protester.

A print depicting an EZLN *comandanta* also conveys the notion of resistance and highlights women's strength. In this specific case, the struggle is against the Mexican authorities who refuse to recognize the rights of Indigenous peoples in Chiapas; however, to the uninitiated viewer, the balaclava worn by the *comandanta* still connotes activism, albeit in a broader sense. Another print also takes up the question of Indigenous peoples, this time the discrimination and racism they experience.[25] The piece depicts an Indigenous woman from the back, her face hidden from the viewer. She wears a bowler hat and traditional clothing. The print reads, "La lucha sigue. Protesta. Resiste. Corazón de mi chola. Chola de mi corazón" (The fight continues. Protest. Resist. Heart of my *chola*. *Chola* of my heart). "Cholo" is a slang term, generally derogatory, that describes people of mixed heritage across Spanish America. Much like *mugre* is used by the collective to mock their detractors, "cholo" has been re-appropriated by sectors of the population. Once derogatory, it is now proudly reclaimed by members of that community. The English-inspired bowler hat is a clear reference to Indigenous Aymara and Quechua women of Bolivia, who were forced to adopt European attire in the 1600s, but who adapted it to their traditions. Historically, they have been marginalized, leaving members of poor rural communities to migrate to cities where they found few employment opportunities, generally on the lower rungs of society. Since the 1960s, they have been advocating for their rights, and the election of Bolivia's first ever Indigenous president, Evo Morales, gave momentum to their advocacy. They can now be seen occupying a variety of professions, from congresswoman (Leal 2018), to wrestler (Haynes 2020), to rock climber (Jourdan and Morales 2024).

The last two prints to feature only one woman specifically tackle bodily autonomy. One depicts a naked woman with the words "Mi cuerpo es mío" (My body is mine) written over her crossed arms and "Yo decido" (I decide) over her stomach. Her posture – she is standing with crossed arms – highlights her determination. Despite the fact that her body, with its wide hips, appears stereotypically suited to child-bearing, she has the option not to bear a child. Another work shows the female reproductive system: uterus, Fallopian tubes, and ovaries, aestheticized as corncobs, linking womanhood to Mother Earth and to Indigenous cultures. On Facebook, MuGre describes the print as follows: "The female reproductive system as a symbol of the appropriation of our body, and therefore, as a way of resistance. The ovaries represented by corn as a reference to the fertility of the land itself." The adequation women – land is a common trope in MUGRE's prints, one that alludes to conquest and colonization, and to the imposition of an external world order onto Indigenous populations. With these prints and the protest writings related to them, the group proposes that, much like the process of decolonization under way in Spanish America, women must begin to assert control over their bodies. The two aforementioned prints demonstrate that bodily autonomy, as well as deciding whether or not to have children, is one way to resist patriarchal standards and expectations. It is a bit naive to think that this would indeed be an actual choice across most of Spanish America, but it is a goal toward which MUGRE and many activist groups are working.

Group Resistance Four prints depict groups of women and highlight the ties – both artistic and historical – that MUGRE has with other activist organizations, as well as the global nature of their cause. A print with the words "Lucha y resistencias" (Fight and resistance) portrays two women breaking chains that are reminiscent of Adolfo Mexiac's 1954 print *Libertad de expresión*, which I referred to previously. By reviving the symbol of the chains, MUGRE is inscribing itself in the genealogy of Mexican activist printmaking. Another work, *Resiste*, depicts sisterhood: Four women are seen in front of a closed, black fist, a metaphor for something greater than the sum of its parts used in many social movements (Stout 2020). The raised fist was first used in 1917 as a logo for the Industrial Workers of the World, an international labour union (Leverette 2021, 1). It is also reminiscent of the Black Power raised fist, and John Carlos's and Tommie Smith's raised fists on the podium at the 1968 Olympics in Mexico. The adoption of the black fist underscores MUGRE's concern for civil as well as basic human rights, as well as its intersectionality. A third piece reads, "Luchar es vivir, aún en la muerte" (To fight is to live, even in death), and portrays two EZLN fighters. In the EZLN, men and women are treated equally, and both can fight and be leaders. The slogan embodies the very nature of activism, where even after death some of the changes one fought for remain. Finally, a print reading "La rebeldía es la vida. No pasarán" (Rebellion is life. They shall not pass) shows two women sitting around a bonfire. I see two ways to interpret this protest writing: Rebellion is a way of life, or the only way to stay alive. "No pasarán" is of course a reference to the Spanish Communist fighter Dolores Ibárruri, better known as La Pasionaria, who spoke these words as she ended a speech against General Francisco Franco's Nationalist army entering Madrid in 1939. Unlike those found on most of the other prints, the women depicted here appear older, indicating that there is no age limit to this fight. It also alludes to the passing down of knowledge to younger generations.

These images line up with the view that MUGRE expressed in the "Invisibilización" statement I analyzed earlier: "We are not an individualized story but a collective one and we work with other groups to position ourselves against the capitalist, patriarchal and globalized system" (Mujeres Grabando Resistencias 2015). This further underscores that MUGRE is clearly aware of its own position in the long genealogy of women activists.

Outliers Two prints do not fit neatly into the categories I outlined above, but they nevertheless deserve our attention. One woodcut tackles disappearances in Mexico, and alludes to gender-based violence, maybe even to feminicide. It shows a man wearing a shirt with the image of a woman named Karla on it. The poster shares the aesthetics of a missing person poster, suggesting that the woman depicted on it has disappeared. In the background, a train – a symbol of migration – is approaching. This print is perhaps most similar to ASARO's works in that it blends the issues of migration and gender-based violence.

The last artwork in the fanzine shows a skeleton with a raised fist standing in front of a star. The text reads, "No puede ser que estemos aquí para no poder ser. She or he is not important" (It cannot be that we are here for not being allowed to be. She or he is not important). With this print, MUGRE positions itself as a trans-inclusive feminist group that recognizes and accepts non-binarity. Indeed, unlike in ASARO's prints, a skeleton erases the gender of the character.

The fanzine, released in 2013–14, serves as a road map for MUGRE. In it, the members laid out the main issues of their advocacy: above all, the need for women to be agents of change, whether by resisting capitalism and patriarchy or defending increased diversity, inclusion, and intersectionality. These acts of resistance take many forms; women can protest on their own or count on sisterhood to have a stronger voice. MUGRE also ties their fight to historical ones, both social movements more broadly and specific women's movements. These unresolved challenges formed the basis for their three #VivasNosQueremos campaigns, which expanded the number of artists featured from the fourteen initially to any woman interested in participating.

#VivasNosQueremos

As discussed earlier, Mexican and Argentinean feminist groups appropriated the hashtag #VivosLosQueremos (We want them alive), which is used to denounce forced disappearances, and updated it to #Vivas NosQueremos (We want ourselves alive). As a reminder, the change in pronoun, from *los* (them) to *nos* (ourselves), enabled female or women-identifying activists to include themselves in the slogan, emphasizing that they are part of the group whose lives are very much at risk, mired in "structural vulnerability" (Fuentes 2019, 182).

As of 2023, MUGRE has issued three calls for prints for its #VivasNosQueremos campaigns. In true MUGRE fashion, the name of the campaign has several meanings. In Spanish, the verb *querer* means both to love and to want. When read as "to want" – "We want ourselves alive" – it carries a notion of the future; the campaign envisions a future in which women stay alive. When understood as "to love" – "We love ourselves alive" – it carries a notion of the present, of enjoyment of being alive as a woman. The word *vivas* (alive) also produces two readings: as the opposite of dead, but also as "fully alive," freed of patriarchy and the social norms that impede women from living up to their full potential.

The initial campaign, launched in July 2014, consisted of sixteen linocut prints; the second, launched in February 2015, garnered fourteen designs. As MUGRE explains in the call for proposals for the second series of prints, "The objective of the project is to create graphics with clear and understandable messages about violence against women, feminicides and for our right to self-defence, to intervene in the streets of Mexico and other countries of Abya Yala. Based on our everyday experiences and the struggles that we face and that touch us, we promote this campaign in the form of prints" (Mujeres Grabando Resistencias 2015).

This language already signals a shift from that used by ASARO, both in the order of the issues MUGRE tackles, and also in terms of actions. First, it presents gender-based violence as something that happens daily, *en lo cotidiano*, a phenomenon made up of multiple small actions that accumulate and can culminate in greater violence. Although they do contemplate feminicides, their interest also lies in the actions that lead to this extreme form of violence against women, and more specifically, to stopping all forms of violence against women. Second, they claim a "right to self-defence, to intervene in the streets of Mexico and other countries of Abya Yala." Where ASARO portrays the phenomena of gender-based violence and feminicides, MUGRE incites women to defend themselves and other women against sexism and misogyny. They also claim a right to intervene against both. The verb *intervenir* has multiple meanings in

Spanish, but three are of particular relevance for my analysis. When discussing street art and posters, to *intervenir* in the street is synonymous with plastering walls with posters relating to a specific cause. *Intervenir* also translates to "taking part," to participating in something, intervening with authority, and interceding or mediating for someone; all are actions that MUGRE presses women to take because of their lived experiences and to help other women. Finally, "Abya Yala" – the name by which Indigenous communities refer to Latin America – expands the scope of their call to the rest of the continent.[26]

The use of the first-person plural *nosotras* in the feminine positions MUGRE as stakeholders in the campaigns. In a way, MUGRE makes the personal political in its search for equality. The online store Electric Machete, one of the few places where it is possible to buy MUGRE's art, presents the collective as one "that uses graphic art to build *our* memory and capture the strength of *our* struggles" (my emphasis).[27] The use of the first-person plural – *us* and *our* – is of the utmost importance in their work, as it positions them as experiencing the very violence they denounce. But they are not victims – they are activists opposing this violence. According to Florencia Laura Rovetto (2015, 31), their political posture "is constructed through the specificity of what they enunciate, denounce and enable in terms of political action." This specific positionality is what differentiates them the most from ASARO. Having experienced the violence they denounce shapes their world view and political positions, both of which find expression in their artistic production.

In 2015, the initial call was extended to "women who want to add their image and voice to the #VivasNosQueremos campaign." By using the verb *sumar*, to add, the group indicates that it is expanding. The subsequent prints are not conceived as a series whereby a second one would replace the first; the catalogue keeps expanding and more prints circulate. In this way, #VivasNosQueremos aims to be a choral production, where multiple voices and experiences coexist and complement each other.

To ensure consistency between the first and second call for prints, the technique and format are specified: "Linoleum or wood engraving, size 28x38 cm, vertical format, black and white. The final engraving must include: 1) the hashtag #VivasNosQueremos; 2) a phrase, text or word(s) separate from the hashtag; and 3) the graphic creation" (Mujeres

Grabando Resistencias 2015). This editorial direction creates a specific visual identity for the campaign, and the hashtag makes the prints easily recognizable, viable on several platforms, and available for cross-posting. This second call gathered fourteen more prints, bringing the total to thirty.

The call concludes by thanking "muchxs cómplices" (many accomplices) for their help with the project. Replacing the *o* at the end of the article *mucho* with the non-binary and inclusive *x* reaffirms MUGRe's intersectional and inclusive position. More than allies, these people are accomplices in subverting patriarchal norms by circulating and posting the prints. Indeed, the prints are now circulating globally. Unlike ASARO and ARMARTE, MUGRe tends not to sell its artworks. The art is distributed under copyleft licence, "a strategy of utilizing copyright law to pursue the policy goal of fostering and encouraging the equal and inalienable right to copy, share, modify and improve creative works of authorship." MUGRe stipulates that the works "will be disseminated on the page of Women Engraving Resistances and on social networks under the terms of the Copyleft license, without commercial gain, for free digital dissemination and reprinting. It should be noted that the posters are not and will not be available for sale, they are intended solely for free dissemination to be pasted up or used in actions" (Copyleft, n.d.). Creative Commons licensing enables MUGRe to further their objective of establishing fruitful connections with other activist groups in Mexico, Spanish America, and the rest of the world.

In what follows, I analyze the output of the first two #VivasNosQueremos campaigns, and, as with the fanzine above, I use the messages that appear on the prints as titles. I will also look at prints from the third campaign, but I have chosen to keep them separate. Although that call fell under the same general hashtag, MUGRe added the notion of *autocuidado* (self-care), one more step toward a feminist ethics of care as theorized by Tronto (2013). I will come back to this shortly.

Artists were free to interpret the thematic line #VivasNosQueremos broadly in their own work. All the prints represent women in their diversity by depicting a range of topics, such as the passing down of knowledge from generation to generation, same-sex relationships, and sisterhood. It is important to point out that most of the prints tackle current issues and hopes for the future, while very few grapple with past struggles. One print that does take a historical outlook, linking past struggles to current ones, is *Somos las nietas de las brujas que no pudieron quemar* (We are the granddaughters of the witches you could not burn). The print depicts a woman wearing a pointed witch's hat and raising her fist in the air. She wears a studded bracelet, which ties her to the punk subculture, indicating that she is a rather modern witch.

The image of the witch is a recurring one in feminist circles, and thus places MUGRE within a broader circle of activism. Calling on the imagery of the witch is also a form of subversive re-appropriation. According to religion scholar Cynthia Eller (1995, 55), "By choosing th[e] symbol [of the witch], feminists were identifying themselves with everything women were taught not to be: ugly, aggressive, independent, and malicious. Feminists took this symbol and molded it – not into the fairy tale 'good witch,' but into a symbol of female power, knowledge, independence, and martyrdom." For feminists, assuming the identity of a witch is to present oneself as powerful and as part of a long tradition of strong women. Ultimately, the figure of the witch is about women both standing together and "owning" their individual strength. Indeed, as Pam Grossman writes, the witch is defined by her individuality and her subjectiveness: "The Witch is arguably the only female archetype that has power on its own terms. She is not defined by anyone else. Wife, sister, mother, virgin, whore – these archetypes draw meaning based on relationships with others. The Witch, however, is a woman who stands entirely on her own" (quoted in Chollet 2002, 72).

In her book *In Defense of Witches* (2002), Mona Chollet claims that, "by reclaiming the story of the women accused of witchcraft, Western feminists have – whether deliberately or not – both perpetuated their subversive effect and defiantly reasserted the terrifying powers accorded them by their judges" (18). One of these powers was to challenge social norms. In a traditional society where gender roles were being codified, medieval "witches talked back, were insolent, perceived like that by a society that expected them to be submissive" (169). Historically, witch hunts have always been a war against women, an unequal fight in which extreme violence was inflicted on women (Federici 2004). Midelfort (1981, 27–31) calls the European ones (1550–1700) a "burst of misogyny without parallel in Western history." These women were persecuted for refusing to know their place. Ultimately, witch hunts have historically been, and still are, a mechanism to enforce social control (Federici 2004).

One contemporary witch figure worth looking at is the group WITCH, Women's International Terrorist Conspiracy from Hell, formed in New York in 1968. While there is no information confirming that MUGRE claims a kinship with WITCH, the parallels cannot be ignored. Not only did they, too, re-signify a loaded figure – the witch – and poke fun at political correctness with their acronym; they also promoted sisterhood and committed to helping other women. Their 1968 "Witch Manifesto" boldly states that WITCH is "an awareness that witches and gypsies were the original guerrillas and resistance fighters against oppression – particularly the oppression of women – down through the ages" (Fahs 2020, 465). It should not come as a surprise, then, that strong women are portrayed as witches, disrupting the status quo. WITCH postulated that all women who "dare[d] to look within" themselves were witches, thus expanding the pool of potential resistance fighters. In their view, any woman willing to reflect could be a feminist. And much like MUGRE, WITCH proposed to use art – "theatre, satire, … stickers, stencils and paint" (465) – to further their message.

Much like MUGRE, WITCH was intersectional and also sought to foster wider social change. For them, patriarchy was but a symptom of deeper structural problems, and the group was fighting for both women and men. As a WITCH, "you are pledged to free our brothers from oppression and stereotyped sexual roles (whether they like it or not) as well as ourselves" (Fahs 2020, 465). Before the expression was coined, WITCH challenged toxic masculinity. WITCH also highlighted that there is strength not only in knowing oneself, but also in being part of a group: "Your power comes from your own self as a woman, and it is activated by working in concert with your sisters. The power of the Coven is more than the sum of its individual members, because it is together" (465). To summarize this perspective, belonging to a group and being open to collaboration were paramount for WITCH, and also resonate with MUGRE.

Although it does not depict a witch, *Si tocas a una respondemos todas* (If you touch one, we all respond) embodies the same ethos of sisterhood and collaboration between women, this time in protecting one another.

The print tells the viewer that sisterhood is one way to go about combatting gender-based violence; there is strength in numbers. The woman's hair is tightly braided, just as sisterhood ought to be tightly knit, and she is pointing her index finger at viewers, both calling to them and having them complete the print as they are on the receiving end of the finger. The pointed finger is reminiscent of Uncle Sam posters popularized during the First World War. Although the original posters are from the United States, the iconography is unmistakable and known worldwide. Whereas Uncle Sam was encouraging young men to enlist, the protester on this poster is pointing at a potential aggressor.

Two other prints further address sisterhood through diversity. *Las mujeres somos la mitad de todos los pueblos* (We women are half of the world) portrays five women from different ethnic backgrounds, represented by their distinct facial features and hair styles and the cultural sign each one wears. For example, one is veiled, hinting that she might be Muslim, one sports an Afro, and another wears a kaffiyeh, a traditional Palestinian scarf. This breadth of representation is a concrete example of how MUGRE's calls for prints result in gathering a diversity of experiences around the world and reinforce that the fight for equality is every woman's responsibility, unimpeded by borders. The fact that the five women are pictured together also shows that resistance does not, or should not, happen in silos.

Exigimos nuestra parte de placeres en el banquete de la vida (We demand our share of pleasures in the banquet of life) also portrays a group of women. Unlike those seen in *Las mujeres somos la mitad de todos los pueblos*, the women are not ethnically diverse, but they do vary in age. Much like in the fanzine, this range of ages underscores that the fight for equality, for what one deserves, reaches across all age groups and is strengthened by a variety of life experiences. The verb *exigir* reinforces the idea of a "right": the Real Academia Española defines the verb as "Pedir imperiosamente algo *a lo que se tiene derecho*" (my emphasis). Using this word implies that women have been denied rights and privileges, and that they are ready to claim them as rightfully theirs.

While the prints analyzed above tie MUGRE and their collaborators to past struggles and/or emphasize sisterhood, the prints I examine next concentrate on the perpetuality of the fight for equality, on the process of emancipation, and on hopes for the future. The print *Construyendo, crecidendo / Nosotras, vivas, libres y fuertes nos queremos* uses the gerund (-ing) form to highlight the never-ending process of evolving toward freedom. The print depicts seven women at different stages on the path to freedom from patriarchal norms. The tagline is written on a flowy ribbon, a visual metaphor for the winding path to freedom. The path is curvy; one woman even appears to be walking on a tightrope, using her arms to maintain her balance. This highlights that it is a complex and challenging path to walk on; but once she reaches the end, the woman is drawn with wings, indicating that she has secured her freedom and is ready to fly on her own. Unlike most of the prints, on this one the *a* in *nosotras* is drawn like the anarchist circle-A, indicating the political ideology of this particular participant.

The print titled *Sembrando rebeldía cosechando libertad* also uses the gerund to reflect the process of moving from rebellion to freedom: One must sow rebellion to reap freedom; one must be one's own agent of change. In this specific case, the rebellion targets sexual orientation: On the right bottom corner, in a much smaller font than the title, the print reads, "La lesbofobia mata" (lesbophobia kills). The print shows a happy lesbian couple; such a public display of affection goes against patriarchal norms and is still considered shameful in some sectors of society in Mexico, particularly the more traditional and/or Catholic ones. Of relevance is the little banner on which the title of the print is written. Indeed, the banner is reminiscent of Frida Kahlo's paintings (Barba 2017; Jimeno 2004). The twentieth-century Mexican painter often chose a flowy banner to make critical comments about Mexican society. Adopting a similar banner might be a nod to Kahlo's bisexuality, which was severely criticized at the time (Herrera 2002), or a reference to her painting *Unos cuantos piquetitos*, a painting about gender-related violence. Kahlo decided to paint *Unos cuantos piquetitos* after reading a newspaper article relating how, after stabbing his wife to death, a man had told the police that the stab wounds were just a few little nips, thus minimizing his fatal actions. In this reading, *Sembrando rebeldía cosechando libertad* reframes gender-based violence as violence due to one's sexual orientation.

Two prints openly look toward a future where women feel safe and their contributions are fully recognized. *Un día ya no tendré miedo de andar por la calle. Ya no tendré miedo de morir por tu machismo* (One day I will no longer be scared to walk down the street. I will no longer be afraid of dying because of your machismo) uses the future tense to describe a time when open spaces, like a city street, will no longer be dangerous for women. On the print, a woman is seen walking alone in the moonlight; a relatively banal situation that can turn dangerous or deadly due to street harassment. A flower protrudes through the spaces between the cobblestones, creating a crack through the word "machismo." I attribute a double meaning to this flower: The small cracks it has made imply that both the processes of overcoming fear and of shattering machismo are underway, and that such a small flower can be very powerful.[28] Once again, the print highlights the strength in elements that are coded as feminine, such as flowers, even if they are sometimes ridiculed. Portraying women taking back the street is a "talk back mechanism" (Ryan 2017) women use not only to take control of, but also to resemanticize this space from which patriarchal power and neoliberalism have historically expelled them (Friedman and Tabbush 2016). The print – specifically the depth of field – recalls Leopoldo Méndez's *New York*, designed while the TGP member was living abroad after receiving a Guggenheim Fellowship (Noack 2009). In the #VivasNosQueremos print, however, the point of view is lower, at street view; instead of creating a sense of claustrophobia in the viewer, the print evokes hope and a future where women will indeed walk without fear.

The second print on the theme of a better future is entitled *Nunca más un mundo sin nosotras* (Never again a world without us women). The message it conveys is twofold: It demands a world where women will never again be excluded, and a world where Indigenous women (depicted in the print) will never again be dismissed.[29] It also reinforces the idea, introduced in *Exigimos nuestra parte de placeres en el banquete de la vida*, that there is no age limit in the fight, and that passing down knowledge to future generations is one way to participate in shifting paradigms and resisting.

In 2016, after issuing two calls under #VivasNosQueremos, MUGRE circulated a third call for prints. However, this time MUGRE made the call more specific by adding the following: "As a female collective we decided to develop the next edition around the topic of 'Self-care as a radical act,' how do I take care of myself in order to take care of all of us?" (Mujeres Grabando Resistencias 2016).

Over the past few years, abiding by a feminist ethics of care (Tronto 2013) has become essential for activists and protesters. Indeed, many women-identifying and/or feminist activist groups brought notions of care to the forefront of their political and social engagement, to recognize how emotionally draining the fight for social justice can be. Groups "care about" the issue of gender-based violence, but also "care for" their sisters by devising various safety measures (be they physical or emotional measures), "give care" to contributors, and "receive care" in return, and most importantly, "care with" by being "consistent with democratic commitment to justice, equality, and freedom for all" (Tronto 2013, 22–3).

Whereas the 2014 and 2015 #VivasNosQueremos campaigns concentrated on agency and sisterhood, the third campaign, *Autocuidado*, depicted much darker themes. There are actual deaths shown in these prints – suicide, murder disguised as suicide – thus making this third series more focused on feminicides than the previous two. This shift can be attributed to the fact that the number of feminicides continued to rise, and that more and more cases made the headlines. Related themes, such as intimate-partner violence and street harassment, are also present.

Three prints call men out directly: *¡Estoy harta de tu violencia!* (I am tired of / fed up with your violence), *No quiero que tu mirada ni tus palabras me incomoden* (I don't want your look or your words to make me uncomfortable), and *No me chifles, cabrón* (Don't catcall me, asshole).

¡Estoy harta de tu violencia! depicts an older woman brandishing a frying pan. She is ready to fight back using the tools at hand – namely, what is in her home. The aesthetic is reminiscent of another print from this campaign, *Defendamos nuestros cuerpos/territorios* (Let us defend our bodies/territories), in which another woman is seen holding a pot. Unlike in *¡Estoy harta de tu violencia!*, this woman does not appear to be wielding it to defend herself yet, but the slogan with the word "defence" is an indicator that there is something dangerous in this situation. Both the frying pan and the pot are re-signified from cooking tools aligned with gender expectations to weapons that women can use to fight off a violent partner. Indeed, the viewer infers from both these prints that the woman is shown in a domestic setting; ironically, this is where women are at a

higher risk of experiencing gender-based violence. The depiction of pots and pans could be a nod to the 2006 "march of the pots and pans" in Oaxaca, where women took to the streets banging with pots and pans to defend the city against the military. More recently, this trope has also been used by the Chilean collective LasTesis in their latest performance, *Canciones para cocinar* (Songs to cook to).

No quiero que tu mirada ni tus palabras me incomoden and *No me chifles, cabrón* both attack street harassment directly. *No quiero que tu mirada ni tus palabras me incomoden* is perhaps the strongest anti-men statement made by the three #VivasNosQueremos campaigns so far. Three men, portrayed as pigs, are seen staring and laughing at a woman, whom the viewer can only see from the back. She appears to be trying to move past them, but they block her, even if the tagline indicates that she demands to be left alone.

No me chifles, cabrón is not as visually bold as its counterpart, but it does use a vulgar term to get its message across. The print has a tripartite organization. At the very top, there are three medallions: On the left, a man is seen whistling at a woman who looks upset (on the right). In the middle medallion, a raised palm calls for the end of street harassment. In the main and dominant section of the print, a woman is seen riding a bicycle, and the path on which she is riding is shaped like wings, indicating freedom from street harassment.

Four other prints from the third series centre on death. The first one I analyze, *Muero por sacar tu moral de mi vida*, relates to the Canadian context. The print refers to the 2012 suicide of a fifteen-year-old girl in British Columbia. On 7 October 2012, Amanda Todd uploaded a video to YouTube in which she used flash cards instead of her voice to communicate how she had been blackmailed into exposing herself online, and the bullying and online harassment that ensued. On 10 October, she hanged herself. The video went viral after her death and sparked a joint Canadian-European investigation by the Royal Canadian Mounted Police and Interpol. The perpetrator was convicted of sextortion, criminal harassment, communication with a young person to commit a sexual offence, and possession of child pornography. He was found guilty and sentenced to thirteen years in prison. This case continues to be reported on and discussed in Canada to this day.

The print itself shows Amanda Todd surrounded by roses and holding a flash card that reads, "Muero por sacar tu moral de mi vida" (I die to get rid of your morals). The text is directed at those who bullied her, slut-shamed her, and perpetuated the cycle of violence by blaming an adolescent for the violence she experienced (Dean 2012).

The print *¿Matarme te hizo más hombre?* (Did killing me make you more of a man?) shows a woman standing with her arms crossed and asking the eponymous question. It openly grapples with feminicide, and questions toxic masculinity and machismo. Both concepts emphasize strength and virility, and the power of men over women. This time, the nod is again to Kahlo's *Unos cuantos piquetitos* (1935), though the use of the flowy banner is even stronger. Both artworks call out gender-based violence and the impunity men can expect after committing such offences.

Yo no me suicidé me asesinaron (I did not kill myself, they killed me) depicts a young woman smiling, standing over a city where crosses, similar to those used to memorialize feminicides, are scattered. The print rejects the narrative about feminicides that women are not killed; rather, they kill themselves because they did something to dishonour their families. Once again, women are blamed for the violence to which they are subjected. Moreover, justice is often denied to these women, as crimes that are made to look like deaths by suicide are not investigated as thoroughly in Mexico.

Finally, *No es suficiente sobrevivir. La vida de mujeres importa* (It's not enough to survive. Women's lives matter) shows a skeletal woman. I read it as a representation of what can happen when societies judge that women's lives do not matter: a limbo between life and death. Much like *Si tocas a una respondemos todas*, *No es suficiente sobrevivir. La vida de mujeres importa* underscores the collective aspects of MUGRE's struggle: solidarity – all women must support each other – and equality – the life of every woman is important. Both prints suggest that a broader change in Mexican society is required. For MUGRE, although paying tribute to the victims is paramount, the time for simply naming or denouncing feminicides has passed. Through the prints, they show ways that women can take care of themselves and their sisters – first, by acknowledging the root causes of gendered violence and the myriad ways it can be experienced, and then by taking a stand against it.

Reflecting on MuGRe's Engagement

MUGRE has adopted a clear political posture – to destroy patriarchy and machismo, to empower women, both artists and viewers, and to foster sisterhood – and both their prints in the fanzine and those they curated for the #VivasNosQueremos campaigns bear witness to that. They aim to illuminate the spectrum of gender-based violence, from street harassment to intimate-partner violence, to feminicides, and to show that violence against women happens everywhere: in the kitchen, on the street, at school. Unlike ASARO's prints, MUGRE's curated works often set out concrete, actionable items. They either speak to women directly or to their aggressors, as with *No me chifles, cabrón*. They also recognize the importance of tying current fights to past ones, and of propelling the feminist project into the future. The fact that they distribute their work freely online ensures a wide circulation; their commitment to Abya Yala and the world appears genuine.

While MUGRE expresses a clear commitment to diversity and inclusivity, the prints do not always explicitly convey this. Granted, the identities of the artists are not known, but, save for a few prints, the women represented appear at first sight to be Caucasian. This highlights another way race is fraught in Mexico: One can both be white and mestiza, and still not be considered white in the Global North. Only *Las mujeres somos la mitad de todos los pueblos* and *Nunca más un mundo sin nosotras* portray ethnic diversity and concentrate on Indigenous identities, respectively. Sexual orientation is not as clear as ethnicity, but still, only *Sembrando rebeldía cosechando libertad* openly tackles it. If this issue were front and centre in a contributor's life, one might assume that they would design prints that illustrate this reality, their reality.

It would not be fair to discredit MUGRE on these points – they can only print what they receive. The same goes for the depiction of sexual orientation and the dynamics of relationships involving gender-based violence; even if it is present in same-sex relationships, statistically it is more prevalent in heterosexual ones, and the male is usually the perpetrator. Are these editorial decisions, or merely an accurate reflection of the prints they received? Does it mean that their calls for prints only reach certain sectors of society? The calls do circulate online, so one must have access to the Internet to see them, which not everyone has. On a more positive side, this could also mean that the artists actually represent their lived experiences and do not appropriate those of other women just to ensure a broader representation of issues in the graphic campaigns. Since I could not interview the members of MUGRE, I can only speculate.

The collective I examine in the next section, ARMARTE, takes us back to Oaxaca, where the lack of women printmaking artists and/or female-only collectives has long been acknowledged. Since 2018, however, ARMARTE has rallied artists around one specific issue: the emancipation of the woman worker from both capitalism and patriarchy.

The Alianza Revolucionaria de Mujeres Haciendo Arte: Making a Place

After considering ASARO and MUGRE, two collectives that have been active since 2006 and 2013, respectively, accumulating a significant collection of designs in the years since, I now examine one of Oaxaca's youngest collectives: ARMARTE, the Alianza Revolucionaria de Mujeres Haciendo Arte (Revolutionary Alliance of Women Making Art).

Despite its relatively recent creation, ARMARTE does not lack in graphic materials. Since 2018, the group has established what I call a posting pattern, or posting calendar, centred around specific dates and/or activities related to Oaxacan, Mexican, and international social justice movements, releasing posters four or five times a year. They issue new *gráficas* around International Women's Day in March, and commemorate the 2006 Oaxaca protests in June, the Ayotzinapa disappearances in September, and, in some years, the International Day for the Elimination of Violence Against Women on 26 November. They have also participated in a few other protests: In 2019, they celebrated the legalization of abortion in the state of Oaxaca, emphasizing that the right to choose is a victory for women; in 2020, unsurprisingly, their posters related to the COVID-19 pandemic and how it affected specific segments of the Mexican population; and in 2021, they posted wheat paste posters denouncing the ongoing crisis in Palestine. All their prints either position women as leaders in these different struggles or denounce the impacts of these situations on women specifically. For instance, unlike other Oaxacan collectives, their prints about Ayotzinapa do not show the missing students at all; rather, they show the mothers still searching for their sons.

In this section, I examine ARMARTE's 2018 Día de Muertas mural, painted on the facade of the Taller de Arte Comunitario in Oaxaca, in collaboration with URT-Arte, and their three #8M series of posters created for International Women's Day in 2019, 2020, and 2021. My analysis of this artistic production is informed both by ARMARTE's artwork and by interviews they have given since their inception. As we will see, there is an evolution in the issues presented in their designs, from a broad notion of struggle, to gender-based violence, and finally to explicitly positioning women as targets of violence.

I argue that ARMARTE's limited scope of activism – releasing a small number of prints on specific occasions each year – is a deliberate decision, one grounded in both the demands of daily life and in their understanding of marketing strategies. On the one hand, as they explained when I interviewed them, some members have day jobs, others study or have caregiving duties, all of which combine to make it more complex to maintain a steady production and be out on the streets every week (Ana [pseudonym], interview with the author, 2018). Depending on its size, it can take from a day to a month to create an artwork, from the first concept to the finished product. This process also takes longer due to the inherent nature of collaboration, as all members must agree before moving forward with a piece. While this makes for fewer pieces, each one is well thought out and meaningful to the group.

On the other hand, having a predictable posting pattern generates an expectation of things to come and builds anticipation. My reading of ARMARTE's posting pattern as a marketing strategy of sorts is reinforced by the visual grammar and repertoires from which they draw, and the repeated motifs, which almost create a brand similar to that of URT-Arte's. This is a tried-and-true technique, one that Guzmán dismissed as stemming from a lack of artistic and political experience (Guzmán, interview with the author, 2018). While this might be the case, using visual codes that are easily and quickly understood by passersby is also politically savvy, further demonstrating that they understand marketing. Adding a few different posting campaigns every year also fuels this marketing strategy, as it keeps viewers in a state of anticipation. There is an inherent tension between the collective's rejection of some aspects of capitalism – which they disavow as a concept, without proposing a full project with which to replace it – and their political savviness, as I explore later in this section.

In spite of appearing limited in terms of numbers of prints and causes embraced, ARMARTE's activism is clearly delineated ideologically. Its ten or so members work toward the emancipation of the *mujer proletaria* (the proletarian working woman) through education, highlighting themes of equality and inclusion. I read their political engagement as one of both learning and teaching. Working alongside URT-Arte and other groups of artists living in Oaxaca enables ARMARTE members to hone their craft and engage with different political perspectives. At the same time, leading creative workshops at the TAC or hosting artistic camps around Oaxaca allows them to impart their knowledge. They are themselves the seeds to which the epigraph of *Pasting Up Protest* refers – shaped by the 2006 protests and their aftermath, they are in turn sowing new seeds, ones that might lead to more gains for women.

By sponsoring the creation of ARMARTE in late 2018, URT-Arte aimed to open more space for women, whose voices often went unheard – or, at least, under-represented – in the Oaxacan engraving scene. Indeed, the idea of creating a space dedicated to women belongs to Mario Guzmán; he identified a gap and then sought to fill it. The female-only collective is ideologically aligned with URT-Arte, with whom they shared a workshop until 2023, as well as some members. A number of artists belong to both collectives, which means they can grapple with similar issues from two different angles. Whereas URT-Arte concentrates on the struggles of the *pueblo* as a whole, most of ARMARTE's prints tackle the challenges faced by a specific segment of the population – women. While the members of ARMARTE do not consider their struggle "una lucha de género" (a gender struggle) (Ana interview, 2018), by predominantly depicting women protesting against capitalism and patriarchy, they demonstrate an acute awareness of how these two systems disproportionately affect women. Unlike MUGRE, ARMARTE sometimes portrays men and women united against patriarchy and gender-based violence, since they believe that men, too, should be at the forefront of these societal changes.

But like MUGRE, and unlike ASARO, ARMARTE presents the full spectrum of gender-based violence – from intimate-partner abuse to feminicide.

As mentioned above, the acronym "ARMARTE" stands for the Alianza Revolucionaria de Mujeres Haciendo Arte. The name is very descriptive and similar to URT-Arte (Unión Revolucionaria de Trabajadores del Arte), thus stressing their affiliation. (ARMARTE later changed its name but retained the acronym, a decision I address in this chapter's conclusion.) The emphasis is first on the notion of a group, an alliance; then its revolutionary nature; and, finally, the medium they choose – art – to power the revolution. Their logo – a red star with a pencil and a paint brush in the centre, a visual echo of the hammer and sickle – also underscores the role art plays in the revolution to which their name alludes (see plate 24).

The acronym the group selected is yet another indicator of their goals as a collective. In Spanish, the verb *armar* means "to arm." By adding the second-person singular reflexive pronoun *te* to the infinitive form to make "ARMARTE," this result is "to arm yourself." To arm oneself – with art or with knowledge – is one way for women to become empowered. This reading is reinforced by the slogan "Ármate mujer" (Arm yourself, woman), which they used to spray paint next to their posters. Another meaning of the verb *armar*, one that is not pronominal, is "to assemble" or "to pull together" – a reference to women coming together in the creation of the collective. These notions of occupying a space that is theirs and coming together through artistic creation reflects both ARMARTE's genesis and the ideas they hope to perpetuate, and ties their praxis to the principles of artivism: training more women in artistic techniques and spreading awareness around social issues through art.

I met the members of ARMARTE during field research over the summer of 2018, when my research assistant and I interviewed them at their workshop. The collective was still in its early days, and this probably was their first interview. They have since been featured in local, state, and national newspapers.[30]

During the ninety-minute interview, our conversation flowed naturally from the role of artists in society, to the process that led to the creation of ARMARTE, to their position in Oaxaca's engraving milieu, and finally to their political affiliations. What I enjoyed most about our conversation was their thoughts on their role as "learners" – as artists learning new techniques, as collaborators learning to make decisions as a group, but also as citizens constantly learning more about issues affecting the Mexican population. The members of ARMARTE continuously reflect on the artworks they create, their purpose, and their significance for viewers; they see artistic creation as a means to educate both themselves and Oaxacans about ongoing social issues.[31]

Unsurprisingly, our conversation revolved around politics, the assembly's mode of organization, their position on vandalism, and their reflections on feminism, which I interpret as forms of political savviness. The artists were still a bit shy and reserved, and they were very mindful of respecting the ideals of collective organization. For instance, they made sure to differentiate between interventions made in the collective's name, and interventions they were making as individuals. This highlighted both their respect of the collective and the other members, and their individuality as artists and activists who hold different perspectives while working together to learn from each other, fostering healthy debates. These constant discussions and the necessity to agree on how to proceed are consistent with the principles of horizontal organizing. As I mentioned above, ASARO was established in 2006 following the model of the *asamblea*, a horizontal way to organize group work and ensure that every member's voice is heard. Like ASARO, and unlike their brother collective URT-Arte, ARMARTE also adopted a model in which there is no hierarchy between members, either artistically or politically.

This approach was articulated by a member who emphasized how, as a diverse group composed of students with part-time jobs, full-time artists, or stay-at-home mothers, the *asamblea* helps them to stay organized:

> The assembly is like making the decision and having a plan … We say as a group that we cannot make spontaneous or anarchic decisions, right? But instead [we must] plan it well and [ensure] that the project has to come out on a given date, and if it doesn't come out on that date, we have to get it out [as soon as possible], right? But there is always a plan to get us involved, right? And to ensure that we are all working. (Ana interview, 2018)

More than a mode of political organization, for ARMARTE the assembly is a mode of organizing themselves. With it, they also model what they want women to do, which is to participate in conversations, take their place, and learn about social issues.

Whereas ASARO's *asambleas* tended to centre more on the political aspects of artistic production and were used to develop and agree on a specific political position – and to mitigate internal dissensions – ARMARTE adopted this model to organize its production, stay on track, and ensure a steady workflow. I believe that they are able to use it for planning purposes, because, unlike ASARO, which was a "coalition" of different political ideologies that coalesced around the idea of anti-capitalism, everyone in ARMARTE is aligned with Marxism-Leninism; this avoids the need to agree on a position.[32]

The *asamblea* not only enables ARMARTE to streamline its production; it also allows the members to plan where a certain poster will be pasted and articulate positions on specific issues related to street art and protest. A case in point is the collective's politically savvy position on vandalism. As we already know, ARMARTE is URT-Arte's sibling. While one could expect ARMARTE to share a similar position to that of its sibling collective, their stances could not be more different. This difference in thinking stems from the historical moment that led to the creation of each collective. URT-Arte emerged in the wake of the 2006 events, shares members with ASARO, and is somewhat more traditional – in the context of the graffiti world – in its position on vandalism; they rarely request permission to post posters, and thus take the risk that they will be promptly removed. Unsurprisingly, this sometimes contradicts their explicit desire for permanence.

Even if Oaxaca still is "un lugar de resistencia" (a place of resistance) (Ana interview, 2018), ARMARTE makes a clear distinction between the 2006 "revolution," a period of political and social turmoil where vandalism was to be expected, even necessary, to put forward the demands of a *pueblo* that was attacked daily by the military, and the prevailing situation in Oaxaca. While there are still several social problems that need attention, activists rely on different strategies to be heard, as the current situation does not lend itself to a social revolution as it did in 2006. Given that their priority is raising awareness around issues that are not given the public space they warrant, ARMARTE wants their message to be heard and to remain on the walls as long as possible. As such, the members ask permission to paste posters in highly visible locations, all the while ensuring that they do not disturb third parties like businesses or the municipality, tactics that in turn ensure that Oaxacan municipal workers do not remove them.

With its twelve hundred inventoried monuments of cultural significance, the Historic Centre of Oaxaca is a UNESCO World Heritage Site (UNESCO, n.d.), and Oaxacans are proud and protective of it. In a city where the variety of colours that homeowners can use to paint their facades is strictly regulated, vandalism is not tolerated. Even though posters are illegal and unsanctioned by the city, ARMARTE's political and social message is better received since the artists do not harm the historical heritage of their city. This acceptance, or at least tolerance, of protest posters also plays in the collective's favour, since their work has greater durability, meaning their message can resonate with viewers for an extended period.

As a member explained to a local newspaper, they respect the community's faith and pride. To ensure that their paste-ups become a semi-permanent fixture in the city,

> one of the strategies we have used … [is] giving respect to certain places, to certain historical places. The fact that we do not use spray paint. Or scratch or paint or put engravings on the stonework or on the churches, right? In places that are historical … We do it more for that purpose, and it's conscious … Because we start to think, "Ah! yes we are young," because I am fifteen or sixteen years old, I feel like going to vandalize and just make a tag of my name. *So, a little bit of the art we do, or the artistic work, does have a message or a goal.* As to why we are posting there, and we also respect the places, and it is also like *asking for permission* [to post], *even in the marches.* I remember going out to march with women and I remember going to a beauty salon, where we went to ask for permission, and not with the aim of vandalizing anything else, because we are in a time of youth or revolt. (Quoted in Morán Ramos 2021; my emphasis)

As this member explains, the decision to seek permission to post on the walls of specific businesses and not to target churches or historical venues is a conscious one. They call it a "strategy" based on "respect," one that positions them as different from other groups in Oaxaca. In a way, by pitting artistic regimes against one another, ARMARTE is playing on the reception of various forms of urban art, from graffiti to street art. There is a value judgment in this reasoning: They believe that their art is better than a tag because their pieces "have a purpose, an objective." Its purpose is educational and aims to elevate women, whereas "a tag of my name" merely shows an individual desire to vandalize, to self-promote, and to rebel. ARMARTE envisages their artworks as contributions to conversations occurring in the public space; asking for permission before affixing it to a wall ensures that the poster, but most importantly the political message it carries, endures. This stance on vandalism and on the use of spray paint, expressed in 2021 in an interview to a local newspaper, signals an evolution in their thinking. Indeed, in their early days ARMARTE did use spray paint – generally black or purple – to sign their installations of prints.

The collective is aware that their work is often overlooked, and they believe in the power of being exposed to critical art, even unconsciously. Like most socially engaged artists, the members of ARMARTE have an acute understanding of their role as cultural producers; as one of the members told us, "It seems to me that it is a very important role because messages are transmitted through paintings or drawings, and they greatly influence people even if they see them unconsciously" (Elena, interview with the author, 2018). The objective is to catch the eye, to capture minds; a project that they conceive as explicitly political, at least eventually. For them, being exposed to artworks on the street is part of a process of awakening, even if at first this process can be, and often is, unconscious. Once again, the spaces the artists select for their posters, as well as the absence of vandalism, predisposes the viewer to being open to the message and not rejecting it the moment they lay eyes on an artwork. Elena added that for her, street art is "a means and a space to protest or to start to act" (interview, 2018), implying that it can be a first step in militancy. This aligns with ARMARTE's conception of social and political action, in which art and activism are tightly intertwined. First comes an exposure to art, either on the streets or in the workshop. Then, as a member becomes more involved with the collective, comes a deeper understanding of the reasons for creating and using art, through political debates or reading circles that allow members to develop a better theoretical grasp of the implications of using art to convey a political message. This trajectory mirrors the path that most of ARMARTE's members followed to the collective; a path they seek to reproduce for new members.

There is a convergence of humanist ideals and ideas concerning broader social transformation in ARMARTE's works that is grounded in their lived material conditions. And while at first sight both their positions and, as we will see shortly, their artistic production can be interpreted as feminist – since their work is centred on the *trabajadora*, the female worker – the members do not consider themselves, or the collective, to be feminist. While they recognize that their prints and discourse have clear feminist undertones, and that this is how most people perceive their production, they reject the label.

A lack of familiarity with the tenets of feminism might explain the collective's avoidance of the term. Indeed, a few members explained that they did not call themselves feminist because they did not feel they knew enough about the topic and its principles to embrace such a label, but they also specified that they were learning about it:

> In my case, I do not consider myself a feminist … From my point of view, *if I choose one term, and say, "Yes I am [that]," then I would have to argue it. And so I think that until now I don't have a basis to say … that I'm a feminist.* (Sara, interview with the author, 2018; my emphasis)

> And as a collective … I in particular … as if taking up what [my colleague] says, I feel that it is not. *I am very illiterate on these issues of feminism. I know there are feminisms and feminisms, community feminism, liberal feminism, radical feminism.* (Elena interview, 2018; my emphasis)

> Right now, I do not have the background to define myself as a feminist, but there is something that I … I question myself, right? The

> fact of counting ourselves as women because we are already committed to a social struggle, a gender struggle, a woman's struggle, which … in the eyes of others is already, like, feminism, right? (Ana interview, 2018)

They refer to their actions and their work as "a social struggle, a gender struggle, a woman's struggle" (Ana interview, 2018), which for many North American or European readers is understood as feminism. But as author Cristina Rivera-Garza provocatively wrote in a 2020 op-ed, feminism is still the "f-word of Mexican vocabularies." Feminism's negative connotations in some sectors of Mexican society are only exacerbated by its relationship with "radical feminism," which connects misandrist ideas, violence, vandalism, and arson in protests with feminism. This perceived link between feminism and radicalism has not only created a rift between those in power and feminist activists but also makes people reluctant to associate with feminism while fighting for equity and equality. Although in Latin America organized feminism as we conceive it today dates back to 1916 (Marino 2019, 4), feminist ideals were still largely rejected by intellectuals in the early 2000s; feminism was associated with crazy women who defied societal norms on all levels (Rivera-Garza 2020). Understandably, activists challenge this description of women. This position aligns with Latorre's observation (2019, 140), who, in her investigation of Chilean street art, claims that the terms "'feminism' and 'feminist' remain[n] … discursive minefields." These same minefields are present in Mexico and indeed most Latin American countries, where it is easier to explain social inequality almost exclusively as a symptom of class hierarchies and capitalism than as a gender issue (140). ARMARTE is taking steps toward integrating more extensive reflections on gender into their thinking, but class remains their main political concern.

That being said, the members of ARMARTE do not sidestep the issue of feminism: Unlike other street artists I met during field research, they are open to discussing it, and they even admit that they question themselves about feminism, and what it means to call oneself a feminist. This reinforces their status as learners, this time about the theoretical underpinnings of claiming this position. The members of ARMARTE are not, to use Rivera-Garza's term, "crazy," but they do defy social norms. They are artists, performing illegal work in the streets, and they have an explicit political position that centres on the emancipation of women, a group that has historically been expected to remain silent. By doing so, they transgress many "rules" of Mexican society, while also trying to reconcile their identity as women artists with a label that would position them even more as outsiders. If they openly position themselves as feminists, they run the risk of their audience misjudging them or their work. Indeed, in Oaxaca alone, feminist activists are often caught smashing windows and destroying property (de la Luz 2019). While some of ARMARTE's work is illegal, they make a point of avoiding vandalism, thus gaining some credibility with the local population. ARMARTE rejects the feminist label but keeps its ideals – equal rights, emancipation, intersectionality – without restrictions regarding the type or wave of feminism with which they identify. Essentially, the "feminist" label could be oppressive for them, and it might harm their efforts. Rejecting it appears to be a well-thought-out decision, one that they seem open to revisiting as they keep growing, and Mexican society evolves.

Día de Muertas Mural (2018)

One of ARMARTE's first creations was a Día de Muertas mural on the facade of the TAC in 2018 (see plate 25). The mural, which stayed up for about eighteen months, was a collaboration between ARMARTE and URT-Arte. Indeed, both collectives worked on the mural, and ARMARTE did the installation with crosses.

The mural is an homage to Meztli Omixochitl Sarabia Reyna, a labour rights defender, member of the Puebla-based UPVA (Unión Popular de Vendedores Ambulantes 28 de Octubre, or Popular Union of Street Vendors 28 October). She was killed in June 2017, during an armed attack on the offices of UPVA. UPVA is an organization that defends the rights of street merchants and organizes various social protests over labour rights (Front Line Defenders, n.d.). On the mural, Sarabia Reyna is surrounded with *cempasúchil* (marigolds) – the traditional orange flower associated with Day of the Dead activities – and white crosses bearing the names of other victims of feminicide (see plates 26 and 27). Unlike in Ciudad Juárez, where the crosses were pink, on this mural they are white.

The mural weaves two issues together: gender-based violence in the form of feminicide and forced disappearances. Indeed, under the stern-looking face, the words "NI UNA MÁS" are written in capital letters, leaving little doubt that the mural tackles feminicide. However, under the slogan, lines from a poem by Uruguayan author Mario Benedetti appear on a white banner, expanding the possible meaning of the artwork: "Están en algún lugar, concertados, desconcertados, sordos, buscándose, buscándonos, bloqueados por los signos y las dudas" (They're out there somewhere, all assembled, disassembled, bewildered, voiceless, each seeking the others, seeking us, hemmed in by their question marks and doubts) (Benedetti 1979).

Anyone familiar with Latin American history and literature will recognize Mario Benedetti's poem "Desaparecidos" (The disappeared). Written at the height of the dictatorship years in the Southern Cone (1979–84), the poem describes the confused state in which victims found themselves and alludes to the forced disappearances carried out by the state in Latin American countries from the 1960s to the 1980s. Taken from the first stanza of the poem, the specific verses chosen by the collectives are likely the best known, their meaning easy to grasp while looking at the white crosses floating above and the "NI UNA MÁS" slogan. People walking by would likely recognize both the source and the context, thus opening up another reading of the mural.

Mexico, Argentina, and Chile all fought dirty wars against their citizens, forcibly disappearing thousands. The poetic voice highlights that many individuals were never found and now exist in a state between life and death ("nadie les ha explicado con certeza si ya se fueron o si no"), a limbo shared by their friends and families. The poem reflects on how the disappeared must feel, lost and voiceless, yet still attempting to find their way home. The poem also includes the voices of nations that collectively experience the loss of the disappeared in their everyday lives. The poetic voice emphasizes that the disappeared are victims of states that put ideology first. "Desaparecidos" criticizes governments not only for the state terrorism that leads to the disappearances of citizens who espoused different ideologies, but also for their silence regarding atrocities stretching back far beyond the 1970s. While the poem is about past events and how they endure in the present, it also resonates with contemporary audiences; feminicides and the disappearance of the forty-three Ayotzinapa students that I already examined also leave families in a state of limbo, searching for their lost loved ones. Citing Benedetti's verses thus broadens the mural's scope of criticism. It is not only about the current feminicide crisis, or a specific feminicide – and surely it would be enough to tackle this issue alone; it also draws attention to the forcibly disappeared and those who are left behind.

The text and hashtags used on Instagram (ARMARTE 2021) offer a thinly veiled criticism of the Spanish-language gender binary and of how, grammatically, the masculine form always supersedes the feminine one. When referring to the disappeared in Spanish the expression *los desaparecidos* is used. While any speaker instinctively understands that both men and women are missing, the formulation is masculine by default. By tagging the post with the #Desaparecidas hashtag, ARMARTE highlights missing women specifically, and criticizes the well-known fact among Mexicans that the disappearance of women is often taken less seriously by the police than that of men.

The mural is political; it denounces feminicides in the state of Oaxaca by portraying a real victim and inscribing the names of real victims on white crosses. However, it is not protest-oriented. Unlike ASARO's *Denunciar la complicidad del gobierno*, the mural is about remembering and commemorating lives lost, in keeping with Día de Muertos traditions, and not about pinpointing guilty parties. In contrast with most of ASARO's prints, analyzed previously, the mural also makes the ubiquity of feminicides visible at the municipal and state levels by presenting actual victims rather than fictional depictions of women. Furthermore, there is an aura of commemoration to this mural that is not repeated in ARMARTE's later work.

The painting and unveiling of the mural coincided with the Día de Muertas initiative, created in 2012, with which it is also ideologically aligned. According to its creator, the objective of the initiative is to shift the focus from remembering the dead to raising awareness about feminicides:

> There is a Day of the Dead for every cause of death, including violence, but until now none expressly dignified women who are

> murdered for the mere fact of being women. Under the neutral nature of our language, the Day of the Dead, of a festive nature, hides another reality, exclusive to women. That is why we believe it is necessary to bring it into the light beyond the inclusive language and create the Day of the Female Dead. (Día de Muertas, n.d.)

This description highlights how women are not recognized as "grievable subjects" (Butler 2016) under the generic masculine form, and that special attention ought to be paid to victims of gender-based violence. During Día de Muertas demonstrations,[33] women call for justice by protesting, marching, displaying posters, and writing the names of victims on pink or white crosses, much like ARMARTE did on their first mural. By linking feminicides to the state-sponsored disappearances of the 1980s, ARMARTE and URT-Arte highlight how the state normalizes violence against its citizens, implicitly saying that it is up to the people to stop it.

As we have already seen, another important feature of early activism still omnipresent today is the use of victims' faces to humanize them. To counter government and police narratives that victims are somehow to blame for their own murders, families started to represent their daughters as human beings, with human faces. Indeed, the more human a depiction appears to be, the easier it is for the viewer to develop a sense of solidarity with the person portrayed. Unlike posters and crosses, murals are often seen as a more sophisticated form of activism and, consequently, are not generally defaced or removed by the government. Lozano (2019) claims that they are often left intact because the murals are a symbol of "haunting" that communicates social violence through viewers' interaction with them. More than creating awareness, this haunting "functions to promulgate members of society into action" to fight that violence (98); in other words, to develop solidarity and build momentum around an issue.[34]

International Women's Day Paste-Ups

Following their Día de Muertas mural in 2018, one of the first activities ARMARTE engaged in was a week-long intensive painting workshop titled "La situación actual de la mujer y los feminicidios" (The current situation of women and feminicides) (ARMARTE 2019c). The workshop took place between 26 February and 3 March 2019, just days before International Women's Day. This kind of event is a concrete example of practice meeting theory. Indeed, by hosting a workshop for women who are not members of the collective, and who are either artists or interested in art, ARMARTE brings women together to raise awareness of gender issues through art. During this workshop, art served as an entry point, if not to militancy, then at least to issues facing women. The workshop also was a space to gather and to experience the community of the collective.

The results of the workshop, a series of gouache portraits depicting oversized faces of women, became part of ARMARTE's 8 March 2019 paste-ups. These were ephemeral works with only one copy of each produced. Much like ASARO's and MUGRE's works, these provide no indication of who the women are. That they could be anyone creates a sense of solidarity with viewers, who can project themselves onto the figures.

Portraits are a departure from ARMARTE's usual work, which generally depicts women standing, denouncing a specific situation. That said, the framing of the faces is identical. These women either look toward the future, at something outside the frame, at each other, or straight at the viewer, as if to draw their attention. The images are posted at eye level, making it easier to catch the viewer's attention and ensuring that the woman on the poster is looking straight at them, forcing the "rapport de face à face" (Levinas 1969) I elaborated on in relation to the Ayotzinapa students.[35]

For International Women's Day, ARMARTE posted a series of prints along with the portraits showing women standing, ready to fight. Most of these prints were surrounded by slogans or calls to action centred on work and unpaid labour. For instance, "La doble jornada nos tiene cansada" (Our double workday keeps us tired) explains that most employed women work two shifts: a first in the paid workplace, and a second at home. To the uninitiated viewer, the slogan is a call to reduce women's workload (ARMARTE 2019a). A second level of reading is available for those sharing in the knowledge that *La Doble Jornada* (1986–98) was also the name of the feminist supplement to *La Jornada*, Mexico's most-read left-leaning newspaper (Millán 2014, 156). Gender politics are present in both versions, but the feminist double entendre is only apparent to a certain audience, who, by the fact that they were reading *La Jornada*, are more receptive to the feminist implications of the inscription. Finally, "La mujer trabajadora lucha contra la sociedad capitalista" (The woman worker fights against capitalist society) embodies ARMARTE's ethos and the reasons for the very creation of the collective (ARMARTE 2019b).

A poster titled *Romper las cadenas de lo indiferente* (Breaking the Chains of Indifference) (see plate 28) depicts a sad young woman with Indigenous features staring up at something beyond the image. She is holding a bolt cutter, and she appears to have just cut the chains of oppression to which the title of the artwork refers. I read the unhappy look on her face, despite having just freed herself, as an indication that she knows there is still work to do before she – and indeed everyone who experiences the same hardships – can be fully free. The poster works within a visual code understood by most Mexican citizens: Chains are a subtle reference to Mexiac's *Libertad de expresión*. The woman could be breaking the chains that were silencing her, a first step toward freeing herself from other forms of oppression now that she has regained her voice. The print, by depicting a woman, departs from Mexiac; it acknowledges that women are victims of oppression, too, and that they can take matters into their own hands to liberate themselves.

To the right of the print are two white sheets bearing the following inscriptions: "Mujer organízate y lucha!" (Woman, get organized and fight!) and "Las calles son nuestras" (The streets belong to us). "Mujer organízate y lucha!" uses the imperative voice to speak directly to the viewer. By using the singular, the slogan is reactivated each time a new woman sees it, making each viewer responsible for organizing and advocating against structural issues. The slogan is, in a way, directed at everyone individually. It is a call to action, but because it is renewed every time someone new sees it, it turns into hundreds of calls to action. "Las calles son nuestras" is, to use Ryan's (2017) expression, a "talk back mechanism," one that ARMARTE uses to reclaim a space that is often coded as masculine in Mexico. These protest writings also speak to ARMARTE's work as a new group of printmakers in Oaxaca. They are claiming their "droit à la ville" (Lefebvre 1968), but more so, their right to be safe while outside. It is one of the ways they articulate their political project.

Equally noteworthy is the fact that these inscriptions were not spray-painted; instead, they were written on 8.5-by-11-inch sheets of paper and pasted with the same mix of flour and water used to glue the prints and posters to the walls. This is a concrete example of ARMARTE's stance against vandalism, which I discussed earlier. Water and flour might leave a sticky residue on walls, but it does not permanently damage them.

Another instance in which a strong message respects the venues where it is posted is a print depicting a *soldadera*, a woman soldier from the Mexican Revolution (1910–20) (see plate 29). The *soldadera* is standing in a field of wildflowers wearing traditional clothing and a large brimmed hat. She is leaning on her weapon, carrying a belt of bullets over her chest. The print serves as a reminder that women have always taken part in revolutions, even if historically their role has been overlooked or underplayed.

In 2019, ARMARTE had completed only a small number of prints, as they were only just beginning and had few members. Nevertheless, they compensated for this limited output by varying the slogans they added with each poster. Even today, this print is the most widely used by ARMARTE. The collective keeps repeating it, changing the banners they place around it, thus expanding the scope of their demands, but always tying it to the figure of the *soldadera* and her erasure from the nation's history. In this 2019 example, multiple slogans surround her, each exposing different facets of gender-based violence. For analytical purposes, I divide them into three categories: gender violence, intimate or institutional violence, and a broader idea of *lucha* against different systems of oppression.

"Disculpen las molestias, es que nos están asesinando" (Sorry to bother you, it's just that they're killing us) and "Ni una agresión sin respuesta. Ni un agresor sin castigo" (No aggression without reaction. No aggressor without punishment) both tackle intimate and institutional violence. While the former is ironic in tone, denouncing the fact that women tend to apologize too much, the latter implies that women do not denounce their aggressors but ought to. By coming forward, women would normalize talking about gendered violence; a first step toward eradicating it. "Contra la violencia capitalista el feminismo socialista"

(Against capitalist violence socialist feminism), "El sistema patriarcal es el hijo del capital" (Patriarchy is the child of capital), and "Ni del Estado, ni de las Iglesia, ni del patrón, ni del marido" (Not the state's, not the church's, not the boss's, not the husband's) encapsulate the multiple oppressions women face daily. Finally, "Contra la crisis y la precariedad ¡Compañera! Luchemos en unidad" (Against crisis and precarity. Comrade! Let's fight in unity) and "ARMARTE, nos organizamos, 8 de marzo combativo" (ARMARTE, we organize, combative 8 March) both show the way: Women must get organized and fight for a better future.

There is a tension between ARMARTE's position on feminism and the protest writings they choose. Though most of the members do not consider themselves feminists, they resort to taglines that make use of the concept or are popular within feminist circles. In our July 2018 interview, the member I refer to as Ana framed the group's need to disseminate knowledge and bring awareness to social issues or problems, such as the ones articulated in the taglines, by directly tying them to gender politics: "We can denounce social problems and also the fact of being a woman because it also pushes us a little to … to get together as women … and if we are in the artistic environment, then use this as a tool and say that … *we are here to transform … a system that oppresses us doubly*." She describes and denounces what they see as the double oppression of capitalism and patriarchy, as well as the role artists can play in dismantling both. ARMARTE conceives of patriarchy as a symptom of capitalism, one of its many tentacles. Any issue affecting the *pueblo* necessarily affects women even more:

> ARMARTE has been conceived as this emancipation of working women, right? Well, I can say that from there we laid the foundations, and … we do support this fight … Has there been talk of a patriarchy as well? … [Yes, but we recognize] that the capitalist system uses it as one more of its tentacles … In patriarchy we have a system that in addition to being capitalist is patriarchal, right? So, we focus not only on a fight against patriarchy but also on a fight against this capitalist position … This is where we see the root of the problem. (Ana interview, 2018)

Without using the word, Ana astutely describes how intersectionality disproportionately affects some women. The first layer of oppression they face is capitalism, the second is gender, and a third is racial background, which in Mexico and the state of Oaxaca means being Indigenous or Black. ARMARTE concentrates on the emancipation of specific women, the ones who, according to them, need it the most:

> Actually, we have taken this word, the emancipation of women, … but now which woman? The women who are privileged, the women who sit as elected members and, in this parliament, the woman … who is the wife of the president? *We are fighting for this emancipation, or we are fighting for an emancipation of working women, of women who, apart from being Indigenous, are coloured; apart from being coloured, they are domestic workers; apart from being a homemaker, she has children, [and] she also dedicates herself part-time to a job, and a job where … she is poorly paid, right?* We, well, we are on this side, I could say as a collective, fighting for – now, yes, for the *emancipation of the proletarian woman*, right? A working woman, right? (Ana interview, 2018; my emphasis)

The conditions faced by working-class woman are at the core of the collective's actions. As Ana indicates, they aim to draw attention to the situation of the woman who often works a double shift – at work and then at home – is underprivileged due to her socio-economic background and limited access to education, and whose race means she encounters more prejudice. Often overlooked by society, these women have fewer resources to help them escape precarious situations, such as gender or economic violence.[36]

The act of placing the figure of the *soldadera* at the centre of such activism is filled with political intent. As I mentioned above, *soldaderas* were instrumental in the outcome of the Mexican Revolution, and yet, as Jean Franco explains, after the revolution their role was largely forgotten: "The Revolution with its promise of social transformation encouraged a Messianic spirit that transformed mere human beings into supermen and constituted a discourse that associated virility with social transformation in a way that marginalized women at the very moment they were, supposedly, liberated ... The very construction of national identity was posited on male domination" (quoted in Linhard 2005, 67). Women had fought along with men and had contributed to winning the revolution, but afterwards they were once again relegated to the private sphere. In more traditional or rural areas of Mexico, this situation endures to this day. By selecting the figure of the *soldadera*, ARMARTE affirms that women have been equal to men all along, not fighting *alongside* them but fighting *with them*, as equals.

Sin mujeres no hay revolución (Without women there is no revolution) (see plate 30) builds on the print of the *soldadera* by showing seven women of different ages and racial backgrounds, each advocating for a different cause. Even if they are found in different settings, here they are depicted standing alongside one another to demonstrate that the fight takes many forms. Two carry weapons, and the woman at the very centre of the print carries wood on her back, indicating that there are many ways to contribute to a revolution. One conceals her features under a scarf, either indicating that police repression is expected or that she might commit an illegal act. In the middle, a young girl is depicted wearing a T-shirt with a hammer and sickle. She represents the future of revolution as understood by ARMARTE.

While their prints are my primary focus, ARMARTE also posts dozens of pictures and videos detailing their creation process to their social media accounts, highlighting that for them, their work is as much about the collective process of making things together as it is about the final product the viewer experiences when they are displayed. Awareness and learning begin with the makers in the workshops and continue on the streets. Depending on the reception of the artworks, the reflection on social issues can extend into the private sphere. The print is a catalyst; it is planting a tiny seed in the viewer's head.

ARMARTE documents their own production not only as part of a duty to remember, but also so that the work contributes to producing an alternative historical and cultural memory, one where women's perennial struggles are recognized. Pragmatically, posting videos from past workshops on social media also helps them promote new ones. Not only does the art remain "present in the digital world" (Pabón-Colón 2018, 38), so, too, do the creation and posting processes, offering future members more complete access to the collective, to what it means to be part of the collective.

The prints that ARMARTE pasted the first time that they took part in International Women's Day celebrations established a presence and introduced the newly formed collective to viewers and other activists in Oaxaca. By drawing on well-known figures like the *soldadera*, they were able to communicate their message effectively, despite their limited resources. Whereas the 2019 prints centred the role of women in various revolutions, in March 2020 their prints concentrated on everyday accounts of gender-based violence and actualized historical figures into revolutionaries. The violence and revolutions these posters depicted were more everyday struggles, and unlike the previous year, this time there were no heroines like the *soldaderas*.

ARMARTE also broadened the scope of their activism by using popular slogans such as "Vivas nos queremos" (used in Mexico and Argentina), "Ni una más" (mostly used in Mexico), and "Ni una menos" (mostly used in Argentina), thus positioning themselves as part of a larger national and continental struggle against gender-based violence. A former member of ARMARTE confirmed that there had been exchanges between that collective and MUGRE, and that ARMARTE's use of "Vivas nos queremos" could have been influenced by MUGRE. Even without a formal meeting between the groups, MUGRE's prints were circulating on social media. This member also confirmed that Argentinean artists had visited Oaxaca the previous year, which might explain the appearance of "Ni una menos," which is not often seen in Mexico. This choice to use slogans from different regions of Spanish America aligns with ARMARTE's tactic of *sumar voces*, adding up voices. The more voices participate, the louder each one becomes.

Mi lucha es por vivir (see plate 31 and figure 3.6) depicts a young woman looking at herself in the mirror after having been punched in the face. She touches her cheek where a black eye is beginning to form. The tagline on the poster indicates that she will fight back, as she wants "to live." This poster is similar in tone to MUGRE's *Sobrevivir no es suficiente, la vida de las mujeres importa*. Indeed, they both claim that gendered violence impedes women from experiencing life to the fullest.

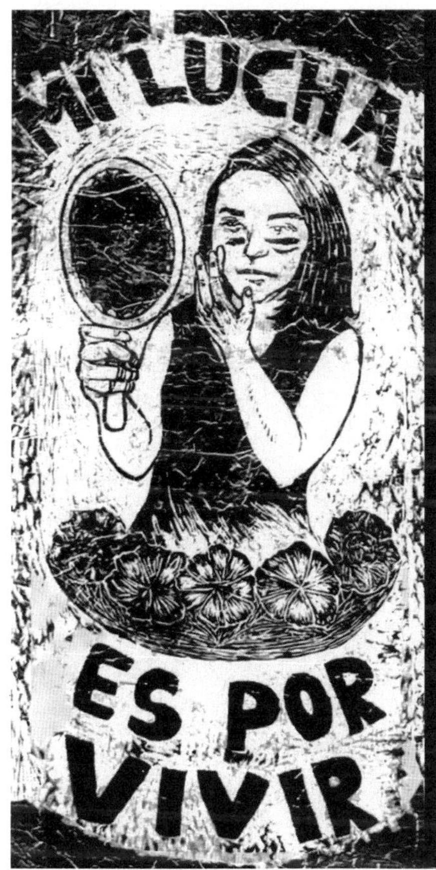

Figure 3.6
"Mi lucha es por vivir" (My struggle is to live).

On the same wall, and adjacent to this poster of a battered woman, we see a very different young woman wearing traditional Mexican dress and with her hair braided. Her depiction is almost doll-like; she has a thin waist and long legs, and she appears to be wearing heels. She looks determined: Standing straight with her hands on her hips, staring out at the viewer. The halo above her head reads. "Ni una menos" (Not one woman less). Each print is interesting individually, but taken together they tell a larger story, one of awakening to activism through lived experience. In my view, the decision to situate them next to each other tells a story that each individual print would not tell alone, a story of activism rooted in personal experience.

The *Ni una menos* print and its creation embody another of ARMARTE's objectives, which is to integrate new members and to teach artists interested in their work. Regularly, artists visiting the city come to their workshop to learn engraving techniques. While *Mi lucha es por vivir* is signed by ARMARTE, *Ni una menos* is the design of Montreal-based artist Élise Rubin. In a brief conversation on Facebook Messenger, Rubin confirmed that while in Oaxaca she worked alongside members of ARMARTE at the TAC. She also designed an untitled print that portrays the same young girl, this time facing a wall, using a paint brush to paint a symbol. It is self-referential, an artwork depicting an artist representing gender-based violence. In a way, it refers to ARMARTE and Rubin, female artists who use art to denounce gender-based violence.

Somos el grito de los que no están (We are the cry of those who are not here) (see plate 32) also embodies ARMARTE's role as the voice of *los*, both men and women who are no longer around to fight for themselves. The print shows women shouting with their fists raised. The slogan is similar to one from 18 August 2018, when feminist protesters took over the Ángel de la Independencia monument on the Paseo de la Reforma in Mexico City and covered it with spray-painted inscriptions. However, in Mexico City, the slogan emphasized murdered women – "Somos el grito de *las* que no están." This slight difference is indicative of ARMARTE's ideology: They fight for everyone, not only for women, since they know that, ultimately, improving women's living conditions will also improve life for their children and families.

In 2020, ARMARTE started actualizing historical figures as advocates for women's rights. Two iconic female figures in Mexican history, Sor Juana Inés de la Cruz and Frida Kahlo, appear on Mexican banknotes: the former on the two hundred peso bill, the latter on the five hundred peso one. Even without having studied literature or visual culture, most Mexicans would immediately recognize these faces, as they quite literally walk with them in their pockets. By resorting to a visual grammar and a repertoire of symbols that are easily recognizable, ARMARTE ensures that at least part of its message is widely understood.

On this large poster (figure 3.7), a young Sor Juana appears as a *Ni una menos* activist. Like all the women portrayed by ARMARTE, she looks serious, gazing straight into the eyes of the viewer. Juana Inés de

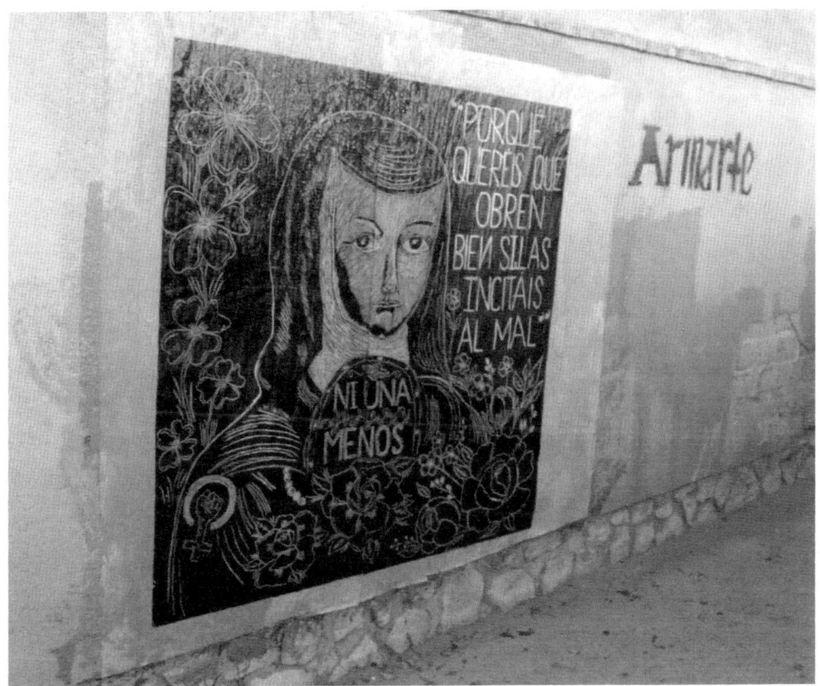

Figure 3.7
Wheat paste poster depicting fifteenth-century nun Sor Juana Inés de la Cruz with the first lines of her famous poem, "Hombres necios" (You foolish men), and a raised fist typical of feminist iconography.

Asbaje (1648–1695), better known as Sor Juana, was a nun in the Order of Saint Jerome during the Spanish Golden Age in New Spain, in what is now Mexico. Most scholars consider her to be a proto-feminist for her work criticizing religion and patriarchy for imposing double standards on women.

On the poster, to her right, we see a verse borrowed from her most famous poem. "Arguye de inconsecuentes el gusto y la censura de los hombres que en las mujeres acusan lo que causan" (An argument regarding the inconsistencies in the taste and censorship of men who accuse women of what they themselves cause) is better known for its opening words, "Hombres necios que acusáis" (You foolish men). The Sor Juana portrayed on the poster asks passersby the following question: "¿Por qué queréis que obren bien si las incitáis al mal?" (Why do you want them to do good if you incite them to do wrong?). The poem criticizes the hypocrisy of men in New Spain and the unequal relationship between men and women at the time, by calling out the foolishness of men for finding fault with women for doing the same things that they themselves do, and for blaming women for problems they themselves create by expecting female perfection. The poem also highlights the double standards men impose on women when it comes to sexual relationships: Women are criticized for being both chaste and promiscuous. The poetic voice gives several examples to highlight that men's expectations are convoluted and impossible to satisfy, so that a woman is never in a position to do right in their eyes, and men's double standards and arrogance prevail. That was true during the Golden Age and remains true to this day, such as through slut-shaming and rape culture.

Just as they had by using Benedetti's poem about forced disappearances, ARMARTE taps into common knowledge of Mexican literature to underscore their argument. The artists crafting this piece expect the audience to recognize Sor Juana's iconic face without having to read the verse taken from the poem. Should they not recognize her, the poem clarifies what the artists mean. They are aware of the limitations some viewers might have, and make sure that even if one is unable to read or has not been exposed to much poetry, the message can be understood based on the image alone.

Frida Kahlo is another figure appropriated by collectives in Oaxaca, and often reframed as a *comandanta*, an EZLN leader, wearing a balaclava. Blending the figure of Frida Kahlo with symbols representing the EZLN is a forceful way to express that "art is [a] weapon," a slogan ARMARTE had previously deployed. While Kahlo depended on art to empower herself and get through difficult periods of her life – and has, since the turn of the 1980s, been appropriated by feminist groups as the epitome of Mexican feminism – the EZLN used mural art as pedagogy to empower farm workers in Chiapas. Much like the depiction of Sor Juana, their visual mention of the EZLN and Frida Kahlo taps into Mexico's history of artists and intellectuals picking up their brushes and putting their pens to paper to oppose the state, the social norms of their time, and the hypocrisy of various leaders. Once again, by relying on a visual grammar

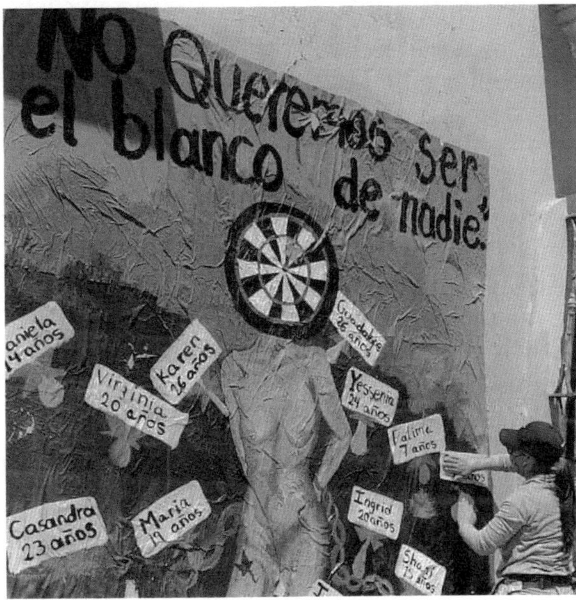

Figure 3.8
"No queremos ser el blanco de nadie" (We do not want to be anyone's target).

and a repertoire of symbols that are easily recognizable, ARMARTE ensures that at least part of the message is understood.

In hindsight, a poster from 2020 portraying a woman in the crosshairs, as if having a weapon aimed at her, indicated ARMARTE's evolution and provided a foretaste of the prints they would release for International Women's Day 2021, in which they address violence explicitly.

No queremos ser el blanco de nadie (We don't want to be anyone's target practice) is more of an installation than a print. It consists of a central hand-painted poster and fifteen smaller white posters affixed to it. The installation depicts a naked woman with a dart board in lieu of a face. Her hands are tied behind her back with chains. I have often interpreted ARMARTE's use of chains as emphasizing the need to break the "chains of oppression," but on *No queremos ser el blanco de nadie* these chains allude to torture. On the smaller white posters, we see the handwritten names and ages of victims of feminicide.

This installation is quite explicit in the specific violence it denounces. It was designed a year after the gruesome murder of Ingrid Escramilla and could have been influenced by the graphic circumstances. Unlike

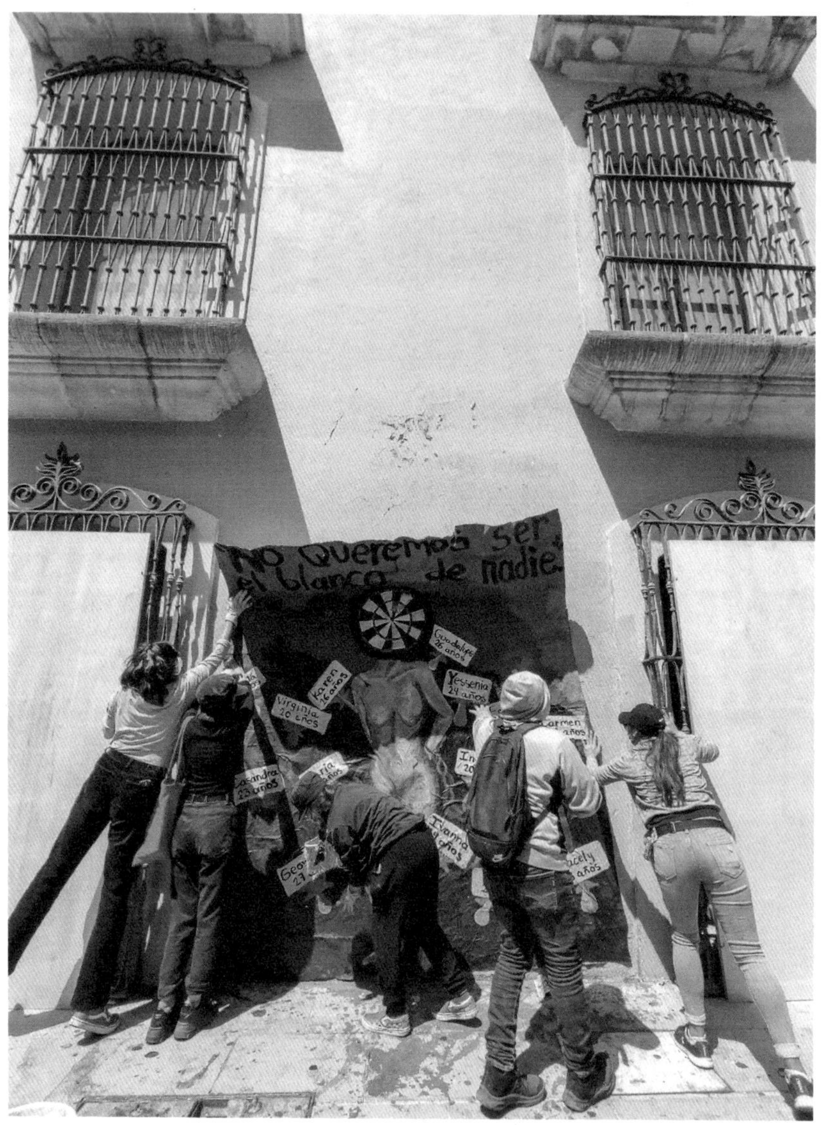

Figure 3.9
Members of ARMARTE pasting up the hand-painted installation *No queremos ser el blanco de nadie* (We do not want to be anyone's target).

most of ARMARTE's prints, which often contain several levels of meaning, *No queremos ser el blanco de nadie* is assertive, almost confrontational in its depiction of feminicide. It memorializes lives lost to violence, and the boldness of the print is an electroshock, telling the viewer that it is up to them to decide to take action against it.

Reflecting on ARMARTE

This section was premised on the following assertion: ARMARTE is a politically savvy collective whose central political project is the emancipation of the woman worker. Its members' work is infused with their lived experiences, and this desire for emancipation starts with them, as women, active on the Oaxaca engraving scene: "So, I think that this [the group's status among local artists] has also been like a … key piece in which progress has been made, even if it is not noticed, but from my perspective, well, if I have seen how … how we have gained a place there … something that, well, for about two years, well, they didn't see" (Ana interview, 2018). During our interview, Elena reflected on her role as a printmaker in Oaxaca. She said that she believed that "the main function of someone who makes street art is above all to disseminate what is happening at that moment as a society." A street artist ought to highlight issues that "we may hear in the news, in newspapers, on many social networks, but it is not given the importance it warrants." Engaged artists, then, act as filters through which to see the world, and, as with any filter, the members of ARMARTE carefully select where to aim the spotlight. In other words, through art they highlight issues to which the public might be desensitized or of which it has never been made aware. Artists must keep going: "It is a very long process. So, it will continue to happen, and it will continue to happen, and it will continue to happen, and we as artists, I think that what we have to do is spread and not leave it there" (Elena interview, 2018). For ARMARTE, repetition and redundancy are not necessarily negative – they illuminate a social pattern, issues that keep repeating themselves, and that must be denounced until they are resolved, until the conditions needed to fix them are met.

ARMARTE members also work toward achieving their goal by releasing prints around specific dates each year, building up anticipation for their work, while a clearly delineated ideological line keeps them on message.

For instance, the homage they paid to murdered women in their 2018 mural aligned well with the Día de Muertos and Día de Muertas, affording the collective exposure to two different types of communities: people who celebrate the Día de Muertos, and people who oppose gender-based violence. Another example, one that also demonstrates how politically savvy the collective is, is the three slogans found in their 2020 #8M posters. While positioning their work as part of the *Ni una más*, *Ni una menos*, and *Vivas nos queremos* campaigns could be interpreted as evidence of a lack of understanding of each campaign, ARMARTE collapses the three movements into one – a fight for women against gendered violence – ultimately highlighting that all three campaigns share the same objectives. And combining them helps ensure that at least one of those objectives will resonate with the viewer and can be shared on social media with hashtags.

Despite following a strict ideological line that keeps the collective focused on its message, its prints raise awareness of the diversity of the female experience. They show that there are different types of strong women: artists and intellectuals, *campesinas* and *soldaderas*, mothers, everyday examples of *lucha* and of women laying claim to their place in the world. There are as many struggles as there are women, and each one deserves her moment in the spotlight. All these struggles are valid and necessary.

Still, the limited number of prints, a repertoire of symbols that draws from URT-Arte, and the scope of advocacy dominated by a single issue could be seen as restricting the future of the collective. These limitations can be attributed to the small number of permanent members, and the fact that they are aligned in a single ideology. There is only so much that can be said with just one ideological line. However, this ideology almost acts as a brand. As a result, ARMARTE is less agile in responding to the nuances of the political landscape, but as their posting pattern attests, it is not something they really seek to do. Ultimately, these constraints work for them because most of their activities take place outside the workshop.

Indeed, art is only one aspect of ARMARTE's fight. Unlike MUGRE, a major aspect of their fight unfolds inside the workshop, within ARMARTE itself and with the members of URT-Arte, and out in the rural regions of the state, with children to whom they teach art. Indeed, ARMARTE seeks to empower the next generation:

> I think that most of the struggles are also in the communities. What ARMARTE is also looking for is a little, well, to work in the community and bring this ... which is a little what I have already worked on with URT-Arte, like going to ... the most impoverished sectors and giving them this tool ... Many times we believe that art is only for people who have money and that's it, but what about the farm labourer's son, what about the worker's son, what about the domestic worker's daughter, right? Well, art doesn't emerge because this boy, this girl is also helping their mother with the chores, right? So, suddenly it's like by doing this, these artistic camps, these workshops ... give the basic tools to the children, and [it is] a bit like introducing them, well, to artistic education, but also that they grasp art as ... that it's for everyone. (Ana interview, 2018)

The art camps are future-oriented, and a very concrete form of activism. While Duncombe (2016) talks about installations mostly elaborated with an external audience in mind, teaching how art can be a tool for empowerment is a form of artivism too, a very embodied one.

As I was finalizing my analysis in 2021, a small change surfaced on the collective's social media accounts. ARMARTE began referring to itself as "Mujeres en el arte," a new name that is not that much of a change in terms of content; they are, after all, women in art. The change to something shorter and less reliant on URT-Arte might be a sign that they are slowly emancipating themselves from their sibling collective. Incidentally, #MujeresEnElArte is also a very common hashtag on Instagram. By tagging their posts with their name, a name that is also a popular hashtag, they ensure that their posts pop up on more feeds and timelines.

Their latest project, *Ellas que luchan* (Those [women] who fight) is also an indication that while they remain close to URT-Arte, they are also creating a healthy distance and solidifying their own identity as a collective (ARMARTE 2022b). The collective released a call for prints, which were then exhibited in the state of Oaxaca as part of a travelling exhibit, reaching more people than posters glued to a wall. The twenty-four prints that form *Ellas que luchan* will be studied in my next book, as will be the collective's participation to the exhibit *El rebozo* (The shawl) at the Museo Nacional de la Estampa INBAL (2023) and Museo de las Culturas de Oaxaca, and their nine-print portfolio titled *amarrarte* (to moor yourself, to tie yourself).

Conclusion

In "Women Empowering Women" I examined the portrayal of gender-based violence in activist Mexican printmaking from 2006 to 2021, through the analysis of a selection of posters and prints designed by ASARO, MUGRE, and ARMARTE. The analysis of this corpus reveals three major shifts. First, the artivists' prints evolved from representing the feminicide crisis by depicting faceless women – either buried or dismembered – in the mid-2000s to portraying activist figures who directly address women. There was an unmistakable progression from depicting women as victims to showing them as agents of change, speaking directly to an audience and urging viewers to become part of the societal movement against structural gendered violence. Second, the scope of activism expanded, from focusing only on feminicides to denouncing all forms of gender-based violence. Finally, the repertoire of contention articulated by the activists progressed from one rooted in motherhood activism – where mothers staged protests to demand that the disappearance or murder of their daughters be taken seriously by the authorities and fully investigated – to one drawing from sisterhood activism – where all women are considered to be potential victims, and they should therefore stand together, shoulder-to-shoulder to dismantle patriarchal structures.

While the acknowledgment that all women were endangered by structural gender-based violence was implicit for earlier generations of activists, for this new generation it is made explicit through their use of the first-person pronouns *yo* (I) or *nosotras* (we) in many of their chosen hashtags and slogans. Changing the grammatical person following the Ayotzinapa disappearances in 2014 disrupted the accepted narrative that victims of feminicides, and more broadly victims of gender-based violence, were somehow anomalies in the social fabric. It also zeroed in on the notion that, similar to the Ayotzinapa disappearances, where every activist could fall victim to state violence, every woman is at risk, since gendered violence is more systemic than specific.

ASARO, MUGRE, and ARMARTE exercise their artivistic practices by "express[ing] outrage" (Naidus 2009, 5) and "reveal[ing] reality" (Duncombe 2016, 122). However, having examined the three groups' endeavours aimed at combatting gender-based violence in parallel, I conclude that the female-only collectives are more fully engaged with their audience. They collaborate with their base by "invit[ing] participation" (Duncombe 201, 1216) – either through their calls for images or their workshops, by "mak[ing] a place" (Duncombe 2016, 121) for women artists to "process an experience" (Naidus 2009, 5), and perhaps to "heal as makers" (Naidus 2009, 5). Their specific lived experience and their positionality colour their work. Since legislative measures taken at the federal and state levels have proven ineffective, they perceive a need to take matters into their own hands and address women directly in order to foster – even force – a decrease in gender-based violence. They do so in a context that is risky for them as female artivists; by exposing and decrying violence, they expose themselves to the very reality they decry. Through art, they offer women the tools – the written inscriptions – to push back against lewd comments, harassment, assault, and extreme violence. Unlike ASARO, MUGRE and ARMARTE not only denounce the issue; they project themselves into the future. In line with Naidus's (2009) criterion, they "envision a different reality or a better future" by inspiring their audience to dream (Duncombe 2016, 122) of a world where gender-based violence has lessened.

The female collectives are attempting to create a cohort effect through the dissemination of their work. Indeed, their artivistic production is directed at Mexican women, and through workshops, lectures, and reading circles, they join forces with women and victims' families. By lending them a political and an artistic voice, these artists are actively creating change on a small scale. My analysis reveals that these artivistic works "express outrage" (Naidus 2009, 5) but also seek to force a new form of "dialogue" on the Mexican authorities (Duncombe 2016, 121), generally by disrupting accepted narratives (122) around women's responsibility for the violence they experience. Based on Duncombe's theorization, which I introduced in chapter 1, I conclude that through their artworks, ASARO, URT-Arte, ARMARTE, and MUGRe demand an "imminent cultural and social shift." That being said, ASARO is perhaps not as bold and outspoken in demanding change as the female-only collectives. Nevertheless, let us not forget that in 2006 ASARO was at the vanguard. While this shift toward a culture in which machismo and patriarchy are constantly challenged is slow in coming, the gains made since 1993 show that the wheels are in motion.

As I come to the end of this chapter, I am left with similar questions to the ones I had in the previous one. What is the invisible the collectives are working toward "mak[ing] visible" (Naidus 2009, 5)? Slowly but surely, and despite the inaction of various levels of government, gender-based violence is being taken more seriously in Mexico (Kloppe-Santamaria and Zulver 2023). Women's groups are working with women to bring more awareness to the various forms of gender-based violence, encouraging them to question, flag, and denounce it. The reality the collectives are revealing is multi-faceted, as are the perceptions they want to alter (Duncombe 2016, 122): There is the reality of systemic injustices but also the reality that women are working toward changing prevailing attitudes.

Conclusion

Pasting Up Protest: The Art of Memorializing Violence in Mexican Printmaking underlines as a point of departure the tensions between two visions of Mexico: an official one, promoted by the authorities, and an alternative one, articulated by artists and activists. For decades now there has been a tug-of-war between these two groups. While the authorities sweep human rights violations under the rug, activist groups work toward unveiling them, in order to give victims the dignity they deserve. Human rights activists and collectives of artists have been especially active since the Tlatelolco massacre of 1968 at the height of the Dirty War.

The artist collectives I have examined – ASARO, URT-Arte, MUGRE, and ARMARTE – embody the new ways in which Mexican artivists contribute to a critical social discourse about state violence in Mexico. After years of massacres, forced disappearances of peasant and student activists, and waves of feminicides that went ignored by successive administrations, activists, artists, and artivists are now more active than ever "to make visible" these occurrences of violence (Naidus 2009, 5), to open a space for civil society to grieve and come to terms with the abuses Mexicans have experienced or witnessed, and to encourage the Mexican people to contribute to the country's political life. By "foster[ing] dialogue" (Duncombe 2016, 121), the collectives contribute to the elaboration of a more complete cultural identity and collective memory that take into consideration events that have been disregarded by the state. They also participate to a shift toward citizen participation in art; a shift consolidated by the Ejército Zapatista de Liberación Nacional in the

1990s with the creation, and subsequent re-elaboration, of their murals.

Similar to many artists who contributed to the EZLN's artistic endeavours, the members of the collectives are one with their audience; they come from similar socio-economic backgrounds, have experienced some of the same hardships, and acknowledge that they could fall victim to the very violence they denounce. Unlike previous generations of artists, who deplored the issues affecting the Mexican people without necessarily belonging to them, the members of the collectives have a lived experience of the violence to which they strive to draw attention and, hopefully, make disappear. Members of ASARO and URT-Arte have experienced police repression, and in some cases been disappeared, and members of MUGRe and ARMARTE are acutely aware of systemic gender-based violence, for it is an aspect of most women's daily lives. These lived experiences create a proximity to their audience, allowing them to tap into shared struggles and repertoires of visual symbols.

I performed a three-step visual analysis to analyze the corpus of prints and posters: I examined context, content, and form. I described each image and created an inventory of symbols, then focused on an image's conventional meaning, and finally interpreted its symbolic meaning. By drawing on intertextual and intervisual connections that I outlined in the introductory chapter, I illuminated the symbolic meaning of the works to situate the interpretation of the visual texts in their socio-cultural context. This analysis also enabled me to determine if and how these collectives could be considered artivists, and their artworks works of artivism.

In chapter 2, "Commemorating Ayotzinapa," I appraised the artistic representation of the September 2014 forced disappearances of the forty-three Ayotzinapa students by ASARO and URT-Arte. I demonstrated that the symbolism – words and images – used in their murals, installations, and posters promoted the surfacing of an alternative collective memory, one that seeks to mobilize citizens to act against systemic violence sponsored by the government. I also established that while ASARO's body of works mirrors the reactions and grieving process of the larger civil society – from making visible the forty-three students, to protesting and denouncing their disappearance, to finally mourning their loss – URT-Arte was only active during the last two phases. I attributed this to the fact that Mario Guzmán, URT-Arte's founder, was still a member of ASARO in 2014 and 2015, when the collective was designing installations aimed at publicizing the disappearances. I also concluded that the type of artworks aligned with each collective's primary purpose: permanency versus recruitment. Indeed, whereas ASARO opted for mural installations and murals located on the facade of Espacio Zapata, URT-Arte's choice of smaller, highly reproducible posters plastered all over the city allowed the collective to reach more people in different sectors of Oaxaca.

In chapter 3, "Women Empowering Women," I examined the portrayal of gender-based violence in activist Mexican printmaking from 2006 to 2021, through the analysis of a selection of posters and prints designed by ASARO, MUGRe, and ARMARTE. I concluded that the slogans deployed by each group are aligned with their depictions of women as either victims or agents of change. Indeed, while ASARO stands in solidarity with victims of feminicide and their families, the taglines deployed by MUGRe and ARMARTE represent calls to action that speak to women directly, enjoining them to denounce gendered violence. Unlike ASARO, MUGRe and ARMARTE envision a world where women will be the ones to put an end to gender-based violence.

Assembling a corpus of artworks designed and disseminated between 2006 and 2022 enabled me to establish the existence of a discursive and pictorial shift in the collectives' production. In the wake of the Ayotzinapa disappearances in 2014, slogans evolved from using the third person – We want *them* back alive! – to using the first person – We want *ourselves* alive! – effectively including the very activist who is demonstrating in the group for which she is demonstrating.

By switching the locus of enunciation, the activists went from demonstrating for the fate of a third party to demonstrating for themselves, bringing into the fight as many lived experiences as there were protesters, effectively broadening their message to include as many issues as there were protesters. The inclusion of first-person pronouns "I" and "we" in protest broadens the scope of advocacy. Indeed, the movement against feminicide expanded its artivism to take into consideration the full spectrum of gender-based violence, from catcalling to online bullying, to economic violence and sexual harassment. This expansion coincided with international feminist movements like #MeToo and contributed –

and still contributes – to highlighting that no occurrence of violence against women is too small.

This new generation of activists brought private issues like grief and shame into the public eye. For protesters, since gender-based violence is not an anomaly of the social fabric, but in fact the norm, acknowledgment of this violence should be public and should not lead to victim-shaming. Following Mexican traditional values, emotions like grief and shame belong to the private sphere; artivists disagree and blame their very existence on the state. With each poster, the protesters are boldly saying that these occurrences of violence should not be dealt with in private; since they are systemic, and state-enabled, they should be discussed and debated in the public sphere.

Despite a long tradition of politically engaged art that can be traced back to the immediate post-independence period (1810–30), artivism is only starting to be used as a lens through which to study Latin American artists. By bringing to bear the concept of artivism, a framework developed in the Global North, to analyze the production and praxis of artivists from the so-called periphery, *Pasting Up Protest* expands our understanding of the ways art can awaken citizens to pressing social issues, turn them into critical-political subjects, and end their self-imposed lack of political participation that stems from a fear of repercussions. A close analysis of the four collectives' mural installations, prints, and posters enriches our understanding of the different ways artists deploy print artivism, a relatively low-cost form of protest, not only to criticize authorities, but most importantly to engage with Mexican citizens at the base, fight apathy, and drive social change at a local level.

These objectives are shared by many grassroots organizations. The political and aesthetic strategies that the Mexican collectives have developed could thus become part of a more comprehensive tool kit that activists from the Global North leverage in their own movements. Unfortunately, systemic violence and missing persons are not solely Latin American issues. North American activists, whether those committed to searching the grounds of former residential schools for human remains or those involved in locating missing and murdered Indigenous women and girls, could adopt some of these same artivistic strategies to raise awareness of human rights violations and garner more support from sectors of the population that are reluctant to join in more traditional political activism. As my analysis has shown, artivism can act as a point of entry into social movements, promoting dialogue and feeding reflection among individuals who might otherwise not meet.

I conclude that the four collectives deploy an artivistic practice, and that their main targets are an "imminent cultural shift" (Duncombe 2016, 124) – a broader awareness of issues affecting the poorer and more marginalized sectors of the Mexican population – and an "ultimate cultural change" (124) – a change in mindsets, where the value of every life is equal regardless of socio-economic background, gender identity, and race (Duncombe 2016). Through the creation process, the artists fulfill most of Naidus's (2009) and Duncombe's (2016) criteria for artivism. The collectives "question" the state of Mexico, "offer solutions" to improve socio-economic inequalities or end systemic violence, "express outrage" at repeated occurrences of violence, and "foster dialogue" (Naidus 2009, 5) between different sectors of society, and in so doing they "build communities" by "invit[ing] participation" (Duncombe 2016, 121) in their various projects.

I did not set out to establish whether the collectives meet all the criteria listed by Naidus and Duncombe, and I do not believe that all twenty criteria ought to be met for a work to be considered artivism or a group to be considered artivist. The criteria provide different vantage points from which to understand the objectives of artivism, but in my view the lists are not meant as a checklist, every item of which must be ticked for an artwork to be considered artivism. Moreover, some criteria are harder to evaluate – "heal the maker" or "process an experience" (Naidus 2009, 5), for example – and one can only assume that the artists are creating art and using it as their main form of activism because doing so is fulfilling.

As I was finishing this manuscript during the winter 2023 semester, I had the opportunity and the joy to teach a seminar on artistic activism in Spanish America. One of my students was adamant that in order for artistic activism to be considered successful, it had to bring about a concrete, measurable change – an improvement, really – to the situation that artivists were denouncing in their work. I kept challenging them. Was a concrete artistic action taken against a problem not enough? Was a greater awareness of the problems plaguing one's society, a reflection on them, not enough? No, for this student there had to be a measurable change. How do we measure change in mindsets?

While I believe that change is hard to quantify in the humanities, especially in the arts, if there is one measurable change that has resulted from the collectives' work it is the visibility and the awareness that they have brought and are continuing to bring to the issues of forced disappearances and gender-based violence and feminicide. With every new poster and installation, the collectives succeed in making what was once invisible visible (Naidus 2009, 5). The systemic violence around the issues of juvenicide and feminicide, and the systems that foster it, are not invisible anymore, as these issues have moved from the private to the public sphere. More citizens are becoming comfortable addressing them head-on, intent on finding ways to decrease the high number of deaths. The fact that conversations around these human rights violations are now mainstream also highlights the collectives' success in "reveal[ing different] realities" (Duncombe 2016, 122): Artivists shine a light on systemic violence while also showing that new artivists are being born every day, influenced by prints and taglines they witness in the streets and online. The collectives demonstrate that activism and politics by other means take many forms, and though some can be smaller in scope, they can nonetheless be impactful. Indeed, the collectives can teach us a lot about online and in-person collaboration, and about leveraging art as an entry point to the discussion of charged topics. By highlighting the similarities between past and current occurrences of violence, they are convincing people to join a struggle they have little chance of winning – through art.

Reader: You, too, can contribute to the collectives', and to many other artivists', work. By staying informed and educating ourselves on issues that matter to us, and sharing our concerns and enthusiasm with family, friends, and colleagues, every single one of us can contribute to making challenging issues more visible and opening up spaces for conversation, slowly leading to, if not a resolution, then at least an awareness that we all need to work together to make the world a better, fairer place where everyone is recognized as a "grievable subject" (Butler 2016). As many countries restrict women's and LGBTQ+ rights, enforce harsher migration laws, turn a blind eye to systemic racism, and ignore calls to address climate change, every action, however small, is needed. Through their work, the collectives show us that no action is too small. Reaching just one person is a victory, as each person you affect is one more who can contribute to bringing greater awareness to the issues that plague our societies.

Like Mario Guzmán, I do not hold a romanticized view of this struggle, and despite my optimism, I also recognize that there are limits to artivism, and that success is subjective and influenced by one's time, place, and positionality. I therefore conclude that despite having a practice rooted in artivism, the collectives' individual artworks do not all meet the threshold for what counts as "successful" artivism and can instead be categorized as political artworks. In my view, this does not reduce their importance or value, only their reception.

While I did not set out to probe the limits of artivism, I am left with questions that could form the basis of future study. My hypothesis is that the time of creation, the visual language used, and the positionality of the viewer and the point in time when the work is experienced can affect the success of a piece (Sontag 1977). For instance, let us reflect on ASARO's 2006 series "Muertas de Juárez." While there is no denying that these prints played an important role in creating greater awareness around the feminicide crisis in Oaxaca and Mexico, they do not resonate *with me* as much as other works by the same collective, or prints by MUGRe and URT-Arte on the same issue. My positionality as a 2020s woman conditions my appreciation of them. It could be that there have been so many images denouncing this issue since 2006 that ASARO's prints almost appear tame in contrast. I wonder, do images lose some of their power over time? Despite my interrogations, I firmly believe that these prints are still relevant in the genealogy of artivist printmaking against gender-based violence. Having an established, credible collective like ASARO giving exposure to the issue of gendered violence might have encouraged other artists to raise their own voices against it.

My positionality as an individual who has grown up with technology and is familiar with social media also conditions my reading of the "Muertas de Juárez" series. Newer collectives like MUGRe and ARMARTE have access to different websites and different means of circulation than ASARO did in 2006. Whereas MUGRE and ARMARTE mostly share their work on Instagram and Facebook – two social media platforms that feed on likes, views, and immediacy – ASARO used Myspace and a blog in the mid-2000s and 2010s, two venues that require a certain "intentionality" on the part of the viewer: One had to open a web browser and know the specific URL one wished to consult.[1] Unlike current social media, Myspace was not an application installed on every smart phone, and the idea of the hashtag did not exist back in 2006; we could not tag images and create larger networks as easily as we can today.

By integrating the language of the Internet – using hashtags on their prints, and concise, sometimes punchy slogans that can be easily shared on social media or transferred onto a T-shirt or a sticker – younger collectives make it possible for their work to become part of a larger conversation, posted online and shared widely. By using concise messaging, they make it easy for viewers to share their work: Snap a picture of the print on the street, use the hashtag as caption, and voila!

The length of inscriptions and messages shared on prints and posters, as well as the use of past symbols, also affect their reception by a specific audience. While younger collectives grab a viewer's attention quickly with text of less than ten words, the older collectives expect viewers to perform a lot of interpretative work, recognizing the symbols and connecting them to previous conflicts to fully understand the message conveyed. Most of these posters present layers of meaning; one can only get the full picture by understanding the caption. The high levels of illiteracy in Mexico, or lack of familiarity with the poetic verses used, might limit reception of the prints to a certain audience, thus lessening their impact.

Finally, I believe that lived experience – that of the artist and that of the viewer – matters when determining whether a piece is a successful work of artivism. By having lived experience of the issues that they denounce, the artists imbue their works with something indescribable. Their messages resonate more, because the changes they demand have a direct impact on them. They are most invested. The viewer might also be more receptive if they share the lived experience depicted on a poster.

There is no abstraction or universalization of an issue; both artivist and viewer are affected in their flesh.

Eliciting compassion and empathy to get people to care about forced disappearances are noble goals, but I wonder, are these goals too big? Is it possible that by framing juvenicide and feminicide as systemic, "universal issues" to reach the broadest possible audience, ASARO and URT-Arte undermine their own work? In trying to reach everyone, could these collectives end up reaching only a smaller, even if more dedicated, crowd? Unlike the works of younger collectives, prints by ASARO and URT-Arte rarely speak directly to anyone – viewers are expected to universalize the issue and put themselves in the shoes of the protesters, or of the victims and their loved ones.

Beyond these unanswered questions, I am still convinced that print artivism is a valuable and effective way to engage citizens at the base, make violence and its consequences easier to talk about, and embed past occurrences of violence into a nation's cultural memory. Activism and art will never fully compensate for states' unwillingness to treat their citizens with basic care. That being said, in the event that the state sponsors violence against its own citizens or chooses to remain blind to systems that harm large sectors of the population, activists and artists perform useful work, work that has a positive impact first on the artists themselves, then on audience members who are receptive to their message.

Feminist activists in Latin America are particularly active in this regard. In this context, a promising venue of inquiry, blending visual analysis with gender studies and feminist philosophy, would concentrate on how collectives contribute to the construction of decolonial feminisms through various networks of solidarity. Indeed, while it has been established that pan-continental non-governmental organizations or government-funded agencies share policies and best practices, smaller groups of artivists or individual artivists who exchange artworks online have received little attention. And yet, they are the ones engaging with the very targets of gender violence: women. Unlike most government campaigns against gender violence, which only target men, the works of women-identifying artivists enter into a direct conversation with women, telling them they can disrupt engrained machismo. A project I would like to develop is the study of knowledge circulation between Chilean, Argentinean, and Mexican collectives and individual artists, specifically around the struggle for abortion rights and against gender-based violence. I believe it would be of interest to study the North-South circulation of protest knowledge about feminicides and the South-North knowledge around best practices to spearhead legislation on abortion rights, and, considering the current world order, how these practices could be adapted to and disseminated in the Global North.

Epilogue

As I was finishing *Pasting Up Protest*, I travelled to Mexico, to a city I would like to include in a future study. Officially, I was on vacation. Unofficially? I was keeping my eyes peeled for the smallest traces of protest art.

On the first day, as I was walking down main street a few minutes after leaving my hotel, my eyes were drawn to slogans, inscriptions, and wheat paste posters that denounced gender-based violence: "Vivas nos queremos" and "Ni una más" written in neon pink, alongside the names and ages of recent feminicide victims. Wheat paste posters were also calling on tourists to open their eyes to the fact that the city they visited to enjoy the sun and the beach was not the safe haven it claims to be; it was, according to the posters, a paradise for men who abuse and kill women. Further along, the protesters had repurposed a stop sign. Under the word *alto* ("stop" in Spanish) they had added letter stickers that spelled out "Ni una más" – a motif repeated throughout the city.

Finally, a few streets away, in a zone with fewer tourists, I stumbled upon a massive billboard – a full wall, not unlike a mural, I thought – sponsored by the municipal authorities. The Violence Meter listed thirty forms of gender-based violence, and categorized them into various "danger categories," from "be careful" and "react" to, finally, "ask for help immediately" (Instituto Nacional de las Mujeres 2020). It urged women to contact various centres to get help. Up to that point, nothing groundbreaking. Unlike most government-sponsored initiatives I had seen until then, however, this one personalized the issue, talking to women directly by using the imperative form. It appealed to them to keep an eye open for these forms of violence, not only in their own relationships but also in those of their sisters and friends. A concise and snappy hashtag also graced the billboard, an attempt to create a community around the issue. I could not help but to see similarities with the strategies used by the collectives I study. Posting an eye-level billboard directly addressing the audience that you wish to reach? Leveraging empathy toward sisters and friends to conscientize women?

I do not know if the municipal authorities of that Mexican city know the collectives analyzed in this book and their various campaigns. My best guess is that they do not; and if they do, they might be wary of deploying techniques successfully used by openly Marxist-Leninist or feminist collectives. Still, these best practices appear to be assimilating into the mainstream.

Change is in motion. It bodes well for the future.

Notes

Preface

1 The slogan is adapted from Ernesto Cardenal's poem (1984, 117), "Epitafio para la tumba de Adolfo Báez Bone." The original reads as follows: "Creyeron que te enterraban y lo que hacían era enterrar una semilla" (They thought they were burying you but what they were doing was planting a seed). Unless otherwise noted, translations from the original Spanish (and in some cases French) are my own. Where I have quoted from a published English translation, I have used an endnote to indicate the source on first occurrence.

2 "Foreigners cannot, in any way, be involved in political affairs of the country" (Unidad General de Asuntos Jurídicos 2011).

3 Since the feminist movement has ties to green movements, the organizers asked participants to bring eco-responsible glitter. Unlike traditional glitter, which is made from plastic, eco-responsible glitter is made of sugar, and thus better for the environment since it degrades with water (*BBC News* 2019; *Deutsche Welle* 2019).

4 Built between 1900 and 1910, the Ángel de la Independencia represents Nike, the Greek goddess of victory. In recent decades, the monument has become a gathering place for Mexican citizens, for both celebrations and protests. The Ángel and the Paseo de Reforma were both considered places of gathering to demand social justice long before the incident in 2019. An earthquake in 1985 destabilized Mexico City's infrastructure amid an ongoing economic crisis, but on the day of the 1986 World Cup, hosted in Mexico, thousands gathered in the Paseo de la Reforma as Mexico beat Belgium. The joy of winning, and pent-up frustration at the recent economic and infrastructural turmoil, led to vandalism and chaos across the city. As Mexico's soccer team advanced in the

tournament, celebrations continued sporadically until Mexico finally lost to Germany. The occupation of the streets in 1986 set a precedent for how that space would be used. Since then, the Paseo de la Reforma has been the space of protest and social justice advocacy, with constant occupations and, more recently, vandalism as a way of expressing the deep political change many citizens feel is necessary (Nagel-Vega 2020).

5 My most recent visit to the monument was in December 2024. Officially, it is open, but the authorities are so anxious to avoid further public demonstrations that they have opted to keep the metal gates up.

6 As the Restauradoras con Glitter (2019), a group of art restorers and conservators, were quick to point out the day after the protests, tomatoes or lemon juice, more traditionally female weapons, would have caused more damage.

7 In a speech, the president addressed the protesters directly:

> I call on those who demonstrate to do so responsibly, without violence, without harming the citizenry, and *to be careful with the cultural and artistic heritage of Mexico, of all of us, of all Mexicans. How can we not take care of the Ángel [de la Independencia]. It is an extremely important monument.* It is part of our cultural and artistic heritage, and we must protect it; this also applies to the Paseo de la Reforma – not vandalizing it, as has been done. The statues, which we are certainly going to rebuild, these are our heroes who fought in the *Reforma*, in the *Intervención*. How could we not respect that? *What does a movement that pursues a just cause, in this case women's rights, have to do with destruction?* Can we not do it peacefully? Does it have to be with violence? I don't believe in that, I don't think that the path of violence is the approach to take. We will continue to act with tolerance; repression is prohibited. (*Periodismohoy* 2019; my emphasis)

Chapter One

1 "En México … caminamos sobre una alfombra de huesos viejos y de otros muy recientes." Poniatowska quoted in Mateos-Vega (2016).

2 According to Amnesty International (2024), by the end of 2023 the number of disappeared reached 114,004 people. For its part, Human Rights Watch (Wilkinson 2019) reports that the Registro Nacional de Datos de Personas Extraviadas o Desaparecidas (National Registry of Disappeared and Missing People) tallies more than 40,000 missing or disappeared people in Mexico – a conservative figure, as not all families file a missing person report.

3 During former President Enrique Peña Nieto's *sexenio*, thirteen people disappeared every day; that is one person every 112 minutes (Campo 2015). During the tenure of Andrés Manuel López Obrador, Peña Nieto's successor, that figure rose considerably, with some estimates putting the number of disappearances at one per hour (Martínez 2023).

4 I explore the multiple layers of meaning behind MUGRE's name in chapter 3.

5 In Mexico, *colectivos* – collectives – are a very common mode of organization in every sector of society, not only in art. Members are usually united by shared goals or beliefs and put the communitarian aspects of their struggle – rather than individual demands – at the centre of their action. Most have a horizontal mode of organization. In *Pasting Up Protest*, I use the word "collectives" to designate groups of artists that work collaboratively in a shared space, and that pursue a clearly established, ideologically and politically oriented objective, generally laid out in a founding manifesto. Since former President Felipe Calderón launched his "war on drugs" in 2006, and mass disappearances began increasing, a new type of collective made up of families of disappeared people demanding justice for their loved ones began to spread across Mexico. When the justice system failed or simply ignored the victims, these collectives started digging in the Mexican countryside, unearthing mass graves. The Comisión Nacional de los Derechos Humanos (CNDH) confirmed in 2018 that more than thirteen hundred clandestine graves have been found since 2007 (CNDH 2018). Most of these graves were discovered by family members of the disappeared, who, using a metal rod, pierce the soil and wait for the smell of death. The umbrella organization Movimientos por Nuestros Desaparecidos en México (Movement

for Our Disappeared in Mexico), created in 2015 and now comprising more than fifty-two collectives, has been at the forefront of the "discovery" of a lot of these mass graves, stepping in despite local authorities' negligence and their desire to conceal mass violence. Where the authorities fail, the citizenry organizes and prevails, finding and identifying their dead, and offering them a decent burial (see Centro Prodh 2021).

6 In street art slang, "getting up" means that an artist is particularly active.

7 Prints were produced in the Viceroyalty of New Spain as early as 1539 (Oles 2013, 62), and Mexico therefore boasts one of the oldest printmaking traditions in the Americas (McDonald 2016). The first school of engraving was founded in Mexico City in 1781 (Ittmann 2006, 3), and lithography was introduced to Mexico by the Italian Claudio Linati (1790–1832) after 1821 (Oles 2013, 158), increasing the "dissemination of visual imagery across all social classes" (172). However, low literacy rates and prohibitive costs still limited the reach of prints, and artworks more broadly.

8 Referring to prints specifically, Mario Guzmán, co-founder of ASARO and founder of URT-Arte, indicated that the objective is to reproduce the prints until the matrix (the original) disintegrates. He also added that now, thanks to technological advances, the problem of disintegration can be solved by scanning the matrix and reprinting it indefinitely using a 3-D printer (Guzmán, interview with the author, 2018).

9 While calling oneself a feminist has become commonplace in North America, in Mexico embracing the label is still a radical political statement, as feminism is often equated with anarchy, misandry, and violent demonstrations that lead to the destruction of private and public property. This is explored in chapter 3.

10 Volk and Schlotterbeck explain that "it is precisely because the state has failed so abjectly in stopping these murders that 'fictional' narratives have become both the site where victims are mourned and the means by which justice can be restored. Cultural producers have filled the vacuum left by state officials who continue either to shun their responsibilities or to conceal the guilty" (2007, 122).

11 While one would hope that people would feel an urgency to act in the world according to their own belief systems, it must be acknowledged that activism can also be used effectively by people who hold opposing views; it does not make it less effective, even if we disagree with their goals. Efficient techniques and strategies can be put to bad use as well as good.

12 The Black Lives Matter movement, which was triggered in the United States in 2012 by the death of Trayvon Martin in Stanford, Florida, gained more exposure in 2020 following the murder of George Floyd in Minneapolis, Minnesota.

13 Although the EZLN was created in 1983, the Zapatistas only gained international visibility on 1 January 1994, when they released the First Declaration and Revolutionary Laws and rose up in the state of Chiapas – the third-poorest state in Mexico – against the implementation of the North American Free Trade Agreement. Unlike other guerilla and social movements, the EZLN had no interest – and still has no interest – in seizing state power. Their political project is rooted in self-determination, and seeks to restore dignity to citizens excluded from and/or oppressed by the nation-state. In that sense, their work – both political and artistic – is an undeniable influence on the four collectives studied in *Pasting Up Protest*. The Zapatistas defend a clearly articulated political project rooted in revolutionary memory. Whereas the 1910–20 Zapatista discourse integrated art in a diffuse manner, spreading ideas of a flattened hierarchy, the contemporary Zapatista artists integrate claims and ideas much more concretely into their practice. Since 1995, the EZLN includes a multidisciplinary artistic group, the Caravana de Artistas (Caravan of Artists), which brings together musicians, dancers, photographers, as well as visual, literary, radio, and other artists. Murals remain the movement's most emblematic art form, both as a vehicle for storytelling and for its ability to highlight alternative visions of Mexican history. I explore Zapatista muralism further in relation to the Ayotzinapa disappearances.

14 For an exhaustive history of graffiti and street art, I recommend Anna Wacławek's *Graffiti and Street Art* (2011). Unlike most monographs on the topic, hers is one of the few books that pro-

vides a visual art analysis of a series of unsanctioned works from all around the world (but mostly Europe). More importantly, her monograph also relies on images of the artworks she studies. For both reasons, her valuable template underpins my own analysis.

15 Political graffiti, both inscriptions and posters, was reactivated during the May 1968 protests in France, and became a staple of the 1968 movements (Kugelberg and Vermès 2012). Graffiti is part of a larger cultural system. In New York in the 1970s and '80s, graffiti was one of the three pillars of hip hop culture, along with break-dancing and DJing (McEwen 2019).

16 The word "graffiti" (usually both singular and plural; the singular "graffito" is rarely used) is from the Italian word *graffiato*, which means "scratched" or "scrawled."

17 I refer to graffiti practitioners as "writers," since most of them reject the title of "artist."

18 And yet, some tags, "throw-ups," and "pieces" are extremely well crafted, demonstrating mastery of a complex medium. Throw-ups often have two colours (contour and background); pieces are the most complex form of graffiti writing, with as many colours, dimensions, and details as the artist can manage. The quality of a graffiti depends on a few variables: its complexity, its size, the danger involved in its execution, and its placement and visibility. Almost any surface can become a canvas: walls, trains, palisades, floors, panels, windows, vehicles, electrical boxes, even mailboxes. These criteria – complexity, size, danger, visibility – also define the "street cred," the subcultural capital, of a work or artist. These criteria are internal to the graffiti community, which further highlights graffiti's status as an identity-building tool for its practitioners (Wacławek 2008, 168).

19 However, this is no longer the case; street gangs have developed other codes, and the very notion of territory has become obsolete. Taggers' "territories" simply have no limits anymore: The whole city – and even beyond – is their playground.

20 For instance, New York City's zero tolerance policy – spearheaded by Police Commissioner William Bratton and Mayor Rudy Giuliani – was based on the "broken windows" theory, which stipu-

lates that building an environment where crime is not apparent is directly related to its decrease (Kelling and Coles 1996). Thus, the only right answer to the spread of graffiti was to launch a war against it, and to erase all of it. Despite the city's best efforts, the epidemic was never contained. In a game of cat and mouse, city workers would paint over graffiti, only to have graffiti writers use the freshly painted wall as a new canvas.

21 The term "graffiti," used pejoratively in the 1970s and '80s, gave way after 1984 to "post-graffiti," which at the time described every artwork that shared the "street aesthetic" but that was not explicitly graffiti. It now corresponds to creations of the same style but made on canvas.

22 For more on Mexico City graffiti, see Arroyo and Arroyo (2015).

23 Franco Ortiz presents a discussion of the possible origins of the term "cholo." The one she deems most probable is that it came from the English "show and low," used in the United States to describe the way people would walk and their "gait" (2011, 74).

24 Cholo writing was easily distinguishable from graffiti writing: While writers used the same spray paint, cholos used Old English letters that *pachuco* and Chicano youth used in Southern California during the 1930s and '40s (Lammons 2012, 38–9). These pieces were not to be written over by other groups; doing so was perceived as a serious offence and a form of provocation (84). This respect for other groups' works might explain the high regard accorded to the collectives' artworks in Oaxaca. Indeed, whereas urban art in North America is often tagged, in Oaxaca most of it remains untouched for long periods of time. I will explore this aspect in more detail when I examine ASARO's and URT-Arte's bodies of works centred on the Ayotzinapa disappearances.

25 The first generation emerged in the 1990s, the second, which continues into the present, emerged in the early 2000s.

26 Their educational background led some graffiti writers to move toward using stencils to convey their messages. The stencil is a hybrid of two traditions: street graffiti and graphic art, because it is reproducible, uses public wall spaces, and has a pluralist technique associated with graphic design (Franco Ortiz 2011, 113).

This provoked a debate to which I already alluded above. Since stencil artists create their designs off-site, with more than spray paint and a valve, stencil graffiti is not considered true graffiti by "purists," who see graffiti as a unique practice, because their pieces are irreproducible (114).

27 In 1985, the expression "street art" – preferred to "graffiti" for its positive connotation – started circulating. At that time, it was still used vaguely to categorize everything that held a certain "street" ethos (Genin 2014).

28 Although street art is directly derived from graffiti, an ideological divide exists between the two worlds. While graffiti purists advocate a complete rejection of fine art codes, other artists are more comfortable with its legality and institutionalization. This disagreement is often identified as the "sell-out problem." It persists today, and serves, in a way, to distinguish each community of practice (Banet-Weiser 2011). This separation between the two regimes does not prevent artists from moving from one to the other (Wacławek 2008). An ethic of cohabitation, even accountability, has been established: "While some writers may not fully support post-graffiti interventions, street artists, many of whom have participated in graffiti subcultures prior to their individualized practices, consciously tend not to interfere with or obstruct graffiti's space" (Wacławek 2008, 214). Street art, then, can be both legal and illegal, and legal street art played a major role in breaking the glass ceiling between low and high art, ending the subcultural isolation of the practice. Wacławek (2008, 2011) highlights the differences that were already growing in the conception of the practice when the documentaries *Wild Style* (Ahearn 1982) and *Style Wars* (Silver 1983) were released. Both were very influential back then, and still are. Merill (2014), for his part, sees an illustration of this debate in the war in London between the graffiti artist King Robbo and street artist Banksy.

29 For instance, most of the time dedicated to interventions involving ceramics, yarn bombing, and even stencils is spent off-site; only the application process and subsequent display happen directly on the street.

30 Even with the fluidity and constant exchange between the two regimes, a degree of tension persists between graffiti and street art, both within the communities of practice themselves and among the public (Banet-Weiser 2011; Wacławek 2008). Often, it is a case of "beauty is in the eye of the beholder" and of a lack of aesthetic literacy on the part of people outside each community of practice. In my view, this hierarchization highlights two issues: On the one hand, we tend to assign more value to interventions that align more closely with our own understanding of "art," while on the other, we do not fully understand the purpose of graffiti writing. While graffiti writing is a form of vandalism, and therefore illegal, it is often also a way for marginalized sectors to make their presence known in an environment that marginalizes them.

31 Dabène fills a gap in the scholarship on Mexico and its particular political landscape by dedicating an chapter to the city of Oaxaca. As a political scientist, Dabène is interested primarily in participatory democracy and resistance.

32 Intaglios are themselves split into two techniques: engraving and etching. Engraving evolved from goldsmiths' practices. In the past, artists used copper, but over time they adopted other materials, such as plastic, plexiglass, zinc, steel, or brass – some of which are inexpensive and widely available, again reinforcing their appeal for creators of propaganda. Using different dry points, burins, or scrapers, artists cut into the surface to create a pattern. Once the cutting work is done, the ink, thick and viscous, is applied over the whole matrix and penetrates the interstices. The ink is then removed from the surface, so that only the hollow pattern appears in the printed output. Etching works the same way as engraving, except that the design is incised not onto the material itself but onto a superficial layer of protective varnish. Etching techniques are quite numerous; however, mezzotint, aquatint, and sugar lift are the most popular. Artists create their design by gently scraping the varnish. They then immerse the matrix in an acid bath called "mordant" (biting). The sections of the surface that are no longer protected are "bitten" by the chemicals, and damaged as if they were cut out. As in intaglio, the surface is then covered with ink

to fill the interstices, only allowing the hollow pattern to appear on the printed output.

33 A note on colour: All the prints I examine in *Pasting Up Protest* were originally produced in black and white. While art history dedicates a great deal of thought to colour, when it comes to Mexican printmaking, there is generally not much to read into this selection. Indeed, most collectives choose to print in black for the simple reason that black is the cheapest ink colour (Guzmán interview, 2018). Moreover, in militant circles, when prints are reproduced quickly and plastered as posters on the streets, activists always run the risk of seeing them removed by municipal workers or very quickly destroyed by the elements. In such situations, there is no added value in using more expensive colour.

34 José Guadalupe Posada (1852–1911) is one of the best-known producers of Mexican popular prints, primarily due to his representation of Mexicans as *calaveras* (skulls). Posada was active from 1871 until his death at the onset of the Mexican Revolution. His creations are easily identifiable by their social commitment, and they directly tackle national and religious political issues. Unlike earlier artworks, they are not explicitly about nation building in a future-oriented way; they depicted the struggles of the Mexican people during Posada's era. In his *Art and Architecture in Mexico* (2013), which covers five hundred years of creative production, James Oles states that unlike earlier artists, Posada generated "a discourse based on particular rather than grand, overarching themes," as was generally found in earlier larger-than-life or national paintings; Oles labels him a "documentarian" (224). Indeed, Posada's cartoons often portrayed social issues from the perspective of the working class, at a time when most artists either ignored or held common people in contempt (Barajas 2009, 399). As he did not sign most of his prints, attributing them is a complex endeavour (Villoro et al. 2014). According to Rafael Barajas (2009), this might make Posada's legacy appear more political than his practice actually was.

35 I draw mostly from Asavei's *Aesthetics, Disinterestedness, and Effectiveness in Political Art* (2018), and Duncombe's (2016) extensive

research on artivism. I also frame the latter in a Latin American context – a task that only a few scholars have undertaken (Latorre 2019).

36 Cuban American and openly gay artist Félix González-Torres says in an interview with Rollins (1993), "There is no such thing as an apolitical or inert artwork. Art always serves a function – it either furthers and helps the master narrative or it tries to disrupt it."

37 My objective here is not to settle debates or propose new definitions for these concepts. Due to its relative novelty in scholarship, the very notion of artivism is still up for debate, as it is being defined, redefined, and expanded with every new investigation.

38 This critical content is not always oppositional in nature. Asavei (2018) identifies three instances of political art: (1) endorsement, where state authorities and artists align; (2) critique, where artists oppose political decisions or outcomes; and (3) portrayal, which is to say representation. In *Pasting Up Protest*, I concentrate on the second category, critique, since this art "critiques and negates the status quo of the moment … and attempts to make visible the injustices that the dominant structures of power tend to obscure" (15). For Asavei, critical political art concentrates on the "antagonistic dimension of the political" (15), where tensions between participants are highlighted, and a critical but constructive dialogue can emerge.

39 Along the same lines, Frank Möller (2016) claims that "art is political if it complicates, not simplifies" (2), our knowledge about the world, and if "this extension does not produce knowledge conventionally understood and instead confuses, irritates, and unsettles the recipient" (19). It is this confusion and irritation that can lead to action.

40 These audiences are many and include the artist(s) themselves, citizens as political agents who could be impacted by the work, either positively or negatively, as well as the authorities and various power structures. These different audiences, and the relationship between power and artists, are further explored in chapters 2 and 3.

41 Hatuka (2018) theorizes and conceptualizes the use of space by

protest movements. She relies on two main concepts: political and social distance. While political distance is "the condition of being at variance with, disagreeing with, dissenting from, and disputing those in power," social distance "refers to an individual's position (high or low) with respect to others" (14). In other words, while social distance is the differing social position and ideology of a social group in comparison to others, political distance is the dissonance, or difference in opinions and tensions resulting from it, between the ruler and the ruled.

42 Some artivists, like Mario Guzmán, are quite open about this aspect of their work: "We do propose that the only emancipatory guide is going to be violent one day. Yes, we claim the revolution, we claim the armed path as the way in which at some point society can change … And to prepare ourselves for these scenarios … we don't know if we're going to see that, but we are preparing the new colleagues who are going to have to … That's how I see it" (interview, 2018).

43 Cécile Van De Velde (2022, 2) uses the expressions "words of anger" and "writings of anger" to describe the various textual inscriptions deployed by protesters.

44 The evolution from the collective "we" to the individual "I" "reflects the growing place of individuality" in social movements and demonstrations (Van De Velde 2022, 3).

Chapter Two

1 #YoSoy132 was the first social movement in Mexico to use social media effectively. In 2012, then PRI presidential candidate Enrique Peña-Nieto visited the Ibero-American University – a private Catholic institution in Mexico City – as part of his campaign. In an exchange with students, he was asked about the 2006 San Salvador Atenco attacks, where two people were killed and dozens of women were raped by police forces. At the time, Peña-Nieto was governor of this state of Mexico and had given police the green light to dismantle the protest. The presidential candidate dismissed the question, claiming that Mexico had the right to use force to restore peace and order. The discussion was filmed, up-

loaded to social media, and subsequently taken up by major news outlets, which did not mention that the questions had come from the students. Upset by this oversight on the part of the media, some 131 students from the university posted a video on YouTube in which they identified themselves with their ID numbers (R3CR3O 2012). Their video went viral, and the protest movement spread to many other Mexican universities. By sharing the video, every protester became the 132nd protester, thus the slogan #YoSoy132.

2 Mexican author and public intellectual Jorge Volpi writes, "If the case of the Ayotzinapa *normalistas* has aroused so much indignation, it is because, in the midst of the endless horrendous deaths that we have witnessed in these years of gunpowder, it embodies the sum of all our fears … Forty-three young people from families mired in ancestral poverty. Forty-three young people who, beyond their radical ideology, represent all those Mexicans who only aspire to a better life" (Volpi 2014).

3 This version of events is based on the first *Informe Ayotzinapa* report (GIEI 2015) presented by the Interdisciplinary Group of Independent Experts (Grupo Interdisciplinario de Expertos Independientes, or GIEI), from 6 September 2015. I also use the Ayotzinapa timeline created by the North American Congress on Latin America (Gallagher, n.d.).

4 Daniel Solís Gallardo and Julio César Ramírez Nava were shot at close range and their bodies left in the open at the crime scene for hours without any protection (GIEI 2015), despite witnesses claiming that the army stopped to confirm their deaths (Hernández 2020). Julio César Mondragón, who had fled the scene during the press conference, was tortured and skinned, then tossed on a trash pile in an industrial zone. The photo of his faceless body began circulating on social media even before his next of kin had been notified of his passing.

5 Three passersby were also killed by mistake. A bus of teenaged soccer players – the Avispones – was mistaken for a bus carrying *normalistas* and riddled with bullets: fourteen-year-old soccer player David Josué García Evangelista and bus driver Víctor

Manuel Lugo Ortiz died from their injuries after being denied transportation to a hospital for treatment. Blanca Montiel Sánchez, who was in a taxi when the attacks happened, was caught in the crossfire.

6 The Liga de Escritores y Artistas Revolucionarios (LEAR) was a gathering of writers and artists organized in the wake of Lázaro Cárdenas's presidential campaign in 1933. They were aligned with the ideology of the Mexican Revolution and the International Union of Revolutionary Writers. The orientation of their resistance was clear: The members opposed fascism, imperialist war, and capitalist invasion. For the LEAR, the social function of art was to be fulfilled by the realism of social representation, which guaranteed its understanding and autonomy. As David Craven points out, art and social change were inseparable for artists: "those who contributed to LEAR and the TGP [Taller de Gráfica Popular] also attempted to alter social and political structures through their use of culture" (quoted in Smith 2017, 227). The LEAR's means of action were numerous, from congresses to theatrical productions, to their monthly magazine, *Frente a frente*. Their work was often ephemeral, serving its fundamental purpose in protests and only preserved in photographs. In terms of their posture, the collectives examined here reflect many influences from the LEAR: They, too, aspire to an intellectual and artistic production in the service of the workers' and peasants' struggle, to an art of the masses made by artists aware of their posture and their role.

However, ideological differences between artists and audience were not without consequences. In its first year, the LEAR struggled to reach the masses despite its members' efforts. Much of their artwork was produced by middle-class intellectuals influenced by Marxism, an ideology that was not resonating with members of the lower classes, although the LEAR explicitly targeted them (Oles 2013, 282). Artistic experimentation also sometimes obscured their intentions. To reach their audience, the LEAR "sent 'cultural brigades' to provincial cities" (282), similar to the workshops hosted by ASARO, URT-Arte, and ARMARTE in the villages around Oaxaca.

Unlike the LEAR, an ideological alignment between artists and audiences has enabled the Oaxacan collectives to use these activities to recruit more members into their respective groups. Due to ideological "differences between its Stalinist and Trotskyite members" (Williams 2006, 15), the LEAR weakened considerably from 1937 onward. Some of the artists went on to create the TGP, a workshop closely affiliated with the political Left.

7 "A Rebel Tradition" is my translation of a sentence from the essay "Tristeza de las generaciones sin maestros. Se necesitan maestros rebeldes": "Ayotzinapa participa de una tradición rebelde" (Moreno Romero 2018, 27).

8 McCormick (2017), in "The Last Door: Political Prisoners and the Use of Torture in Mexico's Dirty War," examines the experiences of Mexico's political prisoners during the Dirty War (particularly in the 1970s) and the many efforts of family members and leaders such as Lucio Cabañas to achieve the release of these individuals. She focuses on two central repressive tools used by the Mexican government in order to nurture a culture of fear: detention and torture. McCormick breaks the war into three stages: 1946–62 (the birth of Mexico's secret police, and growing repression in rural areas far from the public eye [59]), 1962–68 (aggressive guerrilla and military interactions leaving many activists dead [60]), and 1968–82 (the Tlatelolco massacre, urban and rural extension of repressive tools becoming more systematic, family members becoming political prisoners and torture victims, the start of the disappearances leading to a culture built on fear [60]). In her investigation, McCormick points out that the full extent of the violence experienced in Mexico is unknown due to the lack of a truth commission (61). Given the minimal documentation that exists, we only know of seven thousand people who were tortured – often vaguely described as having undergone "applied pressure" or been "interrogated" in official government files – three thousand prisoners, and over three thousand disappeared (most victims coming from rural areas such as Guerrero) (62).

9 The expression *escuela normal* comes from the Spanish *norma*, norm or method (not to be confused with "normal" as a synonym

for "habitual"). The *normales rurales* are different from the *normales urbanas*, which were created a century before. The main difference lies in their location (urban versus rural, as the name implies), curriculum, and the emphasis put on self-sufficiency and democratic life in the *rurales.* One of the main objectives of the system of rural schools – implemented in the 1920s by Secretary of Education José Vasconcelos – was to bring education to the country's impoverished regions, to raise literacy levels. Incidentally, these regions also have larger Indigenous populations. Civera-Cerecedo (2004, 5) postulates that the schools were created to "integrate the rural population into civilization." See also Civera-Cerecedo (2008).

10 For instance, the Mexican government currently contributes 20 pesos (about CAD$1.35) a day for food, and since 2011 has consistently refused to increase funding to the schools, which, in turn, has led to more student protests. The lack of funding is the main cause of protests by the Ayotzinapa students. At every opportunity, they lobby local officials to improve living conditions at the *normal.* At the end of July 2019, the Secretaría de Educación Pública (Secretariat of Public Education) committed over 34 million pesos (about CAD$2.5 million) to improve the installations at the school.

11 The PDLP (1967–74) adopted Marxism, sparking a belief in the need for a revolution inspired by the 1910 revolution. The politics of the PDLP contained "both older local-regional *campesino* translations of social democracy, radical agrarianism, and Cardenista populism and transnational guerrilla New Left visions based on socialism, direct action, national liberation, and anti-imperialism" (Aviña 2014, 2). It broadened the definition of the revolutionary protagonist to include the poor, therefore making success dependent on the participation of rural communities. The objective was to create a socialist world "without that grand theft … the exploitation of the poor by the rich" (3).

12 Before militant and political art went underground in the wake of the 2 October shootings, the 1950s and '60s had witnessed waves of protest art denouncing government decisions. Two main forms

of art coexisted: the Olympic logo – designed by Pedro Ramirez Vazquez, architect and president of the organizing committee for the Games, Mexican architect Eduardo Terrazas, and American artist Lance Wyman (International Olympic Committee, n.d.) – and posters and slogans used in protests, many of which appropriated and hijacked the visual identity of the 1968 Olympics. For instance, one depicted President Gustavo Díaz Ordaz (1964–70) as a gorilla. These posters were conceived as artifacts intended to serve in marches and demonstrations, not as artworks. This is quite similar to ASARO's 2006 stencils, most of which were produced quickly and efficiently, for militant purposes. For more protest designs from 1968, see Museo Universitario Arte Contemporáneo (2018).

13 For more details on the 1968 protests and the Tlatelolco massacre, see Poniatowska (1971), Zermeño (1978), and Monsiváis (2008).

14 In an interview with the magazine *Walker Art*, Wyman (Byrne 2014) stated that "the most powerful subversion I saw was a response to the dove symbol that we created to represent the World Peace cultural program. Shop owners throughout the city were given decals of the dove symbol to put on their storefront windows. The students would walk by and spray a red spot on the white dove and let the red paint drip down the decal. It was an effective image of the violence of the uprising."

15 According to Blacker (2009), Mexico's Dirty War is much less easily categorized than those of other Latin American countries, partially due to the way the government established a corporate structure after the revolution. Since the 1920s, successive governments have failed to fulfill their promises, which has led to widespread discontent across the country. Beginning in the 1960s, activists reactivated agrarian social movements based on the hopes and promises of the revolution. They continued to use nationalist language despite stemming from international socialism in order to appeal to the government to intervene for change "by speaking its language." These contradictory tactics demonstrate an acceptance of the dominant discourse that "the national government is the embodiment of the 1910 revolution and protector of

the democratic rights of the people" while also challenging it to uphold that claim (191). Therefore, "the limited success [of the movements] was both advanced and constrained by the people's retention of faith in the regime" (192); activists urged people to respect the constitution while also revolting against it. To Blacker, the state of Guerrero represents an important link in the nationwide strikes, when people began to really lose confidence in the state's willingness to meet their needs (184). In an attempt to mask its own Dirty War, Mexico reacted to discontent by opening its doors to Chilean refugees in 1973 – focusing on commercial expansion in Mexico rather than political issues. In fact, she describes the Dirty War in Guerrero as "an intricate diplomatic balancing act" (183).

16 While artists had been transparent about their political positions until then, the 1968 and 1971 massacres and the ongoing Dirty War forced political militancy underground – even in the artistic realm. Due to the tumultuous political circumstances, as well as strong influences coming from Europe, artists moved from figurative to abstract artworks. This shift was political, and artists were able to keep creating at a time when they were under greater scrutiny. Many of these abstract works are not openly political, in that what is represented is not necessarily read as political, nor did they necessarily tackle social issues like the collectives under investigation do, because it was not permitted during the period. But while their works are doubtless political, with abstraction used as a means of survival, the abstraction itself makes it hard for the collectives to draw from them – there is no explicit repertoire of symbols to reproduce or remix. And unlike the murals or the prints created by the LEAR and the TGP that circulated widely or were available to the public, the more abstract pieces were exhibited in museums, and therefore were not as widely available. One notable exception to this shift to abstraction is the work of the *Grupos* (Groups), who were more concerned with artistic interventions than with the creation of figurative or abstract works of art. Proceso Pentágono (Pentagon Process), active from 1976 to 1985, and then sporadically until 1997, is perhaps the most relevant

to my investigation, as the group openly tackled political issues outside of the regular art circuit by elaborating a clear posture on artistic creation, one that integrated the viewer into the process of experiencing the work. Proceso Pentágono not only invented new ways of creating art but also rebranded art as a collective process that can critically denounce repression and drive social transformation. The first part of their name, "Proceso," symbolizes their belief that the process of creating a piece could be more important than the object itself, as well as their collective process of creation, which dissolved and transgressed "the ideology of the individual artist as a paradigm of the bourgeois subject" (García de Germenos 2014, 116). Much like the collectives do today, the members of Proceso Pentágono sought to stimulate their audience's aesthetic and political conscience to inform as well as to influence and subvert. Their practice differed from the propagandist tendency of political art in Mexico until then; they focused on the aesthetic approach of production – that is, on the way in which the process is supported by social and political reflection rather than the result. Proceso Pentágono emerged when Helen Escobedo invited it to the 1977 Paris Biennale, whose aim was to exhibit collaboratively created Latin American art. Proceso Pentágono's installation, titled *Pentágono*, consisted of a pentagonal space in the centre of the gallery filled with objects and pieces denouncing the lived repression of Latin American people during the Dirty War, and specifically the torture procedures carried out by the Mexican state. As mentioned in chapter 1, state-sanctioned crimes during the Dirty War went unpunished and were swept under the rug until the PRI was defeated in 2000. A gap was thus left in historical memory, a gap that these artist collectives addressed and investigated, spreading a counter-history that remained relatively undiscussed until recently.

17 Autopsies would later prove that the two killed students had been unarmed, and the CNDH later concluded that the two deaths amounted to a human rights violation.

18 More specifically, they were guilty of arbitrary detention, cruel treatment, and lack of care for the victims. The report led to the

arrest of two officers, who were released sixteen months later when a judge deemed the evidence insufficient. Former State Attorney General Alberto López Rosas resigned on 13 December 2011 and was accused by the CNDH of covering up evidence and facts. He was exonerated in 2013 and remained in Governor Aguirre's office.

19 In March 2024, Ayotzinapa student Yanqui Khotan Gómez Peralta was fatally shot by the police in troubling circumstances, described by the Mexican president as "an abuse of authority" (Lobo 2024). Investigations are ongoing.

20 Maldonado is a known activist for Indigenous rights and often attends events hosted by the EZLN, discussed in chapter 2. He spent four months living in Ayotzinapa after the forty-three's disappearance, and the document resulting from his stay at the school, *El rostro de los desaparecidos* (*The Faces of the Disappeared*, 2015), blends testimonies from witnesses and survivors with his own reflections on Mexican politics and the role of literature in processing trauma. Gibler's *I Couldn't Even Imagine That They Would Kill Us: An Oral History of the Attacks Against the Students of Ayotzinapa* (2017) provides a minute-by-minute recreation of the night, giving a voice to the survivors. Since the book was published, Gibler has continued writing about Ayotzinapa in various media, such as the website of the North American Congress on Latin America and *The Independent*, in both English and Spanish. Finally, Hernández's *Massacre in Mexico* (2020) is a thorough investigation into the state's response that unravels the web of lies spun by the authorities. Over the course of her investigation, Hernández obtained access to secret documents, memos, briefing notes, and reports. She also interviewed public officials and police officers involved in the case. Hernández's book differs from Maldonado's and Gibler's as her primary material is not the surviving students' testimonies. Instead, she focuses on the voices of the "other" Ayotzinapa victims, the many Mexicans who were falsely accused, jailed, and tortured, to demonstrate the lengths to which the authorities went to cover up their responsibility in the case. Hernández's account, as well as the four reports released by the

GIEI mandated by the Inter-American Commission on Human Rights to investigate human rights violations, inform the version of events I present next (see GIEI 2015, 2016, 2022a, 2022b).

21 Earlier that same month, Ayotzinapa had been chosen as a "pit stop" for students from the various *normales* across the country who were planning to protest together in the capital. The *normalistas* believed that they would need between twelve and fifteen buses to transport everyone from Ayotzinapa to Mexico City, which is why they started to commandeer buses a week before the proposed departure.

22 Bus grabbing by Ayotzinapa *normalistas* is a practice tolerated by bus drivers. As part of their studies to become teachers, students are expected to travel to all parts of the state of Guerrero to undertake classroom observations in schools, and to complete their practicums, yet the Mexican government provides no funding for this. Hence, they "borrow" buses for both short and extended periods of time. Drivers usually go along, because in most cases it allows them to visit family members in remote parts of the state. The practice is also tolerated in part because the *normalistas* are not violent. As Alex Rojas explains, during the 26 September bus takeover "I told them [the bus passengers] not to worry, that we never did anything to citizens, to the people, that we only did this action because it was necessary since we don't have any vehicles at the school to use for transportation to our actions, whether it's going to the march to commemorate the student massacre, or fundraising activities, or the classroom observations and exercises" (in Gibler 2022, 52). Paula Mónaco Felipe (2016) points out that the school only has one bus provided by the state: it seats forty students and is not allowed to drive on main roads, as it does not have licence plates.

23 The Juan N. Álvarez and Periférico Norte intersection; the Palacio de Justicia; the Crucero a Santa Teresa; and Camino del Andariego. Overall, the GIEI reports identified nine different crime scenes covering a territory of about eighty square kilometres. Those attacks made 180 direct and over 700 indirect victims (GIEI 2015, 2016).

24 Later investigations showed that the students were being monitored by C-4 – a Mexican intelligence agency that coordinates information received at the municipal, state, and federal levels, as well as by the military – from the moment they entered Iguala at around 8:30 that night.

25 Only two deaths have been confirmed. Alexander Mora Venancio's death was confirmed in December 2014 and Christian Alfonso Rodríguez Telumbre's in July 2020. In both cases, skeletal remains were retrieved from the San Juan River and in a ravine in Cocula (known as "carnage ravine") and examined at the Medical University of Innsbruck (Austria). The identities of the deceased were confirmed by the Equipo Argentino de Antropología Forense (Argentine Forensic Anthropology Team) (Ferri 2020).

26 This version of events is extremely unlikely. Forensic expertise requested by the GIEI showed that in optimal conditions – those of a crematory oven – a fire needs to reach between 800 and 1,000 degrees Celsius, for a period of ninety to one hundred and twenty minutes, for an adult human body to turn to ashes. In the worst possible scenario, like an open-air fire at the Cocula dump, a minimum of 700 kilograms of wood and 310 kilograms of tires, doused with a minimum of 310 kilograms of diesel fuel, would be necessary to obliterate one adult body. This kind of fire would need to burn steadily for about twelve hours. It is hard to imagine this process being multiplied to incinerate forty-three bodies. Moreover, a fire of that size would have created a huge smoke cloud rising to an estimated 300 metres above the Cocula dump. Yet, no one in Cocula, or even workers at the dump who were on-site on 27 September, when the fire was supposedly still burning, ever mentioned seeing such a smoke cloud. According to weather reports, it was raining during the night of 26–7 September. Satellite images of the zone provided by NASA do not show any trace of the massive fire that would have been necessary to burn forty-three bodies in a relatively short period of time. Finally, this modus operandi – completely incinerating bodies – is not normally associated with the Guerreros Unidos; while it is documented that they have burned bodies in the past, it was done

poorly and remains were identifiable. For all these reasons, the GIEI (2015) claimed that this version of events was scientifically impossible.

27 According to Meneses and Castillo-González (2018), over the course of the Ayotzinapa crisis Peña Nieto moulded himself to the mood of both the electorate and international organizations: "the trajectory of his narratives gradually adapted to the level of national discontent and international pressure." Moreover, "the representation of the other was not clearly expressed, but in each of the speeches analyzed [four speeches made in 2014: 6 October, 29 October, 18 November, and 27 November] the president constructed an ambiguous identity for the enemy. The adversaries of the state changed in each speech" (276). This led to confusion among the families of the forty-three disappeared, further creating a climate of mistrust. It also contributed to the generally accepted narrative of events among survivors and activists – that the government took the students, but most of all, that the state knows where the students are and is failing to return them *con vida* (alive).

28 The GIEI experts concluded that the attacks on the Ayotzinapa students were coordinated, the main objective of which was to ensure that the buses in which the *normalistas* were riding did not leave Iguala, and that those that had already left were stopped at all costs (GIEI 2015, 328).

29 The experts also proposed another rationale for the attacks, one that would justify the level of violence perpetrated that night: One of the buses might have been carrying heroin to Chicago, Illinois, or was transporting money from drug sales. It is public knowledge that drug cartels use buses on the Iguala–Chicago route.

30 At the federal level, the experts highlighted major inconsistencies in the authorities' versions of the events. The PGR claims, to this day, that the students went to Iguala to protest and disrupt a political event – an event that ended between 7:30 and 8:45 p.m., about an hour before camera footage shows them arriving at the Iguala bus station. Phone records of the 066 national system for citizens' emergency and the C-4 also disprove the PGR's timeline

of events. Most of those records had not been consulted by the PGR before they presented their report to the media and to family members in October 2014.

31 The report shows how the PGR stalled the investigation by denying request after request to interview persons of interests, how the authorities refused to let investigators approach the 27th Battalion stationed in Iguala, which, according to witness declarations, played an important part in the events of 26 September, how proper protocols and agreements were not respected, and how the fragmentation of the investigation makes it extremely complex to arrive at a clear picture of the events.

32 One major point highlighted by the GIEI reports is that, despite not finding the missing forty-three students, searches did unearth many mass graves in the state of Guerrero, further underscoring the major problems of violence and disappearances in Mexico.

33 For the latest update on Ayotzinapa at the time the book was sent for review, see John Gibler's "Ten Years of Impunity: AMLO and the Betrayal of Ayotzinapa," published online by the North American Congress on Latin America in September 2024, to mark the ten-year anniversary of the students' disappearance.

34 Workshops do not systematically bring together artists who share the same political views. However, the creation of this mode of social organization is directly linked to the influence of the TGP, whose social commitment is still a key element of the *talleres* of Oaxaca.

35 The works I analyze in this chapter were created between 2016 and 2020, at the time that the TAC was located in front of Espacio Zapata, on Calle Porfirio Díaz. The workshop has since moved to a different space, on Avenida de la Independencia.

36 For example, in the Summer of 2019, both collectives celebrated the one hundredth anniversary of the end of the Mexican Revolution (1910–20) by representing the Zapatista leader Emiliano Zapata, and, in November 2018, URT-Arte created the mural about feminicide that I analyze in chapter 3.

37 Indeed, the rules in the *Plan Parcial de Conservación del Centro Histórico de la Ciudad de Oaxaca* (Conservation plan for Oaxaca's

Historic Centre) are strict – for example, only two colours are permitted on buildings – and the sanctions severe (Municipio de Oaxaca 2018).

38 After 2006, tourism fell drastically in Oaxaca, since it was perceived as an anarchist city. The state and federal governments invested significant sums of money to encourage tourists – both national and international – to return to Oaxaca, and even if there is a certain irony to the situation, the collectives born out of the 2006 events – the very same ones that allegedly led to the drop in tourism – are now touted as a reason to visit Oaxaca. My hypothesis is that, ultimately, erasing the murals would indeed harm tourism, since a fair number of people travel to Oaxaca to view them. They may contravene regulations, yet the city permits them because they bring in revenue. I was unable to discuss this topic with city officials, as none of them answered my requests to meet.

39 The title of this section quotes something Mario Guzmán said during our interview in July 2018, when he explained that one of the goals in creating ASARO was to make members feel like they were "construyendo un colectivo de manera colectiva," building a collective collectively.

40 Note the plural "Pueblos" in "Asamblea Popular de los Pueblos de Oaxaca," indicating the plurality of identities within the state of Oaxaca. Indeed, Oaxaca is home to sixteen Indigenous peoples.

41 Magaña (2020, 141) notes that "these cultural exchanges are multidirectional" – Mexico influences the United States as much as it is influenced by the United States.

42 The use of stencils provoked a debate to which I already alluded in chapter 1. Since stencil artists create their designs off-site, with more than spray paint and a valve, stencil graffiti is not considered true graffiti by "purists," who see graffiti as a unique practice because their pieces are irreproducible (114).

43 Arte Jaguar and AK Crew are among the most respected crews in Oaxaca (Magaña 2020, 141). Magaña studies their production in "Mexico: Political Cultures, Youth Activism and the Legacy of the Oaxacan Social Movement of 2006" (2014).

44 For a detailed chronology of the events between May and December 2006, see Martínez Vázquez (2007).

45 Sotelo Marbán (2008) calls URO's way of doing politics "autoritaria y racista" (authoritarian and racist) (62). Using first-person testimonies, his book chronicles the many human rights violations that took place between June and December 2006.

46 Beas Torres (2007) and Denham and CASA Collective (2008) provide testimonies from Oaxacans who lived through these events.

47 See "The Women's Takeover of Media in Oaxaca: Gendered Rights 'to Speak' and 'to Be Heard'" (Stephen 2013, 145–77) for more on the state and commercial media takeover that began following the March of Pots and Pans on 1 August 2006. The march gathered between 2,500 and 5,000 women, some who, in the spur of the moment, proceeded to the COR-TV station to voice their demands on air. When a manager refused to give them airtime, the women took control of the studio, remaining there for twenty days (Gibler 2009).

48 Franco Ortiz (2011) provides a thorough analysis of the street art scene in Oaxaca, and of the 2006 social unrest and the art created during the uprising.

49 For example, they created stencils about the war in Syria and the situation in Palestine, or the Arab Spring. In these cases, *gráficas callejeras* were used to circulate their demands and bring awareness to events happening abroad.

50 Francisco Toledo (17 July 1940–5 September 2019) is one of Oaxaca's most important figures. Until his death in 2019, he was active as an artist, social activist, cultural conservationist, environmentalist, teacher, and philanthropist. He was from Juchitán, was of Zapotec heritage, and settled in Oaxaca in the 1980s after studying and exhibiting in Europe and the United States. He infused twentieth-century modernism with Indigenous tradition. He founded IAGO – a library with exhibition spaces, over sixty thousand art books, and a collection of prints – in 1988 and the Centro de las Artes San Agustín (San Agustín Arts Centre) in San Agustín Etla in 2006.

51 While this is an effective change in written language, it poses a

linguistic challenge for spoken language, as pronouncing an *x* in place of a vowel does not produce a simple sound. In recent years, the use of the vowel *e* to replace the gendered *o* or *a* has become increasingly common. For example, "Todos somos Ayotzinapa" becomes "Todes somos Ayotzinapa."

52 The first murals appeared during the EZLN's Democratic National Convention (Convención Nacional Democrática de la EZLN) held in the village of La Realidad, in San Cristóbal de las Casas, 6–9 August 1994. They were carried out within the autonomous communities as markers of their distinct and rebellious identity. Zapatista murals hold the same ideological function as that of the traditional muralist school of the 1920s – namely, to affirm a clear political position and open a space for dialogue around the issues they depict (Vargas-Santiago 2015, under "Origins: Visual Genealogies"). However, unlike 1920s murals that portray an idealized nation, the Zapatista muralists give voice to workers, peasants, and Indigenous movements, as well as to the resistance and violence associated with them. In this sense, these murals have literally given a face to the EZLN militant identity discourse, often that of resistance figures like the Mexican Revolution's Emiliano Zapata, the Dirty War's Lucio Cabaña, or Subcomandante Marcos, the spokesperson of the movement until his retirement in 2014. (The man behind Marcos, Rafael Sebastián Guillén Vicente, assumed the persona of Subcomandante Insurgente Galeano in May 2014.) Portraits of figures who have opposed the ruling power are recurring symbols in wall compositions, as testimonies to a past culture of struggle, of the anchoring of anti-reactionary and anti-academic postures (Vargas-Santiago 2015, under "Origins: Visual Genealogies"). As Luis Vargas-Santiago explains, "The dead have a lively presence in Zapatista art; like the living, they look the viewer directly in the eye, establishing a link between the then and the now, and bringing about remembrance." This visual strategy is still prevalent in Mexican protest art. Zapatista muralism is artivism in that it blends art and activism and requires community members to actively participate in its production. As such, the process of thinking and creating the murals is often more impor-

tant than the final result; murals are painted directly onto walls, on the plaster, bricks, partitions, or wood, and the paint used is rudimentary, often acrylic or oil (Vargas-Santiago 2015, under "Origins: Visual Genealogies"). Vargas-Santiago explains that the subject matter of the murals he examined between 1994 and 2007 was always developed collectively by the community, through public meetings or informal gatherings. Sometimes, the artists did not even have any power in the decision of what would be represented; their point of view did not matter, since the work had, first and foremost, to embody the experience of the entire community, and not the artists' individual experience. In a way, the artists served as mediators whose technical skills were put to use by the community. The murals were produced as collectively as they were designed, through the voluntary participation of students and teachers. From this perspective, the images created belonged entirely to the communities; and since the community's reflection was always in motion, so were the murals. For instance, if the visual content became outdated or was criticized, the works were altered. Several types of modifications could be contemplated, according to Vargas-Santiago. First, alterations could consist of darkening the skin of certain figures such as Zapata. Second, erasure could cover up or radically modify the work. Finally, the communities could let the murals deteriorate with the weather (Vargas-Santiago 2015, under "Origins: Visual Genealogies").

53 "Volveré y seré millones" is also a poem by Argentinean poet José María Castiñeira de Dios, after a phrase supposedly spoken by Eva Perón.

54 The image can be found in ASARO (2015b).

55 According to Oles (2013, 284), "the TGP was the first organization in Mexico devoted exclusively to the production of radical graphics, considered the most expedient and inexpensive means of communicating pressing social and political issues to a broad popular audience." In June of 1937, the TGP was set up by members of the visual arts division of the LEAR, including Leopoldo Méndez, Pablo O'Higgins, and Luis Arenal. The themes this collective tackled were always political, with an ideological orien-

tation and a realistic aesthetic very similar to that of the LEAR, while thematically and visually, their prints were inspired by the work of José Guadalupe Posada. The works commissioned by the TGP focused on labour conflicts, strikes, and the importance of national unity, but one of the main themes was Mexican workers' fight against fascism. Most of the TGP's prints are in black and white and are didactic, which makes their message easily accessible to all. They also sought to professionalize the work of artists by offering them technical training. As they put in their "Declaración de principios" (Declaration of principles), "considering that the social aim of visual art is inseparable from good artistic quality, the TGP strives to develop the individual technical capacity of its members" (quoted in Williams 2006, 16). In addition, Méndez conceived of artists as workers in the true communist sense: "Workers can also realize that art is a career and a social activity that is useful, and not the idle pastime that the bourgeois philosophers pretend it is" (16), further highlighting the communist leanings of the workshop. In other words, much like Siqueiros before them, artists like Méndez were both artists and "protagonists in the actual political struggles of the day" (21).

56 The title of this section is taken from my July 2018 interview with Mario Guzmán, who said, "somos la continuidad de lo que es ASARO" (we are ASARO's continuity).

57 This corresponds roughly to Guzmán's departure from ASARO. The exact date and reasons for his departure are hard to confirm; in an interview Guzmán mentioned to me that he had left due to internal differences. Both collectives are secretive about this aspect of their evolution.

58 The viewer might notice that the map of Mexico is flipped. This is likely an oversight on the artist's part. When creating a woodcut block print, one must consider that the design is printed like a stamp. In this case, it means that the state of Guerrero appears on the right of the map, on the Atlantic coast, while in reality it is on the Pacific coast.

59 Since the collectives often depict real-life figures, I considered that the male teacher might be a known activist. During a 2024 field

trip I asked URT-Arte whether the male teacher was an activist that I had been unable to identify. They confirmed that in this case, they did not portray any real-life figure.

60 Strictly speaking, most of the images I analyze in this section are untitled, but I treat the text contained within them as titles, so as to facilitate discussion.

61 A video of the unveiling is available in Urtarte (2019).

62 Although many scholars have highlighted the tensions at the heart of muralism, poet Octavio Paz may have best explained its oxymoronic nature: "on the one hand, it was a revolutionary art, or one that called itself revolutionary; on the other, it was official art" (quoted in Coffey 2012, 1), art sponsored by the state. Shifra Goldman posits that the bourgeoisie "discountenanced the militant and revolutionary aspect of muralism and retained only the superficial, sentimental, and nostalgic" (quoted in Coffey 4); there was a clash between the artists' intentions and the audience's reception of their work. The government financed a mural's creation, so they could ask that certain elements be represented, and for the muralists to tone down their militancy. Smith (2017, 13) aptly calls this a "marriage of convenience" between artists and the state. Some muralists worked within these parameters, while others decided against doing so and stopped accepting commissions. Read within Asavei's (2018, 2) framework, muralism, then, is both critical-political art and propaganda, depending on the period examined and the intent of the producer (artist versus state). This marriage of convenience between revolutionary art and political institutions is at the centre of Mary K. Coffey's *How Revolutionary Art Became Official Culture: Murals, Museums, and the Mexican State* (2012). Her investigation explores the institutionalization of mural art as it entered museums, from a political and aesthetic perspective. She explains that as more than a purely artistic movement, muralism also converted violent energies left in place after the revolution into ethical impulses meant to socialize artistic expression. In short, artists, who were often activists aligned with the values of socialism, were "constrained" by their working relationship with the government. While they are in-

fluenced by the muralism of the 1920s, the collectives I study here do not fully align with this movement, or rather with what muralism became in the 1930s as it was appropriated by the state. Their artistic and ideological ideals are more reminiscent of those held by the social realist painter David Alfaro Siqueiros (1923), who called for the collectivization of muralism and the use of the tools of the workers. After returning from Los Angeles and Buenos Aires in 1933, Siqueiros "advocated that murals be produced by collectives, based on a spirit of camaraderie; that they serve the working class rather than the government or bourgeoisie; and that they appropriate the tools of the proletarian worker (such as the airbrush) and methods of mass communication … in order to create truly revolutionary art" (Oles 2013, 281). While Rivera is perhaps the muralist best known outside of Mexico, I read the collectives under investigation as following in Siqueiros's footsteps, since his stance was less about nation building. Indeed, he was more detached from power, and sometimes even resorted to violence to reach his objectives (Folgarait 2022, 10). Siqueiros was a committed Stalinist who believed in direct action. For instance, he "organized and carried out a terrorist act against Leon Trotsky, leading a band of gunmen who left multiple machine-gun bullet holes inside the Trotsky residence" (10).

Chapter Three

1 The term "machismo" – originally from Spanish – is now common in other languages, including English. In Spanish, the word simply means "manhood," but the connotation has evolved, especially as the anglicized term came to depict the stereotypical dominant male figure in Mexico and other patriarchal Latin American cultures. This new definition also conveys an idea of toxic masculinity or hypermasculinization often used to describe the cultural conditions that allow for feminicide and violence toward women in Latin America today (Cowan 2017).

2 Maquiladoras were built on the Mexican side of the border to take advantage of cheap labour costs – a Mexican worker's average daily pay is the equivalent of between three and six US dollars –

and exploitative labour laws in Mexico; about 80 per cent of these factories are US-owned.

3 See, for instance, the documentary *The Three Deaths of Marisela Escobedo* by Carlos Perez Osorio (2020).

4 The slogan "Ni una más" was coined by the group Mujeres de Negro de Chihuahua (Chihuahua's Women in Black) after a poem by Susana Chávez.

5 The Madres de la Plaza de Mayo are a group of Argentinean activists founded in 1977, at the height of the Dirty War (1973–83), to petition for the return of their children abducted by the military regime.

6 For examples, see Blais and Chrétien (2018), Siddons (2018), and Zeilinger (2008).

7 Bueno-Hansen (2010) accounts for this discrepancy in defining the term and describes how *feminicidio* is understood slightly differently in Mexico, Nicaragua, and Peru.

8 The introduction to the section entitled "Femicide" in the published proceedings of the International Tribunal on Crimes Against Women is quite blunt in its description of the phenomenon:

> We must realize that a lot of homicide is in fact femicide. We must recognize the sexual politics of murder. From the burning of witches in the past, to the more recent widespread custom of female infanticide in many societies, to the killing of women for "honor," we realize that femicide has been going on a long time. But since it involves mere females, there was no name for it until Carol Orlock invented the word "femicide." (Russell and Van de Ven 1990, 104)

Attended by over two thousand women from forty different countries, the main objectives of the tribunal that met in Brussels were to bear witness to the myriad forms of gender violence by documenting women's lived experiences and to challenge oppression. Russell and Van de Ven's introduction to the proceedings is brutal in its honesty: Femicides are inherently about women being subordinated to men. For the longest time, there was not even a word to describe the phenomenon. The term was "resurrected" with the publication of the proceedings in 1976 and has remained contentious since then.

9 Feminicides are divided into two main categories: intimate – committed by a partner or an ex-partner – and non-intimate – committed by a close male relative, such as a father, brother, or uncle (most honour or dowry killings fall into this category), or by a male stranger. The latter has given rise to the "crazy serial killer targeting random women" trope so favoured by the media. To identify if a crime is indeed a feminicide, the relationship between victim and perpetrator must be looked at very closely.

10 Replacing "women and men" with "females and males" was meant to highlight that age is not a contributing factor in killings; female infant killings are considered femicides under this definition.

11 See Monárrez Fragoso's and Cynthia Bejarano's extensive bodies of work.

12 For a thorough rebuttal of Lagarde, see Russell (2013).

13 Unsurprisingly, Lagarde's definition, as well as the fact that she blames culture and government for the feminicide crisis, have spurred new debates. While some argue that her definition has an activist and denunciatory connotation that changes the value of the term, others simply say that it makes visible the systematic aspect of the violence experienced by women and the role that the state plays in perpetuating it. Russell is critical of Lagarde's reworking of the term, which she claims renders it too restrictive. Following Lagarde's definition, she argues, when "perpetrators *are* arrested and imprisoned, these crimes are no longer considered feminicides" (2011; emphasis in the original), and a better definition would be one that can be used globally. Finally, she highlights the growing schism between activists and feminist groups that use "femicide" and those that choose "feminicide." She claims that "the solidarity that should ideally exist between feminists working to combat the same misogynist murders of females has been destroyed by the competition that has developed in Latin America between feminists who have chosen to use one or the other of these terms" (2011). While it is true that all women should be

aligned in combat, most universal concepts have local definitions that apply closely to their national/specific contexts. The infighting is regrettable, but Lagarde is right to point out that in Mexico specifically, both the lack of protection for women and the denial of justice are constitutive parts of feminicides.

14 In *Homo Sacer: Sovereign Power and Bare Life*, Agamben speaks of "humanity" and "citizen" in the broadest of senses – in a manner that can be seen as universalizing the concepts. By doing so, the theory explicitly erases women; indeed, the *homo sacer* is male by default. While the erasure of women from the original theory is problematic, the binary is not only applicable to the Mexican context but also provides a useful lens through which to analyze the lack of action on the part of successive governments. Other scholars, notably Stephen Eisenhammer (2013) and Julia Monárrez Fragoso (2020), account for this flaw in the original theory.

15 Their work was exhibited at Kutztown University in Pennsylvania in 2007 (see https://rohrbachlibrary.wordpress.com/2007/10/02/vcc-exhibit-asaro-artwork/) and the University of Oregon in 2014 (https://jsma.uoregon.edu/asaro%E2%80%94asamblea-de-artistas-revolucionarios-de-oaxaca-assembly-revolutionary-artists-oaxaca-prints), among other venues.

16 This print was repurposed in late 2023 to denounce the Israel attacks on Palestine (decentralize culture 2023).

17 The Pasaporte Gráfico initiative brings together twelve collectives and workshops in Oaxaca. Tourists interested in the city's engraving scene can do a self-guided tour or participate in the monthly guided tour. At each workshop, they receive a stamp on their passport, and by collecting all twelve stamps they are eligible for a discount when buying prints. While some of the collectives have an openly political posture, reflected in their creative process, their mode of governance, and their works, others tend to align themselves with the more neutral concept of gallery or co-operative workshop. The pooling of the means of production and commodification in the spaces open to the public is not directly correlated with the political commitment of the members or the groups, who are not all politically engaged, and much less all in the same

way. It is up for debate whether the artists see the tours as a real opportunity to make their voices heard. The activity is not part of a logic of dialogue, but rather of rapid consumption of visual content. Are their works reduced to objects for sale? Do the collectives participate in a form of the "sell-out conflict," marketing the work for exposure, or more pragmatically to sell to tourists and help pay the bills? It could be read as an acute understanding of market logic. When the initiative came to a stop in February 2020 due to the COVID-19 pandemic, there had been thirty-eight guided tours. To learn more about the Pasaporte Gráfico, see https://www.facebook.com/pasaportegrafico.

18 The figure in this print has been read as either an older woman or a clerical figure. Considering the Mexican context, it would likely be a Catholic figure. This would allow for a paradoxical reading of the print; indeed, while Catholicism is a pillar of Mexican society, its teachings are also one of the very roots of the country's strong sense of machismo.

19 While this art does serve to create and maintain memories of those lost to gender-based violence, the artists that Driver interviewed expressed that it is sometimes hard to use art to express anger strongly enough. Driver also notes that participating in the creation of these memorials and in all other forms of protest can be incredibly dangerous; many of the women who do this end up as victims of violence themselves.

20 See Ké Huelga Radio (2018).

21 *La Adelita* was the nickname given to female soldiers who fought during the Mexican Revolution, as well as the title of the famous corrido (a Mexican folk ballad) written to praise their femininity and command their loyalty to the revolution. The song was inspired by Adela Velarde Pérez's role as medic and nurse during the first half of the revolution. The song's popularity contributed to the terms *soldadera* and *Adelita* becoming conflated over time. For more, see Salas (2010).

22 As I mentioned earlier, MUGRE does not interact with scholars from the Global North. While I analyze their images, I do not reproduce any here out of respect for their ideological position.

Since the images in the fanzine are untitled, I refer to them by their main identifier (a rose, a girl with a bob, and so on).

23 MUGRE can be found on Facebook at https://www.facebook.com/mujeresgrabando.

24 The print entitled *Ni rosa romántico, ni rosa que llore, ni rosa mexicana, todos los colores en mí*, from the third #VivasNosQueremos campaign, conveys a similar message: The stereotype that roses are coded as female, thus frail and limited, ought to be disputed.

25 See Curiel Pichardo (2007).

26 See Espinosa Miñoso (2010, 2014).

27 As this book goes to press in March 2025, it would appear that the Electric Machete site (https://electricmachete.com/) has since been taken down.

28 Two prints from the third campaign, *Las calles son nuestras* (The streets are ours) and *Un día caminaremos sin miedo* (One day we will walk without fear), depict the same idea. The former shows a woman with her eyes closed over a background of black windows – the moon indicates it is nighttime – and the latter shows a mother and daughter walking together on the street, holding each other as if to keep each other safe.

29 Incidentally, "Nunca más un mundo sin nosotras" are the very words the president of the committee in charge of writing Chile's new constitution said when she was elected. She, too, is an Indigenous woman.

30 When I interviewed them, they indicated they preferred to remain anonymous. To protect their identities, I refer to them as "members of ARMARTE." Since then, they have given interviews in Spanish where their names are published, but I have decided to respect their initial wish for anonymity because it may have influenced how open they were with me in some of the answers they provided. See ARMARTE (2022a); *Fusilerías* (2024); Morales (2022); Secretaría de Cultura (2024); *Tendencia Oaxaca* (2024).

31 For a young scholar like me, new to the field of visual culture studies, this explicit position as learners shared by both artists and researchers was refreshing, as it allowed for a more open dialogue, in which both artist and scholar asked questions and learned

about each other's positions and world views. Since our interview, they have started to refer to their role as teachers a bit more explicitly in interviews and on social media.

32 This is an assumption, based on my interactions with members. Like most collectives, the members of ARMARTE were not keen to comment on their internal mode of organization, or on that of other Oaxacan collectives.

33 Since its inception, Día de Muertas has become a social movement protesting violence against women, and has garnered enough support that, in 2012, a seventeen-minute documentary entitled *Día de las Muertas* was released. Día de Muertas was created by Voices of Absence, an organization that "pushes prosecutors to investigate cases and helps relatives navigate the judicial process" (Orsi 2019).

34 Lozano claims that if these murals become tourist attractions, they lose their status as calls to action. I disagree with her on this particular point. Murals or street artworks that attract tourists can also serve activistic purposes by drawing attention to an issue and helping to educating a broader public. I see a difference between murals created for tourists as the main audience, and murals by and for a local audience that also happen to become a tourist attraction. I agree that murals about feminicides created with an audience of tourists in mind are in poor taste. However, if murals meant to memorialize victims and shed light on an issue end up drawing tourists, while still remaining sites of memory for families, I believe that the call to action stands.

35 There is also a practical component to pasting at this height – artists can only paste as high as they can reach, unless they carry a ladder. Pasting with a broom is also done, but again, it only extends as high as the artist's arm and the broom will allow.

36 For more cases of activism, see Stephen and Speed (2021).

Conclusion

1 ASARO's Myspace page is available at https://myspace.com/asaroaxaca.

References

Abud Jaso, Juan José, and Homero Vázquez Carmona. 2018. "La masacre de Iguala: Falta y pulsión de muerte." In Martínez Ruiz, Hernández Urías, and Vázquez Carmona, *Pensar Ayotzinapa*, 77–105.

Agamben, Giorgio. 1998. *Homo Sacer: Sovereign Power and Bare Life*. Translated by Daniel Heller-Roazen. Stanford University Press.

Ahearn, Charlie, dir. 1982. *Wild Style*. Rhino Entertainment; Submarine Entertainment.

Aladro-Vico, Eva, Dimitrina Jivkova-Semova, and Olga Bailey. 2018. "Artivism: A New Educative Language for Transformative Social Action." *Comunicar* 26 (57): 9–18. https://doi.org/10.3916/c57-2018-01.

Alfaro Siqueiros, David. 1923. "Manifiesto del sindicato de obreros técnicos, pintores y escultores." Documents of Latin American and Latino Art. International Center for the Arts of the Americas, Museum of Fine Arts, Houston, Texas. Accessed 14 May 2024. https://icaa.mfah.org/s/es/item/751080.

Allier-Montaño, Eugenia, and Emilio A. Crenzel. 2015. *The Struggle for Memory in Latin America: Recent History and Political Violence*. Palgrave Macmillan.

Amnesty International. 2024. "Mexico's Disappearance Strategy Risks Missing Person's Search." 22 January. https://amnesty.ca/urgent-actions/mexicos-disappearance-strategy-risks-missing-persons-search/.

Anderson, Benedict. 2016. *Imagined Communities: Reflections on the Origin and Spread of Nationalism*. Verso.

Animal Político. 2014. "'Ya me cansé': Murillo Karam explica esa frase tres días después." 11 November. https://animalpolitico.com/2014/11/ya-canse-murillo-karam-explica-esa-frase-tres-dias-despues.

Anzaldúa, Gloria. 1987. *Borderlands/La Frontera: The New Mestiza*. Aunt Lute Books.

Appiah, Anthony Kwame. 2010. *The Ethics of Identity*. Princeton University Press.

Arce, Dolores. 2013. "Hace 232 años, la profecía de Tupac Katari: Volveré y seré millones … " *América Latina en movimiento*, 25 November. https://www.alainet.org/es/active/69265.

Arista, Lidia. 2024. "López Obrador: No soy rehén de nadie en la investigación del caso Ayotzinapa." *Expansión política*, 11 January. https://politica.expansion.mx/presidencia/2024/01/11/lopez-obrador-asegura-que-no-es-rehen-de-nadie-en-el-caso-ayotzinapa.

ARMARTE (@Armarte OAX). 2019a. "La doble jornada nos tiene cansada." Facebook, 8 March. https://www.facebook.com/armarte.oaxaca/photos/1006827102834375.

ARMARTE (@Armarte OAX). 2019b. "La mujer trabajadora lucha contra la sociedad capitalista." Facebook, 8 March. https://www.facebook.com/armarte.oaxaca/photos/1006827152834370.

ARMARTE (@Armarte OAX). 2019c. "Taller intensivo de pintura." Facebook, 16 February. https://www.facebook.com/armarte.oaxaca/photos/99545 5507304868.

ARMARTE (@armarte_oaxaca). 2021. "Ni una más." Instagram, 5 April. https://www.instagram.com/p/CNSW63eqj87/.

ARMARTE. 2022a. "ARMARTE: Artistas visuales que tienen como elementos el amor y el arte." 2022. EDUCA: *Servicios para una Educación Alternativa A.C.* 16 March. https://www.educaoaxaca.org/armarte-artistas-visuales-que-tienen-como-elementos-el-amor-y-el-arte/.

ARMARTE (@armarte_oaxaca). 2022b. "Ellas, las que luchan." Instagram, 1 June. https://www.instagram.com/p/CeRKHb3tl3L/.

Arroyo, Sergio Raúl, and Daniel Arroyo. 2016. *Codex: Una aproximación al grafiti de la ciudad de México*. Consejo Nacional para la Cultura y las Artes.

ASARO (@ASARO asamblea de artistas revolucionarios de Oaxaca). 2014. "Pintado por Ayotzinapa." Facebook, 29 December. https://www.facebook.com/asarooaxaca/photos/pb.100063566320729.-2207520000/426679630820 924/?type=3.

ASARO (@ASARO asamblea de artistas revolucionarios de Oaxaca). 2015a. "Memoria gráfica del 'TALLER DE STENCIL,' por AYOTZINPA." Facebook, 9 February. https://www.facebook.com/asarooaxaca/posts/439195819569305.

ASARO (@ASARO asamblea de artistas revolucionarios de Oaxaca). 2015b. "Pinturas – Ayotzinapa." Facebook, 10 February. https://periodicos.ufsc.br/index.php/politica/article/view/2175-7984.2015v14n30p8.

Asavei, Maria Alina. 2018. *Aesthetics, Disinterestedness, and Effectiveness in Political Art*. Lexington Books.

Aviña, Alexander. 2014. "A Poor People's Revolution." In *Specters of Revolution: Peasant Guerrillas in the Cold War Mexican Countryside*, 137–61. Oxford University Press. https://doi.org/10.1093/acprof:oso/9780199936571.003.0007.

Banet-Weiser, Sarah. 2011. "Convergence on the Street." *Cultural Studies* 25 (4–5): 641–58. https://doi.org/10.1080/09502386.2011.600553.

Barajas, Rafael. 2009. *Posada: Mito y mitote: La caricatura política de José Guadalupe Posada y Manuel Alfonso Manila*. Fondo de Cultura Económica.

Barba, Sandra. 2017. "El feminicidio detrás de 'Unos cuantos piquetitos.'" *Letras Libres*, 6 June. https://letraslibres.com/arte/el-feminicidio-detras-de-unos-cuantos-piquetitos/.

Barstow, Anne Llewellyn. 1988. "On Studying Witchcraft as Women's History: A Historiography of the European Witch Persecutions." *Journal of Feminist Studies in Religion* 4 (2): 7–19.

Bautista Martínez, Eduardo. 2008. "El movimiento social oaxaqueño y la participación ciudadana." Universidad Autónoma Metropolitana.

Bautista Martínez, Eduardo. 2016. "Movilizaciones sociales y reconfiguración institucional a 10 años del movimiento de la APPO en Oaxaca, 2006–2016." In *Antagonismo, subjetividades y esperanza*, 135–51. Miguel Ángel Porrúa.

BBC News. 2019. "Mexicans March to Vent Anger at Police over Rape Cases." 13 August. https://www.bbc.com/news/world-latin-america-49327568.

BBC News Mundo. 2014. "Peña Nieto pide 'superar el dolor de Iguala.'" 4 December. https://www.bbc.com/mundo/ultimas_noticias/2014/12/141204_ultnot_mexico_pena_nieto_superar_iguala_jcps.

Beas Torres, Carlos. 2007. *La batalla por Oaxaca*. Ediciones Yope Power.

Becker, Howard S. 1963. *Outsiders: Studies in the Sociology of Deviance*. Free Press.

Bejarano, Cynthia L. 2002. "Las Super Madres de Latinoamérica: Transforming Motherhood by Challenging Violence in Mexico, Argentina, and El Salvador." *Frontiers: A Journal of Women Studies* 23 (1): 126–50. https://doi.org/10.1353/fro.2002.0002.

Bell, Carole Concha. 2022. "Rejection of Chile's Draft Constitution Serves a Blow to Progressive Government Agenda." North American Congress on Latin America, 10 September. https://nacla.org/chile-constitution-rejection-boric.

Bénaud, C.L., and Suzanne Schadl. 2013. "ASARO: Claiming Space in Digital Objects and Social Networks." In *Preserving Memory: Documenting and Archiving Latin American Human Rights*, edited by Nerea A. Llamas, 23–32. Seminar on the Acquisition of Latin American Library Materials.

Benedetti, Mario. 1979. "Desaparecidos." Poemas del Alma. Accessed 18 February 2025. https://www.poemas-del-alma.com/mario-benedetti-desaparecidos.htm.

Bennett, Jill. 2005. *Empathic Vision: Affect, Trauma, and Contemporary Art*. Stanford University Press.

Blacker, O'Neill. 2009. "Cold War in the Countryside: Conflict in Guerrero, Mexico." *Americas* 66 (2): 181–210. https://doi.org/10.1017/s000316150000 6076.

Blais, Mélissa. 2012. *J'haïs les féministes! Le 6 décembre 1989 et ses suites*. Éditions du Remue-Ménage.

Blais, Mélissa, and Marie Soleil Chrétien. 2018. *Votre antiféminisme, nos répliques: De l'humour à l'affrontement physique*. L'R des centres de femmes du Québec.

Boido, Mario. 2018. "Las artes y la construcción de la memoria." *Memoria de la ficción, ficción de la memoria: Entre el ritual y la crítica*, edited by María A. Semilla Duran, Marie Rosier, and Sandra Hernández, 220–41. Alter/nativas, Université Lumière Lyon 2.

Bolos, Silvia, and Marco Estrada Saavedra. 2013. *Recuperando la palabra: La Asamblea Popular de los Pueblos de Oaxaca*. Universidad Iberoamericana.

Brewer, Stephanie. 2023. "Ayotzinapa 9 Years Later: Pending Tasks in the Search for Truth and Justice." Washington Office on Latin America, 26 September. https://www.wola.org/analysis/ayotzinapa-9-years-later-pending-tasks-search-truth-justice/.

Brunk, Samuel. 2007. *Emiliano Zapata: Revolution and Betrayal in Mexico*. University of New Mexico Press.

Bueno-Hansen, Pascha. 2010. "Feminicidio: Making the Most of an 'Empowered Term.'" In *Terrorizing Women: Feminicide in the Americas*, edited by Rosa-Linda Fregoso and Cynthia Bejarano 290–311. Duke University Press.

Butler, Judith. 2016. *Frames of War: When Is Life Grievable?* Verso.

Butler, Judith. 2020. "Judith Butler on COVID-19, the Politics of Non-Violence, Necropolitics, and Social Inequities." Verso Books, 23 July. YouTube, 1:06:48. https://youtu.be/6Bnj7H7M_Ek.

Byrne, Emmet. 2014. "Radiant Discord: Lance Wyman on the '68 Olympic Design and the Tlatelolco Massacre." *Walker Art*, 20 March. https://walkerart.org/magazine/lance-wyman-mexico-68-olympics-tlatelolco-massacre/.

Campa, Homero. 2015. "Con Peña Nieto, 13 desaparecidos al día." *Proceso*, 7 February. https://www.proceso.com.mx/reportajes/2015/2/7/con-pena-nieto-13-desaparecidos-al-dia-143107.html.

Cardenal, Ernesto. 1984. "Epitafio para la tumba de Adolfo Báez Bone." In *Hacia el hombre nuevo: Poesía y pensamiento de Ernesto Cardenal*, edited by Paul W. Borgeson, 117. Tamesis Books.

Centro Prodh. 2021. "Nos llaman las locas de las palas." 3 June. https://centroprodh.org.mx/las-locas-de-las-palas/.

Chollet, Mona. 2002. *In Defense of Witches: The Legacy of the Witch Hunts and Why Women Are Still on Trial.* Translated by Sophie R. Lewis. St Martin's.

Civera-Cerecedo, Alicia. 2004. *La legitimación de las escuelas normales rurales.* El Colegio Mexiquense.

Civera-Cerecedo, Alicia. 2008. *La escuela como opción de vida: La formación de maestros normalistas rurales en México, 1921–1945*. El Colegio Mexiquense.

CNDH (Comisión Nacional de los Derechos Humanos). 2018. "Mediante muestreo hemerográfico, la CNDH revela el hallazgo de cuando menos 163 fosas clandestinas en el país entre 2017 y 2018, de las que se exhumaron cuando menos 530 cuerpos." 7 September. https://www.cndh.org.mx/sites/all/doc/Comunicados/2018/Com_2018_257.pdf.

CNDH (Comisión Nacional de los Derechos Humanos). 2019. "Se crea la Comisión de la Verdad para el caso de los 43 normalistas desaparecidos de Ayotzinapa: Comisión Nacional de los Derechos Humanos – México." https://www.cndh.org.mx/noticia/se-crea-la-comision-de-la-verdad-para-el-caso-de-los-43-normalistas-desaparecidos-de-0.

Coffey, Mary K. 2012. *How a Revolutionary Art Became Official Culture: Murals, Museums, and the Mexican State*. Duke University Press.

Consorcio Oaxaca. 2009. *Feminicidio en Oaxaca: Impunidad y crimen de estado contra las mujeres, informe ciudadano, 2008–9*. Consorcio para el Diálogo Parlamentario y la Equidad Oaxaca. https://consorciooaxaca.org/wp-content/uploads/2017/02/informe-feminicidio-2008-2009-curvas.pdf.

Copyleft. n.d. "What Is Copyleft?" Copyleft.org. Accessed 8 June 2023. https://copyleft.org/.

Costa, Pedro, Paulo Guerra, and Pedro Soares Neves. 2017. "Introduction:

Urban Intervention, Street Art and Public Space." In *Urban Intervention, Street Art and Public Space*, edited by Pedro Costa, Paulo Guerra, and Pedro Soares Neves, 8–14. Urbancreativity.org.

COVAJ. Secretaría de Gobernación. 2022. *Informe de la presidencia de la Comisión para la Verdad y Acceso a la Justicia del caso Ayotzinapa*. Gobierno de México.

Cowan, Benjamin Arthur. 2017. "How Machismo Got Its Spurs – in English: Social Science, Cold War Imperialism, and the Ethnicization of Hypermasculinity." *Latin American Research Review* 52 (4): 606–22. https://doi.org/10.25222/larr.100.

Curiel Pichardo, Ochy. 2007. "Crítica poscolonial desde las prácticas políticas del feminismo antirracista." *Nómadas* 14 (1): 92–101.

Dabène, Olivier. 2020. *Street Art and Democracy in Latin America*. Palgrave Macmillan.

Dean, Michelle. 2012. "The Story of Amanda Todd." *New Yorker*, 18 October. https://www.newyorker.com/culture/culture-desk/the-story-of-amanda-todd.

decentralize culture (@decent_culture). 2023. "Ceasefire Now." X, 31 December. https://twitter.com/decent_culture/status/1741546700337021150.

de la Luz, Erika. 2019. "Otra vez causan destrozos; El vandalismo opaca protesta feminista en la CDMX." *Excélsior*, 29 September. https://www.excelsior.com.mx/comunidad/otra-vez-causan-destrozos-el-vandalismo-opaca-protesta-feminista-en-la-cdmx/1338965.

Délano Alonso, Alexandra, and Benjamin Nienass. 2021. "Memory Activism and Mexico's War on Drugs: Countermonuments, Resistance, and the Politics of Time." *Latin American Research Review* 56 (2): 353–70. https://doi.org/10.25222/larr.534.

De Leon, Jason. 2015. *The Land of Open Graves: Living and Dying on the Migrant Trail*. University of California Press.

Denham, Diana, and CASA Collective, eds. 2008. *Teaching Rebellion: Stories from the Grassroots Mobilization in Oaxaca*. PM Press.

Derwich, Karol. 2015. "Mexico: A Regional Power of a Failed State?" *Política y sociedade* 14 (30): 8–26.

Deutsche Welle. 2019. "Police Rape Allegations Fuel Women's Protests in Mexico." 17 August. https://www.dw.com/en/police-rape-allegations-fuel-womens-protests-in-mexico-city/a-50060670.

De Vecchi Gerli, María. 2018. "¡Vivxs Lxs Queremos! The Battles for Memory Around the Disappeared in Mexico," PhD diss., University College London.

Día de Muertas. n.d. "Día de Muertas: Mejor vivas que Catrinas." Accessed 8 June 2023. https://diademuertas.mx/.

Driver, Alice. 2015. *More or Less Dead: Feminicide, Haunting, and the Ethics of Representation in Mexico.* University of Arizona Press.

Duncombe, Stephen. 2016. "Does It Work? The Æffect of Activist Art." *Social Research: An International Quarterly* 83 (1): 115–34.

Duncombe, Stephen, and Steve Lambert. 2018. "Why Artistic Activism? Nine Reasons." Center for Artistic Activism, 9 April. https://c4aa.org/2018/04/why-artistic-activism.

Duncombe, Stephen, and Steve Lambert. 2021. *The Art of Activism: Your All-Purpose Guide to Making the Impossible Possible.* O/R Books.

Dussel. Enrique D. 1995. *The Invention of the Americas: Eclipse of "the Other" and the Myth of Modernity*. Continuum.

Eber, Christine, and Ana Cristina Vázquez Carpizo. 2015. "Guest Voz: Remembering the 43 Missing Students of Ayotzinapa Is to Recognize the Pursuit of Justice in a Country Wracked with Impunity and Elitism." *Latina Lista*, 2 September. http://latinalista.com/columns/guestvoz/guest-voz-remembering-the-43-missing-students-of-ayotzinapa-is-to-recognize-the-pursuit-of-justice-in-a-country-wracked-with-impunity-and-elitism.

Echavarría Canto, Laura. 2018. "Ayotzinapa: Locas y fantasmas. Duelos y melancolía." In Martínez Ruiz, Hernández Urías, and Vázquez Carmona, *Pensar Ayotzinapa*, 106–28.

Economist, The. 2022. "At Least 100,000 People Are Missing in Mexico." 30 June. https://www.economist.com/the-americas/2022/06/30/at-least-100000-people-are-missing-in-mexico.

Eisenhammer, Stephen. 2013. "Bare Life in Ciudad Juárez: Violence and Space of Exclusion." *Latin American Perspectives* 41 (2): 99–109. https://doi.org/10.1177/0094582x13509786.

Eller, Cynthia. 1995. *Living in the Lap of the Goddess: The Feminist Spirituality Movement in America*. Beacon Press.

Espinosa Miñoso, Yuderkys, ed. 2010. *Aproximaciones críticas a las prácticas teórico-políticas del feminismo latinoamericano*. En la Frontera.

Espinosa Miñoso, Yuderkys, Diana Gómez Correal, and Karina Ochoa Muñoz, eds. 2014. *Tejiendo de otro modo: Feminismo, epistemología y apuestas descoloniales en Abya Yala*. Editorial Universidad del Cauca.

Estrada Saavedra, Marco. 2012. "La estética de los agraviados: Arte callejero y política. El caso de la Asamblea Popular de los Pueblos de Oaxaca, México." In *Cultura, sociedad y democracia en América Latina*, edited by Klaus Bodemer, 135–57. Iberoamericana.

Fahs, Breanne, ed. 2020. "WITCH Manifesto." *Burn It Down! Feminist Manifestos for the Revolution*. Verso.

Federici, Sylvia. 2004. *Caliban and the Witch: Women, the Body and Primitive Accumulation*. AK Press.

Federici, Sylvia. 2022. "Chasses aux 'sorcières' et ordre patriarcal et capitaliste: Aux origines du crime de féminicide." In *Féminicide: Une histoire mondiale*, edited by Christelle Taraud, 57–71. La Découverte.

Feldman, Joseph P. 2021. *Memories Before the State: Postwar Peru and the Place of Memory, Tolerance, and Social Inclusion*. Rutgers University Press.

Ferrell, Jeff. 2004. *Crimes of Style: Urban Graffiti and the Politics of Criminality*. Northeastern University Press.

Ferri, Pablo. 2020. "La identificación de uno de los 43 estudiantes de Ayotzinapa tumba la versión histórica del PRI." *El País*, 7 July. https://elpais.com/mexico/2020-07-07/la-identificacion-de-uno-de-los-43-estudiantes-de-ayotzinapa-tumba-la-version-historica-del-pri.html.

Finnegan, Nuala. 2021. *Cultural Representations of Feminicidio at the US-Mexico Border*. Routledge.

Flores, Demian. 2015. "La gráfica, fundamental en la historia de las artes visuales de México." In Valdez and Aguilar, *A tiro de fuego*, 19.

Folgarait, Leonard. 1998. *Mural Painting and Social Revolution in Mexico, 1920–1940: Art of the New Order.* Cambridge University Press.

Folgarait, Leonard. 2022. "Art After the Mexican Revolution: Muralism, Prints, Photography." In *A Companion to Modern and Contemporary Latin American and Latina/o Art*, edited by Alejandro Anreus, Robin Adèle Greeley, and Megan A. Sullivan, 5–19. John Wiley and Sons.

Foss, Sonja K. 2004. "Theory of Visual Rhetoric." In *Handbook of Visual Communication: Theories, Methods, and Media*, edited by Kenneth Smith, Sandra Moriarty, Keith Kenney, and Gretchen Barbatis, 163–74. Routledge, 2004.

Foucault, Michel. 1991. *The Foucault Reader*. Edited by Paul Rabinow. Puffin.

Franco Ortiz, Itandehui. 2011. "El deleite de la transgresión. Graffiti y gráfica política callejera en la Ciudad de Oaxaca." Honours thesis, Escuela Nacional de Antropología e Historia, México.

Fregoso, Rosa-Linda, and Cynthia L. Bejarano, eds. 2010. *Terrorizing Women: Feminicide in the Americas*. Duke University Press, 2010.

Friedman, Elisabeth Jay, and Constanza Tabbush. 2016. "#NiUnaMenos: Not One Woman Less, Not One More Death!" North American Congress on Latin America, 1 November. https://nacla.org/news/2016/11/01/niunamenos-not-one-woman-less-not-one-more-death.

Front Line Defenders. n.d. "Meztli Omixochitl Sarabia Reyna." Accessed 18 February 2025. https://www.frontlinedefenders.org/en/profile/meztli-omixochitl-sarabia-reyna.

Fuentes, Marcela A. 2019. "#NiUnaMenos (#NotOneWomanLess)." In *Women Mobilizing Memory*, edited by Ayşe Gül Altınay, María José Contreras, Marianne Hirsch, Jean Howard, Banu Karaca, and Alisa Solomon, 172–91. Columbia University Press. https://doi.org/10.7312/alti19184-011.

Fusilerías. 2024. "Colectivo ARMARTE acerca a las mujeres el arte con campamentos." 10 March. https://fusilerias.com/colectivo-armarte-acerca-mujeres-arte-campamentos/.

Gahman, Levi. 2016. "Food Sovereignty in Rebellion: Decolonization, Autonomy, Gender Equality, and the Zapatista Solution." Dorset Chiapas Solidarity, 20 August. https://dorsetchiapassolidarity.wordpress.com/2016/08/20/food-sovereignty-in-rebellion-decolonization-autonomy-gender-equity-and-the-zapatista-solution/.

Gallagher, Janice. n.d. "Timeline." Ayotzinapa. Accessed 6 June 2023. http://www.ayotzinapatimeline.org/timeline.

García de Germenos, Pilar. 2014. "The *Salón Independiente*: A New Reading." In *La era de la discrepancia: Arte y cultura visual en México / The Age of Discrepancies: Art and Visual Culture in Mexico, 1968 – 1997*, 2nd ed., edited by Olivier Debroise and Cuauhtémoc Medina, translated by Christopher Michael Fraga, 51–9. Museo Universitario de Ciencias Arte.

García Márquez, Gabriel. 2007. "El mejor oficio del mundo." *Chasqui. Revista Latinoamericana de Comunicación* 98:26–31.

García Navarro, Santiago. 2008. "El fuego y sus caminos." In *El Siluetazo*, edited by Ana Longi and Gustavo A. Bruzzone, 333–64. Adriana Hidalgo.

Genin, Christophe. 2013. *Le street art au tournant: Reconnaissances d'un genre*. Les Impressions Nouvelles.

Geoffray, Marie Laure. 2013. *Internet, Public Space and Contention in Cuba: Bridging Asymmetries of Access to Public Space Through Transnational Dynamics of Contention*. Freie Universität; desiguALdades.net.

Giacoman, Claudia, and Rodrigo Torres. 2021. "Dance to Resist: Emotions and Protest in Lindy Hop Dancers During October 2019 Chilean Rallies." *Canadian Journal of Latin American and Caribbean Studies / Revue canadienne des études latino-américaines et caraïbes* 47 (1): 46–66. https://doi.org/10.1080/08263663.2022.1996696.

Gibler, John. 2009. *Mexico Unconquered: Chronicles of Power and Revolt.* City Lights.

Gibler, John. 2017. *I Couldn't Even Imagine That They Would Kill Us: An Oral History of the Attacks Against the Students of Ayotzinapa.* City Lights.

Gibler, John. 2022. "How to Destroy an Investigation from the Inside: Ayotzinapa and the Legacies of Impunity." North American Congress on Latin America, 7 November. https://nacla.org/how-destroy-investigation-inside-ayotzinapa-and-legacies-impunity.

Gibler, John. 2024. "Ten Years of Impunity: AMLO and the Betrayal of Ayotzinapa." North American Congress on Latin America, 25 September. https://nacla.org/ten-years-impunity-amlo-and-betrayal-ayotzinapa.

GIEI (Grupo Interdisciplinario de Expertos Independientes). 2015. *Informe Ayotzinapa I: Investigación y primeras conclusiones de las desapariciones y homicidios de los normalistas de Ayotzinapa.* Grupo Interdisciplinario de Expertos Independientes, 12 October. https://nsarchive.gwu.edu/document/27609-2-giei-informe-ayotzinapa-resumen-ejecutivo-spanish.

GIEI (Grupo Interdisciplinario de Expertos Independientes). 2016. *Informe Ayotzinapa II: Avances y nuevas conclusiones sobre la investigación, búsqueda, y atención a las víctimas.* Grupo Interdisciplinario de Expertos Independientes, 24 April. https://nsarchive.gwu.edu/document/27610-3-giei-informe-ayotzinapa-ii-spanish.

GIEI (Grupo Interdisciplinario de Expertos Independientes). 2022a. *Informe Ayotzinapa III: Mandato medida cautelar MC/409/14 CIDH.* Grupo Interdisciplinario de Expertos Independientes, February. https://nsarchive.gwu.edu/document/27665-giei-informe-ayotzinapa-iii-resumen-spanish.

GIEI (Grupo Interdisciplinario de Expertos Independientes). 2022b. *Informe Ayotzinapa IV: Situación actual del caso a los 8 años de los hechos.* Grupo Interdisciplinario de Expertos Independientes, 29 September. https://comisionayotzinapa.segob.gob.mx/es/Comision_para_la_Verdad/Cuarto_Informe.

GIEI (Grupo Interdisciplinario de Expertos Independientes). 2023a. *Informe GIEI V: Una visión global sobre los hechos, las responsabilidades y la situación del caso Ayotzinapa*. Grupo Interdisciplinario de Expertos Independientes, 31 March. https://cdhcm.org.mx/wp-content/uploads/2023/03/Informe-GIEI-V.-Hechos-responsabilidades-y-situacion-del-caso-Ayotzinapa-31-marzo-2023.pdf.

GIEI (Grupo Interdisciplinario de Expertos Independientes). 2023b. *Informe GIEI VI: Hallazgos, avances, obstáculos y pendientes*. Grupo Interdisciplinario de Expertos Independientes, July. https://comisionayotzinapa.segob.gob.mx/work/models/Comision_para_la_Verdad/Documentos/pdf/Informe_Ayotzinapa_VI.pdf.

Goldman, Francisco. 2015. "Mexico's Missing Forty-Three: One Year, Many Lies, and a Theory That Might Make Sense." *New Yorker*, 30 September. https://www.newyorker.com/news/news-desk/mexicos-missing-forty-three-one-year-many-lies-and-a-theory-that-might-make-sense.

Graham de la Rosa, Mike, and Suzanne Michele Schadl. 2014. *Getting Up for the People: The Visual Revolution of Asar-Oaxaca*. PM Press.

Griffin, Alba. 2023. *Reading the Walls of Bogotá: Graffiti, Street Art, and the Urban Imaginary of Violence*. University of Pittsburgh Press.

Gutiérrez Castañeda, Griselda. 2018. "Pensar Ayotzinapa." In Martínez Ruiz, Hernández Urías, and Vázquez Carmona, *Pensar Ayotzinapa*, 62–76.

Gutman, Yifat. 2017. *Memory Activism: Reimagining the Past for the Future in Israel-Palestine*. Vanderbilt University Press. https://doi.org/10.2307/j.ctv16759tr.

Gutman, Yifat, and J. Wüstenberg. 2022. "Challenging the Meaning of the Past from Below: A Typology for Comparative Research on Memory Activists." *Memory Studies* 15 (5): 1070–86.

Harris, John, and Vicky White. 2013. *A Dictionary of Social Work and Social Care*. Oxford University Press.

Hatuka, Tali. 2018. *The Design of Protest: Choreographing Political Demonstrations in Public Space*. University of Texas Press.

Haynes, Nell. 2020. "Ethnographic Exposure and Embodied Solidarity: Getting Into the Ring with the Cholitas Luchadoras." *Latin American and Caribbean Ethnic Studies* 15 (3): 292–308. https://doi.org/10.1080/17442222.2020.1770976.

Hernández, Anabel. 2020. *A Massacre in Mexico: The True Story Behind the Missing Forty-Three Students*. Translated by John Washington. Verso.

Herrera, Hayden. 2002. *Frida: A Biography of Frida Kahlo*. Perennial.

Híjar, Cristina. 2015. "A tiro de fuego: Constancia del crecimiento y fortalecimiento de la tradición gráfica en México." In Valdez and Aguilar, *A tiro de fuego*, 17–18.

Hobsbawm, Eric J., and Terence O. Ranger. 2019. *The Invention of Tradition*. Cambridge University Press.

Hodgkin, Katharine, and Susannah Radstone. 2011. *Regimes of Memory*. Routledge.

hooks, bell, and Amalia Mesa-Bains. 2018. "Day of the Dead." Chap. 9 in *Homegrown: Engaged Cultural Criticism*. Routledge.

Hunnicut, Gwen. 2009. "Varieties of Patriarchy and Violence Against Women: Resurrecting 'Patriarchy' as a Theoretical Tool." *Violence Against Women* 15 (5): 553–73.

Instituto Nacional de las Mujeres. 2020. "Violentómetro. Si hay violencia en la pareja, no hay amor." Government of Mexico, 14 February. www.gob.mx/inmujeres/articulos/violentometro-si-hay-violencia-en-la-pareja no-hay-amor-234888?idiom=es.

International Olympic Committee. n.d. "Mexico City 1968: The Brand." Olympics.com, accessed 12 March 2025. https://olympics.com/en/olympic-games/mexico-city-1968/logo-design.

It's Time Edmonton (@ItsTimeYEG). 2019. "Pyramid of Sexual Violence." Twitter, 24 September. https://twitter.com/itstimeyeg/status/1176492564964417536.

Ittmann, John, ed. 2006. *Mexico and Modern Printmaking: A Revolution in the Graphic Arts, 1920 to 1950*. Philadelphia Museum of Art.

Jelin, Elizabeth. 2003. *State Repression and the Labors of Memory*. University of Minnesota Press.

Jelin, Elizabeth. 2021. *The Struggle for the Past: How We Construct Social Memories*. Translated by Wendy Gosselin. Berghahn.

Jimeno, Myriam. 2004. *Unos cuantos piquetitos. Violencia, mente y cultura*. Universidad Nacional de Colombia.

Jourdan, Adam, and Claudia Morales. 2024. "Bolivia's Cholita Climbers Dream of Conquering Everest in Skirts." Reuters, 6 March. https://www.reuters.com/investigates/special-report/bolivia-cholitas-climbers/.

Ké Huelga Radio. 2018. "Vivas nos queremos – Mujeres Grabando Resistencias." 9 July. https://kehuelga.net/spip.php?article5804.

Kelling, George L., and Catherine M. Coles. 1996. *Fixing Broken Windows: Restoring Order and Reducing Crime in Our Communities.* Simon and Schuster.

Kerkvliet, Benedict J. Tria. 2018. *The Power of Everyday Politics: How Vietnamese Peasants Transformed National Policy*. Cornell University Press. https://doi.org/10.7591/9781501722011.

Kloppe-Santamaría, Gema, and Julia Zulver. 2023. "Beyond Collateral Damage: Femicides, Disappearances, and New Trends in Gender-Based Violence in Mexico." Wilson Center, 27 June. https://www.wilsoncenter.org/article/beyond-collateral-damage-femicides-disappearances-and-new-trends-gender-based-violence.

Krauze, Enrique. 1987. *Emiliano Zapata. El amor a la tierra*. Fondo de Cultura Económica.

Kugelberg, Johan, and Philippe Vermès. 2012. *Beauty Is in the Street: A Visual Record of the May '68 Paris Uprising*. Four Corners Books.

LaCapra, Dominick, 2004. *History in Transit: Experience, Identity, Critical Theory.* Cornell University Press.

Lache Bolaños, Norma Patricia. 2009. "La calle es nuestra: Intervenciones plásticas en el entorno de la Asamblea Popular de los Pueblos de Oaxaca." In *La APPO: ¿Rebelión o movimiento social?* edited by Victor Raúl Martínez Vásquez, 199–217. Universidad Autónoma Benito Juárez.

Lagarde y de los Ríos, Marcela. 1997. "Identidad de género y derechos humanos: La construcción las humanas." *Estudios básicos de derechos humanos* 4:85–126.

Lagarde y de los Ríos, Marcela. 2006. "El derecho humano de las mujeres a una vida libre de violencia." https://catedraunescodh.unam.mx/catedra/CONACYT/16_DiplomadoMujeres/lecturas/modulo2/2_MarcelaLagarde_El_derecho_humano_de_las_mujeres_a_una_vida_libre_de_violencia.pdf.

Lagarde y de los Ríos, Marcela. 2010. "Preface: Feminist Keys for Understanding Feminicide: Theoretical, Political, and Legal Construction." In *Terrorizing Women: Feminicide in the Americas*, edited by Rosa-Linda Fregoso and Cynthia Bejarano, xi–xxv. Duke University Press.

Lammons, William Bishop. 2012. "Entanglements of Urban Art in Oaxaca, Mexico." Master's thesis, University of Colorado at Boulder.

Latorre, Guisela. 2019. *Democracy on the Wall: Street Art of the Post-Dictatorship Era in Chile*. Ohio State University Press.

Leal, Eduardo. 2018. "The Rise of Bolivia's Indigenous 'Cholitas' – in Pictures." *Guardian*, 22 February. https://www.theguardian.com/world/gallery/2018/feb/22/rise-bolivia-indigenous-cholitas-in-pictures.

Lear, John. *Picturing the Proletariat: Artists and Labor in Revolutionary Mexico, 1908–1940*. University of Texas Press, 2017.

Lefebvre, Henri. (1968) 1972. *Le droit à la ville suivi de Espace et politique*. Anthropos.

Lemoine, Stephanie, and Samira Ouardi. 2010. *ARTIVISME: Art, action politique et resistance culturelle*. Alternatives.

Lentin, Ronit. 2006. "Femina Sacra: Gendered Memory and Political Violence." *Women's Studies International Forum* 29 (5): 463–73. https://doi.org/10.1016/j.wsif.2006.07.004.

Leverette, Tru, ed. 2021. *With Fists Raised: Radical Art, Contemporary Activism, and the Iconoclasm of the Black Arts Movement*. Liverpool University Press.

Levinas, Emmanuel, 1969. *Totality and Infinity: An Essay on Exteriority*. Translated by Alphonso Lingis. Duquesne University Press.

Linhard, Tabea Alexa. 2005. *Fearless Women in the Mexican Revolution and the Spanish Civil War*. University of Missouri Press.

Lobo, Andrea. 2024. "Mexican Police Kill Ayotzinapa Student Hours After AMLO Likened Protest to 'Dirty War.'" World Socialist Web Site, 15 March. https://www.wsws.org/en/articles/2024/03/15/avwt-m15.html.

Lozano, Nina Maria. 2019. *Not One More! Feminicidio on the Border*. Ohio State University Press.

Lugones, María. 2008. "Colonialidad y género / Coloniality and Gender / Colonialidade e gênero." *Tabula Rasa* 9:73–101. https://www.revistatabularasa.org/numero-9/05lugones.pdf.

Magaña, Maurice Rafael. 2014. "Mexico: Political Cultures, Youth Activism and the Legacy of the Oaxacan Social Movement of 2006." In *Rethinking Latin American Social Movements: Radical Action from Below*, edited by Richard Stahler-Sholk, Harry E. Vanden, and Marc Becker, 67–83. Rowman and Littlefield.

Magaña, Maurice Rafael. 2020. *Cartographies of Youth Resistance: Hip Hop, Punk, and Urban Autonomy in Mexico*. University of California Press.

Maldonado, Tryno. 2015. *Ayotzinapa: El rostro de los desaparecidos*. Planeta.

Mandolessi, Silvana. 2023. "Latin America." In *The Routledge Handbook of Memory Activism*, edited by Yifat Gutman and Jenny Wüstenberg, 295–9. Routledge. https://doi.org/10.4324/9781003127550-57.

Marino, Katherine M. 2019. *Feminism for the Americas: The Making of an International Human Rights Movement.* University of North Carolina Press, 2019.

Martínez, César. 2023. "Desaparece una persona cada hora en sexenio de AMLO." A dónde van los desaparecidos, 1 June. https://adondevanlosdesaparecidos.org/2023/06/01/desaparece-una-persona-cada-hora-en-sexenio-de-amlo/.

Martínez Arellano, Irma Rosa. 2018. "Over 37,000 People Have Been Made to Disappear in Mexico. *Equal Times*, 29 October. https://www.equaltimes.org/over-37-000-people-have-been-made?lang=en.

Martínez Ruiz, Rosaura, Mariana Hernández Urías, and Homero Vázquez Carmona, eds. 2018. *Pensar Ayotzinapa*. Almadía Ediciones.

Martínez Vázquez, Víctor Raúl. 2007. *Autoritarismo, movimiento popular y crisis política: Oaxaca 2006*. Universidad Autónoma Benito Juárez.

Martínez Vázquez, Víctor Raúl. 2008. "Crisis política y represión en Oaxaca." *El Cotidiano*, no. 148 (March–April): 45–62.

Masters, Cristina. 2009. "Femina Sacra: The 'War on/Of Terror,' Women and the Feminine." *Security Dialogue* 40 (1): 29–49. https://doi.org/10.1177/0967010608100846.

Mateos-Vega, Mónica. 2016. "Laura Restrepo pide construir una ética laica, porque la religiosa se derrumbó." *La Jornada*, 20 May. https://www.jornada.com.mx/2016/05/20/cultura/a05n1cul.

McCormick, Gladys. 2017. "The Last Door: Political Prisoners and the Use of Torture in Mexico's Dirty War." *Americas* 74 (1): 57–81. https://doi.org/10.1017/tam.2016.80.

McDonald, Mark. 2016. "Printmaking in Mexico, 1900–1950." In *Heilbrunn Timeline of Art History*. Metropolitan Museum of Art. http://www.metmuseum.org/toah/hd/prmx/hdprmx.htm.

McEwen, Jérémie. 2019. *Philosophie du hip-hop: Des origines à Lauryn Hill.* Éditions XYZ.

Mendoza, Yobani, and ECPM68. 2018. "Graphics that Resist." In *Signal 06*, edited by Alec Dunn and Josh McPhee, 6–25. PM Press.

Meneses, María Elena, and María Concepción Castillo González. 2018. "Digital Storytelling and the Dispute over Representation in the Ayotzinapa Case." *Latin American Perspectives* 45 (3): 266–83. https://doi.org/10.1177/0094582x18760301.

Merrill, Samuel. 2014. "Keeping It Real? Subcultural Graffiti, Street Art, Heritage and Authenticity." *International Journal of Heritage Studies* 21 (4): 369–89. https://doi.org/10.1080/13527258.2014.934902.

Midelfort, Erik. 1981. "Heartland of the Witchcraze: Central and Northern Europe." *History Today* 21 (2): 27–31.

Mignolo, Walter D. 2007. "Coloniality of Power and De-Colonial Thinking." *Cultural Studies* 21 (2–3): 155–67. https://doi.org/10.1080/09502380601162498.

Millán, Márgara. 2014. "Politics of Translation in Contemporary Mexican Feminism." In *Translocalities/Translocalidades: Feminist Politics of Translation in the Latin/a Américas*, edited by Sonia E. Alvarez, Claudia de Lima Costa, Verónica Feliu, Rebecca Hester, Norma Klahn, and Millie Thayer, 149–67. Duke University Press. https://doi.org/10.1215/9780822376828.

Milton, Cynthia E. 2011. "Defacing Memory: (Un)Tying Peru's Memory Knots." *Memory Studies* 4 (2): 190–205. https://doi.org/10.1177/17506980 10392959.

Milton, Cynthia E., ed. 2014. *Art from a Fractured Past: Memory and Truth-Telling in Post–Shining Path Peru*. Duke University Press.

Mitchell, William John Thomas. 2010. *What Do Pictures Want? The Lives and Loves of Images*. University of Chicago Press.

MND Staff. 2025. "Ayotzinapa Investigation Remains a Priority, Sheinbaum Says: Friday's Mañanera Recapped." *Mexico News Daily*, 17 January. https://mexiconewsdaily.com/politics/ayotzinapa-priority-sheinbaum-friday-mananera-recap/.

Möller, Frank. 2016. "Politics and Art." In *Oxford Handbook Topics in Politics* (online ed.). Oxford University Press. https://doi.org/10.1093/oxfordhb/9780199935307.013.13.

Mónaco Felipe, Paula. 2016. *Ayotzinapa: Horas eternas*. Ediciones B.

Monárrez Fragoso, Julia. 2020. "La *femina sacra* del arroyo del navajo y la política de la visceralidad." In *Genealogía crítica de la violencia. Hacia la liberación del espacio político religioso del cuerpo de las mujeres*, edited by María del Carmen Servitje Montull, 257–72. Universidad Iberoamericana.

Monárrez Fragoso, Julia E., Kerry Carrington, Russell Hogg, John Geoffrey Scott, and Sozzo Maximo. 2019. "Impunity for the Perpetrators and Injustice for the Victims." In *The Palgrave Handbook of Criminology and the Global South*, 913–929. Palgrave Macmillan.

Monsiváis, Carlos. 2008. *El 68: La tradición de la resistencia*. Ediciones Era.

Montes, Rocío. 2023. "Chile rechaza la constitución redactada por la derecha y la extrema derecha con un 55% del voto contra." *El País*, 18 December. https://elpais.com/chile/2023-12-18/chile-rechaza-la-propuesta-de-las-derechas-y-se-queda-con-la-constitucion-nacida-en-la-dictadura-de-pinochet.html.

Morales, Amallely. 2022. "ARMARTE: Mujeres oaxaqueñas pegan grabados en las calles et #8M." *IstmoPress*, 10 March. https://www.istmopress.com.mx/oaxaca/armarte-mujeres-oaxaquenas-pegan-grabados-en-las-calles-el-8m/.

Morán Ramos, Citlali del Rocío. 2021. "ARMARTE. Mujeres en Resistencia." *Somoselmedio*, 27 August. https://www.somoselmedio.com/armarte-mujeres-en-resistencia/.

Morbiato, Caterina. 2017. "Prácticas resistentes en el México de la desaparición forzada." *Revista Trace* 71:138–65. https://doi.org/10.22134/trace.71.2017.100.

Moreno Romero, Cuitláhuac. 2018. "Tristeza de las generaciones sin maestros. Se necesitan maestros rebeldes." In Martínez Ruiz, Hernández Urías, and Vázquez Carmona, *Pensar Ayotzinapa*, 25–46.

Mouffe, Chantal. 2008. "Critique as Counter-Hegemonic Intervention." *Art of Critique*. https://transversal.at/transversal/0808/mouffe/en.

Mouffe, Chantal. 2013. *Agonistics: Thinking the World Politically*. Verso.

Mujeres Grabando Resistencias. 2015. "Invisibilización y posicionamiento de mujeres en el arte." *Hysteria! revista*, 23 December. https://hysteria.mx/mujeres-en-la-grafica-lucha-y-resistencia/.

Mujeres Grabando Resistencias (@Mujeres Grabando Resistencias). 2016. "Convocatoria de Grabado, 3era edición de la campaña gráfica: #Vivas NosQueremos." Facebook, 15 November. https://www.facebook.com/story.php/?story_fbid=1191818207564841&id=525466387533363&_rdrnts.

Mujeres Grabando Resistencias. 2018. "¡Vivas Nos Queremos! (*Art*)." NACLA *Report on the Americas* 50 (4): 418–22. https://doi.org/10.1080/10714839.2018.1551465.

Mulvey, Laura. 1975. "Visual Pleasure and Narrative Cinema." *Screen* 16 (3): 6–18. https://doi.org/10.1093/screen/16.3.6.

Munck, Ronaldo, and Kyla Sankey. 2020. *Social Movements in Latin America*. Sage Publishing.

Municipio de Oaxaca. 2018. "Plan parcial de conservación del Centro Histórico de la Ciudad de Oaxaca de Juárez." https://www.oaxaca.gob.mx/inpac/wp-content/uploads/sites/17/2019/08/PLAN-PARCIAL-ESTATAL.pdf.

Municipio de Oaxaca (@municipiooaxaca). 2021. "Remoción de graffiti." Instagram, 28 April. https://www.instagram.com/p/CYCn70gOodi/.

Museo National de la Estampa INBAL. 2023. *El rebozo: Propuesta gráfica femenina* (Exposición virtual). Flickr. https://www.flickr.com/photos/188203902@N03/albums/72177720310876186/.

Museo Universitario Arte Contemporáneo. 2018. *Gráfica del 68.* Exhibition, 1 September–30 December. https://muac.unam.mx/exposicion/grafica-del-68.

Nagel-Vega, Vanessa. 2020. "De euforias mundialistas y reivindicaciones feministas. El espacio público del Paseo de la Reforma, Ciudad de México, en 1986 y 2019." *Arquitecturas del Sur* 38 (58): 6–23. https://doi.org/10.22320/07196466.2020.38.058.01.

Naidus, Beverly. 2009. *Arts for Change: Teaching Outside the Frame.* New Village Press.

National Security Archive. 2015. "Prelude to Iguala: 'Heavy-Handed Police Tactics' Used Against Ayotzinapa Students in 2011." *Truman*, 7 October. https://trumanfactor.com/2015/prelude-to-iguala-heavy-handed-police-tactics-used-against-ayotzinapa-students-in-2011-15123.html.

Nevaer, Louis E.V. 2009. *Protest Graffiti Mexico: Oaxaca.* Mark Batty.

Noack, Karoline. 2009. "The 'Workshop for Popular Graphic Art' in Mexico – Bauhaus Travels to America." *Bauhaus Imaginista.* https://www.bauhaus-imaginista.org/articles/2444/the-workshop-for-popular-graphic-art-in-mexico-bauhaus-travels-to-america.

Nuñez, Alicia, Patricia González, Gregory A. Talavera, Lisa Sanchez-Johnsen, Scott C. Roesch, Sonia M. Davis, William Arguelles, Veronica Y. Womack, Natania W. Ostrovsky, Lizette Ojeda, Frank J. Penedo, and Linda C. Gallo. 2015. "Machismo, Marianismo, and Negative Cognitive-Emotional Factors: Findings from the Hispanic Community Health Study/Study of Latinos Sociocultural Ancillary Study." *Journal of Latina/o Psychology* 4 (4): 202–17.

Nussbaum, Martha. 1998. "Cultivating Humanity." *Liberal Education* (Spring): 38–45.

Ocampo Arista, Sergio. 2011. "Matan policías a dos estudiantes al desalojar un bloqueo carretero." *La Jornada*, 13 December. https://www.jornada.com.mx/2011/12/13/politica/002n1pol.

OHCHR (Office of the United Nations High Commissioner for Human Rights). 2022. "Mexico: Dark Landmark of 100,000 Disappearances Reflects

Pattern of Impunity, UN Experts Warn." 17 May. https://www.ohchr.org/en/statements/2022/05/mexico-dark-landmark-100000-disappearances-reflects-pattern-impunity-un-experts.

Oles, James. 2013. *Art and Architecture in Mexico*. Thames & Hudson.

Olick, Jeffrey K. 1999. "Collective Memory: The Two Cultures." *Sociological Theory* 17 (3): 333–48.

Olick, Jeffrey K., Vered Vinitzky-Seroussi, and Daniel Levy, eds. 2011. *The Collective Memory Reader*. Oxford University Press.

Olivares Alonso, Emir. 2024. "El caso Ayotzinapa no se concluirá en mi gestión: AMLO." *La Jornada*, 16 February. https://www.jornada.com.mx/noticia/2024/02/16/politica/el-caso-ayotzinapa-no-se-concluira-en-mi-gestion-amlo-1619.

Orozco-Mendoza, Elva F. 2017. "Feminicide and *the Funeralization of the City*: On Thing Agency and Protest Politics in Ciudad Juárez." *Theory & Event* 20 (2): 351–80. https://muse.jhu.edu/article/655776.

Orsi, Peter. 2019. "Demonstrators Demand Halt to Killings of Women in Mexico." Associated Press, 3 November. https://www.ksl.com/article/46666849/demonstrators-demand-halt-to-killings-of-women-in-mexico.

Orsono, Diego. 2007. *Oaxaca sitiada: La primera insurrección del siglo XXI*. Grijalbo.

Osorio, Carlos Perez, dir. 2020. *The Three Deaths of Marisela Escobedo*. Scopio; Netflix.

Pabón Colón, Jessica Nydia. 2018. *Graffiti Grrlz: Performing Feminism in the Hip Hop Diaspora*. New York University Press.

Panofsky, Erwin. 1955. *Meaning in the Visual Arts*. University of Chicago Press.

Pérez Garci, Santiago. 2015. "A tiro de fuego: Espacio de reflexión y encuentro." In Valdez and Aguilar, *A tiro de fuego*, 12.

Periodismohoy. 2019. "AMLO pide a mujeres protestar sin violencia y 'cuidando' el patrimonio." 19 August. http://periodismohoy.com/amlo-pide-protestar-sin-violencia/.

Poniatowska, Elena. 1971. *La noche de Tlatelolco*. Ediciones Era.

Presidencia Enrique Peña Nieto. 2014. "Conferencia de prensa del procurador Jesús Murillo Karam (Ayotzinapa)." YouTube, 7 November, 1:00:41. https://www.youtube.com/watch?v=QNcfdHUiP8c.

Procuraduría General de la República. 2006. *Informe histórico a la sociedad mexicana*. https://nsarchive2.gwu.edu/NSAEBB/NSAEBB209/index.htm#informe.

Reuters. 2022. "Chilean Lawmakers Reach Agreement to Start Work on New Constitution." 13 December. https://www.reuters.com/world/americas/chilean-lawmakers-reach-agreement-start-work-new-constitution-2022-12-13/.

Restauradoras con Glitter (@RGlittermx). 2019. "Pronunciamiento ante las pintas." Twitter, 21 August. https://twitter.com/RGlittermx/status/1164371199054548992.

Riggle, Nicholas Alden. 2010. "Street Art: The Transfiguration of the Commonplaces." *Journal of Aesthetics and Art Criticism* 68 (3): 243–57. https://doi.org/10.1111/j.1540-6245.2010.01416.x.

Rivera-Garza, Cristina. 2020. "On Our Toes: Women Against the Femicide Machine in Mexico." *World Literature Today*, 3 March. https://www.worldliteraturetoday.org/2020/winter/our-toes-women-against-femicide-machine-mexico-cristina-rivera-garza.

Roberts, John. 2014. *Photography and Its Violations*. Columbia University Press.

Rojano Pérez, Rocio. 2015. "La gráfica favorece la formación crítica y social de artistas plásticos." In Valdez and Aguilar, *A tiro de fuego*, 15–16.

Rollins, Tim. 1993. "An Interview with Félix González-Torres by Tim Rollins." Artspace San Antonio. https://artpace.org/exhibitions/untitled-beginning/.

Rose, Gillian. 2012. *Visual Methodologies: An Introduction to Researching with Visual Materials*. Sage.

Ross, Jeffrey Ian. 2016. *Routledge Handbook of Graffiti and Street Art*. Routledge.

Rovetto, Florencia Laura. 2015. "Violencia contra las mujeres: Comunicación visual y acción política en 'Ni Una Menos' y 'Vivas Nos Queremos.'" *Contratexto* 24:13–34.

R3CR30. 2012. "131 alumnos de la Ibero responden." YouTube, 14 May, 10:59. https://www.youtube.com/watch?v=P7XbocXsFkI.

Russell, Diana E.H. 2011. "The Origin and Importance of the Term Femicide." Dianerussell.com, December. https://www.dianarussell.com/origin_of_femicide.html.

Russell, Diana E.H. 2013. "Best Strategies to Advance the Global Struggle Against Femicide." *labrys, études féministes/estudos feministas* (July/December). https://labrys.net.br/labrys24/feminicide/russel.htm.

Russell, Diana E.H., and Jane Caputi. 1990. "Femicide: Speaking the Unspeakable." *Ms Magazine*, September–October, 34–7.

Russell, Diana, and Roberta Harmes. 2001. "Femicide: Politicizing the Killing of Females." In *Femicide in Global Perspective*, edited by Diana Russell and Roberta Harmes. Teachers College Press.

Russell, Diana, E.H., and Jill Radford, eds. 1992. *Femicide: The Politics of Woman Killing*. Open University Press.

Russell, Diana E.H, and Nicole Van de Ven, eds. 1976. *Crimes Against Women: Proceedings of the International Tribunal*. Frog in the Well.

Russell, Diana, and Nicole Van de Ven. 1990. "Femicide: Violence Against Women." In *Crimes Against Women: Proceedings of the International Tribunal*, 3rd ed., edited by Diana Russell and Nicole Van de Ven, 104–8. Russell Publications.

Ruxton, Megan M. 2017. "*Femina Sacra* Beyond Borders: Agamben in the 21st Century." *Theory & Event* 20 (2): 450–70. muse.jhu.edu/article/655780.

Ryan, Holly Eva. 2017. *Political Street Art: Communication, Culture and Resistance in Latin America*. Routledge.

Salas, Elizabeth. *Soldaderas in the Mexican Military: Myth and History*. University of Texas Press, 2010.

Samarrilleres. n.d. "Mujer que avanza." Samarrilleres.org. Accessed 30 April 2024. https://samarrilleres.org/es/zapatista/.

Sánchez Contreras, Josefa. 2024. "Checovaldez: Pinceladas de la vida y obra colectiva del muralero rebelde." Este País, 11 September. https://estepais.com/galeria/checovaldez-vida-obra-colectiva-muralero/.

Schadl, Suzanne M., and Mike Graham de la Rosa. 2014. "Getting Up Pal Pueblo: Tagging ASAR-Oaxaca Prints and Stencils." Exhibition text for *Getting Up Pal Pueblo: Tagging ASAR-Oaxaca Prints and Stencils*, 28 February–7 November, National Hispanic Cultural Center, Albuquerque, New Mexico. University of New Mexico Digital Repository. https://digitalrepository.unm.edu/cgi/viewcontent.cgi?article=1003&context=ulls_fsp.

Schwartz, Barry. 2016. "Collective Memory." In *The Blackwell Encyclopedia of Sociology*, vol. 2, edited by George Ritzer. Blackwell. https://doi.org/10.1002/9781405165518.wbeosc066.pub2.

Secretaría de Cultura. 2024. "Colectivo Armarte, un espacio de mujeres artistas que quieren transformar la sociedad a través del arte." Gobierno de México, 8 March. https://www.gob.mx/cultura/prensa/colectivo-armarte-un-espacio-de-mujeres-artistas-que-quieren-transformar-la-sociedad-a-traves-del-arte.

Siddons, Edward. 2018. "Want to End Sexual Violence? Feminist Self-Defence Is the Only Proven Solution." Solutions Journalism Network, 10 August. https://api.solutionsjournalism.org/stories/want-to-end-sexual-violence-feminist-self-defence-is-the-only-proven-solution.

Silver, Tony, dir. *Style Wars*. 1983. Public Broadcasting System.

SlutWalk Toronto. n.d. "What Is Slutwalk?" Accessed 12 March 2025. https://slutwalkyyz.wixsite.com/slutwalkto/history.

Smith, Stephanie J. 2017. *The Power and Politics of Art in Postrevolutionary Mexico*. University of North Carolina Press.

Sommer, Doris. 2014. *The Work of Art in the World: Civic Agency and Public Humanities*. Duke University Press.

Sontag, Susan. 1977. *On Photography*. Picador.

Sotelo Marbán, José. 2008. *Oaxaca: Insurgencia civil y terrorismo de Estado.* Ediciones Era.

Spivak, Gayatri Chakravorty. 1988. "Can the Subaltern Speak?" In *Marxism and the Interpretation of Culture*, edited by C. Nelson and L. Grossberg, 66–111. Macmillan.

Staudt, Kathleen. 2008. *Violence and Activism at the Border: Gender, Fear, and Everyday Life in Ciudad Juarez*. University of Texas Press.

Stephen, Lynn. 2013. *We Are the Face of Oaxaca: Testimony and Social Movements*. Duke University Press.

Stephen, Lynn, and Shannon Speed, eds. 2021. *Indigenous Women and Violence: Feminist Activist Research in Heightened States of Injustice*. University of Arizona Press.

Stout, James. 2020. "The History of the Raised Fist, a Global Symbol of Fighting Oppression." *National Geographic*, 31 July. https://www.nationalgeographic.com/history/article/history-of-raised-fist-global-symbol-fighting-oppression.

Suarez-Enriquez, Ximena. 2018. "The New Investigative Commission for the Ayotzinapa Case." Washington Office on Latin America, 20 August. Archived 21 February 2020 at https://wayback.archive-it.org/2930/20200221205829/https://www.wola.org/analysis/investigative-commission-ayotzinapa-case/.

Szymanek, Angelique. 2022. "Elina Chauvet." *Latin American and Latinx Visual Culture* 4 (1): 58–74. https://doi.org/10.1525/lavc.2022.4.1.58.

Taibo, Paco Ignacio. 2019. In "Los días de Ayotzinapa." Episode 1 of *The 43*, directed by Matías Gueilburt. Netflix. https://www.netflix.com/ca/title/81045551.

Tate Gallery. n.d. "Art Term: Activist Art." Tate. Accessed 12 April 2024. https://www.tate.org.uk/art/art-terms/a/activist-art.

Taylor, Diana. 2003. *The Archive and the Repertoire: Performing Cultural Memory in the Americas*. Duke University Press.

Tendencia Oaxaca. 2024. "Colectivo ARMARTE, un espacio de mujeres artistas que quieren transformar la sociedad a través del arte." 9 March. https://www.tendenciaoaxaca.com/post/colectivo-armarte-un-espacio-de-mujeres-artistas-que-quieren-transformar-la-sociedad-a-trav%C3%A9s-del-a.

Titelman, Noam. 2022. "Why Did Chileans Reject the Draft Constitution?" North American Congress on Latin America, 8 September. https://nacla.org/why-did-chileans-reject-draft-constitution.

Todorov, Tzvetan. 1995. *Les abus de la mémoire*. Éditions Arléa-Le Seuil.

Tronto, Joan C. 2013. *Caring Democracy: Markets, Equality, and Justice*. New York University Press.

UNESCO. n.d. "Historic Centre of Oaxaca and Archaeological Site of Monte Albán." UNESCO World Heritage Centre, accessed 12 March 2025. https://whc.unesco.org/en/list/415/.

Unidad General de Asuntos Jurídicos. 2011. "Article 33 De los extranjeros." https://www.ordenjuridico.gob.mx/Documentos/Federal/CPEUM_REFORMA_02122024.doc.

UN Women. 2013. *Violencia feminicida en México: Características, tendencias y nuevas expresiones en las entidades federativas, 1985–2010*. United Nations. https://www.unwomen.org/sites/default/files/Headquarters/Attachments/Sections/Library/Publications/2013/2/Feminicidio_Mexico-1985-2010%20pdf.pdf.

Urtarte Oaxaca. n.d. "Qué es Urtarte." Blogspot. Accessed 21 February 2025. https://urtarte.blogspot.com/p/que-es-urtarte.html.

Urtarte Oaxaca (@Urtarte Oaxaca). 2015. "Jorge Luis Gonzáles Parral." Facebook, 8 January. https://www.facebook.com/urtarte.oaxaca/photos/pb.100058155386392.-2207520000./830617393652719/?type=3.

Urtarte Oaxaca (@Urtarte Oaxaca). 2019. "¡a 5 años!" Facebook, 26 September. https://www.facebook.com/watch/?ref=saved&v=788339371600671.

US Embassy Mexico. 2002. "Former President Appears Before Special Prosecutor for Second Time." National Security Archive, 12 July. https://nsarchive.gwu.edu/document/21307-01.

Valdez, Humberto, and Orietta Aguilar, eds. 2015. *A tiro de fuego: Segundo encuentro nacional de talleres de gráfica contemporánea*. Universidad Nacional Autónoma de México.

Van De Velde, Cécile. 2022. "The Power of Slogans: Using Protest Writings in Social Movement Research." *Social Movement Studies* 23 (5): 1–20. https://doi.org/10.1080/14742837.2022.2084065.

Vargas Llosa, Mario. 1990. "Vargas Llosa: 'México es la dictadura perfecta.'" *El País*, 31 August.

Vargas-Santiago, Luis. 2015. "Zapatista Muralism and the Making of a Community." In *Dancing with the Zapatistas: Twenty Years Later* (online ed.), edited by Diana Taylor and Lorie Novak. Duke University Press. https://scalar.usc.edu/anvc/dancing-with-the-zapatistas/zapatista-muralism-and-the-making-of-a-community?path=path-1.

Velez Ascencio, Octavio. 2007. "El IAGO abre sus puertas a *Graffiteros al paredón*." *La Jornada*, 4 February.

Villanueva, Carla Irina. 2020. "To Disappear the Escuelas Normales Rurales: Political Anxieties, the Secretaría de educación pública, and Education Reform in Mexico in 1969." *Americas* 77 (3): 443–68. https://doi.org/10.1017/tam.2020.5.

Villoro, Juan, Mercurio López, Montserrat Gali, and Helia Bonilla. 2014. *Posada: A Century of Skeletons*. RM/BBVA.

Vinthagen, Stellan. 2019. *Conceptualizing "Everyday Resistance."* Routledge. https://doi.org/10.4324/9781315150154.

Volk, Steven S., and Marian E. Schlotterbeck. 2007. "Gender, Order, and Femicide: Reading the Popular Culture of Murder in Ciudad Juárez." *Aztlán: A Journal of Chicano Studies* 32 (1): 53–86.

Volpi Escalante, Jorge. 2000. "El fin de la conjura." *Letras Libres*, 31 October. https://letraslibres.com/revista-mexico/el-fin-de-la-conjura/.

Volpi Escalante, Jorge. 2014. "El desamparo de Ayotzinapa." *El País*, 14 November. https://elpais.com/elpais/2014/11/07/opinion/1415375130_085059.html.

Volpi Escalante, Jorge. 2016. "Escribir Ayotzinapa." *Revista de la Universidad de México* 145 (March): 18–19

Wacławek, Anna. 2008. "From Graffiti to the Street Art Movement: Negotiating Art Worlds, Urban Spaces, and Visual Culture." PhD diss., Concordia University.

Wacławek, Anna. 2011. *Graffiti and Street Art: 211 Illustrations*. Thames & Hudson.

Wilkinson, Daniel. 2019. "Mexico: The Other Disappeared." Human Rights Watch, 15 January. https://www.hrw.org/news/2019/01/15/mexico-other-disappeared.

Williams, Lyle W. 2006. "Evolution of a Revolution: A Brief History of Printmaking in Mexico." In *Mexico and Modern Printmaking: A Revolution in the Graphic Arts, 1920 to 1950*, edited by John W. Ittmann, Innis H. Shoemaker, James W. Wechsler, and Lyle W. Williams, 1–22. Yale University Press.

Wilson, Peter Lamborn. 1991. *T.A.Z.: The Temporary Autonomous Zone, Ontological Anarchy, Poetic Terrorism*. 2nd ed. Autonomedia.

Wright, Melissa W. 2011. "Necropolitics, Narcopolitics, and Femicide: Gendered Violence on the Mexico-U.S. Border." *Signs: Journal of Women in Culture and Society* 36 (3): 707–31. https://doi.org/10.1086/657496.

Zapiain, Marcela, Pedro Quintero, and Benigno Casa. 2007. "Graffiti en México: Arte marginal y transgresor." *Revista digital Cenidiap* 8 (April). https://discursovisual.net/dvweb08/entorno/entmarcela.htm.

Zebadúa-Yañez, Verónica. 2005. "Killing as Performance: Violence and the Shaping of a Community." In "Sexualities and Politics in the Americas," edited by Antonio Prieto Stambaugh. Special issue, *Emisférica* 2 (2). https://hemisphericinstitute.org/es/emisferica-2-2/2-2-essays/killing-as-performance-violence-and-the-shaping-of-community.html.

Zeilinger, Irene. 2008. *Non c'est non. Petit manuel d'autodéfense à l'usage de toutes les femmes qui en ont marre de se faire emmerder*. La Découverte.

Zermeño, Sergio. 1978. *México, una democracia utópica: El movimiento estudiantil del 68*. Siglo Veintiuno editores.

Index